365 Love Letters

365 Love Letters

A Daily Devotional and Much More

William Roberts

XULON PRESS

Xulon Press
2301 Lucien Way #415
Maitland, FL 32751
407.339.4217
www.xulonpress.com

© 2020 by Williams Roberts

All rights reserved solely by the author. The author guarantees all contents are original and do not infringe upon the legal rights of any other person or work. No part of this book may be reproduced in any form without the permission of the author. The views expressed in this book are not necessarily those of the publisher.

Unless otherwise indicated, Scripture quotations taken from the Holy Bible, New International Version (NIV). Copyright © 1973, 1978, 1984, 2011 by Biblica, Inc.™. Used by permission. All rights reserved.

Printed in the United States of America.

Paperback ISBN-13: 978-1-6322-1366-2
eBook ISBN-13: 978-1-6322-1367-9

Preface

When I began writing the letters to my children on January 1, 2011, I had no idea what God would reveal to me about myself. As I looked back on letters that I had written, I found many connections that opened my eyes to things I had not seen before.

On April 21, 2011, I started a four-part series on death. While the stories were sent out on four-consecutive days, the stories were written over a period of about two months and it was not until the third of the letters were written that I could see what God was telling me about what I had learned about death. It turns out that the other three stories that I wrote about death chronicled my own journey of faith and became connected dots even though the events described in the four stories happened over six decades

There was another series of four stories that were sent out starting on August 6, 2011 that chronicled my maturing view of music. Again, the actual stories took place over a period of about forty years and were written over a period of a few months then sent out on four successive days.

Another set of connected dots in my stories were not sent out on successive days and it was not until over a year later that I noticed the strong connection. These stories dealt with key people that God placed in my life at just the right time. These key people came in all shapes and sizes – from our cleaning lady to an executive in a large engineering firm. (See January 7, 8 and November 6, 7)

Yet another set of letters tracked my ill-placed love of sports that unbeknownst to me had taken a position above God in my early years and lasted until my fifties. I had never heard the term "God of Sport" until my wife and I attended a weekend conference led by Voddie Baucham. As I looked back over my stories I didn't like what I saw. (See June 28, January 4 and June 4)

Start your own journey, today.

Introduction

On the morning of December 31, 2010, I had finished my morning devotions and while I was completing my morning prayers, God spoke to me through my spirit and told me that He was proud of the fact that I have prayed faithfully for my two adult children and their families over the last several years. He assured me that He had heard my prayers and in due time my prayers would be answered. However, God also told me that I needed to do more. He told me that He wanted me to send them a letter every day in 2011 to let them know how much I love them and how much He loves them.

After I completed my year-long assignment, I thought my journey was complete; God had other ideas. I discovered that the ending was only the beginning. On December 31, 2011, I sighed with relief as I sent out my last letter. God spoke to be again and said, "Good Job." Now I have another assignment for you. I want you to write letters to all of my children to let them know how much "I am" loves them. With over two thousand letters written and shared with thousands of people via email and Facebook, I am still fulfilling my assignment. When will I stop? God hasn't told me yet.

These original "365 Love Letters" will serve you in many ways. First, and foremost, they are a good way to begin your day with God. When you read a story, ask the Holy Spirit to take you to a place in your own life that may have been spurred on by the daily story you just read. We are all a collection of moments – dots – that we can recall and begin to connect. Once this occurs, we can invite the Holy Spirit to help us find God connections in our stories. For example, in writing the stories of my life I began to see the dots connect and how it has prepared me for the work that I am now doing for the Kingdom.

As you read my stories, take notes because you will be seeing stories through a new set of lenses, the eyes of your heart. I call it redemptive remembrance because God will show you things you had never seen before. Before long you will realize that God is connected to every story of your life. Next, be sure to share your stories with your family friends and anyone who will listen. There is no better way to be a disciple of Jesus Christ than to share with others what God has done for you personally. You may even want to begin to share your letters via email to people you do not see on a regular basis.

True Self

The day we are born we begin a life-long journey to discover our True Self, the person God created us to be. Early in our lives our identity is formed by those around us. We unknowingly develop core values that help us make decisions. As we move through the teenage years, our identity changes like the season and our self-image morphs along the way. If we are Christians, God slowly, but surely, helps us discover our True Self. In its most simple form, God slowly reveals to us the person He wants us to be as He walks along beside us. The speed at which we hear and understand Him is a function of our daily awareness of His presence; He is always there, but we do not take the time and effort to listen. 365 Love Letters puts a simple focus on increasing your awareness of His daily presence.

Early on, you will start to recognize that your life has changed and your key moments and actions are being led by the Holy Spirit. You will know that there can be no other explanation. Use 365 Love Letters as the foundation for writing your own "Love Letters" – they are there and they are amazing!!!

January

January 1

365 Love Letters

Dear Lori and Chris,

Happy New Year! If the date 1-1-11 doesn't symbolize a new beginning, I don't know what does.

A new beginning–I am going on a journey in 2011 and I want the two of you to go with me. I don't know exactly where the journey will lead us and there is no road map. I can tell you that I am excited about the trip and I have been preparing to go with you for some time. Oh, by the way, we do have a tour guide, which is one reason I am so excited. The tour guide is the Holy Spirit.

For the remainder of 2011, I am going to send you an email every day. All you need to do is to read them. Feel free to share them with others in the family or anyone else who might benefit. With the help of our tour guide, I will try to encourage you, enlighten you, entertain you, and, most importantly, equip you for life.

In essence, I am sending you "365 Love Letters" so that you will never doubt or forget how much I love you. Better yet, I will remind you just how much God loves you. No matter what you have done in the past or what you will do in the future, I love you and God loves you even more. God is love and as it says in 1 John 4:7, "loves comes from God."

I have only one disclaimer for my covenant to you. James 4:15, "If it is the Lord's will, we will live and do this or that." As long as I have breath, I will complete this journey.

See you tomorrow, God willing!

Love,

Dad

p.s. Proverbs 19:21 – Many are the plans in a man's heart, but it is the Lord's purpose that prevails.

January 2 — Broken Relationships

Today is my brother Wayne's birthday. I have not spoken to him since his last birthday a year ago, but I do intend to call him again today to wish him a happy birthday and a happy new year! It doesn't say much for a relationship if I only talk to him for five minutes every year.

Why don't Wayne and I have a better relationship? Over the years, I have asked myself that question, but I never seem to get an answer. Of course, I blame him for the situation because I couldn't possibly be to blame. After all, I did call him last and he didn't call me even once.

When I think about my brother, very few pleasant thoughts come to my mind. I wonder why? Growing up, we had a lot of fun together, even though we fought a lot. He must have the same thoughts about me. For whatever reason, the distance between us grows wider and wider and since Mother died; we don't ever see each other.

Matthew 7:3-5 says, "Why do you look at the speck of sawdust in your brother's eye and pay no attention to the plank in your own eye? How can you say to your brother, let me take the speck out of your eye when all the time there is a plank in your own eye? You hypocrite, first take the plank out of your own eye and then you will see clearly to remove the speck from your brother's eye."

As I begin 2011, I need to take a closer look at broken relationships. Why are they broken? What did I do to break them or fix them? God does not want me to be the judge. James 4:12 says, "There is only one Lawgiver and only one Judge, the one who is able to save and destroy." Needless to say, it isn't I.

Do you have any relationships that need to be mended? Let's make 2011 a year of restoration!

See you tomorrow, God willing!

January 3 — Be an Example

Children and grandchildren are gifts from God and it is our role as parents and grandparents to teach them all the things they need to know to love God and live fruitful lives. Unfortunately, children do not come with instruction booklets so we do the best we can to raise them.

Like many parents, I tried hard and failed often. In retrospect, there were two major mistakes that I made and thousands of smaller ones that I could not begin to uncover or articulate.

Mistake one – The other day I was reading John's Gospel and I was reading about the Last Supper in John 13. When Jesus washed His disciple's feet he said in verse 15, "I have set you an example that you should do as I have done." In raising you, I think I too often said, "Do as I say, not as I do." What a difference! Set an example by all that you do – by how you speak, by how you treat others (especially your spouse), and by your acknowledgement of God's role in your life.

Mistake two – The last statement in the previous paragraph was my second big mistake. Even though I was religious, it was not apparent to me just how much God was blessing me. My pride told me that it was solely I who was responsible for my success. How wrong I was. Make sure your children know that everything you have, including them, is a gift from God.

I apologize for all my mistakes, large and small. With God's help, I have changed and am trying to make up for past foibles. To the degree that you need to change, God will help you if you just ask Him. Revelations 3:20 says, "I stand at the door and knock. If anyone hears my voice and opens the door, I will come in and eat with him and he with me."

It is a powerful invitation. I wish I had opened the door sooner.

See you tomorrow, God willing.

January 4 — Eighth Fruit of the Spirit

Golf has been an important part of my life since I first started playing over 50 years ago. On the golf course, I have made many friends and I have learned a lot about myself–some good and some not so good.

For example, one of my coworkers and golfing buddies in Pennsylvania made an astute observation. He said, "At work you are one of the calmest, most patient people I have ever worked with. On the golf course, you are a totally different person." I knew he was right because the expectations I set for myself on the golf course are unrealistic. I want to play my absolute best every time out. That's a noble objective, but not possible.

On another occasion here in North Carolina, a Christian friend reminded me that the eighth fruit of the Spirit is "self-control." He told me that right after I had shown that I lacked that particular fruit. That comment really hit home so I called him the next day and thanked him for his candor and told him that "self-control" was really the ninth fruit of the Spirit." We laughed. I promise to talk more about God's sense of humor in the future.

All of us need a way of checking our spiritual growth. The fruit of the Spirit listed in Galatians 5:22 are a good checklist. "But the fruit of the Spirit is *love, joy, peace, patience kindness, goodness, faithfulness, gentleness and self-control.*"

There is not a day that goes by that I don't come up short on at least one of these fruits, especially on the golf course. However, with God's help, I can strive to be better. 2 Chronicles 16:9 says, "For the eyes of the Lord range throughout the earth to strengthen those whose hearts are fully committed to Him."

See you tomorrow, God willing!

January 5 — Mercies Never Fail

One of the most well known slogans used by Alcoholics Anonymous is "one day at a time." Not surprisingly, that advice works well for all of us – don't get overwhelmed by the problem or task in front of us. Stay in the moment and eat the elephant one bite at a time.

Akin to that slogan is Jeremiah's word to us in the book of Lamentations. Lamentations 3:21-23 says, "Because of the Lord's great love we are not consumed, for His mercies never fail. They are new every morning; great is your faithfulness."

Do you know why his compassions are new every morning? It is because we use up the previous day's allotment every single day. During the forty years that the Israelites spent in the desert, God fed them manna every day. Only on the day before the Sabbath were they allowed to gather enough manna for more than a single day.

God is trying to assure us of several key messages:

1. He is there for us every day, really, every moment of every day.
2. He will provide for our needs.
3. He loves us "for His compassions never fail."

Those are God's promises to us. What does He ask in return? "Love the Lord your God with all your heart and all your soul and with all your mind...Love your neighbor as yourself (Matthew 22: 37, 39).

Remember, you can't use them all up.

See you tomorrow, God willing!

January 6   Bless the Lord at All Times

I woke up very early this morning and my mind began to race. After lying in the bed for awhile, I knew I would not be going back to sleep so I did what I have done many times in the past, I got up and decided to have a quiet time with the Lord. I glanced at the digital clock on the dresser and the time read "2:34."

That time certainly proved that it was early in the morning, but as you will soon understand, the time had much more significance. In late 1981 through the first few months of 1982, the number "34" kept appearing to me everywhere I turned around. It happened so often that I was spooked. I couldn't figure it out for the life of me what it meant. Perhaps it was part of a lottery number. I started to watch attentively for the other numbers to appear magically so I could win the lottery. They never came and I eventually gave up.

Over 20 years later as I was reading my Bible, God told me the meaning; a meaning I was far too immature in my faith to understand in 1982. The first verse of Psalm 34 says, "I will bless the Lord at all times." That is what He wanted me to learn. My blessings were not of my own making, they were from Him. He wanted me to know it in my heart and He reminds me now every time I see the number "34" anywhere.

Another favorite Bible verse of mine that relates to this story is Deuteronomy 29:29. It says, "The secret things belong to the Lord, but the things revealed belong to us and to our children forever......" There are three powerful messages in that verse. One, there are many secret things that happen in our lives that only God will understand. No matter how hard we try or how much these things affect our lives; we will never understand "why." Two, God does reveal things to us when we are mature enough in our faith to understand. Three, once revealed, these things belong to us and to our children, but only if we share them.

I thank God that He woke me up this morning at 2:34 so I could share this revelation with you.

See you tomorrow, God willing!

January 7 — God's Guest List

Debbie Macomber wrote a book titled "God's Guest List" that I read a couple of months ago. The premise of the book is that throughout your life God places people in your path who dramatically influence your development. Sometimes the people are friends who simply help us learn to love and share while others are described as "sandpaper" because their roughness may be used to help smooth our rough exterior. If you happen to read the book, you will start to think about some of the people God has put on your guest list.

The most unlikely person on my own guest list was a cleaning lady my wife used in Pennsylvania. To be quite honest, I didn't like her at first. When she cleaned, she invariably put things away in the wrong places and we had to search for them every week. Despite her instructions, she continued the annoying habit. To make matters worse, Shirley overpaid her because she needed the money.

To make a long story short, she got my wife started in Bible Study Fellowship (BSF), a very disciplined worldwide organization that helps people study God's word. By the next year, my wife had me attending a men's BSF class along with her husband.

From a humble, Christian cleaning lady I was led to begin studying God's word. I doubt that I have missed five days in the last fifteen years and it has changed my life.

What does God have to say about His Word? 2 Timothy 3:16-17 says, "All scripture is God-breathed and is useful for teaching, rebuking, correcting and training in righteousness so that the man of God may be thoroughly equipped for every good work." Nothing equips you like God's word.

Proverbs 30:5-6, "Every word of God is flawless ......Do not add to His words of He will rebuke you and prove you a liar."

2 Peter 1:21, " For prophesy never had its origin in the will of man, but men spoke from God as they were carried by the Holy Spirit."

It's good enough for me.

See you tomorrow, God willing!

January 8 — There Is No One Who Does Good

There was another guest that God sent around the same time. In retrospect, they were a tag team and just what I needed to kick-start a personal relationship with Jesus Christ. The guest was the discussion leader for BSF and he was as different from the cleaning lady as the day is from the night. He was an executive with a company in Bethlehem, PA. Every week when he lectured he was dressed in a suit and tie. I could relate to him and I admired his knowledge of the Bible and his willingness to share it with us.

I grew up being taught that good works would earn you a place in heaven. It was logical to me and, while I didn't think much about it, I lived most of my adult life hanging on to that belief and trying to live my life according to that premise. In fact, I had a pretty high opinion of myself. I went to church every Sunday; gave generously of my time, talents, and treasures; and generally lived a good life. Oh, I was far from perfect, but on balance, I thought I was earning my way to heaven.

One night the lecture was on Romans 3, my eyes were finally opened. Romans 3:12 says, "There is no one who does good, not even one." He didn't just read these words; he pounded them into my heart. How could he say that? I was really a good person. I was dumbfounded and shocked. Was he telling the truth? Did God really mean that?

For a moment, I couldn't hear him anymore. My mind was racing. My heart was pounding. Then something very strange happened. I was free. I didn't need to be perfect; in fact, I couldn't be perfect, no matter how hard I might have tried. As I would later read in Larry Crabb's book, "The Pressure Is Off," I no longer had to earn my way to heaven. It says it very plainly in Ephesians 2:5b, "It is by grace you have been saved."

I don't know when my consciousness returned, but I am sure I heard this verse next, "for all have sinned and fallen short of the glory of God, and all are justified freely by His grace through the redemption that comes by Jesus Christ." (Romans 3:23-24) That was the payoff.

Works aren't wrong! They are just our response to the love God has for us. That night, I became a new man and I will never be the same.

See you tomorrow, God willing!

January 9 — Flaming Torches

Yesterday morning I was up early. I had finished my morning devotions and my daily letter so I went outside on the balcony to watch the sun rise over the ocean. As I saw the sun come out of the water, the whole earth began to come alive. The darkness gave way to a powerful light. At first, just as the sun comes up, the light is soft and diffused. As the sun reflects off the water at a low angle, the beauty is evident. As it rises more, the power is awesome. All darkness is gone; there are shadows where the direct light cannot go. Yet, even there the light permeates so overall visibility is good.

Last week as I was going through some choice scripture for my writings, I found Isaiah 50:11,"But now, all of you who light fires and provide yourselves with flaming torches, go, walk in the light of your own fires and of the torches you have set ablaze. This is what you shall receive from my hand: you will lie down in torment."

I have a mental image of some one walking in darkness with a blazing torch. How much light does it really give off? How far forward or backward can an individual see with their torch? How long will the torch burn? Will the light from the torch be strong enough to reflect or will it be absorbed? The answers are easy, particularly when you compare the torch to the light of the sun. Magnify that difference and you have a pretty good idea of what we are like as individuals without Christ in our lives. God said it, "you will lie down in torment."

It is easy to go through life walking by the light of our own torches. We think we can see okay, since we have nothing to compare it to. We think the torches light our path. However, once we see the true light, we can begin to see life at its best. The difference is overwhelming. Satan wants us to walk in the darkness. God wants us to walk in the light.

"The thief (Satan) comes only to steal and kill and destroy; I have come that they may have life and have it to the full." (John 10:10)

Walk in the light; the darkness destroys. Enjoy the abundant life that God has in store for you.

See you tomorrow, God willing!

January 10 — Mercy and Grace

I am not a theologian. I am not a Biblical scholar. I am not even a very astute Biblical student. In fact as early as 15 years ago, I would have been classified as Biblically illiterate. I am just a hillbilly (or hill Bill) from the mountains of Southwest Virginia whom God has chosen to help tell His story of mercy and grace.

One of the simplest definitions I have heard for mercy and grace is: mercy is not getting what you deserve and grace is getting what you don't deserve. Because God loves us so much and His mercy is so great, He forgives our sin. And, because of grace, we can have an everlasting relationship with Him, a relationship we can never earn, one that He freely gives. No one is able to sin beyond the Lord's redemptive grace. Romans 5:20b says, "But where sin increased, grace increased all the more."

In Charles Stanley's devotion for today, he said, "Grace is not a license to sin. God allows us to experience the consequences of wrongdoing. That's what a loving parent does to be sure a child learns the value of doing right." Disciple exists; love abounds!

When a group of us from our church was preparing for a mission trip to Bulgaria a couple of years ago, we started preparing for the trip through regular group prayer, Bible study and fellowship. At one of our early meetings, a verse from Hebrews set the course for my own personal preparation.

Hebrews 12:15 says, "See to it that no one misses the grace of God." Little did I know how much impact that verse would have on me. It became the foundation for a sermon I would preach in a small church in Dragonia, Bulgaria; the catalyst for my regular walks through the poorest parts of West Greenville; the mirror for my daily actions at work and play; and, yes, even the genesis for "365 Love Letters."

Please don't miss God's amazing grace. It is a gift. Don't leave it unopened!

See you tomorrow, God willing!

January 11 — Unanswered Prayer

When I moved to North Carolina nearly ten years ago, I had a friend in Pennsylvania who called me every week to see how I was doing. He wanted to make sure I was doing okay and he listened to all of my problems and helped me come up with good solutions. After a few weeks, I got comfortable in my new surroundings so when he called, I didn't want to spend the time talking to him so I quit answering the phone when he called. He was really loyal to me and he kept calling for a long time. Finally though, I guess he knew I no longer needed him so he quit calling. A year passed by and then another year. As life would have it, I ran into a problem I couldn't solve so I gave my friend a call. Would you believe the nerve of that guy? He wouldn't answer the phone.

In Zechariah 7:13, God said the same thing to the Israelites, "When I called, they did not listen so when they called, I would not listen, says the Lord Almighty." God wanted a relationship with his people, just like my friend wanted a relationship with me. The good news is, you can reestablish your relationship with God and He will hear your prayers and answer them.

1 Peter 5: 6-7 says, "Humble your selves, therefore, under God's mighty hand, that He may lift you up in due time. Cast all your anxieties on Him because He cares for you." How do you cast your anxieties on Him? You do it through prayer. When you call on God through prayer you are declaring your dependence on Him. When we humble ourselves we demonstrate our need for Him and our faith in Him. Nothing is a challenge for His power.

Matthew 11:28, "Come to me all you who are weary and burdened and I will give you rest." God's phone line is always open. Leave a message and He will get back to you with an answer that is perfect for you and timed just right.

See you tomorrow, God willing!

January 12   About My Dad

Have you ever noticed that I smile a lot? Psalm 16:6 says, "The boundary lines have fallen for me in pleasant places, surely I have a delightful inheritance." I have always been a very happy person and God has blessed me with a delightful inheritance that is comprised of a wonderful wife, two great children and three fabulous grand children.

As I think back on my childhood, I have trouble tracing the source of my happiness. My dad was not a happy man. I can remember vividly being sent away from the dinner table (without food) for laughing at the table. There was no place for laughing when you were supposed to be eating.

My dad was also a disciplinarian. I still remember two whippings I got as a little boy. One of them was for leaving the gate unlatched that allowed the cows to get out of the pasture. The second whipping was for misbehaving in church. In both cases, dad used a leather belt to help me remember not to repeat my wrongful acts.

My dad was also never satisfied with his job or vocation. As a result, we moved eight times from the time I entered the first grade until I graduated from high school. It did teach me how to make new friends, but it also taught me not to make lasting relationships.

No matter how unhappy my dad was or how often we moved, there was a common thread that was woven through our lives. God was always there and as a family, we attended church every Sunday and prayed over every evening meal. Looking back, I suppose that is where my happiness was grounded. Proverbs 22:6 says, "Train a child in the way he should go and when he is old he will not turn from it."

There were a lot of good qualities in my father and it is a shame that I too often recall his frailties. He did, however, train me in the way I should go, leaving me a delightful inheritance.

See you tomorrow, God willing!

January 13   Suitable Helper

Yesterday I made a mistake and I owe my children and their spouses an apology. I said two great children, but I should have said "two great children with great spouses." In a later email I used the excuse that I think of couples as "one." While it was a lame excuse, it really is true. In Genesis 2:24 it says, "For this reason a man will leave his mother and father and be united to his wife, and they become <u>one</u> flesh." When you become one flesh you take on a new identity. People even refer to their married friends as if they were one: Lori & Randy; Chris & Steph; Bill & Shirley; Becky & David; and Raymond and Amelia. There is an earlier verse in Genesis 2 that I love–verse 18. "The Lord said, 'it is not good for man to be alone.' I will make him a helper suitable for him." I want to focus on two key words, helper and suitable.

A helper is one who complements us; one who picks us up when we are down; one who corrects us when we need it; one who loves us when we are not very lovable; and one who encourages us to be the best we can be. When God uses the word "suitable," He means "hand picked" by Him to complement our skills and be the helper we need.

My wife has been my suitable helper for over 40 years. I encourage each of you to look in the mirror and be the spouse that God has chosen you to be.

I'll close with these verses from Ecclesiastes 4:9-12. "Two are better than one because they have a good return for their work. If one falls down, his friend (spouse) can help him up. But pity the man who falls and has no one to help him up. Also, if two lie down together, they will keep warm. But how can one keep warm alone? Though one may be overpowered, two can defend themselves. A cord of three strands is not quickly broken." Isn't it curious that the whole discussion is about two and then ends up with three, "a cord of three strands?" The third strand is God. He is the one who adds strength to the marriage.

See you tomorrow, God willing!

January 14 — Mire and Mud

This will be our last full day on the island of St. Maarten. The weather has been beautiful and the entire trip has been a continual display of God's creation—its complexity, its beauty, its diversity and its wonder. Yesterday we went on a snorkeling trip that was scheduled to be about four hours long. We were supposed to go to three different sites where we would get a close up look at some of the beautiful fish God created. We also anticipated seeing many shapes and sizes of fish, each variety with a purpose in God's big plan.

Unfortunately, God had a different plan. As we got up yesterday we noticed that the wind was blowing a little harder than it had the previous days. The sea was raging and it would be a tough day to be on a boat. As we got to the marina we were told that there was a change in plans. We would be taxied to another part of the island where they hoped we would find calmer seas. The rest of the day was an adventure. To make a long story short, we tried to snorkel at three different locations, but the visibility in the water was about three feet. The small boat that took us to the locations bobbled up and down like a cork and at least one person on board got very seasick. Don't laugh; it wasn't my wife or I. We did have a great time and the four-hour trip actually lasted nearly six hours.

By now I hope you are wondering where the message is for today. Isaiah 57:20-21 reads, "But the wicked are like the tossing sea, which cannot rest, whose waves cast up mire and mud. There is no peace, says my God, for the wicked."

The image of the tossing sea is appropriate for me right now. Try snorkeling when the sea is restless. You can't see anything because the sand is suspended in the water. If you happen to be on a small boat, as we were, you can also appreciate the uneasiness created by the rolling waves.

God speaks to us in many ways. Yesterday's message was clear—turmoil, no visibility, and unrest. That is the final picture for the wicked that have rejected God.

Matthew 7:7–"Ask and it will be given to you; seek and you will find; knock and the door will be opened for you." God says you don't have to settle for turmoil, lack of direction or unrest.

See you tomorrow, God willing!

January 15 — God Speaks to Us in Many Ways

I first started journaling in March 2000 when my wife and I were on a mission trip to Honduras. One night on that trip I was awakened from my sleep by an intense thunderstorm. Even though it was 2 a.m. in the morning I could not go back to sleep. As my mind recalled some of the experiences of the week, I got out of bed and began to write. Immediately, scripture from 1 Kings 19 came to me. Verses 11b-12 read, "Then a great and powerful wind tore the mountain apart and shattered the rocks before the Lord, but the Lord was not in the wind. After the wind there was an earthquake, but the Lord was not in the earthquake. After the earthquake came a fire, but the Lord was not in the fire. After the fire, came a gentle whisper."

That night I learned something very special. God can speak to us any way or anywhere He chooses. He spoke to Elijah through a gentle whisper. He spoke to Moses through a burning bush. He spoke to Pharaoh through signs and wonders. He spoke to Jonah in the belly of a whale. And, He spoke to Daniel in the lion's den.

I suppose what reminded me of that early morning encounter in Honduras was scripture I read a couple of days ago from Isaiah 29:6, "The Lord almighty will come with thunder and earthquake and great noise, with windstorm and tempest and flames of devouring fire." And, like my experience in Honduras, God has once again awakened me in the wee hours to speak with me.

Over the last decade, it is not uncommon for me to awaken between the hours of 2 a.m. and 3 a.m. and be absolutely certain that I will not be able to go back to sleep. I now use that time to pray. I speak to God in a gentle whisper and I know He hears me through all the noise of the world.

Next time you wake up from a deep sleep in the wee hours of the morning, think about it. Is God nudging you? Does He have something special He wants to tell you? Is there someone or something that He wants you to pray for? Turn an early morning wake up into a special time with your best friend.

See you tomorrow, God willing!

January 16 — Women Should Not Be Invisible

Larry Crabb is a well-known psychologist, conference and seminar speaker, Bible teacher, and popular author. I have read a number of his books, including: *The PAPA Prayer, The Pressure Is Off, Shattered Dreams* and *66 Love Letters*.

He came to our church a few years ago to do a weekend conference entitled *Life on the Narrow Road*. Like his books, the conference was a little hard to take and understand. It is hard to argue with his ideas, but hard for me to put them into daily practice.

I am embarrassed to admit, I couldn't tell you too much about the theme and purpose of that weekend conference. One topic that he discussed, however, will forever remain embedded in my soul. It had to do with the difference between men and women.

He said that men live to protect themselves from being hurt. Women, on the other hand, are contentious and vexing to avoid being invisible. That last phrase hit me like a ton of bricks, "to avoid from being invisible." To most men, women are vexing. Some women may even be ill tempered. That really isn't the point. The question is "what are we as men doing on a daily basis to help insure that the women in our lives don't feel invisible." Do we listen without offering solutions? Do we spend quality time with them? Do we go out of our way to do special things for them? Do we love them unconditionally?

I love my wife dearly, but I cannot honestly say that I do all of these things as well as I should. The scriptural basis for Crabb's conference comes from Matthew 7:13-14. "Enter through the narrow gate. For wide is the gate and broad is the road that leads to destruction. But small is the gate and narrow the road that leads to life, and only a few find it." Take the narrow gate with your loved ones and treat them as men of God should treat them and they will "shine like stars in the universe." (Philippians 2:14c)

See you tomorrow, God willing!

January 17 — Toasting and Boasting

On December 31, 1985, we hosted a New Year's Eve party at our home in Pennsylvania. It had been a joyful and successful year and, as the New Year approached, we toasted the grand year past.

On New Year's Day 1986, the next day, the water pump in our well failed. That was the beginning of a bad string of misfortune. In March, my father died of a heart attack at the age of 72. The following month we discovered that our fourteen-year old son was experimenting with illegal drugs. I thought back to New Year's Eve and swore that I would never again toast the good fortune of a year, fearing it would quickly bring on misfortune in the following year.

Fast forward to New Year's Eve 2001. The year 2001 had been another wonderful year. I retired in August and we moved to North Carolina to get away from the harsh weather of Pennsylvania. It also helped that we were nearer our son who lived in Emerald Isle, NC and our daughter and her lovely family who lived in Greenville where we moved

To make a long story short, in a gathering with friends on New Year's Eve 2001, I once again toasted the events of the previous year. However, this time I did not fear a curse of misfortune following the toast. Why? What had changed?

In the intervening sixteen years, I had learned a valuable lesson. All of the blessings I had received in 2001 were from God. They were not of my own doing. He blessed me, and my family, and He continues to bless me today. Of course, He also blessed me in 1985, but that year, I took the credit. Were there any bad times in 2002? Yes. Could I deal with the problems on my own? No. Did God help me through the valleys? Yes. Will He ever leave me or forsake me? No.

Jeremiah 9:23-24–"Let not the wise man boast in his wisdom or the strong man boast of his strength or the rich man boast of his riches, but let him boast about this: that he understands and knows Me, that I am the Lord, who exercises kindness, justice, and righteousness on earth for in these I delight, declares the Lord."

Yes, I had learned a valuable lesson. Isn't it interesting that if you change the one letter in the word "boast" you get the word "toast?" Let not the wise man "toast" of his wisdom ...his strength...his riches...Let him "toast" Me.

Psalm 121:1 – "I lift my eyes to the hills, where does my help come from? My help comes from the Lord."

Where does your help come from?

See you tomorrow, God willing!

January 18 — It's the Heart, Not the Suit

Early in my career when I moved from the research laboratories to the advertising department at the chemical company where I worked, I had to start wearing suits to work every day. That was a big change for me and, having very little money at the time, I had to wear the cheapest suits I could find. My office was in downtown Cincinnati so I often walked by a Brooks Brothers store during my lunch hour. I would look in the windows and think to myself, one day, when I am successful, I'll buy myself a Brooks Brothers suit and wear it proudly.

Time passed by and I switched jobs and moved to Pennsylvania. Although the suits I purchased were of slightly better quality, I still longed for one from Brooks Brothers. One Christmas after my wife had taken a part time job to get out of the house and make some spending money, she bought me my first Brooks Brothers suit. I wore it proudly and began the process of switching my whole suit wardrobe over to these quality suits.

I looked good on the outside, but I was worried more about my outside appearance than my heart. The other day, I was reading a book by Charles Spurgeon, the late English writer and preacher. In his book, he mentioned another English preacher by the name of Daniel Burgess who covered this "suit" topic in a particularly clever way. While I have changed the names of the stores for clarity, I have retained Burgess's meaning. "If any of you want a cheap suit, go to Today's Man; if you want a suit for life go to Brooks Brothers; but if you want a suit that will last to eternity, you must go to the Lord Jesus Christ and put on His robe of righteousness."

"For the kingdom of God is not a matter of eating and drinking (Or what you wear), but of righteousness, peace, and joy in the Holy Spirit." Romans 14:17. Obviously, I added the words in parenthesis. I still have my Brooks Brothers suits, but I only wear them once or twice a year. As I have gotten older, I know Daniel Burgess is correct. Although I am unworthy to wear His robe of righteousness, God allows me to try it on every now and then to remind me "that I have been marked with a seal, the promised Holy Spirit, who is a deposit guaranteeing my inheritance." (Ephesians 1:14).

See you tomorrow, God willing!

January 19   Coincidence or God

Coincidence is defined in the New American Oxford Dictionary as "a remarkable concurrence of events or circumstances without apparent causal connection." It is also a word that many people use to describe events, usually of some remarkable nature, which cannot otherwise be explained. Before one develops his or her faith, we use that word a lot. However, as faith in Jesus Christ grows, we slowly and surely begin to learn that the word probably comes from the devil to help keep our eyes closed to the wonder of our Lord and Savior.

I read the Bible every morning. Sometimes I read the Bible straight through and other times I wander around wherever God leads me. A couple of years ago after finishing the whole Bible, I recalled receiving a book that explained the Psalms in great depths so I decided to use that book as a guide through the Psalms. Twelve days into that personal study I read Psalm 12 and verse 6 really caught my attention. "The promises of the Lord are pure, silver refined in a furnace on the ground, purified seven times." I have been through a lot of trials in my life, as we all have, and that verse helped me to understand how God works to purify us and to demonstrate His power and majesty.

I recalled many times in the Bible where God caused things to happen in such a powerful manner to demonstrate that He alone is God, there can be no coincidence, no other explanation for the events. In Exodus chapters 7 – 13, God rains down disaster after disaster on the Egyptians to prove that their gods could not stand up to Him. In 1 Kings 18, God shows the 450 priests of Baal that they were no match for one servant of the most-high God. In John 11, Jesus raises Lazarus from the grave after four days to show the Jews that He was the real God, since Jews believed that the soul left a dead person after three days. And in Acts 19, Paul was able to heal people by sending handkerchiefs and aprons he had touched to loved ones in need. Corinth, where this happened, was full of false gods, once again proving God's majesty.

That night I was talking to my wife about the great verse (Psalms 12:6) that I had read and memorized that morning. To my surprise she said, "Oh yea, I heard that same verse today at the Women's Conference."

Coincidence?

See you tomorrow, God willing!

January 20   Planting Seeds

You probably don't know much about my early years on a farm in Southern Illinois. My dad was born in that area and raised on a farm with a whole bunch of brothers and sisters, eleven in all. He loved farming, but he was the only one in our family who did.

I do have some fond memories of the three years we lived on the farm and I learned some life lessons. I can vividly remember riding on tractors and riding on pigs. I remember helping with the baling of hay and making tunnels in the stacked hay in the barn. I recall riding my bicycle on the gravel road in front of the house and failing to negotiate the curve resulting in numerous scars on my knees that are still visible today. The first baseball I remember was playing with my brother in the yard. And, I enjoyed fishing for catfish, blue gills and perch in our ponds.

There is one particular adventure that comes fondly to mind. One spring, my brother, two friends and I decided to build a raft in order to voyage across one of our ponds. The ponds weren't very large so it seemed safe enough, so we thought. Either the raft was no good or we were lousy sailors, either way we ended up in the pond and the water was very cold. Frankly, I don't remember the consequences of our foolhardiness, but I'm sure mom and dad weren't very happy with us.

Farmers, perhaps more than any other profession, have to trust in God for their livelihood. They can plant and fertilize, but it is up to God to nourish the crop. Of course, planting the seed reminds me of Jesus' parable in Mark 4:3-8. "A farmer went out to sow his seed. As he was scattering the seed, some fell along the path, and the birds came and ate it up. Some fell on rocky places, where it did not have much soil. It sprang up quickly because the soil was shallow. But when the sun came up, the plants were scorched, and they withered because they had no root. Other seed fell among thorns, which grew up and choked the plants, so that they did not bear grain. Still other fell on good soil. It came up, grew and produced a crop, multiplying thirty, sixty or even a hundred times."

Farmers know where to plant their seeds. However, those of us who spread God's seed are at a slight disadvantage, because we are not always sure of the quality of the soil. Still God tells us to keep sowing the seed; He will take care of everything else.

See you tomorrow, God willing!

January 21 — Who Is Legion?

There was a man in the Bible by the name of Legion. No one really knows what his real name was, but that was the name he was given by the people where he lived. The only thing we know about him is provided in Mark's Gospel, Chapter 5. Legion was demon possessed and lived in the tombs on an island across the lake from Gerasenes. We know he was incredibly strong because no one could bind him with chains. Mark tells us that Legion had often been chained hand and foot, but he tore the chains apart and broke the irons on his feet. No one was strong enough to subdue him.

That's where the story gets good. Jesus had crossed the lake and landed on the island. When Legion saw Him from a distance he ran and fell on his knees in front of Him. He shouted at the top of his voice, "What do you want with me, Jesus, Son of the Most High God? Swear to God that you won't torture me." For Jesus had said to him, "Come out of this man, you evil spirit!" The rest of the story, as told in Mark 5:1-20, is history. Jesus drove out the demons and cleansed Legion. He was a new man, a new creation. As Jesus was leaving the island, Legion begged Him to let him go with him, but Jesus declined and told Legion to "Go home to your family and tell them how much the Lord has done for you and how He has had mercy on you." The Bible says that he did and all were amazed.

There is one more thing I know about Legion that Mark doesn't tell us. I am Legion. You are Legion and so is everyone else whom God has cleansed from the demons that haunt our lives. While we may want to go with Jesus and rest in His Glory that is not what He wants us to do. "Go home to your family and tell them how much the Lord has done for me!"

Quite frankly, I haven't done a very good job of telling the story of what Jesus has done for me, but I am trying to make up for lost time, every day.

See you tomorrow, God willing!

January 22 — The Birthday Party

It is 4 o'clock in the morning and I am lying here in bed looking at the nearly full moon shining through the skylight. The still of the night is broken by the sound of the wind chimes that are just outside the bedroom. Is the music from the wind chimes playing "Happy Birthday"? Is the moon really a large birthday candle? Are they having a birthday party in heaven to celebrate my mother's birthday?

When she left her earthly tent, God assured us that her room was ready. "Do not let your hearts be troubled. Trust in God; trust also in me. In my Father's house are many rooms; if it were not so I would have told you. I am going there to prepare a place for you. And if I go and prepare a place for you, I will come back and take you to be with me that you also may be where I am." John 14:1-3. We read this scripture to mother a lot in the last months of her life and it always made her smile. She knew her room was being made ready just for her.

When you celebrate a birthday, it is natural to think about all of the gifts God has given us. Mother had many gifts and she left many of them behind with her children, grandchildren, great grandchildren and yes, all the significant others.

Mother loved the beach and she taught us how to get the most of it. Our stoop shoulders were obtained by many hours of searching the shore for a prized seashell. She loved to garden and our house and yard a full of beautiful flowers. She loved to play cards and she played bridge until her memory would not allow her to remember which cards had been played. Even that didn't stop her from playing cards. No one in the entire family will ever play "kings around the corner' without thinking of her.

Mother also loved Jesus and as long as she lived with us, she went to church every Sunday. Growing up, I remember her tireless work at her church as a Sunday school teacher, a choir member, and the official baker of a "black skillet cherry cobbler" for every potluck dinner ever held at St. Paul Methodist Church.

"Listen, my son, to your father's instruction and do not forsake your mother's teaching." The shining moon and the music from the wind chimes reminded me this morning of the importance of this verse from Proverbs 1:8.

See you tomorrow, God willing!

January 23   It's A Fool

The year 2000 was to be our last Christmas in Pennsylvania. I had decided to take early retirement from my job and head south. Knowing we were moving my daughter and her family, decided to visit us for Christmas. We made plans to go into New York City and see the annual Radio City Music Hall Christmas production. In order to catch the bus into the city, we had to arise well before sun came up. Getting our youngest grandson up at the hour was no easy task. To make a long story a little shorter, we got him up and dressed. However, when he went outside and saw that it was still pitch black, he exclaimed, "It's a fool!" In his mind, we had pulled a dirty trick on him. You just don't get up before sunrise.

Sometimes, I think we react to things in our life with the same attitude towards God, "it's a fool." Our faith is tested when we try to intellectualize God. It says in 1 Corinthians 1:19 and 25, "For it is written: I will destroy the wisdom of the wise; the intelligence of the intelligent I will frustrate...For the foolishness of God is wiser than man's wisdom, and the weakness of God is stronger than man's strength."

Until we let go of our intellect and allow our heart and soul to experience God, we will never be happy. In the book of Job, Job and his three friends tried to rationalize God's role in all of Job's troubles. Finally, God spoke to Job directly starting in Chapter 38 and ending in Chapter 41. In perhaps the most beautiful prose every written, God asks Job many questions. "Were you there when I laid the earth's foundation? Who shut up the sea behind the door? Have you ever given orders to the morning or shown the dawn its place? What is the way to the place where the lightning is dispersed? Who let the wild donkey go free? Who provides the food for the raven?" Job could only answer, "I am unworthy, how can I reply to You?"

That about sums it up. "I am unworthy, how can I reply to you?" So the next time you are tempted to say, "It's a fool," just remember the definition of faith written in Hebrews 11:1. "Now faith is being sure of what we hope for and certain of what we do not see." It is not intellectual, it's the heart.

See you tomorrow, God willing!

January 24   There's Music in the Air

For many years, I was a big fan of country music. It was all I listened to. I can remember driving my daughter to high school and she would ask me to turn the radio off when I let her off at school so she wouldn't be embarrassed in front of her friends. Country music wasn't pretty, but the words seemed to be about real life. Just look at some of the titles and phrases of some country music songs and you'll see real people with real emotions – *Don't come home drinking with lovin' on your mind*; *Take this job and shove it*; *The girls all look prettier at closing time*; and *There's a place down the road they call Sam's place*.

Country music describes all aspects of life, but it tends to concentrate on the darker side of our lives. And unfortunately, it doesn't offer much in the way of solutions. If I knew anything about rap music, I would describe the same situation with the words and lyrics simply aimed at a group of people with a different set of vices.

There was no magical time when I stopped listening to country music, but there was a reason. I found something better.

"As the deer panteth for the water
So my soul longeth after thee."

*"No weeping, no hurt or pain,
No suffering, you hold me now,
You hold me now."*

"Thy word is a lamp unto my feet and a light unto my path."

Christian music doesn't dwell on the miseries of mankind. It dwells on the solutions to our problems. The majority of Christian music simply puts the words of the Bible to music. Psalm 119:105 reminds us that God's word is indeed a lamp to our feet and a light for our path. *No weeping* tells of the New Jerusalem of Revelations 21. And, Psalm 42 describes our longing for a Savior akin to a deer panting to water.

If you don't already listen to Christian music, tune in your car radio to a Christian station the next time you are on the road and see if it doesn't lighten your day. After all, it's just the Bible put to music.

See you tomorrow, God willing!

January 25   Manna–What is It?

As I have gotten into the rhythm of writing a daily devotion, I have a fear that some morning I will wake up and the cupboard will be bare. Perhaps, I thought, I should go ahead, write some devotions, and put them into inventory for use at a later date, just in case. Would that be cheating? Would I be losing faith in the Holy Spirit to guide me every day?

As always, the answer is in the Bible. While the Israelites were wandering around the desert for forty years, God gave them manna every day to fill their hunger needs. When they first saw it on the ground, they said, "what is it" and the Hebrew word for that is manna. Can you imagine eating the same thing every day for forty years? The Bible doesn't tell us this, but they probably learned to be very imaginative in their food preparation. They made manna stew, manna salad, manna goulash, and their favorite was obviously manna-cotti. (Sorry, I just couldn't resist). In Exodus 16:16, "This is what the Lord has commanded: Each one is to gather as much as he needs".....v19 "No one is to keep any of it until morning."

God wanted the Israelites to learn an important lesson – Trust in me, God says, I will provide for your needs every day of your life. Later in the New Testament when Jesus taught His disciples how to pray in Matthew 6: 11, He said, "Give us this day our daily bread." If God can provide food for two million people in the desert every day for forty years, I suppose it is not a big stretch for Him to provide me with ideas for a daily devotional for one year.

I do keep a notebook of ideas for devotions and as I read other authors, I jot down thoughts from them that I think will be useful. I do a little planning, but not much.

This is what the Bible says in Proverbs 19:21, "many are the plans in a man's heart, but it is the Lord's purpose that prevails." Isaiah 30:1 says, "Woe to the obstinate children," declares the Lord, "to those who carry out plans that are not mine." On a more positive note, Proverbs 16:3 says, "Commit to the Lord whatever you do, and your plans will succeed." All of these verses combined spell out what the Lord said to the Israelites four thousand years ago and what He is still telling us today, "Trust me!"

See you tomorrow, God willing!

January 26   Buy or Build?

When we moved to North Carolina in the summer of 2001, we rented a house so we could get a good lay of the land before we plunged into the housing market. As we looked at houses of all shapes and sizes, we discovered that we had another decision to make. Should we buy an existing house, as we had always done, or should we go "hog wild" and build one just to our liking?

There was one house that my wife really liked, but it had a few flaws, don't we all. Thankfully, we had included God in our planning process, praying daily for His guidance and will. He answered me one morning around 3 a.m. and almost verbally told me "no" about that particular house. When I told my wife about the response from God, she said okay, and we continued our search.

One day as we were driving around looking at houses, she went up to a new house that was for sale and, since it was not open and no one was around, she went up and peered in the windows. Out of nowhere a man appeared, the builder of the house saw my wife and opened the house for her to view the inside. We didn't buy that house, but it opened a dialogue with the builder.

Each time we went to his office to look at house plans, we would pray in the parking lot for God's direction and blessing. Finally, we found a plan we liked and, after making several modifications to the plan, it was time to sign an agreement. The very morning we were to make the decision, God shed His magnificent light on our dilemma. I was reading the book of Samuel at the time and here is what God told us. 2 Samuel 7:27 says, "I will build a house for you." I couldn't believe my eyes.

That day we signed the papers and began to build. A few days later, I ran across another bit of advice. Psalm 127:1, "Unless the Lord builds the house, its builders labor in vain. Unless the Lord watches over the city, the watchmen stand guard in vain." How does the Lord build a house? He starts with a very strong foundation – Him. Then He fills it with His love and watches over it to keep it safe.

If you come to the front door of our house, look down on the sidewalk just before you get to the front porch. You will see 2 Samuel 7:27 scribbled in the concrete. It is a permanent reminder of who rules our lives.

See you tomorrow, God willing!

January 27 — Do Not Be Afraid

When we first got married, we moved from Virginia to Cincinnati, Ohio so I could get a job in the chemical industry. It was a scary move since we would be living over five hours away from our families. Two years later, I faced another traumatic decision. I worked as a research chemist, and the company asked me to move to the advertising department. I was afraid. Ten years later after I finished my MBA program, we made the tough decision to move to Pennsylvania to another job that offered more money and opportunity. It was ten hours away from our families, and we were afraid.

By now, I guess you get the point. There are many times in our lives when we face tough decisions that cause us to be afraid. Not surprisingly, in the NIV version of the Bible, the phrase "Do not be afraid" appears over three hundred sixty-five times. In each case, God is speaking to one of His flock and telling them there is no reason for fear, even in the worst of circumstances. As you look at some of these verses, you will see that the term applies to many situations.

1 Chronicles 22:13 – "Then you will have success…..Do not be afraid." Do not be afraid to step out in life to achieve success.

2 Chronicles 20:15 – "Do not be afraid….of this vast army. For the battle is not yours, but the Lord's." Do not be afraid of the obstacles that get in your way. God will take care of them if you trust Him.

Luke 1:30 – "Do not be afraid, Mary. You have found favor with God." Do not be afraid to accept God's call for your life.

Acts 18:9 – "Do not be afraid. Keep on speaking. Do not be silent." Do not be afraid to share your testimony with others.

Revelations 2:10 – "Do not be afraid of what you are about to suffer." God gives us special instructions about suffering. "We rejoice in our sufferings because we know suffering produces perseverance; perseverance, character; character, hope. And hope does not disappoint us because God has poured out His love into our hearts by the Holy Spirit…" Romans 5:3-5.

Frankly when I was younger, I was afraid of the unknown because I did not call on the Lord for strength. As I have gotten older, I have learned to trust God and live by His instructions and that has made all the difference.

See you tomorrow, God willing!

January 28   Laughter – the Best Medicine

One of the daily devotions that I read had this verse from Luke 6:21. "Blessed are you who weep now, for you will laugh." That verse reminded me of several reasons why I love to read the Bible. The first reason is its ability to stay alive. Since God was, is and will be, the Words in the Bible are not stagnant. They spoke to His people when they were written thousands of years ago and they speak to us today just as powerfully. I marvel at the Bible's teachings, its life instructions, its depth, its poetry, and I love its humor. God wants us to laugh as well as weep.

Have you ever had someone tell you that you have short arms and deep pockets? I hope not, because it's a graphic expression for someone who is cheap. In Numbers 11:23, "The Lord answered Moses, Is the Lord's arm too short?" Moses doubted that God was going to be able to "pay the bill" to feed 600,000 men.

In John 9:27, God uses a bit of sarcasm to deliver His point. The verse takes place after a man blind from birth has his sight restored. The Pharisees refused to believe either the parents or the man and they were working hard to discredit him. The former blind man's final response to the Pharisees dripped with sarcasm. "I have told you already and you did not listen. Why do you want to hear it again? Do you want to become His disciples, too?"

You have to picture the next situation to get a good laugh. God had promised Abraham that he would be the father of nations. Yet years had passed since that promise was made and Abraham had reached the ripe old age of 99 and Sarah, his wife, was no spring chicken. Sarah was standing near the entrance to the tent when she heard God repeat His promise to Abraham. "So Sarah laughed to herself as she thought, after I am worn out and my master is old, will I now have this pleasure." She was laughing not because of the ridiculous nature of the situation but because of her realization that all things are possible with God

Next time you are in a weeping mood, think of Jesus and what He did for us on the cross and it will turn your tears into laughter.

See you tomorrow, God willing!

January 29 — The First Milepost

My wife could tell you some things about me that you may not know. For example, when I get in the car and travel for a long period, I usually don't talk to her very much. I don't understand why I am that way because as a young boy at school I was forever in trouble with the teachers for talking too much. Furthermore, no one has ever accused me of being an introvert. There are exceptions to my "no talking" rule. I talk a lot when I get excited. Yesterday as we traveled to Virginia to see my son and his family, I was excited for two reasons. One, we were going to celebrate Christmas 2010 with them because the weather and other factors had made the traditional time of celebration impractical. However, the real source of my excitement came from my experiences of the last twenty-eight days. Writing to my family on a daily basis has opened my eyes to things I would never have seen or discerned before. It has also opened up lines of communication to levels I never thought possible. That is one reason why my wife and I started talking so much in the car about events in our lives that may be of interest to you. Some of these events will give you a glimpse of yourselves through our eyes and others will be glimpses of things that were part of our own journey to maturation.

Why is it important to tell you of days past? Deuteronomy 11:19 tells us to "teach them to your children, talking about them when you sit at home and when you walk along the road, when you lie down and when you get up." Of course, God was instructing the Israelites to teach their children about Him. One way I can tell you about God is by telling you my own personal stories, some include each of you and some do not. Either way, God is a central character.

That is all for today. Although it is not the end of a month or the end of a quarter, it has turned out to be a milepost. I cannot wait to start the next leg of the journey.

See you tomorrow, God willing!

January 30 — Forsaken? Not on Your Life

Although golf has been my favorite pastime for many years, there was a twenty-year period of my life that I just didn't have the time or inclination to play. It was during that time that I took up tennis. It was far less expensive, but more importantly, I could play all I could handle in less than two hours compared to a commitment of at least five hours to play eighteen holes of golf. One of my favorite tennis stories involves my son.

My best friend and I played most of our tennis at Lennape Park, which was about a mile from our house in Pennsylvania. Lennape Park not only had nice tennis courts, it also had great playground equipment for children. Although my son, who was about seven or eight years old at the time, didn't usually go with us, on the day in question, he wanted to go play on the swings and other equipment while we played tennis. All was well until we finished playing tennis and proceeded to leave for home forgetting that my son was with us. He told me later that he saw us leaving and his heart sank. Before we traveled the mile to the house, we discovered our error and retrieved our prize package.

As a parent, we never want to give our children any reason to believe that we have forsaken them in any way. Our heavenly Father feels the same way. When Joshua was about to lead the Israelites into the Promised Land, he felt alone after taking over Moses' leadership position. God knew that Joshua was feeling like my son did when we left him behind. To comfort him, God made Joshua a promise in Joshua 1:5, "As I was with Moses, so will I be with you; I will never leave you nor forsake you."

That promise is still good today. No matter what trials or tribulations we face; no matter how deep the valleys; no matter how dark the nights; no matter how depressed we feel, God will never leave us or forsake us. There is another related promise that God makes to us in 1 Corinthians 10:13, "No temptation has seized you except what is common to man. And God is faithful; He will not let you be tempted beyond what you can bear. But when you are tempted, He will provide a way out so that you can stand up to it."

There you have it. He won't forsake us. He won't let us be tempted beyond what we can bear. And, He will provide us a way out of our troubles. Sounds like a pretty good Father to me. Oh, that I could measure up.

See you tomorrow, God willing!

January 31   Do Dreams Ever Have Meaning?

Have you ever had a dream that was so real that you woke up during the middle of the night and wondered what just happened?

"Last night I had a wonderful dream. For a brief moment, an angel reached down and took me by the hand. The angel had wings and was dressed in pure white just as I have seen them portrayed in movies and paintings. There was also an incredibly strong white light that surrounded the angel."

When I got up the next morning, I didn't know what the dream meant. My first thought was of impending death, but that seemed too obvious. I prayed for enlightenment because I had a strong sense that God was trying to tell me something. As I was doing my morning prayers that day, I looked at the wall to my right and there was the silhouette of an angel. This one I could explain. In the window above my prayer bench hangs a stained glass angel that my wife had made. When the sun rises in the morning, it hits the angel and casts a shadow on the wall. While this angel was explainable, it confirmed to me that God wanted to tell me something important.

Eight days later, I was once again doing my morning prayers and God told me to go to the story of Balaam in the Bible (Numbers 22:21-41. There are three central characters in this story–Balaam, a donkey, and an angel. In the story, the angel appears to Balaam to oppose him and give him instructions, but the stubborn, lowly donkey sees the angel well before Balaam does. When the donkey saw the angel it was frightened, Balaam sensed that something was wrong and became very angry at his mount.

Finally, it dawned on me. Had I been like Balaam and not seen the angels in my life? Had pride and my desire for possessions kept me from seeing? Had I shown anger to others who have kept me from getting where I need to go? The simple message of the dream was "don't let your pursuit of earthly goals keep you from seeing the angels in your life. Several days later, I came across affirmation in Psalm 32:9. "Don't be like the horse or the mule which have no understanding, but must be controlled by bit and bridle." Verse 8 of that Psalm says, "I will instruct you and teach you in the way you should go; I will counsel you and watch over you."

Two key characters in the Bible, Daniel and Joseph, had the gift to interpret dreams. If God talked about dreams that much in the Bible, there must be something supernatural about some them. The next time you have a dream that seems to wrestle with your spirit; don't assume it was something you ate. Get on your knees and ask God what it means.

See you tomorrow, God willing!

FEBRUARY

February 1 — Tradition or Straitjacket?

A straitjacket is defined as "a strong garment with long sleeves that can be tied together to confine a violent prisoner or mental patient." The word is often used more loosely to describe our habits and beliefs when they bind our ability to think and act in a rationale manner.

Our daughter and her family were visiting us in Pennsylvania one year and on that particular visit, we attended St. Margaret's Episcopal Church, our place of worship for nearly twenty-five years. Let me remind everyone that the praise music more familiar to my son-in-law, which is played at their church, is nothing like the hymns at St. Margaret's. As the worship service progressed that morning, I noticed that my son-in-law was not really singing with us, but rather he seemed to be flipping through the hymnal. After the hymn was over, he poked me in the side to get my attention and said to me, "I found a new one, 1814." The Episcopal Hymnal is full of traditional hymns, written hundreds of years ago, and he had found a new one written in 1814.

His comment was funny, but insightful. When we moved to North Carolina several years later, we began to attend his church. It was then that the stark reality of his earlier observation became apparent. I have since learned that God's people can worship Him in many ways. As his pastor has pointed out on many occasions, there is only one church in Pitt County or any other county for that matter. They go by many names and they come in all shapes and sizes, but they are still one church universal.

In a recent daily devotion, I got a warning about one aspect of getting too set in my ways no matter what church I attend. Colossians 2:8 says, "See to it that no one takes you captive through hollow and deceptive philosophy, which depends on human tradition and the basic principles of this world rather than on Christ."

The moral of the story is this. Be true to God's instruction book when you worship. "God is spirit, and His worshipers must worship in spirit and in truth." (John 4:24) Tradition is just fine, unless it becomes a straitjacket.

See you tomorrow, God willing!

February 2 — Obedience Pays Off

When I was in school at the University of Virginia, I was fortunate enough to be within an hour's drive of my sister's house in Manassas. On more than one occasion, I caught a ride to Manassas with a roommate, who lived in Fairfax, in order for me to spend the weekend with family. One particular weekend remains indelibly inscribed on my memory over forty years later.

My sister gave us the location of a Shell gas station where we could meet her. We arrived at the location she had designated, but we couldn't find the place. After searching for a few minutes, we found the station several blocks away. However, when we got there, she wasn't there. Since there were no cell phones to contact her, my friend drove me directly to her house. She was there and in a very apologetic mood. It seems the gas station where she intended to meet us was in the right place. However, it was a Texaco station not Shell.

That weekend and others like them were a lot of fun. Her husband would ask me to help him clean out the horse stable. I think he got a kick out of getting the young UVa student to humble himself by doing the most menial labor. Before I left on Sundays to return to school, he would slip me a $20 bill and tell me not to tell my sister. A little later, she would slip me a $20 bill and tell me not to tell him. I was obedient and never told either one of them.

I was on scholarship at Virginia, which paid for most of my expenses. However, it didn't pay for food. Mom and Dad weren't able to make much of a contribution because money was scarce. I had a part time job that helped some, but peanut butter and jelly was still a staple. I don't know if my sister knew my plight or not, but the contributions were much appreciated.

Jesus reassured His disciples that God would provide for them. Luke 12:22-24 says, "Therefore I tell you, do not worry about your life, what you will eat; or about your body, what you will wear. Life is more than food and the body more than clothes. Consider the ravens: They do not sow or reap, they have no storeroom or barn; yet God feeds them. And how much more valuable you are than birds."

I wasn't wise enough at the time to realize what was happening, but looking back now I can understand what God is saying. Luke 12:25 goes on to say, "Who of you by worrying can add a single hour to his life." A little faith goes a long way. So does $40 to a poor college student.

See you tomorrow, God willing!

February 3 — Good Question!

Today is the day we would have celebrated my wife's dad's birthday, or was it yesterday? Right up to the day he died at the ripe old age of 90, no one really knew whether he was born on February 2nd or February 3rd. However, there was a lot we did know about him. He was a great storyteller and he told us many a story about his childhood, his days as a young man and stories about his days as both a bus driver and an owner of a bus line.

I can also tell you that her dad could fix anything and he kept spare parts for everything in case he needed them when something broke. I loved to have him visit us because if there were something in the house that needed fixing, he would do it. Once when we lived in Pennsylvania he split a whole cord of firewood for us, pretty good for a man nearly 80 years old at the time.

He was very generous with his time and money. In our early years of marriage, we didn't have a lot of extra cash lying around, but we always managed to visit them on holidays. It was common for him to slip me some cash to help pay for the expenses of the trip.

He never met a man he didn't like and I doubt that there was ever a man that didn't like him. I recall that he met my son-in-law before we did. After meeting my son-in-law, he told my daughter and my wife that "he was a keeper." He was a good judge of people and he loved his family, especially the grandchildren.

He was a good man in every respect. Yet, as his health failed, my wife began to wonder if her dad had been saved. Good men don't necessarily go to heaven. Works don't get you there. Romans 10:9 says, "That if you confess with your mouth, 'Jesus is Lord,' and believe in your heart that God raised Him from the dead, you will be saved." Had he made that confession?

After he died, my wife got the answer from two different sources. She found a card in an old Bible that confirmed the date and place of his salvation. Just so there was no mistake, she learned later from her brother that while her dad was in the hospital before his death, he once again accepted Jesus as his Lord and Savior.

There is no question more important for each of us to answer. Have I accepted Jesus or rejected Him? It is a good question.

See you tomorrow, God willing?

February 4 — Walking in the Light

The year after my son and his wife moved to Southwest Virginia, we spent an autumn afternoon walking with them through the woods enjoying the foliage. It was a gorgeous day and I recall the sun filtering through the trees as God highlighted the magnificent golds, reds, greens, and yellows of the changing leaves. That same light glistened over the waterfalls that we saw as we walked along the path. God's light also showed me something that afternoon that I had seen in our son before, but never so clearly. I saw the gifts that God had given him. He loves the outdoors and everything that goes with it. He loves to use his hands and his mechanical abilities to fix things. He also loves to camp, fish, and four wheel, which makes the mountains a perfect place for him to live.

As I thought about the gifts that God bestowed on him, I thought about how different my gifts were from his. It was apparent to me that our son had inherited many of his gifts from my wife's father. In some respects, life had come full circle. We moved away from St. Paul over forty years ago and our son and his wife had moved to that same town years later bringing the gifts that my wife's father had displayed there until his death over twenty years ago.

As part of a ministry known as "Letters from Dad," I wrote my son a letter that talked about his gifts. The focus of the letter was to encourage him in his new surrounding and let him know that he was special. God's desire is for us to do all we can to "turn the hearts of the fathers to their children, and the hearts of the children to their fathers"...Malachi 4:6

As I have gotten older, I am trying to make up for lost time. Psalm 78:1-7 gives me the instructions I need. "O my people, hear my teaching; listen to the words of my mouth. I will open my mouth in parables, I will utter hidden things, things from of old, what we have heard and known, what our fathers have told us. We will not hide them from their children; we will tell the next generation the praiseworthy deeds of the LORD, his power, and the wonders he has done... so the next generation would know them, even the children yet to be born, and they in turn would tell their children. Then they would put their trust in God and would not forget his deeds but would keep his commands."

It will take a long time for me to tell all the praiseworthy deeds God has done for me. That's the whole premise of *365 Love Letters*.

See you tomorrow, God willing!

February 5 — Three Legs of the Stool

Studying the Bible, praying and journaling serve as the three legs of the stool that support my own personal walk with God. There are many other aspects of that walk – corporate worship, fellowship, and mission/service to name just a few. However, for me, it always comes back to the legs of the stool. Yesterday, the three legs came together in such a startling manner that it drove me to share the experience with you.

In my *365 Love Letter* yesterday, I quoted scripture from Malachi 4:6, "He will turn the hearts of the fathers to their children, and the hearts of the children to their fathers…" After I send out the letter every morning, I read a daily devotional and the Bible, write in my journal, and then finish with prayer. In my journal, I normally summarize the letter that has just gone out and recall events of the previous day that relate to my spiritual journey. I finished yesterday's journal entry with the verse from Malachi.

My practice, as of late, has been to start my morning prayers with my focus on the theme of the daily "Love Letter." That is when God began to reveal to me some of the deeper meaning of Malachi 4:6. The first thing God showed me was the correct sequence that had to take place in order to get our hearts in the right place. Notice in the verse from Malachi that the father's heart must return to the children before the children's hearts return to the father. Are we willing to put forth the effort that it takes to make sure our hearts are in the right place? I'll be honest; I wanted God to do the work, not me. God says that if we do our part the hearts of the children will return to their fathers.

God then proceeded to give me additional insight into Malachi 4:6. There is another father/child relationship in that verse. It is the relationship that all of us have with our Heavenly Father. How does that verse help us with that relationship? The first thing I must realize is that God has already done his part; He doesn't have to turn His heart to us. He already did it at Calvary. It is interesting to note that in Malachi 3:6, just one chapter earlier, God had told His people, "I the Lord do not change."

God is working every day to help us turn our hearts to Him. If we do our part through Bible study, prayer, and fellowship, He will do the rest.

See you tomorrow, God willing!

February 6 — Super Bowl Sunday

My dad was a football fanatic. When he worked the day shift in the coal mines, he would get off work and come directly to the football field to watch my brother and me practice. When he worked the night shift, he would miss work on games days; he couldn't bear to miss a game. Of course, he had his own football stories to tell. In dad's senior year in high school, the Benton Rangers football team went undefeated and unscored on. He even had his high school annual to prove it.

As you might expect, dad's fanaticism had it pros and cons. One of the benefits was his annual fall pilgrimage to visit us in Cincinnati so he could go with me to see the Bengals play. On the negative side, Mother had to plan the timing of Thanksgiving and other holiday meals so we could sit down to eat at halftime. I thought about that nuance as we planned our Super Bowl dinner this evening.

Yes, today is Super Bowl Sunday. Around 6:30 this afternoon, over 100 million people worldwide will tune in to watch the Pittsburgh Steelers play the Green Bay Packers for football supremacy. This particular game is numbered XLV or Super Bowl forty-five. I have no idea why they started numbering the games with Roman numerals, but since the first game in 1967, it has been that way. Being a football fan, I have seen all forty-five.

I will never forget Super Bowl III. That was the year Joe Namath made his prediction that the Jets, a huge underdog, would topple the Baltimore Colts and give the upstart AFL its first victory in a Super Bowl. Those of us who are old enough to remember that game have Joe Willie Namath and his bold prognostication planted in our brain.

Another well-known player made some bold predictions between XXX and XXXIII. His name was Jesus. Here are two of them.

John 2:19–"Destroy this temple, and I will raise it again in three days."

Mark 10:33–"We are going up to Jerusalem," he said, "and the Son of Man will be betrayed to the chief priests and teachers of the law. They will condemn him to death and will hand him over to the Gentiles…"

I have a bold prediction to make. One hundred years from now, no one will remember who won Super Bowl III or today's game. However, Christians everywhere will always remember Jesus Christ and the sacrifice He made to guarantee our salvation.

See you tomorrow, God willing!

February 7 — In Sync

Yesterday, I got up even earlier than my recent pattern–3:55 a.m. to be exact. I don't actually like getting up that early, but when God wakes you up what are you going to do? First, I got the morning devotion finished and sent it out at 4:05. Then I morphed into my morning routine – reading the Bible and my daily devotions, pray, and read the newspaper while I eat breakfast. After all of these activities, it was still early so I decided to lie down on the couch to see if I could catch another hour or so of sleep.

I woke up about 7:15 and wondered if my son-in-law had read and responded to the letter that went out at 4:05. He is an early riser and often responds before he goes to work in the morning and I look forward to his responses because they always give me something else to consider. As I walked to the computer room, I thought about his possible response. Would he say "wow"? What a stupid thought! I don't know why that word came to my mind, but it did.

When I opened the email program and hit the 'send/receive' button, I waited anxiously for a response. Just then, I heard the chime that indicates mail coming in, was it from him? Yes, it was. I clicked to open his email, and there it was; the very first word of the email was "wow." As always, his response was thoughtful and from his heart, but the overall content could have been anything. I was stuck on the word "wow." I'm not sure what it means, but for one second, our spirits were in sync.

Jesus and His Father were always in sync. In the 14th chapter of John's Gospel, there are several verses that help illustrate the point.

"Don't you believe that I am in the Father, and that the Father is in me? The words I say to you are not just my own. Rather, it is the Father, living in me, who is doing his work." John 14:10

"On that day, you will realize that I am in my Father, and you are in me, and I am in you." John 14:20

"But the world must learn that I love the Father and that I do exactly what my Father has commanded me." John 14:31

I believe that the message for today is simple. We can only experience peace and joy in life if we do the things our Heavenly Father wants us to do. To be in sync with Him means we have to develop a personal relationship with Him. How do we do that? Speak to Him often. Read His love letters to us daily. And, help take care of His children.

Should I do any less?

See you tomorrow, God willing!

February 8 — Who Is Your Boss?

Children have a language all their own. My youngest grandson, in particular, has a special way of expressing himself. Some of his phrases are imbedded in our collective memory; we call them "Cody-isms." In the year 2000, when he was five years old, we spent a week at Disney World with my daughter and her family. The days in the park were long and tiring, especially for a five-year old. Tired children do not always have the most pleasant personality, so it was with my grandson. One evening as we tried to get him to rest while my daughter and her husband were out, my grandson told us very emphatically, "You're not the boss of me!"

That turned out to be a prophetic statement. He is now a fine young man celebrating his sixteenth birthday today. He has a mind of his own and he has grown mightily in stature and wisdom. Today, he might express the same thoughts using different words, but the meaning is still the same, "You're not the boss of me."

I've known a few headstrong people in my life. Some people call them independent thinkers to put a positive spin on the situation. In fact, I like to think of myself as an independent thinker. Unfortunately, there are times when it benefits us to accept sound advice from wiser, more mature people who have been through life's struggles and learned how to cope.

How many people do you know who stiff arm God and tell Him, "You're not the boss of me?" I did for a long time. Then I learned that He loves me and wants only the best for me. Proverbs 3:5-6 contains some wise words, "Trust in the Lord with all your heart, and lean not on your own understanding. Acknowledge Him in all your ways, and He will make your paths straight."

Eventually, we have to decide, who is the boss? "I am the LORD your God, who teaches you what is best for you, who directs you in the way you should go." (Isaiah 48:17). He is my boss!

See you tomorrow, God willing!

February 9 — The Good Book

Shepperd's Memorial Library in Greenville has an annual book sale at the Greenville Convention Center. Although I now do most of my reading using an electronic reader, I still read some books in the traditional format, especially rereading books that I already own. Recently I was looking through the house for a book by Larry Crabb titled, *Shattered Dreams*. I had purchased and read the book a couple of years ago and there were some concepts in the book that I wanted to review. I looked from one end of the house to the other and I could not find that book. That brings me back to the library's book sale.

When my wife and I went into the convention center, I went straight for the section of books marked "Religion/Spirituality." As stupid as it may sound, I was hoping to find a copy of *Shattered Dreams*. To my amazement, I walked straight to a copy even though the books were totally unorganized. When I pulled the book away from the others, I noticed a sticker on the front of the cover, Bill and Shirley Roberts with our address. Several months ago, we had donated several boxes of books to the library and that particular book had obviously been included by mistake. I had to pay a dollar to get my book back, but it was worth it.

It wouldn't be right to talk about books without mentioning my mother. Now there was a person who loved to read. When she went to bed at night, there was always a book to accompany her. She told me "as long as you have a good book, you will never be alone." I didn't realize until after she died that what she really meant was "as long as you have THE GOOD BOOK, you will never be alone."

Yes, "The Good Book," The Bible, The Word of God, that is what my mother meant all along. The Gospel of John tells us in the very first verse, "In the beginning was the Word, and the Word was with God, and the Word was God." If we stay in the Word, we abide in Him and He in us. When we share His Word with others, the promise of Isaiah 55:11 plays out, "so is my word that goes out from my mouth: It will not return to me empty, but will accomplish what I desire and achieve the purpose for which I sent it."

See you tomorrow, God willing!

February 10 — Be Joyful Always

In First Thessalonians 5:16-18, Paul gives his fellow Christians the following advice, "Be joyful always; pray continuously; and give thanks in all circumstances." Those words are as fitting today as they were nearly 2000 years ago. It is good advice, but how can we possibly adhere to those three commands when our daily lives take us through periods that make the three directives virtually impossible. I can be joyful when good things happen, that is easy. However, how can I give thanks when something tragic happens like the death of a loved one or terminal illness in a close friend?

Today, I want to talk about the first of the directives. The next two, I will cover on the following two days. "Be joyful always" – People are watching! If Christians can't be joyful, why would others want to become followers? When my wife and I went to Bulgaria on a mission trip, we were told that the people of Bulgaria are not joyful and you would see it in their faces. They were correct. Bulgarians had lived under Turkish rule and communism for centuries, and God was not part of their lives. No wonder there was no joy. As we worked, played and prayed with the Bulgarian people they saw joy. The small group of us from our church who went to Bulgaria had the gift of laughter. If fact, I have never laughed so much in my life. As some would say, it must have been a God thing.

When I was gainfully employed, I received calls daily from our sales people from all over the United States who were looking for information or ideas on how to pitch a particular new prospect. One day I received a call, but I was distracted by something else that I was doing. Therefore, the joy that I usually demonstrate in my voice was missing. The sales person noticed and asked me what was wrong? I told them the reason for my apparent lack of joy. Here is the response I received from them; "It's tough out here selling, sometimes I call you just because I know that your joy and positive attitude about life will invigorate me." From that day on, I never answered the phone with an indifferent tone of voice. People are looking for joy and we can give it to them.

"Then make my joy complete by being like-minded, having the same love, being one in spirit and purpose." (Philippians 2:2). This is what God calls us to do.

See you tomorrow, God willing!

February 11   Pray Continuously

Prayer is nothing more than having a conversation with God – to share your concerns with Him, to thank Him for His many blessings, and to ask him for His favor in getting through the trials of life. It sounds as natural and easy as talking to your best friend. Why then do we go through so many ups and downs in our prayer life? If you took my daily prayer life and turned it into an amusement park ride, you would have the greatest roller coaster ride in the world. On some days, I am at the top of the mountain, while others I am in the valley. I go through long springs of fruitful prayers followed by summers of drought. Why does this happen?

A few years ago for Christmas, my wife commissioned a friend of ours who is an expert woodworker to make a prayer bench for me. It is a work of art and I have it situated in an alcove of my office that faces east. Several days ago, as I was kneeling in prayer on the padded bench, the rising sun warmed my face. It was as if the risen son was acknowledging that He had heard my prayers.

There have been other times in my life when I felt overwhelming evidence that God had heard my prayers. For a week or two after my mother died, God reassured me that prayers for my mother had been heard. As I read my Bible in the days immediately following her death, there were passages that jumped from the pages with clarity and impact like I had never seen before. It was too vivid to ignore and I knew it was God's way of telling me that all was well.

When Paul was telling the Thessalonians (1 Thessalonians 5:16-18) to "pray continuously," he knew that they needed to develop a discipline of prayer. When something great happens to you, thank God for the blessing! When small annoyances get your goat, ask God to calm you down! When life's troubles overwhelm you, seek direction from your Heavenly Father! When a friend tells you he or she has a problem, don't tell the person that you will pray for them, do it right then and there. It is okay to pray for them later, but they may need the support on the spot.

I have a confession to make; I still have my ups and downs in my prayer life. However, they have moved the roller coaster to the children's portion of the amusement park.

See you tomorrow, God willing!

February 12   Give Thanks in All Circumstances

For the previous two days, I covered the first two directives in Paul's message to the Thessalonians. Today, I will take on the hardest of the three – "Give thanks in all circumstances." The "giving thanks" part of the verse isn't too hard on most days. However, there are times and situations in our lives that giving thanks can be virtually impossible.

How about this situation? A good friend of my daughter had terminal cancer, how could she possibly give thanks for those circumstances? How about giving thanks for the courage and faith that her friend displayed every time she saw her? How about giving thanks for having known her and having received the fruits of her friendship? How about giving thanks for the Christian brothers and sisters who stepped into the gap with prayer, food, the running of errands or simply being by my her friend's side when she needed someone to talk to? How about giving thanks that my daughter was able to show love and compassion to her friend's daughter for years after her mother's death?

Is it easy? No way José. It is much easier to give thanks when our cups runneth over. Unfortunately, we can't afford to be fair weather Christians. Psalm 118:29 ends with the following verse, "Give thanks to the Lord, for he is good; his love endures forever." And, I can add, in all circumstances.

See you tomorrow, God willing!

February 13 — The Money Jar

One morning last week it was too cold to go to the golf course so I decided to show up for work. When I pulled into the parking lot and got out of the car, there on the pavement was a shiny new dime. I immediately thought of my father-in-law and his "money jar" where he kept all the money he had found over the years. It was full of pennies, nickels, dimes, quarters and even a little folding money. What he found, he kept. For years and years, he walked the streets of St. Paul with his head down searching for money to put in his jar. Although he died in 1990, it wasn't until my mother-in-law died in 2005 that the "money jar" passed on to my daughter. She still has it and its original contents. As far as I know, she has neither added to nor taken away from its content.

I often wondered why my father-in-law never spent any of his collection. What did he think about when he added another dime or quarter? He did not need the money so why did he get such a kick out of finding coins. He was a numismatist but to my knowledge, he never found a coin for his collection. I wonder what would have happened had he found a rare coin. He would have been torn between putting it in the jar or adding to his treasure trove of coins. I guess I'll never know for sure.

He never told me this, but I think I know why he got such a kick out of adding to the "money jar." Every time he added to the jar, he was reminded of the many blessings God had given him. And, by keeping them in the jar, he could see those blessings grow. Furthermore, even after he was gone, those blessings would be passed on for generations to come.

In Bible days, they didn't have glass jars, but they did have jars of clay. Paul mentioned clay jars in his second letter to the Corinthians, Chapter 4 verse 7, "But we have this treasure in jars of clay to show that this all-surpassing power is from God and not from us." My father-in-law knew this intuitively and was reminded of it every time he added to his jar of clay.

Perhaps we should all have a "blessings jar" that we make additions to on a regular basis. I think we would be amazed at how fast it would grow. Before we knew it, it would be overflowing.

See you tomorrow, God willing!

February 14   Happy Valentine's Day

Today is the day of love, so I am going to show you how much I love each of you by sparing you the time it takes to read one of my daily stories. Instead, I am asking each of you to take a moment and tell everyone who is near and dear to you just how much you love him or her. And, while you are at it, don't forget to tell them how much God loves them. For those whom you see every day, tell them in person. If you talk to them on the phone regularly, give them a call. However, if you can't for some reason do either of the first two options, just forward this email with a note or draft your own. Don't forget, you love them and so does God.

"By this all men will know that you are my disciples, if you love one another."
John 13:35

See you tomorrow, God willing!

February 15 — It Wasn't Me!

At sixteen years of age, I wasn't as respectful of adults as I should have been, as the following story will demonstrate.

Here is the scene. It is the library of St. Paul High School and it just happens to be my study hall period. As usual, my friend and I take a seat at a table as far away from the librarian as we can get. We had no intention of studying, our goal was mischief. On that particular day, we decided to whistle at a very low volume, just loud enough to disturb our fellow classmates without being heard by the librarian. It appeared we had accomplished our goal until she stopped us as we were leaving the library at the end of study hall. She asked me point blank, "Bill, was that you whistling at the back of the room?" I answered, "No maam, it wasn't me." She replied in a correcting tone, "It wasn't I!" I replied in a smart aleck tone, "If it wasn't me and it wasn't you, I wonder who it was." Her mouth dropped as I turned and walked out of the room. It is a funny story, but today, I am not proud of the disrespect I showed her. She didn't deserve it.

Often, I go back and read entries in my daily journal. On many occasions, I react to the content of the writing much like my response to the lovely librarian, "It wasn't me." I realize that God reveals many things to me when I sit down and allow Him to use my hand to write His words. When I have shared this experience with other people who journal on a regular basis, they tell me that they experience the same thing. Yet another person who is an artist told me that he looks back on his paintings and realizes that God must have been the one using the brush.

"For the Holy Spirit will teach you at that time what you should say." (Luke 12:12)

This scripture is true not only for our journaling, but everything we do. If you are in a tough situation and don't know what to do our say, allow the Holy Spirit to shine through! Don't know what to say or do with a troublesome child, allow the Holy Spirit to shine through.

The next time you say, "It wasn't me," remember, it is not bad grammar; it is a reminder that the Holy Spirit is with you.

See you tomorrow, God willing!

February 16   Don't Pick the Unripe Fruit

When I first committed myself to writing and sending out a daily "Love Letter" to you, I knew I had taken on a task that would be hard for me to accomplish on my own. If the Holy Spirit didn't show up every morning, I was going to be in big trouble.

It went fine for a couple of weeks, but then I began to get uneasy again. I had completed about twenty days of devotions, but I had three hundred and forty-five to go. I got an idea! Why not write some of the devotions ahead of time and put them in inventory just in case I came up dry some morning. My spirit quickly told me, "not a good idea, Bill!"

More days went by and the ideas for new devotions began to flood my mind. On a trip to Virginia to see my son and his family, my wife and I brainstormed about events from our past that would help me communicate the messages and values that were circling around in my head. Not only did the ideas come, but also the whole stories were developing in my mind and I could not take a chance on forgetting what God was obviously telling me.

So, I began to write new letters for use at a later date against the earlier prodding of the Holy Spirit. Or, was I? Had I misinterpreted the message or just viewed it too narrowly?

When I lived on a farm in Illinois as a little boy, I vividly remember wild persimmon trees that grew along some of our fence lines. I can also remember picking unripe persimmons and biting into them. There is nothing that will pucker your mouth like a persimmon that is eaten before it is ripe. Unripe persimmons make lemons seem sweet. Through the parable of the persimmon, (I now call embellished stories, parables), God was telling me it is okay to write when the Spirit moves me. Just don't take the easy way out and grab something from my inventory without making sure it is ripe.

"There is a time for everything, and a season for every activity under heaven..." Ecclesiastes 3:1. There is also a time for every story to be told, in God's time not my own.

See you tomorrow, God willing!

February 17 A Friend in Need Is a Friend Indeed

Yesterday morning I went to see a friend who had thoracic surgery later in the day to remove the lymph nodes from the areas around the throat. Several months ago, he had been diagnosed with stage four cancer of the throat and for the last seven months, he has been undergoing aggressive chemotherapy and radiation treatment to rid his body of the cancer cells. A biopsy performed last week indicated that he is now cancer free, but the precautionary surgery will reduce the chances that the cancer will spread.

I arrived at the hospital around 8:45 am to pray with him and his wife before the surgery. As we prayed, I recalled something I read in Phillip Yancey's book on prayer. He said, "When you pray for someone, envision taking that person by the hand and presenting them to God*." What a wonderful image! It was a sweet time and I'm sure all of us felt a little better after our conversation with God. After I left, I had a little time to kill before a doctor's appointment that I had later in the morning. My mind conjured up events from the past when I had prayed for other people who faced life-threatening diseases. Some of these folks recovered beautifully, but others did not fare as well. Why? Does God only hear certain prayers? Is prayer really important?

I have read a number of books on prayer, and none of them answers the questions directly. However, I have gotten some very keen insights. I believe the most important thing I learned is this – Jesus prayed. He never missed an opportunity to talk to His Father. If it is good enough for Him, it is good enough for me. Better yet, here is what the Bible says about what Jesus is doing now. "Christ Jesus ...is at the right hand of God and is also interceding for us." Romans 8:34

Many Bible verses stress the importance of prayer to the believer and each of them gives us additional reasons to pray. "For the eyes of the Lord are on the righteous and his ears are attentive to their prayer...." (1 Peter 3:12) He does hear our prayers.

"Come near to God and he will come near to you". (James 4:8) God wants us to be in personal relationship with Him. Prayer helps bring us into that relationship.

It is clear that God wants us to be in communication with Him on a regular basis, to speak and to listen. And remember as you pray, "Nothing lies beyond the reach of prayer except that which lies outside the will of God."*

See you tomorrow, God willing!

*Prayer – Does It Make a Difference? Phillip Yancey

February 18   Give Me a Sign

In the late 1990's, our family began to worry that Mother's health was failing and she would not be able to live much longer by herself. However, she continued to manage and we celebrated her 80th birthday with a big party at her church. Most of the family was there for the celebration and we gave her a birthday party to remember. Two months after her birthday, in March 2002, the bottom fell out. Mom contracted double pneumonia and while she was in the hospital, she had a minor stroke. She was released from the hospital in the care of my wife and me and we took her to North Carolina to recover.

For a short time, she lived with us and then my sister took care of her for a year. When she suffered additional serious health issues, she came back to North Carolina to live with us. By this time, Mom had been diagnosed with Alzheimer's disease. We took good care of her and even found bridge players for her. However, it wasn't long before her short-term memory was insufficient to play her favorite card game. As the disease progressed, we were able to keep her at our house with the help of two excellent caregivers. Unfortunately, we knew the time would come when she would need to be in an environment where she could receive 24-hour a day professional care. Finally, we were able to move her to assisted living. When that day came, I prayed to God that He would give me a sign that we had done the right thing. I asked Him to send Blue Birds for assurance. In the next two weeks, we saw in our backyard, two pairs of Blue Birds, a Blue Grosbeak, an Indigo Bunting, and several Blue Jays. Before that week, we had never seen either the Blue Grosbeak or the Indigo Bunting in our yard. We had received our assurance.

Asking for signs is not uncommon in the Bible. When God chose Gideon to lead the Israelites against the Midianites, Gideon asked for several signs. "If now I have found favor in your eyes, give me a sign that it is really you talking to me." (Judges 6:17) First, he asked for a dry fleece and then a wet fleece. (Judges 6) King Hezekiah had a similar experience when he asked God for a sign that would assure him of anther fifteen years of life. Hezekiah had asked Isaiah, "What will be the sign that the LORD will heal me and that I will go up to the temple of the LORD on the third day from now?" (2 Kings 20:8) In this case, God had the sun go back an hour in the sky. It must have been pretty dramatic.

Does God still give us signs? Ask the blue birds why they came to my house?

See you tomorrow, God willing!

February 19 — The Race

As I write this morning's message, my daughter and her husband are in Myrtle Beach getting ready to run the Myrtle Beach Half Marathon. Two years ago, I had prepared for that same race with eager anticipation, because it was going to be the first time I would run any race with my daughter. Unfortunately, her whole family got sick a few days before that race and they couldn't even make the trip to Myrtle Beach, much less run the half marathon. I kidded my son-in-law that he skipped the race because he was afraid to compete with me. Given the fact that he runs these long races at a pace of about eight minutes a mile compared to twelve minutes a mile for me, the joke was really on me.

I have not run at all since the Myrtle Beach race two years ago. After waiting two months for my hip to recover, I grudgingly went to an orthopedic doctor to see what was wrong. The diagnosis was simple; I had no cartilage remaining in my right hip and would need a hip replacement. I waited until August and had the surgery done. It was a success and I have resumed all of my former activities except for one. Running is too hard on the new artificial joint, so no running–doctor's orders.

I have to admit, there are days when I really miss going out for a long run, particularly at the beach where I am writing this letter. The biggest disappointment, then and now, is not getting the enjoyment of running with my daughter. I know she would have beaten me that day and that would have been okay with me. For me, running races was never about winning, it was always about participating.

In his first letter to the Corinthians, Paul talked about running a race that was more like a super marathon. It is the race we run our entire lives to gain the biggest prize of all. Paul said, "Do you not know that in a race all the runners run, but only one gets the prize? Run in such a way as to get the prize. Everyone who competes in the games goes into strict training. They do it to get a crown that will not last; but we do it to get a crown that will last forever." (1 Corinthians 9:24-25) Everyone who finishes the Myrtle Beach Half and Full Marathon gets a medal. Likewise, everyone who trains properly and finishes God's super marathon receives a crown that will last forever.

My daughter and her husband have been training for the Myrtle Beach race for quite a while and they will receive a medal for their effort. All of us train every day for the other race and one day we will receive our crown.

See you tomorrow, God willing!

February 20   A Fish Story

To all of the ladies in my family, I apologize if what I am about to say offends you, but since men are from Mars, we often see and do things a little differently than you do. Women bond by going shopping together. That just doesn't cut it for men. We go camping and the more difficult the trip, the better.

When the men of my family invited me to join them on a camping expedition, I gladly accepted. We went to Swansboro, NC, and rented ocean-going kayaks. We loaded the kayaks with food, water, cooking and eating utensils, tents, fishing gear, and sleeping bags. It was enough to fill every kayak to the brim. After loading up, we proceeded to make our way to an island you can just see from Emerald Isle. It was a small island and we were the only inhabitants, except for crabs.

After kayaking for about an hour, we made it to our destination. When we arrived to set up camp, I played the role of patriarch and let the younger men do all the work; I looked for shells. I would later learn that my wife and my daughter were watching this play unfold from the Point at Emerald Isle with a pair of binoculars. As dusk approached, the anglers attempted to secure our dinner. They were successful and my son-in-law did a great job of frying the fish.

When Jesus began to call His disciples, He started with a bunch of fishermen. "As Jesus was walking beside the Sea of Galilee, he saw two brothers, Simon called Peter and his brother Andrew. They were casting a net into the lake, for they were fishermen. 'Come, follow me,' Jesus said, 'and I will make you fishers of men.' ... Going on from there, he saw two other brothers, James son of Zebedee and his brother John. They were in a boat with their father Zebedee, preparing their nets. Jesus called them." (Matthew 4:18-19, 21).

Why did Jesus begin His earthly ministry by choosing four fishermen as His first disciples? I suspect there were several reasons. First, these were rugged men who would not quit when the going got tough. Second, fishermen are persistent and accustomed to failure, if the fish aren't biting on a particular day, they come back the next day and try again. There is one last character trait that was of utmost importance to Jesus, they knew how to bond.

As Christians, it is not enough for us to go to church every Sunday to meet our weekly obligation. We need to bond with our fellow brothers and sisters in Christ.

See you tomorrow, God willing!

February 21   The Shock of His Life

Living on a farm as a youngster was quite an experience, particularly when it came to animals. We had several varieties of cattle and pigs, chickens, dogs (mostly strays) and cats (also strays). We also had a pony that dad won through some job he had, but the pony wasn't too friendly so we got rid of him in a hurry. We may have sold him to get money for food for all I know.

Of all the animals that we had, one stood out from all the rest. It was a cat that had been crippled since it showed up at the farm. It was a nice cat, but it limped noticeably no matter where it went. As is the case with most farms, there is very little separation between the yard and the barnyard. To keep the pigs from getting out, we had an electric fence that was about a foot off the ground. Although it was low voltage, it would give you a shock and the pigs certainly knew better than to approach the fence. The pigs knew, but apparently, the crippled cat didn't. When my favorite crippled cat hit that fence, he took off as if he had been shot out of a cannon. Funny thing, when he stopped running and started to walk, the limp was gone, forever. I swear that is a true story.

At creation, God gave man dominion over the animal kingdom. In Genesis 1:28 God said to man, "Rule over the fish of the sea and the birds of the air and over every living creature that moves on the ground." You really learn how to care for animals on a farm. You feed them; you give them water; you talk to them as if they are people; and you care for them when they are sick. So, when I saw my favorite cat healed of his infirmity it made me feel good. I also had learned at a very early age that God works in some mighty strange ways.

See you tomorrow, God willing!

February 22   Blessed Are the Children

My wife and I have had the good fortune of going on three international mission trips – one to Honduras, one to the Dominican Republic and one to Bulgaria. The first trips, to Honduras and the DR, reminded us of what it means to live in poverty. The faith of the folks in those two countries was strong because in their poverty they had learned a valuable lesson – to depend on God for all of their needs. The situation in Bulgaria was quite different. While living under communism for decades, life settled to the lowest common denominator. Unlike many Hondurans and Dominicans, the Bulgarians had housing–cookie cutter concrete apartment building with just enough space to meet the most basic needs of a family. They had food, nothing fancy, just enough. Unlike the Hondurans and Dominicans, the Bulgarians had no joy or hope. Communism had met their physical needs at the most basic level, but ignored their spiritual needs completely.

The story for today does not deal with the differences in these two societies, but with a striking similarity. In each of these countries, we had the good fortune to visit an orphanage. The children in these countries were well cared for in terms of food and the necessities, but all of them were starved for affection. I remember forming a quick bond with a young girl about eight years old in Honduras. Having had some experience with young children, I knew how much they like to be swung around by their arms. I should never have started. Before I knew it, I had become a human merry-go-round. Did I get tired? Yes, I did. Was I enriched? Yes, I was.

My wife had a similar experience in Bulgaria when she was strangely attracted to some teenage girls at the orphanage who were accustomed to being ignored by visitors in lieu of the younger children. Despite the language barrier, she began to teach this group of teenage orphans how to do the hokey-pokey. It was hilarious and boy did they have fun. My wife was exhilarated and for a moment, the girls felt loved.

Two verses in the Gospel of Mark give us a picture of how Jesus felt about children. Mark 9:37 says, "Whoever welcomes one of these little children in my name welcomes me; and whoever welcomes me does not welcome me but the one who sent me." A little later in Mark 10:14, Jesus clarifies His attitude even more, "Let the little children come to me, and do not hinder them, for the kingdom of God belongs to such as these."

If you ever have the opportunity to go on an international mission trip, I highly recommend it. You will never be the same; I guarantee it.

See you tomorrow, God willing!

February 23 — Scars are Proof

There was a man in my car who wasn't supposed to be there. When I approached the passenger door, the man jumped out, and the next thing I knew I was bleeding profusely and air bubbled from my side. It wasn't a pretty picture.

As many of you who know me can attest, I have been known to tell a tale or two and I have also embellished stories that were actually true. The details I listed above are true. The evening that this crime took place I was returning to my car around 10 pm having completed another evening at the University of Cincinnati where I was pursuing my MBA in marketing. I happened to be at the wrong place at the wrong time. I still have the scars on my side and back to prove the story.

It is human nature to doubt stories of an outrageous nature, especially when the credibility of the storyteller is suspect. Thomas, one of Jesus' disciples, was that way, "Unless I see the nail marks in his hands and put my finger where the nails were, and put my hand into his side, I will not believe it." (John 20:25). He wanted to see the scars.

Then Jesus told him, "Because you have seen me, you have believed; blessed are those who have not seen and yet have believed." (John 20:29) When our faith wanes, wouldn't it be great to see those nail scarred hands? Wouldn't it be great to put our fingers where the nails were? All we really have to know is this–because of those nail scarred hands, our sins are forgiven. As far as the east is from the west, so far has he removed our transgressions from us. (Psalm 103:12)

See you tomorrow, God willing!

February 24   Respect You Elders

About the age of thirty-three, I was hitting my stride. My career was beginning to take shape; we were settling into a new set of surroundings; we were establishing new sets of friends; and we had found a church family where we were welcome.

As I began to get more involved in the life of our new church family, I offered my services in areas of church life where my "gifts" might be used most appropriately. Since I appeared to be a bright young businessman, I was invited to join the finance committee. I accepted the invitation and joined a committee that was composed of four other gentlemen, the youngest of which was probably over sixty years old (I thought that was pretty old at the time). Like many small churches, a shortage of money to meet on-going expenses was always a problem. Most months, cash in-flow was less than expenses for the month. There was neither a budget to understand expected expenses nor a record of past giving to get a fix on expected revenue. To put it plainly, the church was living from week to week depending on God's grace to survive. Thirty years later, I can appreciate that concept. However, at that time in my life, it wasn't acceptable so I jumped in with both feet to "fix" the situation.

One night following one of our heated finance committee meetings, God spoke to me during the night. I don't know if it was an audible voice or not, but it sure seemed like it was. All He said was "respect you elders." It would be a great story if I told you from that day on I have had the utmost respect for my elders. It wouldn't be true, but I can tell you, that night God made an impression on me and I think about that message any time I get out of line.

When I was thirty-three, I was a child in terms of my spiritual growth, "When I was a child, I talked like a child, I thought like a child, I reasoned like a child. When I became a man, I put childish ways behind me" (1st Corinthians 13:11). I no longer can hide behind my immaturity or my lack of knowledge about how God wants me to behave. The Bible has much to say about love and respect, particularly concerning our elders. "Rise in the presence of the aged, show respect for the elderly and revere your God. I am the LORD" (Leviticus 19:32). "Remember the days of old; consider the generations long past. Ask your father and he will tell you, your elders, and they will explain to you" (Deuteronomy 32:7)

"Fear of the Lord is the beginning of wisdom....." is a phrase that appears several times in the Psalms and Proverbs. It could just as easily be read, "A healthy respect for the Lord is the beginning of wisdom."

See you tomorrow, God willing!

February 25   Stormy Relationships

Every family has one. No matter whether you like it or not, you have to deal with it. You can't ignore it; you can't pretend as if it isn't there. You can't live with it and you can't live without it. Yes, I'm talking about an eccentric aunt or uncle. My Aunt Fran was just such a person.

Don't get the wrong idea from my introduction. I loved my Aunt Fran dearly and I had wonderful memories of her. She lived in Virginia most all of her life, but when we lived in Illinois on the farm, she visited us at least every other year. When she came, she always brought us presents

At one point in our lives, when we lived on Virginia, our house was only a block or two from where Fran and her husband lived. She had a Siamese cat named Tasie, short for Tasmanian devil. As much as I loved animals, I was afraid to go in her house because the cat would literally be purring on your lap one minute and attacking you the next.

I am telling you the story about the cat for one reason; Fran's personality was often like the cats. She could be the kindest, most generous, thoughtful person in the world. However, the next minute she could slice you up like a cat. The relationship between Mom and her sister was stormy at best, but they sure loved each other.

Stormy relationships are all a part of life. Just recall Jesus' relationship with Peter. It was all over the place. Here are a few examples.

> "Get behind me, Satan! You are a stumbling block to me; (Matthew 16:23)

> Jesus answered, "I tell you, Peter, before the rooster crows today, you will deny three times that you know me." (Luke 22:34)

> "But what about you?" Jesus asked. "Who do you say I am?" Peter answered, "You are the Christ." Mark 8:29

> "The third time he said to him, "Simon son of John, do you love me?" Peter was hurt because Jesus asked him the third time, "Do you love me?" He said, "Lord, you know all things; you know that I love you." Jesus said, "Feed my sheep." (John 21:17)

As you all know, there are many more verses in the Bible that give us a picture of this stormy relationship. In a period of only a few hours, Peter cut off a man's ear in the Garden with his sword defending his Master and then a short time later denied knowing him three times. Yet, God loved him and Peter became the foundation upon which the church was built.

The moral is this. God loves us no matter what we do or how irrationally we act, and He has a plan for lives. It helps me to think about the people around me when they do something to irritate me.

See you tomorrow, God willing!

February 26   The Violin

When my daughter was in the sixth grade, she asked if she could take violin lessons. We said absolutely and purchase a full-sized violin rather than rent one, which might have been smarter. Within three months, she tired of the screeching and asked if she could quit. I had a better idea; I would begin violin lessons independently of her and we could encourage one another. She thought it was a capital idea so I arranged for private lessons with a young man about twenty years younger than I who gave lessons at his home. My great idea turned out to be a not so good idea when my daughter again asked if she could quit two months later. After much discussion, we opted to let her quit, but I was hooked.

For the next two years, I continued with my violin lessons and my wife will tell you I really wasn't very good. I did try hard and I will tell you it was one of the most challenging undertakings of my life. If I were asked to speak in front of 1000 people about a subject I knew nothing about, I would not have been as nervous as I was for every violin lesson. I was out of my comfort zone! Eventually I quit taking lessons because I just couldn't find the time every day to practice.

In retrospect, I learned a lot from that experience. One, I learned to read music. By the time I quit, the notes were finally going directly from my eyes to my fingers, seemingly skipping the brain. Two, I learned that it is good to take on a project at which you do not excel. For many males, that is a real challenge. Three, I learned that it is okay to take instructions from someone far younger than you are. That is another good lesson for male pride.

God often calls us from our comfort zone to do His work through the body of the church. And, He gives us these instructions in 2nd John 1:6, "And this is love: that we walk in obedience to his commands. As you have heard from the beginning, His command is that you walk in love." Walk in His commands. It doesn't matter whether or not the command fits our current abilities; walk in His commands. It doesn't matter if we have adequate resources; walk in His commands. It doesn't matter if we are comfortable in the place he sends us; walk in His commands. It doesn't matter if no one else has walked the path before; walk in His commands. Remember the old Christian song, *"Children Go Where I Send Thee."* That is the essence of today's message.

See you tomorrow, God willing!

February 27 — The Chess Game

My oldest grandson couldn't have been much more than eight years old when he and I began to play chess. Being a very smart grandson (aren't they all), he picked up the game very quickly and it wasn't long before he challenged my skills and then began to beat me. I can assure you now, as I have always done, I never let anyone beat me at anything. My philosophy is simple, beat me fair and square and you will appreciate the victory even more. Just to let you know I have gone soft in my old age, I did routinely let my mother win at "Kings Around the Corner" before she went to be with her Maker just to see the joy it brought her.

I was recently reading a book by Charles Spurgeon where he quoted an old Italian proverb. "When the chess game is over, the pawns, the rooks, the kings and the queens all go into the same box." I could add my own proverb, "when the game of life is over it won't matter who won the chess game" or any other game for that matter. The high and mighty, the winners and losers, and the rich and famous will all "stand before God's judgment seat. It is written, As surely as I live, says the Lord, every knee will bow before me and every tongue will confess to God." (Romans 14:10-11)

The chess analogy only gets you so far. Because as Christians, we don't believe the game is actually over when our life here on earth ends. We believe in life eternal and God tells us what happens at judgment. "Let them grow together until the harvest. At that time I will tell the harvesters; first collect the weeds and tie them in bundles to be burned; then gather the wheat and bring it into the barn." Matthew 13:30

It is clear; not all the pieces go into the same box. Furthermore, the game is not won based on our performance in the game, but rather by God's grace that is available to all who believe in Him.

See you tomorrow, God willing.

February 28   How May I Serve You

My wife's mother was a throwback. Just so there is no misunderstanding, a throwback is defined as a person having the characteristics of a former time. Like many women of her generation, she was totally dedicated to her husband and family. If her husband got up a four o'clock in the morning to go hunting or fishing, she fixed his breakfast and packed his lunch before he got on his way. I remember quite clearly the occasions when my father-in-law ran out of iced tea at a meal. He would very casually shake the ice cubes in the glass to indicate to her that he needed a refill. Without hesitation, she would notice the cue and refresh his drink. There was nothing sinister about it, and it was in no way meant to be chauvinistic. For my wife's mother and women of her generation, it was the norm.

That desire to please carried over into other aspects of her life. We visited her and my wife's dad on so many holidays and long weekends over the years that I couldn't begin to count them. She made us feel welcome every time and never failed to have a feast to fill our hungry stomachs. And, when she cooked, she always made one-two-three salad especially for me. It was her way of making me a part of her family.

Like all grandparents, my wife's mother would do anything to make her grandchildren or great grandchildren feel at home when they came to see her. There was a little closet under a stairway in the living room that housed a large collection of toys. There were Fisher Price barns, houses, and parking garages to keep little ones busy. There was also a black train you could sit on and ride around the living room, and it had the noisiest horn you would ever want to hear (or not want to hear). I'm sure my daughter and son could tell you about some other toys that were there to keep them happy when they visited their grandmother. Her ultimate show of servant hood wasn't the cooking or the toys; it was her ability to make every one feel at home. And that included preparing a bed in a chest of drawers for a tiny great grandchild.

Jesus said, "Whoever wants to become great among you must be your servant" (Matthew 20:26). He must have known my wife's mother.

See you tomorrow, God willing!

February 29 — Victory in Jesus

When I was a freshman in college, two of my friends were on the freshman basketball team and oddly enough, their first names were both Bill, and one of them was even Bill R. Bill R, not I, was the star of the team and its leading scorer. He was a lightning quick guard who could score at will. No one could handle him one-on-one. The other Bill, Bill M., was a second string forward who was too short and too slow to compete successfully at the college level.

One day following an upset victory over a more talented opponent, Bill M. came up to me with excitement overflowing. He said, "Did you hear about the game last night? We knocked off so-and so and Bill R. and I scored fifty points. I was impressed both by his excitement and the fact that the duo had scored fifty points. It was then that he provided more clarification, "Yea," he said, "Bill R. scored forty-eight points and I scored two."

As I thought about what I heard that night many, many years ago, I realized that there is an important learning from what Bill M. told me. In our life-long walk with Jesus, we are asked to do many things. Quite often, we are ill-equipped to handle what God is asking us to do. Like Bill M., we are too short, too slow or too anything to feel like we are adequate. However, when we walk beside Jesus and He is our teammate, it is always enough. He will always be the one scoring forty-eight points, but it doesn't matter. As a team, we always win. Furthermore, He loves the fact that we contribute two points to the victory.

"But he said to me, 'My grace is sufficient for you, for my power is made perfect in weakness.' Therefore I will boast all the more gladly about my weaknesses, so that Christ's power may rest on me." (2 Corinthians 12:9) He is sufficient to overcome all of our weaknesses. There is victory in Jesus.

MARCH

March 1 — The Messenger

It was the last Sunday in February and it was our Sunday to serve as greeters at our church. It had been a long cold winter for Eastern North Carolina, but this Sunday was warm and sunny so we were actually outside greeting people as they came to church. You could see it in their faces and you could hear it in our voices, the reappearance of good weather was having a positive impact on all of us. Everyone was talkative and full of smiles as we greeted them with a "good morning," "welcome," "glad to see this beautiful morning."

After greeting many people, I saw an older man approaching the doors, a man I had never seen before. Our church is large so it wasn't too surprising that I didn't know him. For some strange reason, I struck up a conversation with the man and asked him how he was doing? He said, "I'm above ground for another day." Then he hesitated before entering the door being held open for him and we began to talk. As we talked, he told me he had experienced several near death experiences in the last couple of years. Since I didn't know him, I responded, "God has really looked after you." He replied, "Not at all, He is mad at me. He has thrown me back three times." I laughed and told him what an interesting response and bid him to have a good day.

The next morning as I was doing my morning devotions, God brought this man back into my mind. Who was this man that I had never seen before? Was his story true? Why had he stopped to talk to me? Why had he told me about near death experiences? Was there a message that God was trying to send me? Frankly, I don't know the answers to any of these questions.

However, here is what I do know. This is what Paul told the Philippians, "For to me, to live is Christ and to die is gain....... I am torn between the two: I desire to depart and be with Christ, which is better by far..." (Philippians 1:21, 23). Paul knew that death was not the end, it was the beginning. God wasn't finished with him yet.

The new friend I met at the door on Sunday was right about one thing and wrong about another. He was right about the attractiveness of sitting at the feet of Jesus. He was wrong about God being mad at him. He wasn't mad, He just wasn't finished using him.

The next time a stranger tells you something that may seem a little strange, listen, "Do not forget to entertain strangers, for by so doing some people have entertained angels without knowing it" (Hebrews 13:2).

See you tomorrow, God willing!

March 2 — Measure Twice, Saw Once

Our first home in Cincinnati was a small, three-bedroom starter house in a neighborhood with at least a million kids. It had a fenced in yard for our two children, and an unfinished basement, which is the focal point of this message.

The unfinished basement played an important part in our life on Fourson Drive. First, it gave us room to spread out. The basement covered the entire length of the house so I laid out a plan to add a playroom and a large family room. Finishing the basement also gave me a place to unwind when I got home from night classes around 9:30 or 10 pm. It is amazing how easy it is to shut off your mind and relax by hammering a few nails or sawing a few boards or sections of paneling.

Everyone in my family will tell you that mechanical skills are not at the top of the list of talents that God gave me. However, if I take my time, and plan accordingly, I can get the job done. The best carpentry advice I ever received was from my father-in-law. He simply told me to "measure twice and saw once." As long as I followed that advice, I was okay.

As I have gotten older, I have learned to appreciate the wisdom of his advice in many aspects of my life. The Bible also tells us the same thing. Luke 14:28 says, "Suppose one of you wants to build a tower. Will he not first sit down and estimate the cost to see if he has enough money to complete it?" Additional advice is provided three verses later, "Or suppose a king is about to go to war against another king. Will he not first sit down and consider whether he is able with ten thousand men to oppose the one coming against him with twenty thousand?" Planning is an important aspect of making one's life easier.

The Bible gives even clearer advice in Proverbs 19:21, "Many are the plans in a man's heart, but it is the Lord's purpose that prevails." Pray for God's direction in your life, and then listen for His reply. It will come in His time.

See you tomorrow, God willing!

March 3   A New Calling

Last summer, my wife and I rented a mountain cabin in Boone, NC for a weekend birthday celebration for our granddaughter and her mom and dad. The cabin was situated on the side of a mountain overlooking a picturesque valley where a herd of cows was grazing. You may think it strange for me to talk about a herd of cows in the same sentence as a mountain cabin, but it isn't strange for me at all. I often see things a little differently than others. I often hear things a little differently and I often speak a little differently.

That's where the cows come in. You see, I have a gift. I have the ability to talk to cows. Since I was a little boy on a farm in Illinois, I could speak in "cowenese," that's the language of cows. When I moo, they moo back, every time. Not only do they moo, they begin to move toward me as if I am saying, "Come here!" When we used to visit my sister in Eastern Virginia, her house was near a farm that had cows. We would stop the car by the road near her house and I would moo out the car window, here they came; it cracked me up.

Our visit to Boone brought me to a new higher level in my granddaughter's eyes. I could talk to cows. She got so excited when she heard the cows return my calling; it wasn't too long before she was mooing as well. Now when I talk to her on the phone, she wants me to speak in "cowenese" to bring back memories of that weekend.

The Good Shepherd calls us in a language that is familiar to those who know His voice. He speaks only what His Father directs Him to say. "The watchman opens the gate for him, and the sheep listen to his voice. He calls his own sheep by name and leads them out. When he has brought out all his own, he goes on ahead of them, and his sheep follow him because they know his voice. But they will never follow a stranger; in fact, they will run away from him because they do not recognize a stranger's voice" (John 10:3-5).

If you don't happen to know this particular language, it is taught in churches around the world. The lessons are free and the benefits you receive will change your life.

See you tomorrow, God willing!

March 4 — Can I Have a Witness?

It wasn't too long ago that our pastor preached a sermon about the markers you have in your house to indicate to visitors that you are a Christian. I immediately thought about the wall of crosses near our bedroom. My wife started this collection over ten years ago and there are about eighty crosses of all shapes and sizes displayed for all who enter. There are wooden crosses; there are ceramic crosses; there are metal crosses; and there are glass crosses. There are big crosses and little crosses. There are crosses from Israel, Mexico, Canada, Bulgaria and the United States. It is a beautiful sight.

Now for the story. The other day I was going out to run a few errands and my wife asked me to pick up some dry cleaning since the store was near where I was going. When I entered the store, the proprietor greeted me and I told him my wife sent her greetings. He smiled and pointed to the back wall where a large cross was hanging. He said to me, "Your wife gave me that cross." I was curious so I asked her about the cross when I got home. She told me that when she first started getting our dry cleaning done there, another cross was on that same wall. However, when she returned the next time, it was gone and she asked the proprietor where the cross was. He told her that some of his customers had complained about the presence of the cross so he had taken it down. She politely told him that one of the reasons she brought our cleaning to him was the presence of that cross on the wall.

After a couple more trips to the cleaners, she brought him the large cross that is now on his wall. While she fell short of telling him that he should display it, she did encourage him to do so. She also told him about a Bible verse she had just heard in the class she was taking at the time. It is a well-known verse from Paul's epistle to the Romans, "I am not ashamed of the gospel, because it is the power of God for the salvation of everyone who believes: first for the Jew, then for the Gentile" (Romans 1:16).

God calls each of us to be a witness to His love, His mercy, and His grace. We do it every day by how we look, by what we do, and by how we act. As the old saying goes, "Preach the Gospel at all times, and when all else fails, use words."

See you tomorrow, God willing!

March 5   The Crown

It has been my observation that as women get older their need for a weekly trip to the "beauty parlor" increases exponentially with age. This was particularly true of my mother and my wife's mother.

When my mother-in-law was undergoing radiation treatment for breast cancer, she stayed in Pennsylvania with us because it was much easier for us to take her to her radiation treatment in Allentown five times a week. Since my wife worked on Saturday mornings, the task of getting her mom to the beauty parlor for her weekly shampoo and set was often up to me. She greatly appreciated my efforts and she felt and looked beautiful every time she went.

We had a similar experience with my mother. Every Friday it was off to the beauty shop. This particular lady is more than a hairdresser. Her shop is her ministry. She doesn't work every day and her clientele is composed exclusively of elderly ladies who look forward to both physical and spiritual treatment. My mother loved going there and many of us shared the responsibility of getting her to her weekly appointment. As mother's memory faded, I could still get her to recognize the beauty shop "way out in the country."

"Your head crowns you like Mount Carmel. Your hair is like royal tapestry; the king is held captive by its tresses" (Song of Songs 7:5). Yes ladies, we do notice and we are held captive by your tresses. Not to be outdone, the Bible also has something to say about men's gray hair. Proverbs 20:29 says, "The glory of young men is their strength, gray hair the splendor of the old." So, the next time you are tempted to ask me why I don't dye my hair, you already have my answer.

See you tomorrow, God willing!

March 6 — Man in the Mirror

When you are eight years old, there is a lot of stuff you don't know and a lot more that doesn't matter. Baseball cards mattered a lot and I had a collection that was the envy of all my friends. The only thing that mattered as much as the baseball cards was playing the game. The summer that I was eight years old, I tried out for my first organized team and made it. Was I excited! Making the team meant you got a tee shirt and a cap with an iron-on emblem.

I couldn't wait to get home and get the emblem affixed to the cap to make me official. Mom wasn't home so I got out the ironing board to take care of it myself. All went well until I looked at myself in the mirror with my cap on and noticed that I had put the emblem on backwards. I took off my cap, removed the emblem and tried again. I held the cap in my hand and looked it over and it seemed okay so I put it back on my head and once again went to the mirror to admire myself. Much to my chagrin, it was on backwards again. What had I done wrong? I took off the cap once more and looked at the emblem and it looked okay. That is when I finally figured out the mystery of the mirror. As far as I know, I have never told this story to another person in my whole life, but it is time to come clean.

Grown ups use mirrors to check their appearance. Sometimes we like what we see and sometimes we don't. In the Book of James Chapter 1:23-24 he writes, "Anyone who listens to the Word but does not do what it says is like a man who looks at his face in a mirror and, after looking at himself, goes away and immediately forgets what he looks like." When we don't see what we want to, or better yet, don't hear what the Bible tells us, our tendency is to walk away and forget what it says. That is called disobedience and is not pleasing to God.

How often do I walk away from the mirror and forget what I look like? I'm afraid it is more often than I would like to admit. How about you?

See you tomorrow, God willing!

March 7 — I Can See Clearly Now

My dad was a coal miner for much of his life. For many miners, vacation time was always the two weeks in July when they shut down the mines for annual maintenance. Those two weeks became an annual family get together at Myrtle Beach. My sister and her family would drive from Manassas; my brother and his family from wherever they were living; and my family would drive from Cincinnati to St. Paul and complete the journey to the beach with mom and dad. It was not unusual for us to drive all night and arrive in Myrtle Beach just as the sun was rising out of the ocean. There was a little diner right on the beach that was perfect to watch the sun rise and to celebrate the beginning of our vacation.

Riding in dad's car was a treat for the kids because he had a cassette player that he loved to have on at all times. His favorite cassette was one recorded by the Ray Coniff singers, and all of the children loved one song in particular – "I Can See Clearly Now." The words were classic, "I can see clearly now, the rain has gone. I can see all obstacles in my way. Gone is the black cloud that has passed me by. It's gonna be a bright, bright, sun shiny day."

I know this song wasn't meant to be Christian music, but the message rings true with the gospel. Once we find Jesus, the black cloud has passed us by, it's gonna be a bright, bright sun shiny day. Revelation 22:16 describes Jesus in this manner, "I am the Root and the Offspring of David, and the Bright Morning Star."

My dad understood the power of music and he was in church every Sunday singing praise to the "Bright Morning Star". Unfortunately for those who sat around him, including me, he couldn't carry a tune in a bucket. However, my dad knew that God didn't care about the quality of the music; he cared about the quality of the heart. Matthew 12:34 says, "Out of the overflow of the heart, the mouth *speaks*." It could also mean *"sings."*

See you tomorrow, God willing!

March 8 — Water from the Rock

There is a special bond that develops between grandparents and grandchildren. When our kids were little, one of their special treats was to have my wife's father take them for rides in his truck. He made the trips extra special by taking them individually to special places. For my son, he would drive up to High Knob and get off the main road to show him deer, quail, waterfalls, and mountain streams where he often fished for rainbow trout. These places were some of the same places he took my wife's brother when he was a boy.

For our daughter, the trip was often to a mountain spring where you could get water out of a rock. She was fascinated by the cold, clear water that poured right out of the mountainside. My wife's dad even took gallon jugs along so they could bring some of the treasure home with them.

I can not see water flowing out of the side of a mountain without thinking of Moses in the wilderness trying to get fresh water for the throng of two million people he was leading. The first few verses of Numbers 20 describe the negative attitude that the Israelites had. They had been in the desert for over a month, and they were tired, thirsty and upset about their plight. As He always does, God came through. He told Moses to speak to the side of the mountain and water would pour forth. "Take the staff, and you and your brother Aaron gather the assembly together. Speak to that rock before their eyes and it will pour out its water. You will bring water out of the rock for the community so they and their livestock can drink" (Numbers 20:8). And, the few quail that Chris saw on High Knob was nothing compared to the quantity that God delivered in the desert. "Now a wind went out from the LORD and drove quail in from the sea. It brought them down all around the camp to about three feet above the ground, as far as a day's walk in any direction" (Numbers 11:31). The sound of flapping wings and the sight of that many quail must have been incredible.

I have had some wonderful memories with my grandchildren, but nothing compared to water out of a rock or quail on a sun-filtered mountainside.

See you tomorrow, God willing!

March 9 — Ghostwriter or Spiritwriter?

When I worked for a Fortune 200 company as Worldwide Director of Communications, I often wrote speeches for high-level executives of the company. If the speeches were well received by the audiences in attendance, the executive took credit for the wisdom in the speech. If, however, the speech laid an egg, the executive quickly called attention to the real source of the material. That is the fate of a ghostwriter.

The dictionary defines a ghostwriter as a person whose job is to write material for someone else who is the named author. The ghostwriter often lives in anonymity, but his or her words are heard and read by many people and the ghostwriter can often bask in the personal knowledge that they have made a difference.

Since I began writing 365 Love Letters, I have received many compliments on the quality of my writing and the interesting and thought provoking ideas I have presented. I chuckle to myself every time I receive one of these comments because I know that I don't deserve them. I have coined a new word to describe writers like me – most of whom are graduate students compared to my status as a child in kindergarten. The new word is Spiritwriter and here is the definition. A Spiritwriter is a person who writes messages inspired by the Holy Spirit, but puts his or her own name on it. Unlike a ghostwriter, the Spiritwriter gets credit for the writing knowing that the actual writing is not his or her own, but inspired by the Holy Spirit. In fact, the Holy Spirit enables the Spiritwriter to see circumstances and people from a divine perspective.

We all know many writers who are Spiritwriters – Moses, Isaiah, Jeremiah, Solomon, David, Paul, Matthew, Mark, Luke and John. You see, "All scripture is God-breathed …." (2 Timothy 3:16) and "no prophecy of scripture came about because of the prophet's own interpretation. For prophecy never had its origin in the will of man, but men spoke from God as they were carried along by the Holy Spirit" (2 Peter 1:21). By definition, all of the writers of the Bible are Spiritwriters.

In no way do I want to imply that I am on any level with the authors of the Bible or other well known Christian writers. However, God does call each of us to do His work with the skills He has given us. You see, God doesn't call the equipped; He equips those whom He calls. The Bible says it a different way in James 4:10, "Humble yourself in the sight of the Lord, and He will lift you up."

See you tomorrow, God willing!

March 10 — Always Remember

Spring is about to spring here in North Carolina. The Bradford Pears are in full bloom; there is a little red starting to show in the Red Bud trees; there is a hint of green in the dormant grasses that are prevalent in the eastern part of the state; and yes, the temperature is finally high enough for a comfortable round of golf.

Every year when the Bradford Pears begin to bloom, I like to take a short drive by a little house in Winterville to see how a couple of trees are doing. It was the first house my daughter and her husband had purchased and it came at a time when she was pregnant with their first son. When he was born, my wife and I purchased and planted a Red Bud tree in the front yard of their house in honor of his birth. That tree is a favorite of my wife because the red buds turn into small heart-shaped leaves. A couple of years later when their second son was born, we added a Bradford Pear tree to the yard, just a few yards away from the Red Bud.

Last night, we took a drive by that house on Vale Court to see how the trees were doing. The Red Bud tree looks great and is just beginning to sprout. Like all the Bradford Pears in the area, that tree is also in full bloom. We thought to ourselves, just like the boys, mature and healthy.

As part of their heritage, the Israelites often left markers behind as a remembrance of important events in their lives. The first memorial was built by Abraham, "The LORD appeared to Abram and said, 'To your offspring I will give this land.' So he built an altar there to the LORD, who had appeared to him. (Genesis 12:7). Moses also got into the act, "Moses built an altar and called it The LORD is my Banner" (Exodus 17:15). After Gideon's might victory over the Midianites, he also built an altar. "So Gideon built an altar to the LORD there and called it The LORD is Peace. To this day it stands in Ophrah of the Abiezrites" (Judges 6:24). It was their way of acknowledging that God was the source of their blessings.

That is exactly why we planted those trees in the yard of a little house on Vale Court, to help us remember that God is the source of all of our blessings!

See you tomorrow, God willing!

March 11   Nothing Is Impossible

The weather in Pennsylvania in the winter is cold, snowy and gray. For some people who suffer from "seasonal affect disorder" (SAD), it can be a difficult time of the year. To some degree, my wife had this disorder so we tried to break the winter in half by taking a February vacation to a warm climate. For several years, we went with friends to the Yucatan Peninsula on the east coast of Mexico. In the very small village of Akumal, about 30 miles due south of Cancun, we rented a house that was right on the Gulf Coast. We could literally walk out the front door, across the lava rock and snorkel in a magnificent lagoon that was full of incredible fish – Parrot Fish, Grouper, Cardinal Fish, Trumpet Fish, Angel Fish, and an occasional Barracuda. If you like to snorkel, it was paradise.

However, if shelling is your game, it was not so good. There was a large beach about a mile away, but there were no shells there. The beach close to the rented house was tiny - about eight feet wide and about ten feet deep. Nevertheless, my wife went out every morning to drink her morning coffee and pretended to be looking for shells (it is in her blood). One morning she ran back to the house as excited as I had ever seen her. There in her hand was a rare rooster shell conch that she said she had found on that little stretch of beach. We accused her of buying it earlier and then presenting it to us as if it were a prize find. I knew better, God had presented it to her as a way of telling her that nothing is impossible with Him.

Jesus had told his disciples, "It is easier for a camel to go through the eye of a needle than for a rich man to enter the kingdom of God" and they were concerned. Knowing their fears, He assured them, "With man this is impossible, but not with God; all things are possible with God" (Mark 10:25-27). The angel told the Virgin Mary the same thing in Luke 1:37, "For nothing is impossible with God."

The rooster tail conch that Shirley found that morning in Mexico sits proudly in our bookcase even today as an eternal reminder that nothing is impossible for God.

See you tomorrow, God willing!

March 12   What's in A Number?

Today is the 71st day of 2011. Normally, that would have no particular meaning for me. In fact, in previous years, I would never have known that March 12 was the 71st day of the year, except for leap years. Nothing is normal for me this year. Every day I am looking at the world through a new set of lenses; I am seeing things I have never seen before; I am remembering things buried deep in the recesses of my mind; and I am feeling emotions once untapped.

Today is a good example. The number seventy-one evoked memories of both of my parents. For mother it was the reading to her of Psalm 71 on a regular basis toward the end of her life. Verse six says, "From birth I have relied on you; you brought me forth from my mother's womb. I will ever praise you." However, it was verse nine that caught my attention, "Do not cast me away when I am old; do not forsake me when my strength is gone." Then, the psalmist delivered the key line in verse eighteen. "Even when I am old and gray, do not forsake me, O God, till I declare your power to the next generation, your might to all who are to come." My mother lived verse eighteen; by her actions, she declared God's power to all of us.

One of the most compelling images of my dad that is imprinted in the scrapbook of my mind is a photo taken in 1971. That was the year that all three Roberts' children added to the grandchildren pool. Two grandchildren were born in March followed by another birth in July. We must have all been together for Thanksgiving in St. Paul when the picture was taken. It was a picture of a beaming grandfather with all five of his grandchildren sitting on his lap or in close proximity. He was in heaven; he sure loved his grandchildren.

Now that I am a grandfather of five, I can appreciate why it was so easy to capture his smile on that day. Would it surprise you to know that it in Bible times they already understood this special relationship? Proverbs 17:6 says, "Children's children are a crown to the aged, and parents are the pride of their children."

One of the most compelling things I have learned from reading the Bible daily is this.

Man's knowledge of the world we live in has grown incredibly since Bible times and it will continue to grow as God's reveals the scientific mysteries of His creation. However, human nature has not changed one iota.

See you tomorrow, God willing!

March 13   Spring Forward or Fall Back?

The clock over my shoulder says that it is 5 a.m., but it sure looks dark outside for this time of day. Oh yeah, it is that dreaded day of the year when our clocks "spring forward" to give us an extra hour of daylight at the end of the day. I really do not understand why they call it "daylight savings time." We do not save any daylight; there will be the same amount today whether or not we change the clocks. No matter, it is what it is!

Do you have any funny memories about a day when the time switched over? I do. When I was on the golf team at the University of Virginia, we were scheduled to leave on a Sunday morning to travel to Columbia, South Carolina to play a three-way meet with the University of South Carolina and Clemson on Monday. I was on my way back from an adjoining dormitory where I had just completed a load of laundry when I saw a car full of my teammates yelling at me. They had been looking for me since I did not show up at the appointed place for the trip. You guessed it; I had forgotten to reset my clocks so I was running an hour late. Monday was no better; I lost both of my matches. It must have been the time change.

For most of us, it takes a few days to get used to the new times. Getting up an hour earlier is no fun for the first couple of weeks. Likewise, it is hard to stay up an hour longer at night. Yet, every year we move the clocks ahead in the spring and "fall back" in the fall. We try our best to create something which only God can create, an extra hour of daylight. God is in control of the sun and everything else in the universe. He is omnipotent, omnipresent, and omniscient. The prophet Amos said, "In that day," declares the Sovereign LORD, "I will make the sun go down at noon and darken the earth in broad daylight." That is how you control the number of hours of daylight.

See you tomorrow, God willing!

p.s. If you have a funny daylight savings story, share it with members of your family, today.

March 14   Rivalries

Yesterday, for the second time in just over a week, Duke and North Carolina played an intense basketball game; this one for the conference championship of the ACC. Last week, my wife and I attended a friend's 60th birthday party and that night the Duke-North Carolina regular season game was the object of most people's attention. In a room of about thirty people, the crowd was about evenly split between the two intrastate rivals. I don't completely understand the reason why so many seemingly sane individuals become momentarily insane during contests of this nature. Is it jealousy? Is it the desire to feel a sense of superiority? Is it envy? Or, is it simply a deep-seated hatred of losing?

I remember many of the annual rivalry football games between Castlewood and St. Paul, but the fondest remembrance had nothing to do with the outcome of the game. It was my senior year in high school and the game was being played at St. Paul. We were already on the field when the Castlewood team burst onto the field through the traditional paper banner. When the first couple of players burst through the paper, they tripped and fell down. When the majority of the rest of the team fell over them, I couldn't have been happier. It turns out, that was about my only happy event of the evening, as they beat us soundly that evening.

If we think the rivalries in today's sports are too intense, we should look at Bible stories to put it into perspective. It starts in Genesis 4 verses 3, 5, and 8. "In the course of time, Cain brought some of the fruits of the soil as an offering to the LORD, but on Cain and his offering, he did not look with favor. So Cain was very angry, and his face was downcast. Now Cain said to his brother Abel, "Let's go out to the field." And while they were in the field, Cain attacked his brother Abel and killed him." This was the first case of brotherly rivalry in the Bible and it ended with murder.

Rivalries were not limited to the Old Testament or to brothers. Even Jesus' disciples got caught up in discussions about who was the greatest. In Luke 9:46 this it what it says, "An argument started among the disciples as to which of them would be the greatest." Jesus didn't wait long to straightened out the situation, "For he who is least among you all—he is the greatest."

Sports rivalries can be fun if we don't take them too seriously. However, beware those rivalries in your own life that can lead to strife and broken relationships. We should all take Jesus' advice, "whoever is the least, he is the greatest."

See you tomorrow, God willing!

March 15 — Lost but Found

When my son and his family were with us during Christmas, his wife shared a story with all of us that I later realized contained powerful symbolism about how much God loves us and cares for us.

Here is the story. On one of her return trips from Columbia, SC to St. Paul, VA she got a late start and was forced to make a large portion of the drive after dark. And as my mother used to say "everything sure looks different at night." At some point during the trip, she missed one of her route changes and found herself totally lost with no idea how to get herself headed in the right direction. Literally not knowing which way to turn, she called my son on her cell phone for help.

My son first tried to get her to calm down and tell him exactly where she was. He then stayed on the phone with her as she described to the best of her knowledge where she was. Once he was able to ascertain where she was, he patiently walked her through the process of finding her way back on track. In her words, my son was so patient and helpful; he knew I was lost and he took the time to calm me down and help me find my way.

All the time this was going on, their daughter noticed how upset her mommy was and tried to console her – "it's alright mommy, daddy will help us find our way." Once they were back on the right road, her response changed, "Mommy, you are just a big crybaby."

Does this pattern sound familiar? When we are in the darkness, things do look a lot different and it is all too easy to get lost. When we do get lost, our first response should be to acknowledge that we are lost and call upon someone to help. Are you getting the point? Of course, the phone call often takes the form of a prayer and our God is always there to answer. There is never a voice mail or a busy signal. He is always there to calm and reassure us, no matter how badly we are lost. He is also patient with us and He stays on the line until we are back on the right road. And, when it is all over, He doesn't call us a crybaby.

"For the Son of Man came to seek and to save what was lost." (Luke 19:10) "He stilled the storm to a whisper; the waves of the sea were hushed. They were glad when it grew calm, and he guided them to their desired haven." (Psalm 107:29-30)

Next time you are lost in the darkness or in trouble of any kind, dial G-O-D and He will walk you back to the light.

See you tomorrow, God willing!

March 16 — I Got Shoes

An old Negro spiritual starts with these words:

> I got shoes,
> You got shoes,
> All of God's children got shoes.
> When I get to heaven, gonna put on my shoes,
> Gonna walk all over God's heaven.

I thought about that song today when I was reminded of an event that took place at Pinehurst Country Club, home of the 2005 U. S. Open. We had gotten tickets for the whole gang – my daughter's family, and my wife, and me. We left Greenville early in the morning so we could make the three hour drive to Pinehurst, NC and be there in time to watch a full day of golf. All went well until we parked the car and got ready to enter the grounds. Our youngest grandson had no shoes. Thinking he had left a pair in the car the previous day, he got dressed and then got in the car without any shoes. The tension was so thick you could cut it with a knife.

It was at that moment I saw the picture of patience and grace. My son-in-law calmly told us to go ahead without him and my grandson. He would drive into town with him and get him a pair of tennis shoes. About an hour later, they joined the rest of us and we enjoyed the day devoid of any other conflict, or in this case, potential conflict.

Can you imagine how many times in your own life God has said, "It's alright, I forgive you and I will take care of your needs. Conversely, how many times have we failed to forgive those who have harmed us in some way, real or imagined? I don't know what your answer might be, but as for me, I can't count that high.

Paul's instruction to the church in Colosse were, "Bear with each other and forgive whatever grievances you may have against one another. Forgive as the Lord forgave you." (Col 3:13) It's a lesson in grace.

See you tomorrow, God Willing!

March 17   Forty – Good or Bad

Today, someone in my family has a birthday and he will be forty years old or forty years young, take your pick. A pessimist will tell you that when you turn forty, you are over the hill; your best years are behind you; your teeth will begin to fall out and so will your hair; you will forget the things you ought to remember and remember the things you ought to forget. To the pessimist, it isn't a pretty picture.

What does the optimist say? He says that life begins at forty. You are not getting older; you are getting better and wiser. The rocky roads of your youth are becoming paved highways. Your vision is becoming clearer and clearer, not because your eyesight is better, but because you are seeing more things through the eyes of your heart. Your hearing is better because you listen more attentively to the important things in life. Moreover, your heart is stronger because you are beginning to understand just how much God loves you.

Most of you know that the number forty is used prominently in the Bible. Does it give us a clue to what God thinks about the number? Here is my take on the question. The first use of the number forty in the Bible was in Genesis 7 where God tells Noah about the flood. "Seven days from now I will send rain on the earth for forty days and forty nights, and I will wipe from the face of the earth every living creature I have made." What happened at the end of the forty days, life sprang anew on the whole earth. How about Deuteronomy 9:11, "At the end of the forty days and forty nights, the LORD gave me the two stone tablets, the tablets of the covenant." Moses brought down the Ten Commandments, a legacy of law that still guides us today. What happened to the Israelites after forty years in the wilderness? They entered the Promised Land. Last, but not least, Matthew 4 describes Jesus forty days in the wilderness. When those forty days were over, Jesus began his earthly ministry. New Life. New Directions. New Land. New Ministry.

Happy Birthday, my son! May you have–New Life. New Direction. New Land. New Ministry.

See you tomorrow, God willing!

March 18 — What Was I Thinking?

One day this last winter, my youngest grandson and two of his friends made an executive decision on the way to school to forgo the boredom of school for a day of playing hooky. During the day, they made a stop by Wal-Mart. While they were in the store they ran into the vice principal of the high school who wanted to know why they weren't in school. I can hear my grandson now, "What was I thinking?" Because it was a first offence, none of the guilty parties received severe punishment,

A week or so later, my daughter's family was having dinner at our house and we talked about that day off. The question was raised, had any of us ever played hooky from school? The story my wife told made my grandson's look lame.

One day many years ago, my wife and two of her friends decided to skip school and go to Bristol, fifty miles away, to see "West Side Story." Since none of them had a driver's license, they hopped on a bus and in an hour or so had arrived at their destination. They saw the movie and returned to St. Paul, having been seen by no one of importance during their little escapade. That evening was the annual sports banquet at the high school, which honored all the athletes and cheerleaders for all sports. Since my wife and her friends were all cheerleaders, they, of course, got ready and attended the evening's festivities. Just like my grandson, they were busted and my wife was heard bemoaning her plight, "What was I thinking?"

"One evening David got up from his bed and walked around on the roof of the palace. From the roof he saw a woman bathing. The woman was very beautiful, and David sent someone to find out about her. Then David sent messengers to get her. She came to him, and he slept with her. (2nd Samuel 11:2-4) This is not in the Bible, but later David obviously said, "What was I thinking?"

Jonah, a prophet of God, was called to go to the city of Nineveh to preach repentance to his dreaded enemies. Since that didn't suit his desires, he ran the other way and boarded a ship to Tarshish. The rest is history. Again, you won't find this in the Bible, but if you had been there when Jonah was vomited onto dry land, you would have heard him exclaim, "What was I thinking?"

I have done some stupid things in my life and I'm sure all of you can admit to the same thing. Isn't it wonderful that God forgives us? In his Psalm of contrition David hit the nail on the head, "The sacrifices of God are a broken spirit; a broken and contrite heart, O God, you will not despise." (Psalm 51:17) That is all that God requires, a broken and contrite heart.

See you tomorrow, God willing!

March 19 — Down on Your Knees

The average height for a boy in the first grade in the United States is three feet eleven inches. When I am on my knees, my height is approximately three feet eleven inches. I suppose that is why little children are much more comfortable with adults when they are on their knees. They can look you right in the eyes. One of my son's favorite pastimes when he was little was playing with his collection of "Matchbox" Cars. I can remember many times when he would stand at one end of the hall of our house in Pennsylvania, and I would kneel at the other end seeing who could roll the cars the greatest distance. I was on his level in more respects than one. I also think he enjoyed beating me at his game.

We still have his collection of Matchbox Cars and we bring them out whenever our neighbor brings their young son over for a visit. Their son and I play the same game that my son and I played over thirty years ago. Some things never change; kids are more comfortable with us when we are on our knees.

Of course, kneeling is also the natural posture of prayer. The dictionary defines prayer as "a solemn request for help or expression of thanks addressed to God." For many of us, kneeling helps make the action more solemn; it also brings me to the place I need to be. A popular Christian song of a few years ago had it right. Here are first words, "Down at your feet Oh Lord is the most high place.

Two of the most quoted verses in the Bible about prayer are found in Philippians 4:6 and James 5:16, respectively. "Do not be anxious about anything, but in everything, by prayer and petition, with thanksgiving, present your requests to God," and "The prayer of a righteous man is powerful and effective."

Not too long ago, my brother-in-law sent me this message in response to an earlier devotion, "You cannot stumble if you are on your knees!" Oh, how true that statement is.

See you tomorrow, God willing!

March 20   Don't Cry Granny

> Sugar and spice
> and everything nice
> that's what little girls are made of.

That is the first line of a well-known nursery rhyme. For those of us who have had the good fortune to be around daughters and granddaughters, we know just how true those words can be. As I write these words, my granddaughter lies asleep with my wife in a nearby bedroom. She has been visiting for a few days and we are enjoying her company.

When we lived in Cincinnati, we visited both sets of parents on a regular basis. Since they both lived in the same town, it made it very convenient to see both of them on the same visit. No matter how many times we visited them, the farewells at the end of the visit were always filled with tears. The visits were precious especially when the kids were little. By the time our daughter was about three years old, she had noticed the tears, which seemed to accompany each farewell. In a tone of voice that only a three-year old girl could replicate she ended each visit with this phrase, "Don't cry granny, I'll be back!"

There is a famous grandmother in the Bible who had every reason to cry. First, she, her husband, and their two sons had to move to a foreign land to escape a severe drought that was occurring in their country. Then, her husband died and her two sons died after marrying women from the foreign country. As a bitter woman, she moved back to her homeland accompanied by one of her daughters-in-law who refused to leave her side. As fate would have it, Ruth, her daughter-in-law, would marry Boaz, a kinsman redeemer, and bear her a grandson – "The women living there said, 'Naomi has a son.' And they named him Obed. He was the father of Jesse, the father of David" (Ruth 4:17).

Naomi had heard the advice, "Don't cry, Granny!" and she had become the great, great grandmother of David. I suppose the moral to this story appears in the Book of Genesis. It is a famous verse from the 50th chapter as Joseph is forgiving his brothers for their evil treatment of him. "You intended to harm me, but God intended it for good to accomplish what is now being done..." (Genesis 50:20).

Joseph and Naomi had learned the hard way, but they had learned a valuable lesson. When things get a little tough, remember both of these stories. God is in control and He has plans for us to prosper.

See you tomorrow, God willing!

March 21 — Comfort from God

Dave, a friend of mine, passed away a couple of days ago. Dave had been diagnosed with fourth stage cancer in his throat a little over six months ago, but I had seen him at church two weeks ago and after going through a severe regime of treatment, he had been declared cancer free. Last week, Dave went into an unexplained coma and although he did briefly wake up, he never recovered. Only God knows what really happened.

I got to know Dave when we first moved to North Carolina nearly ten years ago. He and his wife sang in the choir and, like me, Dave was a bass. Dave was also like me in some other respects. He was always in a good mood, and he loved to joke around with people. His good nature was infectious so you couldn't help but enjoy your time with him. When my mother moved to assisted living a few years ago, it was Dave who blessed us by agreeing to take Mother's dog and give her a new home. I stayed in pretty close touch with Dave during his six months of treatment, but not as much as I should have. As the old saying goes, "I'm not as bad as I once was, but not as good as I am going to be."

"Praise be to the God and Father of our Lord Jesus Christ, the Father of compassion and the God of all comfort, who comforts us in all our troubles, so that we can comfort those in any trouble with the comfort we ourselves have received from God. For just as the sufferings of Christ flow over into our lives, so also through Christ our comfort overflows. If we are distressed, it is for your comfort and salvation; if we are comforted, it is for your comfort, which produces in you patient endurance of the same sufferings we suffer." (2nd Corinthians 1:3-6) To paraphrase, God comforts us in our times of need so we can comfort others in their time of need.

See you tomorrow, God willing!

March 22   Not My Dog

For those of us in the Baby Boomer generation, we have no trouble recalling the characters on the Andy Griffith Show. One of my favorites was Barney Fife, Andy's trusty deputy sheriff. Here is something you don't know about Barney Fife, his brother was a deputy sheriff in St. Paul. Like Barney, Butch Fife was small in stature; he was probably about five foot three and weighed about one hundred ten pounds without his holster and gun. He was also like Barney in his zeal to enforce the law.

One day about thirty years ago, Butch was patrolling the area of Gray Hill where my mother lived. On the day in question, he spotted a dog running loose in my mother's yard without a leash. My dad was working in the yard so Butch asked dad if the loose dog was his. My dad replied, "It's not my dog." Of course, he was correct, it was Jill Number One, mother's dog, but because dad didn't like the dog, he denied any ownership. Since the owner was not to be found (Mother was at work), Butch left a ticket on the door of the house which mother had to pay later. I don't have to tell you that she was not pleased.

My dad passed away a couple of years later. On the day of his funeral, Jill also died and we buried her in the backyard of the house on Gray Hill. Through our tears, we laughed that even in death, Dad could not get away from Jill.

The scoffer would quote Matthew 25:46 ("Then they will go away to eternal punishment, but the righteous to eternal life.") and say that my dad had gone to eternal punishment by having to put up with Jill for eternity. They would be wrong, my dad was a believer.

"I tell you the truth, whoever hears my word and believes him who sent me has eternal life and will not be condemned; he has crossed over from death to life" (John 5:24).

See you tomorrow, God willing!

March 23 — Not My God

It has become my routine to pray each morning using the title of that morning's "Love Letter" as the theme for my prayers. Yesterday's title was "Not My Dog." How was I going to use that as a theme for my prayers? What was God trying to tell me? Had I finally gone off the deep end? As rapidly as those questions ran through my head, the answer came. I was being dyslexic! The real theme for my prayers was supposed to be "Not My God!"

There is a brief joke that I have told often in my life that captures the humor in this situation. It is actually a riddle. What does an agnostic, dyslexic, insomniac do at night?

He stays up all night wondering if there is a dog.

I am neither agnostic, dyslexic nor an insomniac, but I am sure there have been times when I have said "Not My God" by the way I live my life. How often have I said "No" or "Not Now" to His call on my life? How often have I questioned God's existence when terrible things happen to good people? How many times have I taken credit for successes in my life when all along they were blessings from God? Every time I have failed under the foregoing circumstances, I have effectively said "Not My God."

The Bible is full of examples of God-fearing people forgetting their God. Saul started out strong, but finished weak. "Saul then said to his attendants, "Find me a woman who is a medium, so I may go and inquire of her." (1 Samuel 28:7) He had lost his trust in God. In 2nd Kings, the God-fearing Kings Ahaz and Hezekiah also lost trust and paid off the king of Assyria rather than seek protection from God. "And Ahaz took the silver and gold found in the temple of the Lord and in the treasuries of the royal palace and sent it as a gift to the king of Assyria." (2 Kings 16:8) "So Hezekiah gave him all the silver that was found in the temple of the Lord and in the treasuries of the royal palace." (2 Kings 18:15). If those examples aren't enough, how about John the Baptist, "When the men came to Jesus, they said, 'John the Baptist sent us to you to ask, Are you the one who was to come, or should we expect someone else?'" (Luke 7:20) And, the worst was Judas Iscariot who sold Jesus for thirty pieces of silver. Kings, prophets, and disciples all sent forth the same message, "Not My God!"

The next time you have trouble sleeping, I urge you to ponder this important question, and how often do I say "Not My God?"

See you tomorrow, God willing!

March 24   It's All A Blur

The summer between my junior and senior years in high school gave me my first experience with an institution of higher learning. To be precise, I spent six weeks on the campus of Virginia Tech participating in a National Science Foundation summer program for "gifted students." We spent two weeks each studying the basics of ceramic, metallurgical, and mining engineering. One early morning I was sitting in the classroom and I noticed all of the other students writing voraciously. What were they doing? Did they know something I didn't know? Had I forgotten some instructions from the previous day? When the professor came into the room and turned on the lights, the mystery was solved. The blackboard was covered with notes about the day's class that I had not seen.

When I got home after the summer session was over, I had my eyes checked and discovered that I had a bad case of near-sightedness and needed glasses to correct my vision for distances. I wore glasses from that time (1963) until the early 1970's. If you have ever played tennis on a hot day, you can appreciate one of the reasons I finally was tired of glasses and switched to contact lenses. Contact lenses served me well for well over twenty years until my eyes started to rebel against them. So, I took the next step – Lasik Surgery. I had one eye fixed for distance and left the other one alone so I could read without reading glasses. I simply see distances with my left eye and read with my right eye. The brain does all the work; I simply look.

It's amazing what we will do to improve our eyesight. Yet, we do far too little to open the eyes of our hearts. When Jesus was asked by His disciples in Matthew 13:13 why He spoke to the people in parables, He replied," This is why I speak to them in parables: Though seeing, they do not see; though hearing, they do not hear or understand." He went on to say in verse 13:15, "For this people's heart has become calloused; they hardly hear with their ears, and they have closed their eyes. Otherwise they might see with their eyes, hear with their ears, understand with their hearts and turn, and I would heal them."

For over three decades, I took great pains to improve my eyesight. Finally, I started to work on the eyes of my heart. I can assure you it has made all the difference.

See you tomorrow, God willing!

March 25   Driving Miss Lucille

My mother, Lucille, started spending her summers at Emerald Isle, NC beginning in the summer of 1990, the year my daughter got married. Her annual pilgrimage usually began in late March or early April and ended some time before Labor Day. She loved the beach, and her "permanent" spot at the Holiday Inn Travel Park afforded her the luxury of having the same neighbors every year. She spent countless hours looking for seashells and walking her dog on the beach. It was her getaway and her place of refuge.

It was about an eight-hour drive from St. Paul to Emerald Isle, but despite her advancing age, Mother made the trip with no apparent problems (for a while). However, by the late 1990's, it became obvious to all of us in the family that the drive was becoming too difficult for her. Our response was to take turns driving her to and from St. Paul when she was ready to go. We all took our turns and it really wasn't a hardship on any of us.

One particular year, my wife convinced our son to drive Mother from St. Paul to Emerald Isle. She would follow in our car with her mother and bring him back to Pennsylvania after a brief vacation. He joyfully agreed and the trip began. About three hours into the trip, they stopped for a bio-break. My wife will never forget our son's remark when he got out of the car, "She hasn't stopped talking for three hours!" Since we all knew her very well, we knew he wasn't exaggerating. Mother could talk your ear off and some people say I might have inherited that gift of gab.

When Moses delivered the Ten Commandments to the Israelites, the first four commandments pertained to our relationship with God and the fifth pertained to our relationship with our earthly parents. It was also the first commandment with a promise. "Honor your father and your mother, as the Lord your God has commanded you, so that you may live long and that it may go well with you in the land the Lord your God is giving you" (Deuteronomy 5:16). When we drove Miss Lucille back and forth to Emerald Isle every year, we were honoring her with our time and our ears.

I am thankful for her life and my heritage.

See you tomorrow, God willing!

March 26 — The Game of Life

Playing card games and board games has been a part of my life for as long as I can remember. My mom and dad spent hours playing card games with the extended family in Illinois. Likewise, all of the cousins played board games of which Monopoly was a favorite. While I don't think there is a Monopoly gene that is passed on from generation to generation, I must admit that my two grandsons must haven gotten their love of Monopoly from somewhere.

When they were adolescents, they played with great skill and fervor. It wasn't too long ago that I learned just how good a player my youngest grandson is. As we were completing a game that he was winning, he announced to me, "I have never lost a game of Monopoly in my whole life." Like me, he has been known to exaggerate on occasion so I asked him to clarify his statement. He said again, "I have never lost a game of Monopoly in my life. If I see that I am going to lose a game, I quit before it is over." There is nowhere in the rules of Monopoly that it says you can quit and avoid a loss.

The game of life (the real game, not the board game) is just the opposite of my grandson's approach to Monopoly. For in real life, it is not important that we win the battles, the importance lies in obeying the rules and honoring the game. "Those who honor me I will honor, but those who despise me will be disdained" (1st Samuel 2:30b). "Then you will have success if you are careful to observe the decrees and laws that the Lord gave Moses for Israel. Be strong and courageous. Do not be afraid or discouraged" (1st Chronicles 22:13). "If they obey and serve him, they will spend the rest of their days in prosperity and their years in contentment" (Job 36:11).

Just because you may be losing a few battles, don't give up. Trust in God and live by His rules and honor Him and you will spend the rest of your days in prosperity and contentment.

See you tomorrow, God willing!

March 27 — A Charmed Bracelet

Last weekend when our granddaughter was with us, we were able to get her up early enough to go to church with us on Sunday morning. After she was dressed, she came into my wife's dressing area where she often gets to try on high-heel shoes and other "big girl" clothing. While there, she spotted two necklaces that she wanted to wear to church. Being a doting grandmother, my wife allowed her to wear both of them. Then she saw a charm bracelet from my wife's high school days that she also wanted to wear. Now, she was ready for church.

Since it was too noisy for her in the sanctuary, one of us had to stay on Main Street with her and let her wander around and play with some other little children. First, my wife stayed out with her and then my daughter and I took our turn. Our granddaughter had a great time, especially interacting with another little girl who was also spending the service time outside.

Right after church, we invited our daughter's family to have lunch with us. Little did my son-in-law know that our granddaughter was going to give him her full attention. She had seen him on the TV screen in the lobby when the camera panned the musicians during the last song of the service and that must have gotten her started. As she always does, she made us all laugh and we enjoyed the extra time together.

When we got home from church, we noticed that the charm bracelet was missing. We looked in the car and around the house, but it was nowhere to be found. After our granddaughter left on Monday, we searched around the house some more for the bracelet, but again to no avail. Frankly, we were not overly concerned, she had enjoyed wearing it so "what the heck!"

On Friday night, we were back at church for a special speaker our church had brought in to speak on family values. While there, we checked in "lost and found," but again, no bracelet. Saturday morning we were back at church for the Saturday morning session of the conference. After it was over, my wife was sitting on one of the couches on "Main Street" and decided to pull up the main cushion to see if the bracelet might have fallen there. To her surprise, there it was.

Perhaps God had rewarded her for attending the conference. "The Lord rewards every man for his righteousness and faithfulness." (1 Samuel 26:23). I'm sure He also rewarded her for bringing our granddaughter to His house. "Jesus said, 'Let the little children come to me, and do not hinder them, for the kingdom of heaven belongs to such as these.'" (Matthew 19:14)

See you tomorrow, God willing!

March 28   Letters from Dad

Several years ago at our church, I led a small group called "Letters from Dad." The group was based on a ministry started by a man in Texas whose father had passed away leaving behind no personal mementos of his life. To make a long story short, Greg Vaughn made a decision that he was not going to let that happen to his children. With a few of his friends, they began writing letters of love and encouragement to their children, wives, and parents. The response from family members was so positive that the idea soon grew into a nationwide ministry.

"Letters from Dad (LFD)" was a great experience and I suppose it set the stage for "365 Love Letters." The two main differences in LFD and 365 LL are the frequency – LFD is occasional versus 365 LL, which is daily – and the method of delivery – LFD is hand-delivered and 365 LL is email. In Greg Vaughn's book, he uses a verse from Malachi to describe the intent of his ministry, "He will turn the hearts of the fathers to their children, and the hearts of the children to their fathers;" (Malachi 4:6). I could not agree more.

This weekend my wife and I attended a conference on Family Values led by Voddie Baucham. Most of the discussion revolved around the things parents need to do while raising their children to help their children become God-loving adults. He talked in depth about the gods of education and sports that we too often allow ahead of the one true God. It made my wife and me realize that we made a few mistakes along the way and for that, I am sorry. Nevertheless, we can't go backwards; we can't change the past; we can only attempt to influence the future.

As I listened to Voddie speak, I thought about the last letter that Greg Vaughn of LFD recommends that each of us write. It is a letter to be read at our funeral. I have not yet written that letter, but if I had, it would contain some of the scripture that Voddie talked about. For example, when Moses gave the Israelites the Ten Commandments, he gave the men some clear instructions. "Impress them on your children. Talk about them when you sit at home and when you walk along the road, when you lie down and when you get up." (Deuteronomy 6:7) Later, in the New Testament, Paul gives us similar instructions. "Fathers, do not exasperate your children; instead, bring them up in the training and instruction of the Lord." (Ephesians 6:4). My last letter would give my children and my grand children that advice.

See you tomorrow, God willing!

March 29   Size Doesn't Matter

During the early 1960's, when I was in high school, scholastic sports teams in the state of Virginia were classified by size in four different categories. Group 3 was for the smallest schools and Group 1 and 1a were the largest. If there had been a Group 4, St. Paul High School would have been in that category. With less than 200 students in grades 9 through 12, it is fortunate that we were able to field teams in football, basketball, baseball, and track and field. To make matters even worse for us, there were no other Group 3 schools in our region so we competed in Group 2.

In the spring of 1962, my brother and one of his friends who were seniors convinced the school to field a golf team. Not only were there no Group 3 teams in the region, there were no Group 2 teams and only one Group 1a. That meant if we wanted to compete, it would be David versus Goliath. We didn't care; at least we would get to play on some new golf courses. To make a long story short, we won every match that year except one. We were finally beaten in the last match of the year at Abingdon, but that didn't deprive us of the right to compete in the state tournament that was held that year at a Chantilly Country Club near Fairfax, Virginia. Four country boys had made it to the big time. It would be a fairy tale ending if I told you we won the state tournament, but we didn't.

Underdogs in sports very often defeat their larger opponents. In the Bible, smaller forces often defeated larger armies. Since I mentioned David and Goliath earlier, I'll pass on that well-known story and tell you of another that is equally impressive. Here is the gist of the story as told in the Book of Judges. First, God called on Gideon to lead his troops and here was Gideon's response. "But Lord," Gideon asked, "how can I save Israel? My clan is the weakest in Manasseh, and I am the least in my family" (Judges 6:15). To prove His might, God sent Gideon forth with a small, but mighty army. "The Lord said to Gideon, "With the three hundred men ... I will save you and give the Midianites into your hands." (Judges 7:7) How big was the opponent? It says in Judges 8:10, "a hundred and twenty thousand swordsmen had fallen." "What, then, shall we say in response to this? If God is for us, who can be against us?" (Romans 8:31).

It's not the size of the dog in the fight; it's the size of the fight in the dog that matters, especially if the small dog has God on his side.

See you tomorrow, God willing!

March 30 — A Birthday Event

Playing golf with my family members has always been a treat. My son and I have played at many courses. My son-in-law and I have played many times, but the ones at Myrtle Beach were probably the most memorable. My brother-in-law and I have played for years and when he still belonged to Lake Bonaventure, we played every year in the Member Guest with mixed results. I have also played quite a few times with other family members. Last, but not least, I have had the good fortune of playing many rounds with my two grandsons.

Since today is my oldest grandson's birthday, it's appropriate to recall a very special round that took place on his 12th birthday. Let me set the stage. My grandson's game had been improving very rapidly since he started playing. He took the game very seriously and had taken numerous lessons from the pro at the course where we played. Although he had come close to shooting in the 70's he had never quite made it, and he had never managed to beat me. All of that changed on March 30, 2004. When we got to the 18th hole at Brook Valley, he had a one shot lead, but he faced a par three of nearly 200 yards, all over the water. With his knees knocking and his hands shaking, he hit his first shot onto the green about 20 feet from the hole. He was home free, or so he thought. I hit my tee shot into the sand trap just to the left of the flagstick. I am a good bunker player so I didn't give up just yet. I popped the ball out of the sand and it headed right for the hole. As it was rolling, I glanced at my grandson and I saw his countenance drop. At that moment, the ball lipped out of the hole and I had to settle for a par. He two putted and held onto his one stroke lead. He had beaten me and in the process shot his first round in the 70's – a round of 78. What a birthday present! I had not given it to him, he had earned it.

He had worked hard to beat me, and I think that as Christians, we think we have to work hard to earn our way to heaven. But, Paul makes it abundantly clear in both his letter to the Romans and to the Ephesians. "And if by grace, then it is no longer by works; if it were, grace would no longer be grace" (Romans 11:6). For it is by grace you have been saved, through faith—and this not from yourselves, it is the gift of God" (Ephesians 2:8).

See you tomorrow, God willing!

March 31   Can You See?

Today, instead of devotion, I am going to give you a quiz. It is a word phrase quiz, and you get ten points for every phrase you define correctly. The one who gets the most points wins three months of free "*365 Love Letters.*"

Here goes.

1. Bucket brigade.
2. Bucket line.
3. Bucket list.
4. Bucket handle.
5. Nose Bucket.
6. Bucket Seat
7. Buckethead

If you think you have seventy points, send me your answers. In case of ties, everyone wins.

You may notice that there is one word in the list that you may not recognize; it is the word buckethead. It is a special word coined in 1969 by a young father as he watched his two-year old daughter bounce off walls because she was wearing a bucket on her head. She would run into a wall, fall down, take the bucket off her head and laugh hysterically. I can still see her walk around the room until she hit something. If she was trying to get my attention and entertain me, she did a great job. By the way, not once did she ever hurt herself.

How many of us go through life with a bucket over our heads failing to see either the obstacles in front of us or the blessings that God bestows on us every day. Are we foolish and senseless people? Are we a rebellious people? Are we missing the secrets of the kingdom?

Listen to what the Bible tells us.

"Hear this, you foolish and senseless people, who have eyes but do not see, who have ears but do not hear." Jeremiah 5:21

"Son of man, you are living among a rebellious people. They have eyes to see but do not see and ears to hear but do not hear, for they are a rebellious people." Ezekiel 12:2

"The knowledge of the secrets of the kingdom of God has been given to you, but to others I speak in parables, so that, though seeing, they may not see; though hearing, they may not understand." Luke 8:10

How did you do on this final quiz?

See you tomorrow, God willing!

April

365 love letters

April 1 — Caught or Bought?

When we lived in Pennsylvania, I couldn't wait for summer to roll around. The winters were cold, snowy and dreary and it seemed as if the sun never shone. Summer not only meant sunshine, it meant it was time for our annual pilgrimage to North Carolina for a week or two at the beach. One summer vacation stands out because it was the year my wife's brother, his wife and their friends scheduled their summer vacation to coincide with ours.

Although I am not a fisherman, all the adults and their male children went on a half-day fishing trip out of Swansboro. We had a lot of fun fishing and laughing with each other. At the end of the day we brought home a mess of sea bass for everyone to enjoy for dinner that evening. That's where the story really begins. The three fathers and their three sons told slightly different versions of the day's catch to our collective families. Some said that we had caught the fish while out on the ocean and had them cleaned at the dock, while others said we had caught nothing and had bought the cleaned fish on returning to Swansboro. It was a funny ending to the day and the fish we ate that night was superb. However, the story did not end that day. It has now been about thirty years since that day and the ladies still do not know whether the fish were caught or bought. The men formed a pact that day that has not been violated. So much time has now passed that, even if we told them the truth, they wouldn't believe it.

The Son of God came to this earth nearly 2000 years ago to die for our sins. He was the Promised Messiah that had been prophesied for centuries and Jesus' birth and life fulfilled these prophesies. Let me list just a few.

Micah 5:2 – "But you, Bethlehem Ephrathah, though you are small among the clans of Judah, out of you will come for me one who will be the ruler over Israel, whose origins are from of old from ancient times."

Isaiah 7:14 – "The virgin will be with child and will give birth to a son and will call Him Immanuel."

Hosea 11:1 – "When Israel was a child, I loved him, and out of Egypt I called my son."

Psalm 22:18 – They divide my garments among them and cast lots for my clothing."

It has been 2000 years since Jesus walked this earth and gave us the hope for eternal life. His story is told in every nation around the world and many believe. Unfortunately, many still do not put their hope in the Risen Lord. They still ponder the question, Son of God or great prophet? Caught or Bought?

See you tomorrow, God willing!

April 2   Happy Birthday, Tommy

Today is my brother-in law's birthday. I won't tell you how old he is; I will only tell you that he is one year older than I am; not quite as old as dirt, but getting closer and closer. I can say these things about him because I have actually known him longer than I have known my wife. In grade school, he and I were part of a group of St. Paul kids who played tackle football in the town park where the Piggly Wiggly was later built. I can remember playing one hot fall day when the cheap football we were using actually exploded putting an end to that day's game. We also played baseball in that park and the bigger kids could smash balls across the road and hit the front of Domer Molinary's corner grocery store.

As we got older, he and I played on the high school football team together. His senior year, he played tight end and I was the quarterback. We weren't great, but we did have a winning season. It wasn't until after he graduated from high school that I began to date his sister. Perhaps as long as he was there, he kept me away from her; I never really thought about that before. He is a bright guy.

As I got to know him better and better after his sister and I were married, I got to see another side of him. I saw a man who loved and honored his Father and Mother; I saw a man who loved his wife and cherished his children; and, I saw a man who loved to play golf with me. Every year while he was a member of Lake Bonaventure Country Club, he would invite me back to St. Paul to play in the member quest tournament. It gave my wife and me a good excuse to visit our parents so I gladly accepted the invitation. It was our custom to dress identically on the last day of the tournament and by the third or fourth year, the regular participants in the tournament began to kid us about the way we were dressed. It didn't bother us; we simply told them that we were so old it was the only way we could remember who our partner was.

For well over fifty years, he has been more than a friend to me; he is also more than a brother-in-law; he is my brother in Christ. "Whoever loves his brother lives in the light, and there is nothing in him to make him stumble." (1 John 2:10) Amen!

Happy Birthday, Brother!

See you tomorrow, God willing!

April 3   Stiff-Necked or Hard Headed

The other day I was looking through a pile of pictures and I was amazed at the changes that have taken place in photography. Some pictures in the pile were black and white taken with an old Kodak box camera. It would often take weeks between the time a picture was taken and the time the entire roll was processed. Now, as soon as a picture is taken with a digital camera, you can see the picture and immediately. Then, if you so desire, you can process the picture in your own home.

Just for kicks, I went to a dictionary to see if the definition of photography had changed. Here is what it said, "photography is defined as a picture made using a camera, in which an image is focused onto film and then made visible by chemical treatment." That sounded old to me, so I decided to write a new definition that speaks particularly to Baby Boomers. A photo is a visual Google entry into your mind that unlocks a memory of a person, place, thing, or event.

This is what I saw when I looked through that pile of pictures. My second grade school picture showed me with a Band-aid on my forehead. My third grade school picture showed me with a Band-aid on my forehead. Those two Google entries unlocked my memory. I have had more stitches in my head than Betsy Ross had on the first American flag. In addition to the two accidents shown on the school pictures, I had stitches when my brother accidently whacked me in the side of the head with a baseball bat. I had stitches when a grape vine I was using for a swing broke and toppled me into some rocks. I had stitches when I ran head long into a brick wall while playing "kick-the-can" one night with my cousins. And, to complete the cycle, I had several more stitches when slammed in the head with the ramp to a rental truck (you don't want to hear that full story).

The Bible uses the word "stiff-necked" nineteen times in the NIV to describe the Hebrew nation. For example Nehemiah 9:16 says, ""But they, our forefathers, became arrogant and stiff-necked, and did not obey your commands." It took God years to hammer into my head what He was all about! The Hebrew nation walked in the wilderness for forty years, so did I. Once my heart opened up to receive God's love and forgiveness, my hard head quickly followed. "For it is with your heart that you believe and are justified, and it is with your mouth that you confess and are saved" (Romans 10:10).

If any of you are stiff-necked, take a long look at yourself and see if it is time to open your heart to Jesus.

See you tomorrow, God willing!

April 4 — Just Comb It Over

There was a time when baldness was considered a highly undesirable trait for men. However, much has changed in the last thirty years. It is common to see men with their heads completely shaved. It is not just older men who are balding who shave their heads, but younger men who either like the look or don't want to mess around with combing their hair.

My wife's dad was from the old school. By the time he had reached his seventies, he had lost most of the hair from the top of his head. He didn't shave his head, nor did he get a toupee. He simply let his hair grow long in the back and on the sides and combed it over to cover most of his bald spot. He was a man of great ingenuity and his "comb-over" was one of the best I have ever seen.

Speaking of ingenuity, her dad could fix anything. During his years of owning and running a small bus line, he had learned how to make the most out of everything. When mechanical parts failed, he kept them around knowing he could use some part of that item to fix something else in the future. If he couldn't find the item he needed to fix something, I can remember him fabricating what he needed to get the job done. He had a rare talent and an even better attitude.

There is a Biblical character, Elisha, who reminds me of my wife's dad for two reasons. One, the Bible tells us he was baldheaded. "From there Elisha went up to Bethel. As he was walking along the road, some youths came out of the town and jeered at him. "Go on up, you baldhead!" they said. "Go on up, you baldhead." (2 Kings 2:23) However, it is the second reason that is more important. "When they had crossed, Elijah said to Elisha, 'Tell me, what can I do for you before I am taken from you?' 'Let me inherit a double portion of your spirit,' Elisha replied." (2 Kings 2:9) Her dad received a double portion of the spirit of ingenuity and generosity and he never hesitated to use that spirit for others.

See you tomorrow, God willing!

April 5   The Tornado

The Bible is full of stories about natural disasters. As the Israelites were leaving Egypt at the beginning of the Exodus, God controlled the sea, "Pharaoh's chariots and his army He has hurled into the sea. The best of Pharaoh's officers were drowned in the Red Sea" (Exodus 15:4). Later while they were roaming the desert, God used His power over nature to punish disobedience, "and the earth opened its mouth and swallowed them, with their households and all Korah's men and all their possessions" (Numbers 16:32). And in 1st Kings 19:11, God controlled the wind, "Then a great and powerful wind tore the mountains apart and shattered the rocks before the Lord, but the Lord was not in the wind. After the wind there was an earthquake, but the Lord was not in the earthquake."

All of this is leading up to an experience we had as a family when we lived in Cincinnati. It was dinner time when the phone rang and an excited neighbor told us to go immediately to the basement, there was a tornado in sight. We wasted no time in heeding his warning. From the patio door, you could see an ominous sky, but no tornado was visible. My wife went upstairs to open some windows and while she was there, she looked out of the living room window, which faced the opposite direction as the patio door. There the tornado was in all its power and glory. It changed directions before it got to our house, so it spared us. However, many families were not as lucky as the tornado indiscriminately destroyed houses, trees and anything else in its path. You have to see the destruction first-hand to appreciate the power of a tornado and the images of destruction lie in your brain forever.

When things get destructive in our lives, we have at least three choices. One, we can question God as Job did throughout his ordeal and finally acknowledge His sovereignty. Two, we can call on Jesus to calm the storm as the disciples did when they were crossing a wind-blown lake (Luke 8:24) "The disciples went and woke him, saying, "Master, Master, we're going to drown!" He got up and rebuked the wind and the raging waters; the storm subsided, and all was calm." Or, we can wallow in our self pity and say "why me God?"

We have choices; I know which one I will choose!

See you tomorrow, God willing!

April 6   Test Me on This

After we moved to Virginia in 1955, we lived in a series of houses and apartments until four year later when my dad decided it was time to buy our own place. I can still see the piece of paper that my dad used to go through the calculations to see if we could afford the house the ultimately bought. Over the years, I know that there were some rough financial times and many missed mortgage payments. However, God was faithful and mom lived in that house for nearly 50 years before moving to North Carolina.

Fast forward to 2002 and you will see my wife and me attending a Crown Financial Seminar to learn more about God's way of helping manage one's finances. God has blessed us in many ways and finances have rarely been an issue since our early days of marriage. However, we decided to attend the financial planning program in order to see what God had to say about money.

Here is what the prophet Haggai told his fellow Israelites when they were so focused on their own needs that they failed to take care of the rebuilding of the temple. "You have planted much, but have harvested little. You eat, but never have enough. You drink, but never have your fill. You put on clothes, but are not warm. You earn wages, only to put them in a purse with holes in it." It seems to me that while they had all they needed, they chased more, never satisfied.

In the New Testament, Jesus warned His followers in Matthew 6:24, "No one can serve two masters. Either he will hate the one and love the other, or he will be devoted to the one and despise the other. You cannot serve both God and Money." The verse from Haggai 1:6 and Jesus' words from Matthew are simply restatements of the same thing; Haggai tells us what happens on earth when we don't use our gifts correctly and Jesus tells us what happens in eternity,

Malachi 3:10 provides us with the answer. "Bring the whole tithe into the storehouse, that there may be food in my house. Test me in this," says the LORD Almighty, "and see if I will not throw open the floodgates of heaven and pour out so much blessing that you will not have room enough for it."

I will admit that I did not always live by this principle, but since attending the Crown Financial Seminar nearly ten years ago, I changed my attitude and my giving pattern. If I offered to give you $100 right now, would you take it? How about if I added the requirement that you give me $10 back, would you still take it? That is all that God is asking of us. It is not a requirement; it's just an indicator that we fully understand where all of your blessings come from.

See you tomorrow, God willing!

April 7 — Million Dollar Quartet

My wife and I try to get to New York City once a year to see a Broadway show; do a little sightseeing; and perhaps some shopping. The last two years, I have had the good fortune of combining business and pleasure to make the trip more affordable. Last week was our annual trek and two friends of ours made the trip with us.

The Broadway show we saw this year was "Million Dollar Quartet." It was the story of four well-known musicians, who came together in the recording studio for one special night, early in their respective careers. The play included flashbacks about each of the musicians that let you see how each of them had come to be recording artists for the Sun Recording label headed by Sam Phillips. The focal point of the play was December 4, 1956. Our friend reminded the other three of us that she was born in 1956, a fact that could have been left unsaid, since the rest of us were born well before that date.

The four musicians in the "Million Dollar Quartet" were Elvis Presley, Johnny Cash, Carl Perkins, and Jerry Lee Lewis. Listening to the actors and musicians sing and play the music from the mid-fifties was pleasant; it was a walk down memory lane. At the end of the play as three of the four recording artists were leaving Sun Records for other recording labels, Sam Phillips flashed a photo of the artists around Jerry Lee Lewis's piano. As a brilliant flash of light on the stage captured the fake photo session, a picture appeared on the screen stage showing a black and white photo of the actual recording artists taken on December 4, 1956. It was a very theatrical ending to the story.

The flash of light on the stage made me think of another flash of light and another quartet in the Bible that would have made the one we saw pale by comparison. "After six days Jesus took with him Peter, James and John the brother of James, and led them up a high mountain by themselves. There he was transfigured before them. His face shone like the sun, and his clothes became as white as the light. Just then there appeared before them Moses and Elijah, talking with Jesus." (Matthew 17:1-3) That's a picture I would love to have seen.

God reveals Himself to us everyday in small ways – not always through a blinding flash of light. It may be a baby's cry; it may be the presence of a Bluebird at your feeder; or something as beautiful as the sunrise. He is everywhere; we simply have to open our eyes to see Him – no flashbulb required. Look for Him today.

See you tomorrow, God willing!

April 8 — It's the Law

Even though it was light outdoors, my son and I were walking around with flashlights under a bridge about a quarter of a mile away from our home in Pennsylvania. He had seen some crayfish in the area the day before and he wanted me to come back and see them. It wasn't until we heard the voice of a game warden yelling at us that we knew we had done something wrong. It seems that some people use flashlights to cause fish to freeze, making them easy targets for spearing. While that certainly wasn't our intent, we were in the wrong and with no argument we turned off the flashlights and left the area with only a mild warning. No tickets were issued and we had learned a valuable lesson.

There was yet another time that my son and I went fishing without knowing the rules. This time it was in Cincinnati and I was unaware that I needed a fishing license to help him fish. Thinking back on the situation, it was pretty dumb of me to think I could assist him with fishing without taking the time to purchase a license for me. The end-result of this encounter with the law was the same, a warning but no ticket.

Can you imagine how the Israelites must have felt every day of their lives? They had to live with over 600 obscure laws about everything you can imagine. Don't touch this. Don't eat that. Don't converse with her. Don't help him. Don't work today. Don't wear this and don't wear that. It must have been enough to make you scream. In Ezekiel 20:25, God tells Ezekiel to pass along the following message to his rebellious people, "I also gave them over to statutes that were not good and laws they could not live by." God had another plan.

When He was asked which commandment is the greatest in the law, "Jesus replied: 'Love the Lord your God with all your heart and with all your soul and with all your mind.' .....And the second is like it: 'Love your neighbor as yourself'" (Matthew 22:37, 39). Jesus had simplified the code; love was the answer. However, while He simplified the law, He did not come to do away with it. "I tell you the truth, until heaven and earth disappear, not the smallest letter, not the least stroke of a pen, will by any means disappear from the Law until everything is accomplished" (Matthew 5:18).

The laws that I broke with my son were for the common good and as a civilized nation, we need all kinds of laws to maintain a sense of order. However, after Jesus died for us on the cross, we knew that our hope of glory rested in God's amazing grace, not in obeying the law.

See you tomorrow, God willing!

April 9 — Pilgrimage to the Master's

I once had the good fortune of attending the Master's golf tournament. For a golfer, a trip to the Master's is like a pilgrimage to Mecca for a Muslim or a trip to Jerusalem for a Jew. Since the Master's occurs every year during the first week in April, the azaleas are in full bloom and when you add the impeccable manicuring of Augusta National golf course, you have beauty unrivalled at any golf course in the world.

Last week, when my wife and I were in New York, we went to the Brooklyn Tabernacle Church to hear one of the most esteemed church choirs in the world. We also went to hear Jim Cymbala, founder and lead pastor at the church. Pastor Cymbala spoke about the absolute requirement of each Muslim to make at least one trip to Mecca in his or her lifetime. Likewise, in the Old Testament, Israelites were required to make a pilgrimage to Jerusalem. Using Psalm 84 as his text, Pastor Cymbala gave me new meaning for the word "pilgrimage." *"Blessed are those whose strength is in you, who have set their hearts on pilgrimage. As they pass through the Valley of Baca, they make it a place of springs; the autumn rains also cover it with pools. They go from strength to strength, till each appears before God in Zion."* (Psalm 84:5-7)

For Christians, the pilgrimage is no longer to a physical place. We don't find God in any particular place; we find Him in our hearts. I learned from the sermon that the Valley of Baca is the valley of despair or the valley of tears. All of us have been there at some point in our lives. However, when we are on a pilgrimage to find God, He makes the Valley of Baca a place of springs. Living water comes up to surround us and give us peace and comfort. Then to make it even more beautiful, the autumn rains shower us with blessings. If you can see that in your mind's eye, it is far more beautiful than Augusta National. In the seventh verse of Psalm 84 shown above, the Psalmist states that the pilgrim goes from strength to strength, till each appears before God. Pastor Cymbala said that means, even in our despair, we need not stumble toward the finish line, but rather live our lives from strength to strength.

I doubt that I will ever see The Master's quite the same after thinking about my own earthly pilgrimage. I have been to the Valley of Baca and, sure enough, God raised up springs of living water to get me through the valley. Likewise, He has showered me with blessings that are far too numerous to count. And praise God, I am not stumbling toward the finish line.

Think about your own pilgrimage in terms of Psalm 84.

See you tomorrow, God willing!

April 10 — Old One Hundred

My wife and I were members of the Episcopal Church for ten years in Cincinnati and another twenty-five years in Pennsylvania. There are many positive aspects of the Episcopal Church, especially the liturgy. Because of the repetition, there are certain parts of the Bible that one can recite or sing with amazing ease. The 100th Psalm is one such example. I am typing the words as I sing them.

Oh be joyful in the Lord all ye lands,
Serve the Lord with gladness and come before His presence with a song.
Be ye sure that the Lord He is God,
It is He that hath made us and not we ourselves.
We are His people and the sheep of His pasture.
Oh, go your way into His gates with thanksgiving and into His court with praise.
Be thankful unto Him and speak good of His name.
For the Lord is gracious; His mercy is everlasting; and His truth endureth from generation to generation.

Today is the one hundredth day of 2011 and the one hundredth "Love Letter." On day one I said, "In essence, I am sending you "365 Love Letters" so that you will never doubt or forget how much I love you. Better yet, I will remind you just how much God loves you. No matter what you have done in the past or what you will do in the future, I love you and God loves you even more. God is love and as it says in 1 John 4:7, "loves comes from God."

My desire was to tell you stories of the past and relate the stories to God's wonderful presence in all that we do. Guess who is getting the most blessings? Yes, it is I.

I can't begin to tell you how many times I have received a return email from someone letting me know that the message they received that day had been meant for them.

The letters have required me to open my mind to all possibilities in terms of input for the letters. I can tell you with no fear of contradiction that when I begin to write I am unaware of where the story is leading me or rather where the Holy Spirit is leading me.

I have also started a small group that is comprised of mature men with adult children who have now started a similar ministry with their adult children. Several of them have committed to sending out a story a week. They have also reported a wonderful response from their children.

Thank you to each member of my family for your love and encouragement. Writing these letters is one of the most enjoyable activities of my entire life.

See you tomorrow, God willing!

April 11 — Threads of Comfort

My wife's grandmother lived in a nearby town. The house was something special and way too big for her alone. I guess you could say she had one of the first "bed and breakfast" lodgings in Southwest Virginia. They called them boarding houses in those days, but it was really the same thing.

When she was eight or nine years old, my wife would often spend time at her grandmother's house in the summer time. She would help with laundry, make up beds, wash dishes and generally assist her with the work. When the day's activities were completed, her grandmother would sit down with her and teach her how to knit. The first project she can remember was a bright red scarf that lacked the refinement that should have gone into its preparation. Nevertheless, through loving guidance and patient attention, the ugly ducking of a scarf turned into a beautiful swan. By the time her grandmother had finished training her, my wife could knit and crochet a wide variety of items.

Sadly, the skills taught to her by her grandmother laid dormant for many years, finally emerging after we were married and living in Cincinnati. By the time, we moved to Pennsylvania in 1977, she had graduated to the big time. She could do gloves, hats, sweaters, and shawls. Virtually everyone in the family had some item that she had knit for them. To this day, I still have many beautiful wool sweaters that are a legacy of her work.

In the last few years, God has begun to use the talent that He had been developing in her for decades. With a group of six to eight other women, who love to knit, a small group at our home church was formed to make prayer shawls for individuals who are going through tough times in their lives. Each shawl is hand knit; prayed over as it is made; prayer over again after its completion by the entire group; and then prayed over one last time as it is delivered to the recipient. "Threads of Comfort," as the group is known, has become an integral part of the church's healing ministry. My wife's grandmother would really be proud of her.

If my wife's knitting group had a mission statement it would be this verse from Isaiah 49:13. "Shout for joy, O heavens; rejoice, O earth; burst into song, O mountains! For the Lord comforts his people and will have compassion on his afflicted ones." That is exactly what "Threads of Comfort" does; they bestow comfort on His afflicted ones."

All of us as Christians are called upon to use our talents to have compassion on His afflicted ones. Have you thought about which talents to use? Are you still in the development stage? Or, are you afraid to listen?

See you tomorrow, God willing!

April 12 — Tell No One What You Have Done

There is a certain satisfaction that comes from doing nice things for other people, particularly people you don't even know. Often times when my wife and I were returning from North Carolina to Pennsylvania, we would pay the toll for a car behind us just to see what their reaction would be. Some people would catch up with us and give us a wave of thanks, while others would seemingly ignored the small gesture.

My grandson told us about an assignment that he and his girl friend (now his wife) were given at a senior high meeting at church one evening. Those attending the meeting were told to split up into small groups and come up with a way of showing kindness to strangers with no expectation of either being found out or thanked. My grandson's group decided to go to Wendy's and buy a bunch of hamburgers and fries and take the food to the emergency room at the hospital. While their intent was to give the food to persons in the waiting room, that goal was outside the rules. Instead, they were able to treat a group of doctors who serve long hours taking care of individuals who are in dire straits. What a lesson they learned that night and what a gift to those unsuspecting doctors!

In the New Testament, Jesus gave specific instructions to people He had healed not to tell anyone about what He had done for them. In Matthew 8:1-4, Jesus heals a man with leprosy and in verse 4 He says, "See that you do not tell anyone." Again in Matthew 9:30, Jesus restores the sight of two blind men and He tells them, "See that no one knows about this." In the Gospel of Mark, we see it again when Jesus heals a man who is both deaf and mute and instructs him in Mark 7:36, "Jesus commanded them (the man and the crowd) not to tell anyone." Finally, in Mark 8:26, Jesus restores sight to another blind man and tells him, "Do not go into the village." Although the words and the situation vary, the message is the same, "Don't let anyone know what I have done for you."

I have often wondered why Jesus gave those instructions. Perhaps now I know. He was setting an example for us to follow, "make sure your motivations for helping others are pure." If you want others to know about what you have done, you could be falling into the trap of the Pharisees, "Everything they do is done for men to see: They make their phylacteries wide and the tassels on their garments long." (Matthew 23:5)

What good deed can you do today and not be found out?

See you tomorrow, God willing!

April 13 — Who Is Your Hero?

The human mind is a marvelous creation. I just can't get my hands around how "evolutionists" can actually believe that all of creation just happened during the "big bang." It is amazing that we are able to recall the year certain mundane events happened if we can relate them to some larger event that is clear in our mind.

In 1989, the preacher where my wife and I attended church spoke one Sunday about heroes in the Bible and concluded the sermon with a question; who is your hero? On the way home from church, my wife said one of her heroes was an elderly lady at our church who had cancer and who had also lost most of her vision as a result of another illness. The lady had also cared for her husband's mother for years before her mother-in-law finally passed away. To add to her life woes, her husband passed away shortly after his mother. Despite all of her woes, she was the sweetest, happiest person you would ever want to know. She was worthy of being a hero.

My wife then asked me who my hero was. I told her that I had thought about the question and come to the conclusion that I was my own hero. Unfortunately, I wasn't kidding. I was proud of all that "I" had accomplished and I couldn't think of anyone else that I admired as much as myself.

Late in 1989, I heard my wife talking on the telephone to our daughter who was living in North Carolina. She was telling my wife about this new young man she had met and how smitten she was with him. When I heard my wife exclaim over the phone "marry him," I couldn't wait to hear what exchange had taken place. Somehow, our daughter was recalling a conversation that she and her new boyfriend had had about heroes. He had told her that he was his own hero. My wife figured I was a good catch so if this new young man was anything like me she should grab him.

They were married a couple of years later and many years later I talked with my son-in-law about this "hero" conversation. We both acknowledged that our answer of twenty plus years ago would not be the same today. Today, we would acknowledge Jesus as our hero.

It took us far too many years to get the right answer, because our pride got in the way. We didn't understand that all of "my help comes from the Lord, the Maker of heaven and earth." (Psalm 121:2). We also didn't appreciate where pride might take us. "Pride goes before destruction, a haughty spirit before a fall. (Proverbs 16:18) "The arrogance of man will be brought low and the pride of men humbled; the Lord alone will be exalted in that day." (Isaiah 2:17).

Who is your hero?

See you tomorrow, God willing!

April 14 — The Tower of Babel

In 1985, I was transferred to London to work on a six-month project. The project took me all over Western Europe and, as a family, we saw a lot and collected memories that will stay with us for a lifetime.

Traveling through foreign countries is both exciting and challenging. In Holland, we had been invited to a coworker's house for dinner. After becoming hopelessly lost, we finally arrived for dinner over an hour late. Of course, the most difficult part of the journey is communications. You can't read the road signs if you happen to be driving, and you can't stop and ask directions, because you don't speak the language spoken in the various countries we visited.

On one trip to the Continent, we heard five different languages, not counting English – French, German, Dutch, Spanish, Flemish, and Danish. When we visited Eastern Europe (Bulgaria) two years ago, we added numerous additional languages to our lexicon, none of which we could read or understand.

You only have to look in the first book of the Bible to find out why we have so many languages. Beginning in Genesis 11:1, the story unfolds. "Now the whole world had one language and a common speech..." As people grew more proud, they decided to make monuments for themselves. "Come, let us build ourselves a city, with a tower that reaches to the heavens, so that we may make a name for ourselves and not be scattered over the face of the whole earth." But God was not pleased with their plans. "The Lord said, 'If as one people speaking the same language they have begun to do this, then nothing they plan to do will be impossible for them.' Come, let us go down and confuse their language so they will not understand each other." And, He foiled their plans. "That is why it was called Babel–because there the Lord confused the language of the whole world. From there the Lord scattered them over the face of the whole earth."

Man's desire for self-gratification led to the creation of many languages around the world and an inability to understand each other. Did you know that at Pentecost, God removed that barrier? "All of them were filled with the Holy Spirit and began to speak in other tongues as the Spirit enabled them...When they heard this sound, a crowd came together in bewilderment, because each one heard them speaking in his own language." (Acts 2:4-6) Through the power of the Holy Spirit, we can set aside the barriers that separate all peoples. I have heard others who have been on mission trips say that they feel as if they understand a foreign language when corporate prayers are being said. I have experienced the same sensation.

God only speaks one language; the language of love!

See you tomorrow, God willing!

April 15   Bargain Night

St. Paul, Virginia. Population Approximately 1500. Location. Southwestern Virginia, fifty miles from Kentucky, Tennessee, North Carolina, and West Virginia. Why am I telling you all of this? It's because that is where my wife spent her entire childhood and I spent my teenage years. Although I knew my wife for a long time, it wasn't until the last few months of my senior year in high school that I finally got smart and started dating her.

Although St. Paul was a very small town, it had something that the two nearest towns did not have – a movie theatre. The Lyric Theatre was in the heart of downtown St. Paul and attached to the theater was the Lyric Shoppe, the local hangout for all teenagers. It was a typical soda shop complete with jukebox, pinball machine, a counter with spinning seats, tables, and booths where chess games, deep conversation, and laughter was in vogue. The Lyric Shoppe was run by a lady by the name of Ma Whitenack. Everyone who knew her understood why she had her nickname; she adopted everyone who came in the place as her children and she didn't take any lip from anybody. If you crossed her, you were banned, and that meant ostracized.

For all of you young folks, there were no VCR's and no DVD's, no X-Boxes, and only three channels on the television. Entertainment meant going to the movies as often as you could afford it. Since Monday was "Bargain Night", we went to the movies every Monday night to avail ourselves of the twenty-five cent price of admission. Since I was a man ahead of my time, I often let my wife pay our way on those date nights and, perhaps, I would spring for the popcorn and Coke. The whole date might have cost me a dollar! What a deal!

The only thing better than twenty-five cents is free and the last chapter in the Bible, Revelations 22:17, sums it up the best. "The Spirit and the bride say, "Come!" And let him who hears say, "Come!" Whoever is thirsty, let him come; and whoever wishes, let him take the free gift of the water of life." The free gift, the gift of eternal life, the gift available to all who confess Jesus as their Lord and Savior.

"Come, all you who are thirsty, come to the waters; and you who have no money, come, buy and eat! Come, buy wine and milk without money and without cost. Why spend money on what is not bread, and your labor on what does not satisfy? Listen, listen to me, and eat what is good, and your soul will delight in the richest of fare... Seek the Lord while he may be found; call on him while he is near." (Isaiah 55:1-2, 5) It's free and it's good. Now that is what I call a bargain!

See you tomorrow, God willing!

April 16 — Ribbons of Light

There is a line in one of the songs from the Broadway musical "Les Miserables" that includes the words, "I am agog, I am aghast." As I write this letter, those words fit my mental state. As I was driving to the golf course a few days ago, I was confounded and confused by what I saw through the windshield of my car. It was about 8:20 am and the sun was shining very brightly; I was driving east on Firetower Road and I saw two ribbons of light about an inch or two wide streaming from the left and right side of my windshield wiper with each ribbon connecting all the way to the sun. As I drove and changed direction slightly, the ribbons stayed connected to the exact spot on the wipers and seemed to bow slightly as if they were swaying in the wind. I took out my cell phone to try to take a picture of the phenomenon but I only succeeded in taking a picture of myself off the reflection on the windshield. For a few minutes, I felt as if I were directly connected by streams of light to something unknown.

Since the odd event occurred, I have asked a number of people if they have ever experienced something like this and each one assured me that have never seen the phenomenon or heard about a similar situation. If anyone reading this letter has an explanation, I would appreciate your feedback. In the meantime, I will just pray and wait for God to tell me what it means.

I don't know if this was a supernatural event or not, but as of now, it seems a little strange. It reminded me of a dream that Jacob had one night on his way to Paddan Aram to find himself a bride. "He had a dream in which he saw a stairway resting on the earth, with its top reaching to heaven, and the angels of God were ascending and descending on it." (Genesis 28:12) He saw a stairway, what I saw looked more like a cable connection. Later in Genesis 28:17 it says, "He was afraid and said, 'How awesome is this place! This is none other than the house of God; this is the gate of heaven.'" Right now, I don't know what I saw or why I saw it. Perhaps it was nothing or perhaps it was a sign. Only time will tell.

See you tomorrow, God willing!

April 17 — Bad News Travels Fast

For the last several days, the news in the sporting world has been full of negative stories. First, it was the news about Barry Bonds and his Federal trial for lying to a Grand Jury. He was convicted on one count of obstruction of justice. The next news clip would be about the on-going lockout in the National Football League. The third story, though negative, turned out to be a fun story. It seems that Kevin Na, a professional golfer on the PGA Tour made a sixteen on a par four hole at the Valero Texas Open. Since hole-by-hole records have been kept, it was the second highest score on one hole in PGA tour history, topped only by John Daly's eighteen at Bay Hill. As luck would have it, Kevin Na was wearing a microphone and his handling of the misfortune was incredibly pleasant, even funny.

I am telling you the Kevin Na story because in a few hours I will be playing golf with my son-in-law and grandson. On another day while playing with them, I made an eleven on the seventh hole. I would not normally have played the hole to completion, but my son-in-law was still trying to beat me for an eighteen-hole match so I was compelled to finish and take my medicine. I won't say that he was happy when I made the eleven, but I will tell you it gave him hope. By the time the round was complete, the results were the same as always. He had failed to take advantage of the opportunity.

For his sake, I will tell you that he did eventually beat me in an eighteen-hole match while we were on a golf trip to Myrtle Beach. While the victory in the record book does have an asterisk, it is nevertheless a victory. You may ask "why the asterisk?" The eighteen holes were the last nine holes one day and the first nine holes the next day on two separate courses. He claims it and I accept it.

There have been times when my behavior on a golf course has been less than perfect. Making an eleven on one hole certainly tested my patience. As I watched the video clips of Kevin Na making his sixteen, I was proud of his demeanor. He even laughed with his caddy and said that he had made somewhere between a ten and a fifteen on the hole, but probably closer to fifteen. He was an example to every young golfer in the world on how to behave when adversity strikes. "We put no stumbling block in anyone's path, so that our ministry will not be discredited." (2 Corinthians 6:3) No one could blame him for being a bad role model. I must keep that in mind today.

See you tomorrow, God willing!

April 18   What Are Your Eating Habits?

In the Old Testament, God gave the Israelites many laws to follow concerning the food they were to eat, The Book of Leviticus provides us with many of the details. Here are just a few. "You may eat any animal that has a split hoof completely divided and that chews the cud" (Leviticus 11:3). "And the pig, though it has a split hoof completely divided, does not chew the cud; it is unclean for you" (Leviticus 11:7). "Of all the creatures living in the water of the seas and the streams, you may eat any that have fins and scales" (Leviticus 11:9). "These are the birds you are to detest and not eat because they are detestable: the eagle, the vulture, the black vulture...." (Leviticus 11:13).

"All flying insects that walk on all fours are to be detestable to you (Leviticus 11:20).

"Any food that could be eaten but has water on it from such a clay pot is unclean, and any liquid that could be drunk from it is unclean" (Leviticus 11:34).

I would suspect that by now you are beginning to wonder where I am going with this discussion. Here is the tie-in. I was having dinner the other night and as my wife brought out the dessert, I thought of my dad. When it came to eating, he had his own laws concerning the food he ate and how it was presented to him. Here are a few.

"My morning coffee must be brought to me in a cup and saucer; at any other time of the day it may be served in a mug." "There is a special spoon that must be set for me to use in stirring my coffee, all other spoons we will be declared unclean." "The lunch that you pack for me for work must contain a sandwich, an oatmeal cake, and a thermos of coffee, no substitutions, please." "I will not get up from the supper table until some dessert is served. It may be as simple as a bowl of fruit or something more substantial such as a piece of homemade cake or pie." "At bedtime, I must have a snack just before I rest for the night. I cannot go to bed on an empty stomach."

These were dad's rules for himself only and I don't mean to make fun of him in any way. It was a pattern of life that worked for him. My own personal eating habits are as far from my dad's as the east is from the west, but it doesn't matter. "What goes into a man's mouth does not make him 'unclean,' but what comes out of his mouth, that is what makes him 'unclean' " (Matthew 15:11).

See you tomorrow, God willing!

April 19 — Church Hunting

My wife and I had been living in Cincinnati for nearly four years and we still did not attend church on a regular basis. For the first two years of living there, we had a good excuse; we couldn't find a church that both of us liked. We tried several varieties, but nothing seemed right. Looking back on the situation, I suspect we weren't trying very hard; we had an excuse for not liking each church we graced with our presence.

Finally, we settled on an Episcopal Church by the name of St. James. We still didn't attend on a regular basis, but at least we had our daughter baptized and when our son came along in 1971, we also had him baptized. On the day of our son's baptism, God spoke to us through the pastor. As we walked out of the church that morning, he very politely said, "You know you don't have to come to church just on the days you are having a child baptized." It was not meant to be a mean statement, God was simply telling us to get our butts back in church where we belonged.

To make a long story short, we did start to attend St. James on a regular basis, every week in fact. We made many friends there; some of whom became life-long friends. We still exchange Christmas messages with two couples after thirty-five years of absence.

Paul talked about God's intent in creating the church in Ephesians 3:10, "His intent was that now, through the church, the manifold wisdom of God should be made known to the rulers and authorities in the heavenly realms…" In other words, the church would serve as foundation for spreading God's love and wisdom to the world. At its very outset, the church provided early Christians with more than teaching; it also provided a place for fellowship. Acts 2:46-47 described the early church. "Every day they continued to meet together in the temple courts. They broke bread in their homes and ate together with glad and sincere hearts, praising God and enjoying the favor of all the people. And the Lord added to their number daily those who were being saved."

Since God spoke to my wife and me the day of our son's baptism, we have been enjoying the fellowship of other Christians and I am thankful for all of my brothers and sisters in Christ.

See you tomorrow, God willing!

April 20 — The Parable of the Lost Child

After our son was born, we knew our two-bedroom apartment was not going to be big enough to meet the family's needs. We started looking for houses and before too long, we found one we thought we could afford. There was just one catch; we didn't have enough money for the down payment. Knowing my wife's father's generosity, we approached him for a loan to help with this problem. With no hesitation, he gave us the money we needed and we became homeowners.

Our first house was a small, three bedroom, brick ranch in a large subdivision with a thousand other homes that looked amazingly like ours. It did have a lot of advantages though. It had a large backyard for kids to play. Secondly, because of the large subdivision, there were plenty of other children in the neighborhood. And the elementary school was only blocks away.

One day when our son was about three years old, he was playing in the fenced back yard while my wife was doing a load of laundry. She left him in the yard for just a moment to check on the wash. When she came back, he was gone. She was in a panic as she checked with other neighbors to see if they had seen him or if he had come to their house to play. Still, he was nowhere to be found.

At school, our daughter was in her classroom when an announcement came over the loudspeaker; "There is a little boy in the office by the name of Chris McRoberts. If anyone knows him, please come to the principal's office." Our daughter didn't move; she didn't know a Chris McRoberts. About that time, a friend of our daughter who knew our son suggested to her that it might be her brother. The mystery was solved; he had walked to school with my wife enough to know the way so he had made the trip on his own that afternoon.

For a few minutes, he was lost. In Luke 15, Jesus tells three parables about the reaction of human beings to lost items or people. The first is about a lost sheep; the second about a lost coin; and, the third parable is that of the prodigal's son. It is a long parable, but it ends in the same manner as the first two, "But we had to celebrate and be glad, because this brother of yours was dead and is alive again; he was lost and is found."

I have never thought about what it must feel like to be lost. However, I do know what it feels like to find a lost loved one.

See you tomorrow, God willing!

April 21 — The Truman Wingo Story

This is a story that I have never told before. It has been buried deep in the recesses of my mind for over fifty years. Frankly, I don't exactly know why it is coming out right now, but somehow the Holy Spirit encouraged me to share it with you. Perhaps each of you have a similar experience that will be triggered by reading what is about to follow.

When I was in the second grade, I went to a small two-room country school that housed grades one through seven. Grades one through four were taught in one room and grades five through seven were taught in the other. As you can imagine, there weren't many students in the school so you got to know all of them pretty well. In fact, if there were families, you got to know the entire children well.

There was a boy in the second grade named Truman Wingo. He had several brothers and sisters in the school, but I can't remember any of their names. I thought that my family lived in a very modest farmhouse (we were poor, but I didn't know it), but the Wingo residence was several steps down on the housing scale. One winter morning when I got to school, I got the shock of my young life. During the night, the Wingo house had burned down and all of the family members had perished.

I am sure I shed a few tears. I am also sure that I asked the question "why?" All I actually remember is that the seat where Truman sat everyday at school was now empty. I also recall that other students, including myself, had made fun of Truman because his clothes were tattered and he often came to school a little dirty.

The death of Truman Wingo was my first recollection of death. I didn't know how to handle it, but it clearly made an impression on me because I have carried the story in my heart and mind for over fifty years. "I gave you milk, not solid food, for you were not yet ready for it. Indeed, you are still not ready." This verse from 1 Corinthians 3:2 is important. As we grow more mature physically, mentally and spiritually, we are able to view life's circumstances from different perspectives.

Over the next three days, I will tell you three other stories that chronicle this progression.

See you tomorrow, God willing!

April 22 — Uncle Jack Was a Cool Guy

Uncle Jack was one of the early heroes in my life. In my childhood days, I didn't see him very often, but when I did, he brought me presents. That was a very good start. When we moved from Illinois to Virginia, I saw him regularly and he seemed bigger than life. He was well to do in every respect. He smoked a pipe and I can still smell the wonderful aroma. Somehow or another he was always dressed up; I can never remember him in work clothes and because he was an executive with the local coal company he might not have had any real work clothes.

Uncle Jack was well educated having graduated from Yale University; he was Ivy League through and through. He played the banjo and performed every year in the Minstrel put on by the Lion's Club to raise money for local charities. He also played golf, but not very well. He often invited me to go and caddy for him, which may have been the impetus for me to become a golfer. Overall, Uncle Jack was a cool guy.

I tell you all of this, because Uncle Jack's death was the second time in my memory of a death was that near to me. It was in the early 1970's and we were living in Cincinnati at the time. When he died, we came to St. Paul for the funeral and I was honored by being chosen to be a pallbearer along with seven other men who were all much older than I was. I made it through the funeral very well until it was over and I rejoined the rest of the family. It was then that I began to weep uncontrollably for minutes. As I write these words today, tears come to my eyes. Psalm 55:4 captured my frame of mind that day, "My heart is in anguish within me; the terrors of death assail me."

My faith was not mature enough to understand the reality of death; I was in anguish. Later in my life I would start to appreciate the words of John 5:24, ""I tell you the truth, whoever hears my word and believes Him who sent me has eternal life and will not be condemned; he has crossed over from death to life."

The last chapter has not been written, but chapters three and four have.

See you tomorrow, God willing!

April 23 — The End of the Journey

One of the neatest things I have done in the last five years is participate in a program called "Letters from Dad." It was started by a man in Texas who had lost his father and discovered that he had nothing left of his father's life of any value except an old tackle box. He had great times with his dad, particularly when they went fishing. However, there was no hard evidence–no cards, no letters, no signatures anywhere. He was determined not to repeat the mistakes of his father so he gathered a bunch of his friends and they began to write letters to all of their loved ones to let them know how much they loved them. A gathering of friends to share their love with others turned into a national initiative.

I became a leader/facilitator for "Letters from Dad" and wrote letters to everyone in my immediate family, including my mother. I read a letter entitled "Queen of Hearts" to mother on Thanksgiving Day 2008, had it framed and placed it in her room at the assisted living home where she could see it every day. It helped her recall memories from her past that Alzheimer's disease was stealing.

As Alzheimer's disease progresses, it is not uncommon for an individual to say they want to go home. It is believed that the person is talking about a childhood home since the memory has been erased backwards to an early year of his or her life. Although I knew what she probably meant, I would read to her from John 14:1-2, "Do not let your hearts be troubled. Trust in God; trust also in me. In my Father's house are many rooms; if it were not so, I would have told you. I am going there to prepare a place for you." I would tell Mother she could go home, but not just yet, her room wasn't ready.

On the day she died, we knew that she only had hours to live. My wife, our daughter, and I spent the last hours with her and I reassured her that her room was almost ready. I also told her that the room was in the New Jerusalem and that God would "wipe every tear from her eyes. There will be no more death or mourning or crying or pain, for the old order of things has passed away." (Revelations 21:4). She would have a new body and a new mind.

Death was not the end; it was the beginning. At Mother's funeral, we celebrated her life. Yes, we wept because we would miss her, but we celebrated because we know she is at the feet of Jesus.

Three true stories, one person's reaction to death, and a journey of faith, do you have a similar story? Where are you on this journey? Tomorrow, the last installment.

See you tomorrow, God willing!

April 24   Victory Over Death

Truman Wingo. Uncle Jack. Mother. Three very different people at three very different times in my life. Their stories have now been told. There is one more story to tell.

When I was a little boy, in the Truman Wingo era of my life, my memories of Easter are full of Easter candy, Easter baskets and new sets of clothes. In the 1950's, Easter was all about wearing your finest set of clothes to church on that day. While I didn't get too many new sets of clothes each year, I do remember vividly getting new clothes to wear on Easter Sunday.

By the Uncle Jack era of my life, Easter had changed for me. Now, my memory was of sunrise services on Easter morning. These services were almost always outdoors and often quite cold, depending on the particular date that Easter was being celebrated on any given year. As I got older, I can also remember the Easter breakfasts we had every year at St. Margaret's Episcopal Church in Pennsylvania. I could name the men who helped prepare the breakfast every year. Sadly, some of those men only appeared in church once or twice a year.

By the time Mother died in 2009, my memories of Easter had changed yet again. On Palm Sunday evening last week, my wife and I watched *The Passion of Christ*, the movie directed by Mel Gibson. Watching the punishment that Jesus received on my behalf, brought the message of the cross back into full focus for me. In his daily devotion of April 12th of this year, Charles Stanley had this to say, "When we hear the word resurrection, most of us instantly think about Jesus rising from the dead, but His victory over the grave shows what will happen to us as well. One day every believer who has died is going to experience a bodily resurrection like His, and those who are alive when Christ returns will be changed from mortal to immortal in the twinkling of an eye."

As I approach my sixty-fifth birthday in November, this is what I now know about death.

"Death has been swallowed up in victory. Where, O death, is your victory? Where, O death, is your sting?" (1 Corinthians 15:54b-55) "...in a flash, in the twinkling of an eye, at the last trumpet. For the trumpet will sound, the dead will be raised imperishable, and we will be changed." (1 Corinthians 15:52). That is the Easter story.

See you tomorrow, God willing!

April 25 — Meet the Parents

My daughter and her boy friend had been dating for a few months and were beginning to get serious in their relationship so it was time to "Meet the Parents." You have probably seen the movie that was based on our daughter's experiences, but I'll tell you the story anyway. First, our daughter was to meet her soon-to-be husband's parents. The evening after she met them she called us in Pennsylvania to let us know how the meeting transpired. I will never forget her comment, "They are really nice; they are not like you at all." My wife and I were both on the phone at the time and we couldn't help but laugh. We knew what she meant and as soon as she realized how it came out, she tried to backpedal. She was correct about one thing; she could not have gotten finer in-laws.

The next "Meet the Parents" episode actually turned out to be a "Meet the Grandparents" trip. My daughter took her soon-to-be husband and went to Virginia to attend my wife's father's ninetieth birthday party. Her dad was at the top of his game and, he immediately took a liking to her new man. He showed him his guns, knives, and coins and told him stories only my wife's dad could spin. Since we were in Mexico at the time, we still had not met this new young man.

Finally, our turn came and in the spring of 1990, we finally met him on a special visit they made to Pennsylvania to get our approval. I told him that he could marry our daughter but he would have to abide by our family's long heritage, one that we had gleaned from Genesis 29:18. "Jacob was in love with Rachel and said, 'I'll work for you seven years in return for your younger daughter Rachel.'" He agreed and he worked for me for seven years, then another seven, and then another seven. Twenty-one years he has been working for me. Of course, the only work I actually require of him is that he take good care of my daughter and two grandsons as well as laugh at my lousy jokes.

See you tomorrow, God willing!

April 26 — The Jokes on Him

My first job out of college was in a research and development laboratory in Cincinnati. The transition from college to the workplace is always a challenge and no doubt we are greatly influenced by our new found surroundings. One of the other laboratory technicians was a real comedian. To him everything was a joke; unfortunately, his comedy depended on downgrading people around him to make himself look better. In our labs, there was another young man who was very strong in his faith and made it a point to share his beliefs with all of us in a non-threatening way. That young man was constantly the brunt of the joker's wrath. I was guilty of laughing, and I learned a bad lesson; don't let anyone know you are a Christian or you too will face ridicule.

The joker also liked to misquote scripture to make fun of the Bible. Here are some examples. Matthew 5:15 "Don't hide your candle under a basket …but let it give light for all to see "His version was "don't hide you candle under a bushel lest you catch the basket on fire." Or, Luke 4:4, ""It is written: 'Man does not live on bread alone.'" His version was, "Man does not live by bread alone, he must have peanut butter." I am ashamed to say that I thought he was funny. Today, I deeply regret my insensitivity.

This fear of ridicule shaped my witness or lack thereof for over thirty years. However, once I discovered what it meant to have a personal relationship with Jesus Christ, my attitude changed. I was not afraid to let anyone know that I was a Christian and I tried to live into that lifestyle. Guess what happened? People who I had worked with for years began to approach me with prayer requests. Others confessed that they too were Christians and had felt the same as I had, fear of ridicule. God had removed the chains from my feet and I could dance, not literally; I never could dance.

One of Paul's shortest letters was the book of Philemon. Although it is only one chapter long, it contains the following nugget in the 6th verse. "I pray that you may be active in sharing your faith, so that you will have a full understanding of every good thing we have in Christ." Until we learn to share our faith, we will never have a full understanding of Christ.

See you tomorrow, God willing!

April 27   Things Sure Look Different at Night

Alzheimer's is a brutal disease because you are forced to see your loved one fade away into the depths of their own mind. Because their short-term memory is the first to go, you learn to hear and answer the same questions many times in the course of a day or, in some cases, in a span of only a few minutes. You learn to deal with it by answering the question each time as if it were the first time you ever heard it. It takes a little patience, but it allows you to treat your loved one with the love and respect they are due.

Sometimes it was not questions that Granny Roberts would ask, but rather statements she would make. For example, when we were riding around Greenville she would always say, "it sure is building up a lot around here." Bless her heart, she very likely thought she was in some small town she had grown up in and didn't realize that she really had no history of Greenville. There was another classic statement that Shirley and I repeat often to remind ourselves of the time Mother spent with us. When we would go out at night, Mother would always say, "Things sure do look different at night." If she said it once, she must have said it a thousand times, and we never got tired of hearing it. And, you know, she was right, things do look different in the dark.

It has now been well over a year since Mother went to be with the Lord and I finally figured out why things looked so different to her at night. Mother spent her whole life walking in the light.

"When Jesus spoke again to the people, he said, "I am the light of the world. Whoever follows me will never walk in darkness, but will have the light of life." (John 8:12)

"I have come into the world as a light, so that no one who believes in me should stay in darkness." (John 12:46)

"This is the message we have heard from him and declare to you: God is light; in him there is no darkness at all." (1 John 1:5)

Mother was absolutely right, "Things sure do look different at night." She was a smart lady.

See you tomorrow, God willing!

April 28   Miracle on High Knob

My wife's parents were not exactly dog lovers so it was a huge concession when they allowed her to keep a stray dog that had shown up on their doorstep. They could keep the small black and white dog, but it would not be allowed to come into the house for any extended period of time. Neither my wife nor her brother recalls how the dog got its name or who named him, but the dog's name was Tippy.

In my wife's family, it was traditional to spend Sunday afternoons in the summertime at High Knob where my wife's dad had several lots. The routine was set. Her mom would prepare fried chicken, potato salad, and green beans for the picnic. For drinks, they used a metal Coca Cola ice chest filled with drinks of all varieties. There were orange pops, grape pops, cherry pops, lime pops, and even peach pops. On the way to High Knob, it was also tradition to stop and pick up fresh homemade donuts to eat on the way.

On the way to High Knob, there was another special stop to pick up her grandmother so she could also enjoy the day. Here is where it got sticky. Her grandmother claimed to get car sickness if she did not get to ride in the front seat with her son. My wife's mother was relegated to the back seat and she seethed. If they happened to take the truck, her grandmother sat in the middle next to her son and my wife's mother sat by the window. I think you get the picture.

Back to the dog. On one of those Sunday afternoon, Tippy had jumped off the walkway that led into the house and injured his legs. Because of the way the dog was yelping, they were sure he must be badly injured. As they made their Sunday pilgrimage they prayed for that little dog. To their dismay, by the time Tippy jumped out of the truck at High Knob he was much improved.

"If my people, who are called by my name, will humble themselves and pray and seek my face and turn from their wicked ways, then will I hear from heaven and will forgive their sin and will heal their land." (2 Chronicles 7:14). If God can heal an entire nation because of their prayers, He can certainly heal a little dog when He hears the prayers of two little children. Likewise, we need to make sure that our children learn at an early age that "The prayer of a righteous man is powerful and effective." (James 5:16) Pray for somebody today.

See you tomorrow, God willing!

April 29   Hitchhiker

Back in the ancient time of 1966, I was a student at the University of Virginia in Charlottesville and my wife was attending East Tennessee State University in Johnson City. Since it was about 300 miles from one school to the other, we didn't get to see each other very often. The situation was further complicated by the fact that I did not have a car.

That is the background; here is the story. For those of us in the "Baby Boomer" generation, "The Lettermen" were a well known quartet. They were appearing at East Tennessee State one weekend in the spring and my wife invited me to come to the concert because both of us were big fans of their music. Accepting was the easy part. How was I going to get from Point A to Point B? First, there was no car; second, there was no train; third, a bus trip would take forever; and finally, I didn't know anyone who would loan me their car for the weekend. Have you ever heard of hitchhiking? Believe it or not, it was still relatively common in the mid-sixties. All you needed was a good sign and a little patience. So, I made a sign that told drivers of my ultimate destination and I polished up my thumb. I made it to Johnson City easily on Friday night, well in time for the concert the following night.

As Saturday night rolled around I went with my wife's brother (also a student at ETSU) to the girl's dorm to pick up my wife and her brother's date. I will never forget the conversation we had with the housemother. She came out and asked us if we had blind dates. Her brother (not I) responded very quickly, "No ma'am, I think they can see pretty well." It was all I could do to keep from popping a gut. At last, our dates came out and we went to the concert, which was fabulous. I can still hear the words and music of one of their most famous songs, "When I fall in love, it will be forever. For I'll never fall in love, 'til the moment I can feel that, you feel that way, too. That's when I'll fall in love with you." Those words were already true. Before that weekend, I was already hooked.

God didn't wait to hear us say we had fallen in love with Him. He loved us before we were even born and He proved it on the cross. "But God demonstrates his own love for us in this: While we were still sinners, Christ died for us." (Romans 5:8) If you are waiting to hear that God loves you, let the wait end right now, He does!

See you tomorrow, God willing!

April 30   A Tale of Two Businessmen

For the last couple of weeks, I have been reading the book of the prophet Jeremiah. As I was reading Chapter 17:5-8, I was reminded of two businessmen I know. One of these men had a very lucrative business that was growing steadily and profitably. Although he paid his employees well, he was an intolerant taskmaster who left employees feeling incompetent at times and downright useless at other times. When the economic downturn hit, his business was not immune. To make matters worse, his family life also began to suffer and his health began to deteriorate. He was bitter and miserable; and so was everyone around him.

The second businessman experienced almost the same set of circumstances. After all, it was the same economic environment. And, when stress piles up, it isn't too surprising that family and health matters also go down the tubes. However, there was something entirely different about the second man. While he didn't like what was happening, he was relatively happy. He set about the business of living each day with an attitude of gratefulness. Although the situation was bad, those around him drew strength and peace from his confidence in the future.

Now, here is the catch. The two businessmen were the same person. When he thought life couldn't get any worse, he found Jesus. That was when the happy person showed up. As Paul Harvey used to say, "Now you know the rest of the story."

Now it is time to reveal the verses from Jeremiah that reminded me of this beautiful story.

Jeremiah 17:5-8 -This is what the LORD says: "Cursed is the one who trusts in man, who depends on flesh for his strength and whose heart turns away from the LORD.

He will be like a bush in the wastelands; he will not see prosperity when it comes. He will dwell in the parched places of the desert, in a salt land where no one lives.

But blessed is the man who trusts in the LORD, whose confidence is in him. He will be like a tree planted by the water that sends out its roots by the stream. It does not fear when heat comes; its leaves are always green. It has no worries in a year of drought and never fails to bear fruit."

Quite a contrast isn't it?

See you tomorrow, God willing!

May

365 love letters

May 1   A Tale of Two Businesses – Part 2

Here is a response I received from an early review of yesterday's letter.

Wow. I'm humbled that you would want to share my story with others. I wouldn't change a thing and the verses from Jeremiah really hit home and are personally very inspirational to me.

It's funny because on Friday, we sat down and talked about the upcoming months ahead. My partner basically said we have enough work from a financial perspective to keep us in the black through March 15th. I looked at him and said jokingly, "Well, we should probably just close our doors and end things on a positive note." He looked at me in a way that only he can. It was a look like, "Oh no, not the old partner!" I acknowledged the look by laughing and then said, "No my friend, we don't have anything to worry about because the Lord will guide us if we put our trust in him. He has a plan for us." Then I said, "And until we know what that plan is, it looks like we need to get to work trying to find some new business."

I was still a little worried, but I just said a prayer. I took that nagging feeling home with me that night. I was really quiet when I got home. A friend who is staying with me picked up on it immediately. She said "something is bothering you." I told her about the situation. She then hugged me and while she did, I said another prayer. I asked for guidance and let God know that I was putting my trust in his hands. I felt the peace wash over me like so many times before. As she let go of me, she said "you just said a prayer didn't you?" I said "yes" and she said she felt it.

I prayed about it again and again all weekend. By weekend's end I was no longer worried about it at all because I knew that HE had a plan for us.

When I got to the office on Monday morning an email was sitting in my inbox telling me that an important prospect had chosen us to do a significant amount of work for one of his clients.

"Therefore I tell you, do not worry about your life, what you will eat or drink; or about your body, what you will wear. Is not life more important than food, and the body more important than clothes? Look at the birds of the air; they do not sow or reap or store away in barns, and yet your heavenly Father feeds them. Are you not much more valuable than they? Who of you by worrying can add a single hour to his life? (Matthew 6:25-27) God really cares.

See you tomorrow, God willing!

May 2 — Rainbows and Floods

Four years ago today on my wife's birthday, we were looking over one of the most magnificent bodies of water in the world – Niagara Falls. Before we made the trip to celebrate her birthday, we made sure that we knew where to stay, and what to do.

The first thing we learned is – don't stay on the American side. We quickly learned why it is important to stay on the Canadian side. For starters, the view of the falls is limited from the American side. From the Canadian side you can see all three falls clearly and get the full effect of the beauty of the falling water. You also learn that the amenities on the American side are lacking.

One of the smart decisions we made for the trip was upgrading our hotel accommodations in order to get a room on an upper level. This made it possible to see the falls from our balcony. Every evening after dusk there was a multicolored light show beneath the Horse Shoe Falls that was spectacular.

Although it was early May, there was still ice on the river below the falls, which meant it was too early for the Maid of the Mist boat to carry passengers to the foot of the falls. We had to settle for a close view of the falls from observation decks below the falls.

Looking back on the trip, there are two distinct images that are burned into my memory. Each afternoon, when the sun was shining brightly, there would be many rainbows formed by the mist generated by the falling water. I couldn't help but think of the promise God made to Noah after the flood, "I have set my rainbow in the clouds, and it will be the sign of the covenant between me and the earth. Whenever I bring clouds over the earth and the rainbow appears in the clouds, I will remember my covenant between me and you and all living creatures of every kind. Never again will the waters become a flood to destroy all life." God had made a promise and every time we see a rainbow we can rest in the assurance of that promise. (Genesis 9:13-15)

The other image I see is the incredible power of the volume of water that passes over the falls. Our God is powerful enough to shut off this water at His command. When the Israelites were set to cross the Jordan into the Promised Land, God stopped the water long enough for them to cross without incident. "Now the Jordan is at flood stage all during harvest. Yet as soon as the priests who carried the ark reached the Jordan and their feet touched the water's edge, the water from upstream stopped flowing. It piled up in a heap a great distance away ...." (Joshua 3:15-16)

We serve a Mighty God and I will never cease to be amazed at His Creation.

See you tomorrow, God willing!

May 3   Who Are We, Really?

This message is about my oldest grandson. He has always been a character, but not in the sense that most of us use that word. As a child, he was always some one else. When he was Amos Slade, he dressed in a plaid shirt, a leather vest, boots and cowboy hat. If anyone asked him his name, he answered defiantly, "Amos Slade."

My favorite character was Santa Claus. When he played Santa Claus, he wore a red stocking hat and a red vest and carried around a "Santa Sack" filled with toys. He was always in character and my daughter had a very difficult time getting his outfit off to be washed. One Christmas we had traveled from Pennsylvania to North Carolina to celebrate Jesus' birthday. If my grandson could be Santa Claus, so could I. I proceeded to ask him to sit on Santa's lap and tell me what he wanted for Christmas. I did the whole spiel. I will never forget his response." In a very serious tone he said, "that was very good Bobpo." I had entered his world and spoken to him on his level.

Throughout the Bible, God communicated with His people always getting closer and closer to our world. God's first communications were often indirect. For example in Exodus, God spoke to Moses through a burning bush. "There the angel of the LORD appeared to him in flames of fire from within a bush." (Exodus 3:2)

Later, in the Old Testament, God spoke to His people through the prophets. It was God's way of getting nearer to us by having His words spoken through His spokespersons. Out of the thirty-nine books of the Old Testament, seventeen are God speaking through the prophets.

Finally, God sends His only Son to speak to us in a language we should all be able to understand. No simpler words could ever be spoken. "I am the way and the truth and the life. No one comes to the Father except through me!" (John 14:6)

When Jesus left this earth on Pentecost, He left behind the Holy Spirit to speak through us to the world. The church is now His voice. It is the only plan He has.

See you tomorrow, God willing!

May 4 — Friendly or Forewarned

When the McKay's moved from Reading to Zionsville, we were ready for them even though we had never met. They had attended an Episcopal Church in Reading and another friend of ours had found out they were moving to Powder Valley. The day we saw them moving in, we stopped by the house and introduced ourselves. They were shocked to say the least. Were we really that friendly or had someone warned us that they were coming?

The McKay's turned out to be dear friends that we have now known for well over twenty-five years. My wife worked with her in the nursery school that she was instrumental in starting at St. Margaret's and I worked with her husband at a Fortune 200 company. When they were going to celebrate their fiftieth birthdays, we were invited to help them celebrate in Bermuda.

Enough background, now for the story. While Mrs. McKay was still in college, she worked summers as a waitress in a resort hotel at the Jersey shore where her mom and dad had a summer home. Each morning, a lovely elderly lady came into the hotel dining room and Mrs. McKay learned to anticipate the lady's needs. As you would expect, over time the two became friends. One day Mrs. McKay announced to the lady that she was getting married soon. The lady was thrilled and invited her and her Mother to have lunch with her one day. When they were finishing lunch the lady announced that they were going to an upscale jewelry store to buy her a wedding gift. Reluctantly, she agreed. When they arrived at the store, the lady asked her what her china pattern was and then proceeded to buy her twelve entire place settings of the fine china and six sets of her Sterling silver flatware. Although Mrs. McKay tried to refuse the generosity, the lady would have none of that. It was not until this incident that she learned the lady's last name. It was Bostitch of the Bostitch Stapler Company. Little did she know whom she had befriended.

Here is what Proverbs 31 has to say about Mrs. McKay. "A wife of noble character who can find? She is worth far more than rubies... She opens her arms to the poor and extends her hands to the needy... She is clothed with strength and dignity; she can laugh at the days to come... She speaks with wisdom, and faithful instruction is on her tongue. Charm is deceptive, and beauty is fleeting; but a woman who fears the LORD is to be praised... Give her the reward she has earned, and let her works bring her praise at the city gate." Mrs. Bostitch gave her a reward and at some future time, God will give her an even greater reward.

See you tomorrow, God willing!

May 5 — Pure Joy

A couple of days ago, we decided to go watch our neighbor's young son play in a tee-ball game. Matthew is five years old and his dad coaches the team. When we got to the field where the game was being played, we ran into several other families from our church who also had young boys playing in the game. That made our foray even more enjoyable

An inning consisted of nine players going to bat for each team. There was none of this three out stuff; if they had waited for three outs each half inning, the game would still be going on. Each batter got three swings from a pitching machine and if they failed to make contact from a pitched ball, the ball was placed on a tee and the batter was allowed to swing until the ball was put into play. When the ball was finally hit, everyone in the infield headed for the ball. If they happened to catch it, that was enough. Who knew what to do with it? There was one occasion when a ball hit toward second base was fielded cleanly and the young man catching the ball raced toward first base, just in time for an out. It was the fielding play of the game. As far as I know, no one kept score so there were only winners, no losers. When the game ended, you only had to look on the players' faces to see what pure joy looks like.

As we watched the game, it reminded us of a time about thirty-five years ago when our son played tee-ball. The game played by five-year olds has not changed. In one particular game in which he was playing, he came to bat with the bases loaded. He happened to smash the ball off the tee and it took off through the infield toward the recesses of the outfield. My son flew around the bases never stopping to see where the ball was. He had only one thing on his mind – a home run. As he crossed home plate, his face, like those of the young men we had seen in Greenville, was pure joy. It didn't matter that he had passed all three of his fellow teammates on the bases and was therefore technically out.

"Let the fields be jubilant, and everything in them. Then all the trees of the forest will sing for joy..." (Psalm 96:12). How appropriate! Let the fields be jubilant. Every one on that baseball field and in the stands was jubilant because there was love and compassion. So what if a young man wanted to stand on top of home plate to bat. So what if they didn't know where to throw the ball. It didn't matter. They were playing for all the right reasons.

See you tomorrow, God willing!

May 6 — Footprints

February in Pennsylvania is not a good place to be so we decided to use the bad weather as an excuse to go to North Carolina and purchase a condominium at Point Emerald Villas, a place where we had been renting for years. We called the realtor and told him we were coming to purchase a unit and asked him to be prepared to show us all the units that were currently on the market.

Once we got to Emerald Isle, we found out that our timing was good. The original builder had just released his last ten units for sale and they were priced about twenty percent below other units on the market. As we looked at the individual units, there were pros and cons. Some were on the third floor and others were on the first floor. Some had nicer furniture than others and some were closer to the ocean. Finally, after seeing all there was to offer, we made our decision. With elderly parents and our first grand child on the way, we decided on a first floor condo to make access much easier.

However, once we picked the specific unit, our work wasn't finished. The dining room table in the unit we chose seated only four people and that just wouldn't work. My wife also wanted twin beds in one of the bedrooms to accommodate children. The solution was simple. She just asked the realtor to move furniture from other units to ours. While I was a bit skeptical that he would agree, to my dismay he quickly said, "Yes."

We had our first foot in the South and we had learned an important lesson. "You do not have, because you do not ask God" (James 4:12). About two months later, we brought our first little bundle of joy to the beach. Two more have followed in his "footprints," the name we gave to the condo.

See you tomorrow, God willing!

May 7   Goose or Duck?

Oh, the Raggedy Man! He works fer Pa,
An' he's the goodest man ever you saw!
He comes to our house every day,
An' waters the horses, an' feeds 'em hay;
'An he opens the shed–an' we all ist laugh
When he drives out our little old wobbledy calf,
An' nen–ef our hired girl says he can –
He milks the cow fer 'Lizabuth Ann.
Ain't he a awful good Raggedy Man?
Raggedy! Raggedy! Raggedy Man

This was the first verse of one of my daughter's favorite nursery rhymes from Mother Goose. It was one of many that my wife and I would read to her, a pastime that she truly loved. On a visit from my parents, I learned something else about my daughter's two-year old personality and it involved that same book of nursery rhymes.

My mother also liked to read to her granddaughter and point to the pictures to teach her some of the words. On the very front of the book was a picture of Mother Goose. Mother pointed to the picture and said, "Goose." My daughter answered adamantly, "duck!" Mother said, "No, it's a goose." My daughter answered even more adamantly, "duck!" After this verbal battle went on for several more rounds, Mother finally gave in and allowed Mother Goose to be a duck. By the time the last salvo was fired, we were all in stitches.

Little children are expected to act in the ways of a child. They are funny and precocious and we love to watch them grow up. That same conversation that my daughter had with her granny years ago would not be funny today. "When I was a child, I talked like a child, I thought like a child, I reasoned like a child. When I became a man, I put childish ways behind me." (1 Corinthians 13:11)

Sometimes I have to remind myself of this verse when I am acting like a child.

See you tomorrow, God willing!

May 8 — Mother's Day

The first North American Mother's Day was conceptualized with Julia Ward Howe's Mother's Day Proclamation in 1870. Despite having penned The Battle Hymn of the Republic 12 years earlier, Howe had become so distraught by the death and carnage of the Civil War that she called on mothers to come together and protest what she saw as the futility of their sons killing the sons of other mothers.

At one point Howe even proposed converting July 4th into Mother's Day. Eventually, however, June 2nd was designated for the celebration. In 1873 women's groups in 18 North American cities observed this new Mother's holiday. Howe initially funded many of these celebrations, but most of them died out once she stopped footing the bill. The city of Boston, however, would continue celebrating Howe's holiday for 10 more years.

Despite the decided failure of her holiday, Howe had nevertheless planted the seed that would blossom into what we know as Mother's Day today. A West Virginia women's group led by Anna Reeves Jarvis began to celebrate an adaptation of Howe's holiday. In order to re-unite families and neighbors that had been divided between the Union and Confederate sides of the Civil War, the group held a Mother's Friendship Day.

In 1908 a U.S. Senator from Nebraska, Elmer Burkett, proposed making Mother's Day a national holiday at the request of the Young Men's Christian Association (YMCA). The proposal was defeated, but by 1909 forty-six states were holding Mother's Day services as well as parts of Canada and Mexico. In 1912 West Virginia became the first state to officially recognize Mother's Day, and in 1914 Woodrow Wilson signed it into national observance, declaring the second Sunday in May as Mother's Day.

We made it a habit of visiting our mothers in Virginia virtually every year no matter where we were living. It was a special time that neither of us will ever forget. They loved to have us visit and we loved giving them the attention they so deserved.

All mother's are special because they care for us; they love us when we are unlovable; they feed and clothe us; and they teach us many life lessons. There are many wonderful stories in the Bible about mothers. There is also sage advice in Proverbs. "My son, keep your father's commands and do not forsake your mother's teaching." (Proverbs 6:20)

We love you all no matter where you are!

See you tomorrow, God willing!

May 9   Know-It-All

A month or so ago, I finished reading the Book of Hosea, the first of the Minor Prophets. The last verse in the book really caught my attention. "The ways of the Lord are right; the righteous walk in them, but the rebellious stumble in them" (Hosea 14:9). That verse caused me to pause and think back on my life and recall how obstinate I have been over many things. It seems that I always had to be right. It's sad because in most cases, it didn't matter whether I was right or wrong; it is impossible to be right all the time; and you hurt other people with your "I'm always right" attitude.

My best friend in Cincinnati once asked me, "Why am I always wrong and you are always right?" Here was my response, "You are not always wrong; you are only wrong when you disagree with me!" I thought that response was funny at the time. However, as I have continued to mature and look back on that comment, I see it as the height of arrogance.

My dad's nickname was Little Bull, a name he was given because of his prowess in football. Perhaps the nickname also came from his bull-headed nature. I'd like to use the excuse that my "know-it-all" attitude was inherited from my dad, but I would only be kidding myself. I have no one to blame but me.

Here it is for everyone to see and read. I apologize to everyone I have ever offended for being a "know-it-all." This apology is especially aimed at my wife, but it also goes out to the rest of my family as well as friends, and coworkers. My actions are indefensible and reprehensible. I pray that God will help me improve. I can't promise any of you that I will achieve perfection, but I can promise you that I am sorry for my past behavior and with God's help, I will improve.

While I am at it, if I have offended any of you by any of my actions or lack of response to someone's needs, I am also sorry for that transgression and I ask your forgiveness. I no longer need to be right, just forgiven.

"Godly sorrow brings repentance that leads to salvation and leaves no regret, but worldly sorrow brings death." (2nd Corinthians 7:10). I assure you that my repentance is of God, not the world.

See you tomorrow, God willing!

May 10 — Soaking Wet

My daughter and her husband were headed for Cancun to celebrate their 10th wedding anniversary with good friends who also happened to be celebrating their 10th anniversary. It was our good fortune to be asked to host our two grandsons, who were five and eight, respectively.

Since we lived in Pennsylvania, we planned a day outing to Knoebel's Amusement Park – an outing that will never be forgotten by any of us. Knoebel's is advertised as the largest admission-free amusement park in the country. In other word's, you buy tickets for each ride rather than paying a flat fee. The park has a long distinguished history.

At some time during the turn of the twentieth century, the Knoebel farm began to be visited by "tally-hos." A tally-ho was a Sunday afternoon hayride with a destination. On those tally-hos destined for the Knoebel farm, participants would sit along the creek banks, picnic in the woods, and some of the more daring would even jump from the covered bridge to the swimming hole below. It was a version of the swimming hole that made our day so memorable.

Being somewhat uneducated as to what happens at the "modern" amusement park, neither my wife nor I imagined that a change of clothes for each of us would be necessary. Had we stayed off of the log flume, we would have been okay. On the first trip down the flume, we got a little wet, and on subsequent trips, we got wetter and wetter. However, it wasn't until the boys insisted that we watch the rides come down the flume from a bridge over the water ride that we got drenched. Each time a car came down the flume it produced a wave of water at least ten feet high that totally drenched everyone on the bridge. To no one's surprise, it was the highlight of the day for the boys.

On the way back from the park, which was about fifty miles from Allentown, my wife had our grandsons hang their shorts and their underwear out the window of the car to help it dry. It was a sight none of us will ever forget.

Three of Jesus' disciples, Peter, James and John, saw a sight they would never forget on the mountain where Jesus was transfigured. "As He was praying, the appearance of his face changed, and His clothes became as bright as a flash of lightning... Peter and his companions were very sleepy, but when they became fully awake, they saw His glory. While he was speaking, a cloud appeared and enveloped them... The disciples kept this to themselves, and told no one at that time what they had seen." (Luke 9:29-36)

It was certainly more powerful than wet underwear hanging out a car window.

See you tomorrow, God willing!

May 11 — Orphans – Not on Your Life

The story I am about to tell is not unique. Although I cannot be absolutely sure, I imagine it happens in households all over the world and it has been happening for centuries. Before I tell the story, I also need to provide an apology to my brother and sister if they are in any way offended by this story. I do not tell the story to offend them; I only tell the story to make an important point.

I am the youngest of three children. My sister is six years older than I am, and my brother is three years older. While three and six years isn't very much to those of us who are over sixty, it was a very large difference when we were six, nine, and twelve. Being the youngest of three has its advantages, but it has its disadvantages. When two older siblings decide to team up on you, the results can be nasty. A favorite pastime of my siblings was to tell me I was adopted. It was cruel, but effective. I believed them and I longed to see my birth certificate to see if I could prove them wrong. All of us long to be loved and it really doesn't matter if our parents are "biological" or adopted. I admire people who make the supreme sacrifice of adopting children who have lost their parents. It is the ultimate act of love.

I was recently reading a book by Charles Spurgeon who included a chapter titled "The Believer Not an Orphan." In that chapter, he pointed to a verse of scripture in the Gospel of John that brought new meaning to the whole topic. In the NIV John 14:18 says, "I will not leave you as orphans …" The King James version says, "I will not leave you comfortless…"

Now that all of our parents have all passed away, we would technically be orphans. Fortunately, we know better. God will not leave us orphans; He will not leave us comfortless. Furthermore, "God has said, "Never will I leave you; never will I forsake you." (Hebrews 13:5)

Those are promises I will never forget and I hope you won't either.

See you tomorrow, God willing!

May 12 — Waves of Life

Since 1968, the ocean has been part of my entire family's life. From 1968 until 1977, we made the trek to Myrtle Beach every summer along with my parents and the rest of the family. When we moved to Pennsylvania and my brother lived in Raleigh-Durham, we moved our annual beach trip to Emerald Isle. For my mother and my wife, the prime attraction of the beach was hunting for treasured shells. For the kids, it was playing in the sand. For Dad and me it was body surfing, which he taught me to do.

At Emerald Isle, the waves are generally not good enough for surfboards, although my son has certainly surfed many times, but the waves are strong enough to body surf. As I would learn the hard way, the waves were more than strong enough. I can't recall what year it was, but I can vividly remember the incident. On the day in question, the waves were unusually large and powerful and each ride to the shore was better than the previous ride. That soon ended when a large wave picked me up and drove me head first into the sand. When I shook the sand and water from my face, I knew all was not well. My first response was to check to see if my neck was working properly. Thank God, I was not seriously injured. Next, I began to spit blood out of my mouth that was coming from a split lip. Then, I began to feel blood flowing down my face from a large "strawberry" on my forehead right between my eyes. Some of family members who were up on the beach at the time couldn't help but laugh at my appearance; they also didn't realize how close I had come to being hurt badly.

"Therefore let everyone who is godly pray to you while you may be found; surely when the mighty waters rise, they will not reach him. You are my hiding place; you will protect me from trouble and surround me with songs of deliverance." (Psalm 32:6-7) *When the mighty waters rise*, that sounds like a wave on the ocean to me. *You will protect me*, I was not harmed; yes, I was beat up a little and there is a picture of my injured face on the wall of our condominium for all to see, but God had indeed protected me.

When the waves of live come crashing down on you, just remember Psalm 32:6-7.

See you tomorrow, God willing!

May 13 — Storytelling or Parables?

Storytelling is becoming a lost art. For entertainment, families used to sit around and listen to the more mature members of the family talk about "the good old days." Now because of the hectic pace of our society and the plethora of electronic games available to youngsters, hardly anyone takes the time to listen to a good story. It has been my experience that everyone likes to hear a good story and the responses I have received during the first 132 days of "365 Love Letters" confirm that opinion.

Of course there is Biblical precedent. In the New Testament, Jesus told fifty-five different parables. The dictionary defines a parable as an earthly story with a spiritual truth. Every time Jesus told a parable, it was to define a spiritual truth for His disciples, who often needed the parable to be translated before they understood what Jesus was trying to say. When he was alone, the Twelve and the others around him asked him about the parables. He told them, "The secret of the kingdom of God has been given to you. But to those on the outside everything is said in parables so that, "'they may be ever seeing but never perceiving, and ever hearing but never understanding; otherwise they might turn and be forgiven!'" (Mark 4:10-12)

I have now told 133 stories; some of them have been good and some of them not so good. However, I am going to keep telling them for another 232 days until my commitment has been met. For those of you who have gotten some benefit from reading the stories, praise! For those of you who have not seen any benefit, I am sorry that I have not been able to connect with you.

In a recent Charles Stanley devotion, he ended his story with an encouraging thought for each of us. "Look for an opportunity to share your insight with a friend or a loved one." I echo his advice. Share your treasures. "The kingdom of heaven is like treasure hidden in a field. When a man found it, he hid it again, and then in his joy went and sold all he had and bought that field." (Matthew 13:44)

See you tomorrow, God willing!

May 14 — Speak, Lord

For as far back as I can remember I have been an avid reader. In middle school there was something called *The Weekly Reader* that encouraged young minds to develop the habit of reading books. My first books were almost all stories about sports heroes. It didn't matter; I was hooked.

By the time I was in high school, I had graduated to deeper reading. About this time I began to experience the joy of sharing what I had read with other people. One of my golfing buddies was also an avid reader so we not only played golf together; we also discussed the books we were reading.

There have been periods of my life that I have consumed books. When I worked in downtown Cincinnati, I rode the bus to work each day. It was about a thirty to forty minute ride, which gave me a lot of free time to read. That free time translated into two to three books a week. I loved to read the classics and had ready access to many books since I worked close to the Cincinnati Public Library.

By the time we moved to Pennsylvania, my taste in books had continued to progress so I began reading Christian books. Our church had a small group that met regularly to discuss books we were reading. At one of those meetings, the discussion became focused on how God speaks to people. One of the ladies said, "God has never really spoken to me." I replied in a very positive tone. "Perhaps He has spoken to you, but you just haven't realized it. For example, God speaks to me through other people. I think God knows that I need to pay more attention when other people talk." Frankly, it was a very strange response for me, because I had never before thought about that need of mine.

While my wife and I were both at that meeting, we had come in separate cars so I was riding home alone. Just before I got home, I heard very strongly in my spirit, "I revealed that to you." Cold chill bumps ran through my body and it was all I could do to keep the car on the road.

When God first spoke to young Samuel, he did not recognize God's voice so he came running to Eli. After the third time this happened, Eli sent Samuel back to bed and told him that it was God speaking to him. Eli also gave Samuel this advice, "So Eli told Samuel, "Go and lie down, and if he calls you, say, 'Speak, LORD, for your servant is listening.'" (1 Samuel 3:9) If you don't hear God speaking to you, here are two pieces of advice. One, learn His language. Read the Bible every day and He will speak to you. Two, make sure you listen. "Be still and know that I am God." (Psalm 46:10)

See you tomorrow, God willing!

May 15 — Such a Time as This

Children love to play games. When our children were growing up, we played all sorts of games. Therefore, it was no surprise that when we went to visit my daughter's family when her boys were little, games were part of the fun time. On one visit, the youngest got out one of his favorite games, *Mouse Trap*, and invited me to play. As he got the game out to play, my daughter told us that the game was broken so we would not be able to play. However, in no uncertain terms my grandson told us, "If you still have it, you can still play with it." Somehow or another, we managed to fix the game well enough to play.

I have often wondered why some seemingly innocuous statements stick in one's memory while others quickly fade away. I have come to the conclusion that there are bits of wisdom buried in the statements that we remember. My wife's mother suffered from Alzheimer's disease for several years, and the last couple of years of her life, she was bedridden. As we watched a loved one suffer, we often asked ourselves "why?" Our faith in God did not waver so we had to assume that God still had use for her, regardless of how difficult it was for us to see what that purpose was. While there is no way of ever really knowing what His purpose for her was, we think we know the answer and one day when we get to heaven we will know for sure.

Here is our guess. Her mom's health was continuing to fade so we convinced our son to make the trip to Virginia with us to see his grandmother one last time before she went to be with Jesus. Since he loved her, he agreed. While we were there, we were repairing the white picket fence that was along the walkway leading to the entrance door to her mom's house. As we worked, this pretty young blonde lady, the niece of her mom's caregiver, came to visit. Our son was smitten and invited the young lady on a date that evening. The rest is history. A few months later, they were married. Somewhat later, after living in North Carolina for a few years, they moved back to Virginia and now live in the little town where my wife and I grew up.

If we are still living, God can still use us. That is how I would paraphrase the wisdom in my grandson's statement. In the book of Ester, God says it another way, "And who knows but that you have come to royal position for such a time as this?" (Ester 4:14) Ester was used by God to save the entire Hebrew race from destruction. My wife's mom was used to help our son find his helpmate.

See you tomorrow, God willing!

May 16 — Water, Rice and Dirt

Have you ever attended a church where there was no controversy? If you have, praise God things must really be going well. However, if there is no controversy, it is also possible that Satan has declared a "hands-off" because it is already dead. In *The Screwtape Letters*, C. S. Lewis wrote a series of letters that were from Satan to his workers on earth. The letters were instructions on how to disrupt the work of the church. In one of the letters, he instructed his workers to leave certain churches alone lest they wake them up.

After we were married, the first church we attended on a regular basis was St. James Episcopal Church in Cincinnati. As fate would have it, a terrible rift occurred in that church when the rector refused to baptize the grandchild of a well-to-do family when the parents would not agree to bring the child up in the church. First, the family went to the bishop of the Southern Ohio diocese and requested that the rector be removed. When that action failed, the family threatened to leave the church and take all of their wealthy friends with them. That threat triggered a Saturday afternoon meeting at the church presided over by the bishop. The church was full; on one side of the church were the friends of the "wronged family;" on the other side of the church were the rest of us waiting to see what would happen.

As long as I live, I will never forget the opening statement of the bishop. He said, "There are some people who complain that every time they come to church somebody is throwing something at them. The first time they came, water was thrown on them. The second time they came, rice was thrown on them. And, the last time they came, dirt was thrown on them." After saying that, he announced that the current rector would not be relieved of his position and the rector had his full support.

While the friends and family of the child made good on their threat to leave, the story had a happy ending. There were a couple of lean years that followed their leaving, but to no one's surprise, the church went through a growth spurt and managed to recover very nicely. As always the precedent for such recovery was promised in the Bible. "I will restore to you the years which the swarming locust has eaten, the hopper, the destroyer, and the cutter, my great army, which I sent among you. You shall eat in plenty and be satisfied, and praise the name of the LORD your God, who has dealt wondrously with you. And my people shall never again be put to shame." (Joel 2:25-26)

What a promise! If we remain steadfast in our faith in the face of great loss, we can rest in the knowledge that God will restore us.

See you tomorrow, God willing!

May 17 — Caught or Bought: Revisited

This is a follow up from my April 1st story.

Caught or Bought, Day 91 excerpt
Although I am not a fisherman, all the adults and their male children went on a half-day fishing trip out of Swansboro. At the end of the day we brought home a mess of sea bass for everyone to enjoy for dinner. That's where the story really begins. The three fathers and their three sons told slightly different versions of the day's catch to our collective families. Some said that we had caught the fish while out on the ocean and had them cleaned at the dock, while others said we had caught nothing and had bought the cleaned fish on returning to Swansboro. It was a funny ending to the day and the fish we ate that night was superb. However, the story did not end that day. It has now been about thirty years since that day and the ladies still do not know whether the fish were caught or bought. The men formed a pact that day that has not been violated. So much time has now passed that, even if we told them the truth, they wouldn't believe it.

After my brother-in-law received the letter on April Fool's Day, he innocently told his wife all of the details of that day and emailed me his recollection of those details. Here is the content of the email he sent me. "I cannot remember if it was you or your son or maybe our son that had caught the ugly fish the kid would not clean? I remember being impressed with the little league aged kid that cleaned the fish that day. The cat was out of the bag; the mystery was solved; the intrigue was gone; we were finally found out.

For nearly thirty years, our wives and daughters had not been able to discern the truth from fiction. I wondered why? Finally, I got it. We brought the fish home already cleaned. They had not seen the young man at the dock with his electric knife. They knew we were incapable of filleting the fish so they automatically believed they were bought. I guess you can say they were "doubting Thomases."

As you know Thomas was the last disciple to believe that Jesus had risen from the grave.

"Unless I see the nail marks in his hands and put my finger where the nails were, and put my hand into his side, I will not believe it… Then he said to Thomas, Put your finger here; see my hands… Stop doubting and believe. Thomas said to him, "My Lord and my God! Then Jesus told him, "Because you have seen me, you have believed; blessed are those who have not seen and yet have believed." (John 20:25, 27-29).

It has been nearly two thousand years and there are still those who do not believe, not I.

See you tomorrow, God willing!

May 18 — Parting Instructions

It was Sunday evening, March 17, 1986 when I got a call from my brother that dad had had a heart attack and was in the hospital. According to the doctors, he was okay for the time being so I made the decision not to immediately travel to Southwest Virginia to be at his bedside. It was a bad decision, one that I will regret for the rest of my life. Dad passed away the next day and I missed the opportunity to be with him when he went to be with the Lord.

I had a good relationship with my dad and there were no regrets that needed to be discussed. There were no apologies to be made and I had not missed the opportunity to tell him how much I loved him. By the mid 1980's my family had gotten pretty good about verbally expressing our love for one another. My only regret in not being there when he died was this; I was not there to help usher him into God's kingdom and I was not there to receive any final instructions he might have had for me.

When King David died, he had some pretty pointed instructions for Solomon, "I am about to go the way of all the earth," he said. "So be strong, show yourself a man, and observe what the Lord your God requires: Walk in his ways, and keep His decrees and commands, His laws and requirements, as written in the Law of Moses, so that you may prosper in all you do and wherever you go …(1 Kings 2:2-3) Solomon, the wisest man that God ever created, did prosper in the ways of the world, but he failed miserably in walking in the ways of God.

For too much of my life, I too have prospered in the ways of the world and failed miserably in following the ways of God. Fortunately, God removed the scales from my eyes in time to see the error of my ways. I'd like to think that if I had had those last instructions from my Dad, things would have been different. I know better. All along, God had a plan for me and He revealed himself to me before it was too late. "Seek the Lord while he may be found; call on him while he is near." (Isaiah 55:6). God has a plan for each of us, but it is our responsibility to seek Him. Don't miss the opportunity.

See you tomorrow, God willing!

May 19 — Precious Cargo

Another of our favorite pastimes at the beach is kayaking. On many occasions, my wife and I have rented kayaks at Swansboro and kayaked to Bear Island or, better yet, to "Sharks' Tooth Island." Sharks Tooth Island is a small island just off the inland waterway near Emerald Isle. For some strange reason, this small island is a repository for fossilized shark's teeth. We have been to this little island many times, and have never failed to find plenty of fossilized shark's teeth of all sizes. I'm sure the biologists have some explanation for this phenomenon, but I have never heard it.

One of our most memorable kayaking excursions took place during the late 1990's and involved several friends from Pennsylvania. It also included Mother. There were seven of us in all and we rented six kayaks out of Beaufort, and we took along a guide. We were transported by boat to Shakelford Island, about a mile from Beaufort. From there we toured the perimeter of the island, stopping often to look for shells. Once we finished the tour of the island, it was back across the inlet to Beaufort. Did you catch the reference to seven people and six kayaks? Guess who was riding in the double kayak with me! If you answered my Mother, you are correct. Double kayaks are great if you have two people paddling. If one person is a passenger, the chore for the "paddler" is quite heavy. To be honest, I wasn't the only one who was finding the trip to be a challenge. My wife is used to riding with me in a double and we do quite well as a team. Kayaking by herself is more of a challenge. However, she is a good sport and she made the trip back without incident, just a little tired.

Now that I have told you the details of the story, let me share with you the rest of the story. I want you to picture a lady nearly eighty years old who was brave enough to go on a kayak trip that involved about a mile of open ocean travel. To her, it was like riding to the grocery store, and she loved spending the day with her family, particularly looking for sea treasures. She may not have paddled, but she provided encouragement for me as I carried my precious cargo.

"For physical training is of some value, but godliness has value for all things, holding promise for both the present life and the life to come." (1 Timothy 4:8) By the time our day of kayaking was finished, all of us were physically drained, but we had endured. However, our spirits were greatly enriched by the time we had spent with one another. It was a day none of us will ever forget.

See you tomorrow, God willing!

May 20   Blue Cadillac

My wife's dad was a class act and you could tell it by the car her drove. From the 1950's until he went to be with the Lord in 1990, he always had a new Cadillac and his wife loved to ride in it with him. Like clockwork, he traded in his car every two years so his cars always seemed to have that new car smell. Furthermore, he kept his cars as clean as a whistle and in tip-top shape. Since he drove his truck a large percentage of the time, the cars he traded were impeccable. In fact, if I am not mistaken, a friend of his always followed him to the car dealer when he knew he was getting a new car because the friend knew he was going to get a great used car.

When her father died, my wife inherited his 1988 Blue Cadillac and her brother got the truck. We broke the cycle of trading the Cadillac every year and kept it until we finally let go of it in 2004. It had served us incredibly well and it was a sad day when we made the decision to trade it for a new vehicle because it was more than a car. It was a daily reminder of a lost loved one. All of us loved and cherished her dad and it was a very difficult season for all of us.

In the King James Version of the Bible, God makes a promise to us that we must never forget. Psalm 16:7 says, "I will bless the Lord who gives me counsel; my reins also instruct me in the *night seasons*." In other words, I will remember to give God the credit for the happy times, the times of prosperity. Better yet, I will rest in the comfort of knowing that he is with me in the night seasons, those periods of our life where darkness seems to linger for a long time and there is no apparent source of light. Rest in the assurance that the Light is always there, especially in the night seasons.

See you tomorrow, God willing!

May 21 — Fear of the Lord

In the late 1980's, my wife and I used to take a winter vacation with friends to the Yucatan Peninsula of Mexico to the small village of Akumal located about 50 kilometers south of Cancun. The area is now well developed, but in the 1980's there were no telephones in the rental houses; there was no access to newspapers; and there was certainly no television. To be in Akumal was to be in a little world of your own.

We rented a three-bedroom house right on the Caribbean. Because of its proximity to the equator, the house had no glass windows, simply large open windows for good air circulation. Obviously, there was also no air conditioning, but in February when we were usually there, none was needed. The house was built right on lava rock and we could walk out the front door of the house facing the ocean; slip on our gear; and snorkel in the most marvelous lagoon you could imagine.

The lagoon was somewhat protected from the ocean by a coral reef, so most days the water in the lagoon was crystal clear, which made for great vision. We saw parrotfish, grouper, cardinal fish, trumpet fish, sea turtles, lobster, and even a Barracuda. Unlike most fish, the Barracuda has no fear of people in the water; in fact, the opposite is quite true. When my wife spotted the Barracuda, she pointed to the fish and asked our friend what it was. When he told her it was a Barracuda, she asked him if she should be afraid, he told her there was no need to be afraid if she could swim faster than he could. She decided it was time to move on. The Barracuda swam slowly in one direction and my wife swam faster in the other direction.

Fear is a wonderful motivator. Sometimes fear motivates us to do things we would not normally do, while in other circumstances, fear keeps us from doings things we should not do. Proverbs 9:10 tells us that "The fear of the LORD is the beginning of wisdom, and knowledge of the Holy One is understanding." Fear, in this case, means giving God proper respect in all aspects of our life. Once we begin to give God His proper place in our lives we begin to gain wisdom about how our life is to be lived. With that comes understanding and knowledge of our Lord and Savior.

After awhile the fear of God turns into an unquenchable love.

See you tomorrow, God willing!

May 22   Await the Revelation

The year was 1976, the two hundredth anniversary of our nation, and the year I completed by Master of Business Administration degree in marketing at the University of Cincinnati. Since I had an undergraduate degree in chemistry it took me six years of night school to complete all of the business classes required to get my sheepskin.

I was now educated and ready to take on the world. Unfortunately, my employer of the last ten years didn't appreciate my new found intellect. While I very much enjoyed my job, I had a hard time seeing where that job would lead me. My boss, whom I admired and respected greatly, was only fifty-five years old and not even thinking about retirement. To make matters worse, I was now doing most of the work so his incentive to retire was even less than normal. I can't begin to tell you how many sleepless nights I endured trying to decide what to do and where to go. Had I prayed about the situation, I'm sure the agony would have been lessened. Too bad, my Christian walk at that time was insufficient to help me through the trials.

After going to my boss and explaining my predicament, he promised to help me look for other positions in the company that would allow me to grow and progress. Here came the next roadblock. The company was in the process of being acquired by another company and all positions of interest were put on hold until the acquisition was completed. My patience had reached an end so I made the decision to contact a headhunter and begin the process of finding another job. Within three months I had found a new job in Pennsylvania at a company that was rapidly growing and desirous of the skills I brought to the table. It had taken me only a year to make the transition, but as a thirty-year old whipper-snapper, it seemed like forever.

The prophet Habakkuk endured much more trouble over a much longer time frame. He watched as the nation of Israel shamelessly disobeyed God's law and fell deeper and deeper into the clutches of sin. He cried out to God in his impatience and God answered him with a word that all of us should remember. "For the revelation awaits an appointed time....Though it linger, wait for it; it will certainly come and will not delay." (Habakkuk 2:3). I made a tremendous mistake. I didn't even seek the revelation so it was impossible for me to wait on it. It is so much easier now that I have a personal relationship with Jesus Christ. I now have enough sense to seek His plan for me, and I am getting better at waiting.

How are you doing?

See you tomorrow, God willing!

May 23   Grandfather's Bible

Even though our son's family lives nearly four hundred miles from us, we try to see our granddaughter about every two to three months. It is our normal practice to rent a house in Abingdon with a couple of bedrooms so we can have her spend the night with us. During these briefs encounters we are able to develop a relationship with her that will last her entire life. With our two grandsons, we had similar opportunities to develop lasting memories. Now, since we live close to them and they are both teenagers, I know that they will remember us long after we are gone. Our children were blessed to have great relationships with both sets of grandparents

If you can corner my wife, she will tell you about both her grandmothers and one of her grandfathers. On the other hand, if you ask me about my grandparents, I have no first hand stories to tell. All four of my grandparents died before I was old enough to remember them. Since I was named after my two grandfathers, William Roberts and Joseph Coffman, I do have a link to those two grandparents. Sadly, I don't even know the first names of either grandmother. My only other link to my grandparents is a photo of mother with her father taken around 1939 and a leather-covered King James Version of the Bible that was William Roberts' Bible.

I can't tell you how many Bibles we have in our house, but I can assure you that it is a large number. Yet, the Bible that I received from my grandfather has always been special. As I grew up, I can remember looking through the many drawings that were in that Bible depicting famous Bible scenes. For some reason, those drawings made the Bible come alive and perhaps in some respect they made my departed grandfather come alive as well. By around 1996, the Bible was beginning to show its age and was suffering from deterioration. For my fiftieth birthday, my wife surprised me by having the Bible reconditioned. She had kept my keepsake alive.

There is no better keepsake than the Bible. God gave His children for all ages very explicit instructions and He gave us responsibilities for keeping His Word alive. Deuteronomy 4:9 says, "Teach them to your children and to their children after them." Later in Chapter 6 verses 7-9, He expounded on those instructions, "Impress them on your children. Talk about them when you are at home and when you walk along the road, when you lie down and when you get up. Tie them as symbols on your hands and bind them on your foreheads. Write them on your doorframes of your houses and on your gates."

I am thankful for a Godly heritage and I pray that I will leave behind the same heritage for my children, grandchildren, and children for many generations to come.

See you tomorrow, God willing!

May 24 — Sleep Walker

For most of us, our earliest memories of childhood go back to about the age of three or four. In the story I am about to tell you, I don't really know how old I was but I remember where we were living at the time which pinpoints the event to about the age of three or four.

Perhaps it was a space issue; perhaps we couldn't afford another bed; or perhaps I needed to be corralled at night. Whatever the reason, I still slept in a baby bed. At that age, I could easily crawl out of the bed whenever I wanted to get out, so I am surmising that the reason was options one or two mentioned above.

As I was sleeping one night, I had a nightmare that put me into a panic. I can vaguely remember shaking the door knob of what I thought was my mother and dad's bedroom in an attempt to be soothed. The next thing I remember was the neighbors bringing me back home. I had apparently gotten out of my bed in a sleep walk; gone out the front door; walked two houses down to a neighbor's house, and then I had tried to get into their house. To my good fortune, they knew who I was and returned me home unscathed.

Jesus talked about children a lot in His time on earth and used them as an example of how to follow Him. Too bad that it takes us so long to understand the message. Little children are so dependent on their parents and other grown ups that they yield their will without even knowing it. It isn't until we start to mature physically that we think we can make it on our own. "I will search for the lost and bring back the strays. I will bind up the injured and strengthen the weak, but the sleek and the strong I will destroy. I will shepherd the flock with justice." (Ezekiel 34:16)

I know that God brought me home that dark night and He has been bringing me home ever since. I only stay lost when I fail to seek His direction. Who brings you home?

See you tomorrow, God willing!

May 25   Rental Trucks, Kayaks, and Mailboxes

By May of 2001 all of the pieces were starting to fall into place. I had been promised by the vice-president of the division that I could have an early retirement package if I could legitimately eliminate a position in the company and thus reduce headcount. By moving several people across international boundaries, I was able to eliminate a sales position in Czechoslovakia. Much to my dismay, the plan was approved and I was given until September 1, 2001 to complete all the transfers.

By late June, our house was prepared for sale, hoping to complete the sale prior to the August 31 deadline. God had better plans. Within three days on the market our house sold for the asking price. Very quickly we contacted our daughter and asked her to look around in Greenville for houses to rent. She found one in a good neighborhood with plenty of room for all of our "stuff," but when she told us about the house, she informed us we would have to see the house to understand why she wasn't too enthusiastic. It did have a few flaws, but since we only intended to rent it for about a year, it was okay.

The next hurdle was getting out of our house in Pennsylvania. We had no problems hiring a reputable moving company, but once again there was a small glitch. We had numerous items; including two kayaks that the moving company would not take. Not a problem, I would rent a truck and move the kayaks myself along with a few other items.

Between all the moves, the time crunch was starting to become real. After spending a week in Europe on business, I returned home on a Friday afternoon in time to pick up the rental truck. By late evening, the truck was packed and ready to go. Despite the fact that I had been up for over twenty-fours hours the previous day, I got up very early the next morning for the nine-hour drive to Emerald Isle to drop off the kayaks. By late afternoon, I was ready to make the one and a half hour drive to Greenville. Jet lag and too little sleep were starting to catch up with me, but I made it to my daughter's house with not one single incident during the entire trip. Well, almost. While backing the truck into the driveway, I demolished her mailbox. I had come so far!

As I look back on that summer of my life, it is easy to see God's hand in every step of the way. We had prayed and listened; He had answered. As I ran over the mailbox and heard it crunch, I knew it was a gentle reminder from God. "In his heart a man plans his course, but the LORD determines his steps." (Proverbs 16:9) That last step let me know who was in charge.

See you tomorrow, God willing!

May 26 — Coach of Encouragement

I believe they call people with my son's personality "thrill seekers." The trait is with them from birth and it manifests itself early in life. For example, when we first moved to Pennsylvania from Ohio we knew the winters would be cold and snowy. My wife said that we should learn to enjoy the snow so she took the kids to Doe Mountain, a ski resort about five miles from our house. While I wasn't there, my wife told me he was going down the regular slope within minutes at breakneck speed. He didn't know how to turn and he didn't know how to stop, but he did know how to go fast.

After my daughter got married, our son went with his new brother-in-law to go sky diving. With absolutely no hesitation, he was out of the plane like a flash, ready to experience the thrill of falling through space with only the parachute to catch the fall.

Of all of the "thrill-seeking' activities he tried, I think playing football was the best. Football is not a game for the weak of heart. To play effectively, you must play fearlessly. There can be no concern for injury and no hesitation when it comes time to hit or be hit. He began playing when he was about ten years old and he was fortunate enough to play with a group of young men who shared his enthusiasm.

For several of the years I helped coach this group of young men and despite my coaching, they were champions. Our son was an excellent halfback on offense which is where he got the nickname, Snake.

While not everyone is inclined to play group sports, I do believe it is a great way to learn about the ups and downs of life. Coaches teach young men the skills they will need to cope with winning and losing in life. All of us need encouragement, but I think young men need more than their share. On a football team, different coaches have the skills to coach different positions–there are line coaches; there are receiver coaches; there are quarterback coaches; you get the picture. My title should have been "encourager" coach.

In the Bible, Paul was the great encourager; in his letter to Titus there was as much encouragement as there was instruction. "He must hold firmly to the trustworthy message as it has been taught, so that he can encourage others by sound doctrine and refute those who oppose it." (Titus 1:9) Here Paul was a position coach. "Similarly, encourage the young men to be self-controlled." (Titus 2:6) Play within yourself, not with abandon. "These, then, are the things you should teach. Encourage and rebuke with all authority. Do not let anyone despise you." Every coach of youth sports should become familiar with Paul's letter to Titus.

See you tomorrow, God willing!

May 27 — Green Thumb

For the past few weekends, my wife and I have spent a lot of time in the yard picking weeds, trimming the flowering shrubs, replanting flowers that were brought inside for the winter, and planting new flowers to enhance the overall appearance of our yard. While I am not a gardener, my wife is. She does a remarkable job of choosing the right mix of shapes and colors to paint a beautiful canvas that lasts the entire summer and into the fall.

I suppose she always had some latent skills in gardening and she will tell you that she first became interested when, as a child, she would visit her grandmother. After they finished supper, her grandmother would walk her around her neighbor's yards looking at their gardens. I think now she was just being nosey too make sure they did not have any plants that she didn't have!

However, it wasn't until after we were married that she really got the bug. Whenever we would visit my parents during the spring or early summer, my mother would take my wife around the yard and tell her about each flower that was blooming and why the particular flower was planted in a certain spot. My mother had a "green thumb" and her yard was full of a variety of plants. Not surprisingly, the inside of the house was also quite full as well.

As we moved to different locations – Ohio to Pennsylvania to North Carolina – my wife also learned that certain plants don't fare well in different climates. It is a real treat to live in Eastern North Carolina where you can have flowers and shrubs blooming almost year around. Unfortunately, some of her favorite flowers don't do well in the summer heat. She has tried in vain to grow Bleeding Hearts, but they always withered away. It was one of the first flowers that bloomed in the early months of spring in Pennsylvania.

I am always a little sad as the Bradford pears lose their blooms followed quickly by our many different colored azaleas. One by one, the flowers bloom and then fade away. Only the rose bush holds onto its blooms for an extended period. The Bible compares the Word of God to flowers and grass. "The grass withers and the flowers fall, but the word of our God stands forever." (Isaiah 40:8) "All men are like grass, and all their glory is like the flowers of the field; the grass withers and the flowers fall...(1 Peter 1:24).

I have learned to appreciate the beauty of God's creation, but even more importantly, I have learned about the staying power of God's Word.

See you tomorrow, God willing.

May 28 — Cincinnati Zoo

One of our favorite places to visit when we lived in Cincinnati was the zoo. The Cincinnati Zoo and Botanical Garden holds among its many distinctions an honored place in zoo history as the second zoo in the United States, having opened not long after the Philadelphia Zoo in 1875. Cincinnati Zoo has a vast collection of endangered species and plants, including macaws, Indian rhinos, cheetahs, Brazilian ocelots and Western Lowland gorillas. However, it wasn't any of these animals that caught our attention when we took houseguests there as part of their visits to Cincinnati.

The first animals that come into my memory are the giraffes. Not only were they beautiful animals, they also loved vanilla wafers. Back in the early 70's, it was still okay to feed the animals and I can clearly remember the enormous tongue of a giraffe as they leaned down to accept our offering of food. My daughter loved to sit on my shoulders and hand off a vanilla wafer to one of these majestic creatures.

Perhaps second on my list of favorite animals were the polar bears. They were kept in an outdoor setting with plenty of water in which they could swim. For the bears, it was not possible to hand them food, but the vanilla wafers could be sailed through the air like a Frisbee and often caught in the mouth of an appreciative bear. If you have never seen a live polar bear, you just can't imagine how large they are.

I think our son's favorite attraction was the reptile house. As the name implies, it was full of snakes of every variety – from giant anacondas to small coral snakes, from powerful to deadly. Personally, I was thrilled that they were all safely behind the glass. My wife's favorite animals were the white tigers and the Cincinnati Zoo was one of the only zoos in the United States to house these cats.

I mentioned earlier that the first zoo in the United States was in Philadelphia. Do you know where the world's first zoo was located? If you answered, Noah's ark, you are correct. In the 6th chapter of Genesis, God instructed Noah how to populate the floating zoo. "You are to bring into the ark two of all living creatures, male and female, to keep them alive with you. Two of every kind of bird, of every kind of animal and of every kind of creature that moves along the ground will come to you to be kept alive." (Genesis 6:19-20)

See you tomorrow, God willing!

May 29   Warning Signs

I began running again in 2007 and participated in my first 5K races in a very long time. By the fall of 2008, I began to notice some pain in my right hip that would cause me to take a few days off on a regular basis to let the hip heal. Still, I didn't see any reason to quit, so I kept going and the distances kept getting longer. I was feeling so proud of myself that I committed to run a half marathon. When my training runs began to stretch to seven and eight miles the soreness in my hip began to increase. I was getting more warning signs, but I couldn't stop now. To make a long story short, I ran the Myrtle Beach half marathon in February of 2009. The pain in my right hip was with me from the time the race started until I finished. This time, the recovery did not come. More warning signs.

Finally, I visited an orthopedic surgeon who told me that I had no cartilage left in my right hip I needed hip replacement. He also told me that there was no urgency. I could have the surgery done whenever the inconvenience of a hurting hip made me decide to choose replacement. I thanked the doctor and told him I would wait until the following winter since I didn't want to miss the upcoming golf season.

By early summer, the warning signs were more obvious. I could no longer walk when I played golf. I couldn't swing properly because the pain in my hip would not allow me to make a proper turn. And, I could no longer sleep comfortably because the only position that didn't hurt was flat on my back. Just how many signs did I need?

The Minor Prophet Amos delivered many warning signs to the Israelites in Samaria and they were even more stiff-necked than I was. "I gave you empty stomachs in every city..., yet you have not returned to me." (Amos 4:6) "I also withheld rain from you when the harvest was still three months away ...but you have not returned to me." (Amos 4:7-8). "I sent plagues among you as I did to Egypt. I killed your young men with the sword....yet you have not returned to me." (Amos 4:10). There were many warning signs, but they did not return to the Lord. What was the result?

"Your land will be measured and divided up, and you yourself will die in a pagan country. And Israel will certainly go into exile, away from their native land." (Amos 7:17b)

I was a little slow on reacting to the warning signs that God was giving me, but I finally got it and had my hip fixed and I am doing very well. Is God giving you any warning signs that you are ignoring? I certainly hope not.

See you tomorrow, God willing!

May 30 — Symbol of Love

A picture sits in a prominent place in our upstairs family room that shows my wife's dad sitting on a stump whittling. Back to back with him was our son, also whittling. At the time, our son was about eight years old and his grandfather was about eighty. The picture is striking for a number of reasons. First, it captures the bond that exists between young men and their grandfathers as they sat back-to-back. Second, it captures the desire of young men to mimic the behavior of special men in their lives.

Whittling was a common way that my wife's dad used to help him relax and pass time. He had a lawn chair on the walkway leading up to the door of his house that was his favorite place to whittle. To my knowledge, he did not have a favorite whittling knife. Rather, he had a whole pocketknife collection that he used. And, he was proud of that pocketknife collection. If you came to visit him and you showed any interest in knives, he would treat you to a viewing, complete with everything you ever wanted to know about the various knives.

As he got older, he was very generous with the knives. Our son was given several knives and I am sure the one our son used that day on the stump was one of them. He also gave me several knives that I still have; my favorite is a commemorative "Statue of Liberty" knife that he got in conjunction with the celebration of America's 200th anniversary. My wife's brother, of course, is the holder of the bulk of the knife collection.

In Biblical times, a slightly larger knife was the weapon of choice. Throughout the Old Testament, swords were mentioned in conjunction with the many wars that were fought between the Israelites and pagan nations. The sword became symbolic of punishment and destruction. For example in the book of Nahum, God spoke to His people with a warning, "I am against you," declares the LORD Almighty. "I will burn up your chariots in smoke, and the sword will devour your young lions. I will leave you no prey on the earth. The voices of your messengers will no longer be heard." (Nahum 2:13) Later in the New Testament, the sword took on a different more positive image. When Paul advised fellow Christians to put on the armor of God, he used the sword in his symbolism. "Take the helmet of salvation and the sword of the Spirit, which is the word of God." (Ephesians 6:17)

The picture of our son and his grandfather on the stump with their knives was also a symbol; it was the symbol of a bond of love between a grandfather and his grandson.

See you tomorrow, God willing!

May 31   The Tree

I think that I shall never see
A poem lovely as a tree.
A tree whose hungry mouth is prest
Against the earth's sweet flowing breast;
A tree that looks at God all day,
And lifts her leafy arms to pray;
— Joyce Kilmer

Trees are beautiful. I have never seen a Giant Sequoia but their mammoth size and their life span put them in a very special category. Most of the trees of grandeur that I have seen have been Oak trees. There was a large old Oak tree at Lake Bonaventure Country Club where I learned to play golf. At the end of March, we celebrated our oldest grandson's birthday at his other grand parent's house. As we approached the house, something was missing. When we pulled into the driveway, we saw the remains of an Oak tree that had been on their property for well over one hundred years. As each car arrived for the dinner, we all felt the same sadness; it was as if the entire family had lost a friend.

We talked about the tree over the dinner table where stories were shared about that tree. Our son-in-law recalled climbing the tree when he was a boy. He would climb as high as he could and survey the world as all young men are prone to do.

We also heard stories of work that took place in the shade of its limbs. We were told of slaughtered hogs being hung from the tree for cleaning prior to them being divided into edible parts. We heard of hours spent under the tree placing tobacco on sticks for curing in the barn that was at one time adjacent to the tree. It also served as an automobile maintenance area for many generations of shade-tree mechanics.

Mighty oaks from little acorns grow. The Bible says it a little differently; "Though it is the smallest of all your seeds, yet when it grows, it is the largest of garden plants and becomes a tree, so that the birds of the air come and perch in its branches." (Matthew 13:32). This was no ordinary tree; it was part of the family. Sadly, lightning had struck the tree a couple of years ago causing a large split in the main trunk; decay set in and the tree had to be cut down to insure that the tree would cause no harm to the family it had served for many years. So the story has been told; the family perched in the branches of that tree for decades and now it is gone. Perhaps its physical presence is gone, but not the memories.

See you tomorrow, God willing!

June

365 love letters

June 1 — Summer Love

I think it is generally the spring of the year when young folks fancy turns to love. However, that was not true for our daughter in 1984. It was in the summer of 1984, not the spring. To make matters worse, she had fallen in love with a male that was much younger than she was; to add insult to injury, the newest love of her life happened to reside in Virginia, nearly 500 miles away from our home in Pennsylvania.

Here is how it happened. She had gone to Virginia to spend a week with both sets of grandparents. At my mother's house, the neighbors had a nine-month old Great Dane puppy that was starved for affection. When they bought the puppy, they did not realize how much time and affection a Great Dane needs. Once they saw my daughter interact with "Josh," they knew that the best thing for him was to offer to let her take the dog back to Pennsylvania with her. When she called to ask permission to accept Josh, we were dumbfounded. We told her maybe and planned our trip for the following weekend to see the dog and make a decision.

During this same week, her two grandfathers got the bright idea to buy her a 1971 Volkswagen convertible as an early high school graduation present. By the time we reached St. Paul on the following weekend, there was a shiny red VW convertible and a black and white harlequin Great Dane. We, too, fell in love with Josh and adopted him into our family. She and I rode back to Pennsylvania in the convertible with the top down and Josh riding happily in the back seat. You had to be there to appreciate the goofy looks we got that day on the interstate highway as people saw Josh's head towering out of the car.

When we got back home that evening, the fun had just begun. She took Josh in the house and immediately took him upstairs to show him her bedroom. He went up the stairs with ease, but coming down was quite another problem. Apparently, he had never been down a set of stairs before; he was mortified. Finally, with the aid of some raw hot dogs, she was able to coax him down the stairs. To our delight, he never had fear of stairs again after that first episode.

I searched long and hard for the Biblical moral to the story of Josh and the red convertible and finally I found my answer in the Wisdom of Solomon. "Be happy, young man (lady), while you are young, and let your heart give you joy in the days of your youth. Follow the ways of your heart and whatever your eyes see...." (Ecclesiastes 11:9) Josh and the little red VW convertible are pleasant memories of the past.

See you tomorrow, God willing!

June 2   Musical Memory Lane

Our grandson came over to the house the night before last to have dinner with us and the conversation turned to music. Since he is a musician, he has much more appreciation of music than most of his peers. As he was telling us about his likes and dislikes, he mentioned some recording artists that were from our time frame. We told him that we had some "records" upstairs that were original work of "The Beatles," "The Rolling Stones," "Pink Floyd," and many other groups of the 1960's through the 1980's. He got really excited and asked us if we still had a record player. (We weren't sure he knew what one was!). We told him that we did have one upstairs, so up we went to haul out the record player and our remaining albums.

We spent the next hour listening to songs from many of the artists and we looked through the whole stack of records as we strolled down musical memory lane. We listened to The Lettermen, Gene Pitney, Roy Orbison, The Beatles, The Rolling Stones and Pink Floyd. Not only did we find music, we also found comedy. There were three albums of Steve Martin and another of The Smothers Brothers. Finally, my wife popped the big question – would you like to have the record player and the albums? It was Christmas in May as far as he was concerned. With no hesitation, he accepted the gift and a little while later we were loading up his car. At least one more generation will get to hear some quality music.

Our grandson was really excited about this treasure trove of music that we had stored away. It was clear to my wife that he would get more enjoyment from it than we would, since we had not listened to any of the music in ten years. Although he did not ask for the gift, it was clear that he would like to possess it. "So I say to you: Ask and it will be given to you; seek and you will find; knock and the door will be opened to you. For everyone who asks receives; he who seeks finds; and to him who knocks, the door will be opened. Which of you fathers, if your son asks for a fish, will give him a snake instead? Or if he asks for an egg, will give him a scorpion? If you then, though you are evil, know how to give good gifts to your children, how much more will your Father in heaven give the Holy Spirit to those who ask Him!" (Luke 11:9-13) The Holy Spirit – now that is a gift worth asking for.

See you tomorrow, God willing!

June 3 — Mañana

Procrastination is a word that I do not like. The word has a harsh sound and an even harsher meaning. If I want to put something off until a later time, I much prefer the Spanish word mañana. It sounds so much nicer and it only implies that I will do it tomorrow, not postpone the activity forever.

Back in the late 1990's, God had been encouraging me to begin a discipline of capturing my daily experiences and insights in a journal. It seemed like a really good idea, but I didn't know what to write; I didn't think the writing would be very interesting; I didn't know what kind of notebook to use; I didn't know whether to write in pen or pencil. You get the picture; I was really procrastinating.

When we moved to North Carolina in late summer 2001, an event occurred that pushed me over the line. Every year in the church we attended in Pennsylvania, they hold a "Talent Auction" to reinforce the use of one's time, talent, and treasure. It is a fun event and a good fund raiser. When late October rolled around, I sent a check to a friend of ours who always attends the auction and asked him to bid on anything he felt might be of interest to us and to donate any money left over to the church. The auction took place in early November and I did not hear anything from him until a package arrived at our house around Christmas.

Inside the large box was a basket full of Christian items. It contained a Bible, a coffee mug with scripture on it, pens and pencils, several pamphlets to help study books of the Bible, a few other items, and a journal. On the front of the journal is this verse from Romans 10:15, "How beautiful are the feet of them that preach the gospel of peace, and bring glad tidings of good things!" When I saw the journal and the scripture verse, I could only laugh out loud. When God asks you to do something, He will provide the necessary tools to make you journey possible.

On Thursday, December 20, 2001, I wrote my first words in a journal. "Today marks yet another milepost in my walk with God – the beginning of a journey that will begin to capture all of the awesome things God continues to do in my life." While I do not write very day, I have nine volumes of journals that help remind me of what God means in my life. On occasion I get out one of the volumes and read through the entries. As I read them, I am always amazed at what God has written down for me.

If you don't journal, I encourage you to do so and don't wait until a package comes in the mail to get started.

See you tomorrow, God willing!

June 4 — Golf – More Than a Pastime?

Since I was twelve years old, I have been playing golf. As a teenager, it was the norm for me to play at least thirty-six holes a day during the summer. I literally caught a ride to the golf course before 8 am in the morning and went home when it got dark. When it rained, I was lost. During my college years, the frequency decreased, but not the importance. Playing on the golf team at the University of Virginia became almost as important as going to class.

When I got married and I began to work full time, golf became a weekend sport, but I still managed to find a game. When our daughter arrived, the time pressures began to increase another notch, but I still found time to play. Finally, after our son arrived, it was time to give up the game for a while. The "while" lasted nearly twenty years. Finally, after our daughter got married in 1990 and our son had fled the nest, I told myself it was time to dust off the clubs and start playing again.

After a couple of frustrating years of trying to play at public courses, I was invited by a couple of friends at work to play with them at Berkleigh Country Club. It only took one round to remind me of what it was like to play under good conditions. It didn't take much encouragement on my friends' part to convince me to join. Before long, I had a regular tee time at 7:30 am on Saturday morning with the same friends who invited me there in the first place. All was going well; at least I thought so.

In the fall following my first summer at Berkleigh, I started my first real group Bible study as a part of Bible Study Fellowship. It was a breath of fresh air and by the latter half of the study year, around March, I was invited by the leadership to become a substitute discussion leader. I was pleased until they told me that the leaders met every Saturday morning from 7 am until 9 am to review the following week's lesson. What to do? If I accepted the invitation, I would have to miss my regular golf game from March through May. If I didn't accept, I would be putting golf ahead of God! At that point in my Christian walk, it was a tough decision and deep down I knew that God was teaching me a very valuable lesson.

The Biblical principle is pretty simple. "You shall have no other gods before me." (Exodus 20:3) On more than one occasion, God has tested me to make sure I never put anything in front of Him. It's the first and greatest commandment.

See you tomorrow, God willing!

June 5 — Two Dollar Bills

My dad was a hardworking man so it should come to no surprise to anyone in the family that he did not have time to do very much reading. I think he read the newspaper every day, but not much else. I can never remember him reading the Bible although he certainly went to church every Sunday.

Once Dad retired in his early sixties with chronic knee pain and a mild case of black lung, he had more time to read and the Bible was his book of choice. One year for Christmas, he asked us to get him a book on the history and geography of Biblical times. The book was "The Wycliffe Historical Geography of Bible Lands" and he used the book as a reference document to help give perspective to his Bible study. When Dad died in 1986 at the age of seventy-two, we kept the book as a lasting memory to his life.

As we looked through the book after his death, it was clear that Dad had read the entire five hundred plus pages. On virtually every page there were key words, phrases and sentences that were underlined with a ball point pen. I always find it interesting to see what other people consider important enough to underline in the books they read. I should also mention that as I went through the pages of the book, I found two dollar bills neatly tucked into the book. I wish Dad were around to tell me why those dollar bills were there. If you go upstairs in my office area, you will find Dad's Wycliffe Historical Geography book in my book collection with the original two dollars sticking out the top of the book. As far as I am concerned, those bills will be there forever in lasting memory of my Dad.

I suppose that I should make a copy of this letter and paste it on the inside front cover of the book so future generations will get the full picture. "I will perpetuate your memory through all generations." (Psalm 45:17)

See you tomorrow, God willing!

June 6 — Run the Race

I was only a year away from my fortieth birthday and my finely tuned athletic body was no longer fined tuned or athletic. So, I made a decision that by the time my fortieth birthday rolled around, I was going to be in the best physical shape of my life. Making the decision is the first step; actually doing something is quite different.

Being the hard-headed, obstinate person that I am, I had very little problem keeping the promise to myself. I began to run several times a week. At first, the distances were short, typically one to two miles. However, it wasn't long until the distances began to get longer and the speed at which I ran increased rapidly. A friend of mine convinced me to participate in a local five kilometer race to give me a goal for my times and distances. My first race was a 5K race through downtown Harrisburg. Little did I realize how much fun it would be to participate. Before long, I was participating in 10K races, a 10-mile race on St. Patrick's Day in Kutztown, and later a half-marathon in Allentown.

My fortieth birthday came and went and I was in great shape. My weight had dropped below 180 pounds, my lowest weight since my junior year in high school, and I could eat like a pig and not gain an ounce. By my early forties, I was running 3 – 5 times per week and averaging about 20 miles per week. And, I was running in some pretty cool places. The summer we spent in England, I ran from our flat at Pitt Place to and from Epsom Downs, the famous race track. Wherever I went on business, my shoes and running gear came along.

I set a long-term goal of running a 10K race at a sub-seven minute /mile pace. After a number of failed attempts, I found a perfect race to attempt to accomplish my goal. It was a race run down an old switch-back railroad line just above Jim Thorpe, PA. The first four miles of the race were downhill on somewhat unsure footing. The last two plus miles were a slight uphill grade. The key was to go out fast and hope for the best at the end. I finished the race in 42 minutes and 42 seconds, a pace of 6 minutes and 53 seconds per mile. That was my one and only 10K race under seven minute miles.

Since my body is now falling apart, I no longer run physical races. Now, I run a race that is far more important. "However, I consider my life worth nothing to me, if only I may finish the race and complete the task the Lord Jesus has given me—the task of testifying to the gospel of God's grace." (Acts 20:24) I now run this race seven days a week and I can never lose.

See you tomorrow, God willing!

June 7 — Dead Pigs Don't Lie

It was a beautiful summer day and everyone there had come to celebrate our daughter's upcoming wedding. There was plenty of food for everyone and my friend had made large wooden hearts and strategically placed them around his property as part of the overall décor for the day. Finally, it was time to toast the bride and groom to be. As father of the bride-to-be, the responsibility to make the first toast was mine. However, before I made the toast, I decided to tell the folks gathered around me a terrible thing that had happened to my daughter as she drove back from Emerald Isle during one of her visits there to finish some of the wedding plans.

Here is what happened. The back roads from Emerald Isle are rural, to say the least, and there are many farms along the highway. As she was driving back at dusk one day, a pig ran onto the road and she struck and killed the pig. In North Carolina, the law says you must notify the owner of an animal if you happened to kill the animal with your automobile. She looked in every direction, but no farmhouse was to be seen any where near the scene of the accident, and there was no one in sight who could have witnessed the accident. Thinking she had done all she could, she got back into her slightly damaged car and proceeded on her way back to Greenville. About five miles down the road, she noticed a car with a flashing blue light closing in on her rapidly so she pulled over and the state policeman likewise pulled over. After checking her driver's license and registration, he asked her if she had hit a pig a few miles back. She said, "Yes, I did." He asked her if she was familiar with the law with respect to notification of the animal's owner. Again, she said, "Yes, I am." He proceeded to write her a ticket, got back in his car, and pulled away.

The suspense was hanging over the crowd like fog on a cool North Carolina morning. Finally, one of our lady friends shouted to me, "How did the policeman know that she hit the pig?" With tears of laughter rolling down my face, I answered, "The pig squealed on her!"

We don't have to worry about anyone squealing on us when we commit an illegal act. God already knows. "And even the very hairs of your head are all numbered." (Matthew 10:30) The amazing thing is this; He forgives us and loves us anyway. "Who is a God like you, who pardons sin and forgives the transgression of the remnant of his inheritance? You do not stay angry forever but delight to show mercy." (Micah 7:18). Isn't it great to be a part of His family?

See you tomorrow, God willing!

June 8 — Can You Hear Me Now

A baby boomer is person born in the demographic post World War II baby boom covering the period 1946 through 1964. In 1946, the United States experienced one of the highest birth rates per 1000 population of any time in the country's recorded history. It doesn't take a genius to figure out why so many babies were conceived and born in 1946.

While I was born in 1946, and by definition am a baby boomer, my dad was not in the service so my birth is not related to a return from military service. My dad wore a hearing aid for most of his adult life and his inability to hear made him ineligible for military service. Back in the 1950's, hearing aids were not as inconspicuous as they are today. Dad's hearing aid was about the size of a pack of cigarettes and it had a visible cord that was attached to the portion of the device that went in his ear. He carried the hearing aid in the front pocket of his shirts and you can imagine the nuisance value of the cord always being in the way. Since he worked in the coal mines it was also difficult to keep the earpiece clean. I don't know why, but I was always embarrassed around my friends because of the sight of the cord dangling from his ear.

At some point after we moved from Southern Illinois to Virginia, Dad went to an ear doctor who told him that a simple operation would take care of his problem. All the doctor had to do was remove a bony growth in the ear canal that caused the loss of some of his hearing. Dad had the operation and it was a huge success. No more hearing aid.

In the Gospel of Mark (7:32-37), Jesus was able to restore hearing without the aid of any sophisticated surgery. He simply used the power His Father had given Him.

"There some people brought to Him a man who was deaf and could hardly talk, and they begged him to place His hand on the man. After he took him aside, away from the crowd, Jesus put his fingers into the man's ears. Then he spit and touched the man's tongue. He looked up to heaven and with a deep sigh said to him, 'Ephphatha!' (which means, 'Be opened!'). At this, the man's ears were opened, his tongue was loosened and he began to speak plainly. Jesus commanded them not to tell anyone. But the more He did so, the more they kept talking about it. People were overwhelmed with amazement. 'He has done everything well,' they said. 'He even makes the deaf hear and the mute speak.'" After all Jesus is the Great Physician.

See you tomorrow, God willing!

June 9   Here Comes the Judge

Have you ever had the opportunity to see the U. S. legal system from the inside? I have. I have been a defendant; I have supported other family members while they were in court; and I have been a member of a jury. I want to share my experience concerning my role as a juror in Federal Court.

Despite the fact that I had been a registered voter since the late 1960's, I had never been called for jury duty until the 1990's. It was a responsibility I was eager to fulfill. So, when the call came to appear for a jury pool at the Federal Court House in Philadelphia, I answered. After getting my assigned number and waiting for a day in the "waiting room" my number was called. Much to my surprise, I was selected as a juror for a case involving the manufacture of methamphetamines in the Philadelphia area.

The defendant was smuggling the chemicals needed to manufacture the drugs from Costa Rica across the Texas/Mexico border at Brownsville, Texas. The chemicals were hidden in a spare gasoline tank of trucks used to haul eighteen-wheel trailers carrying legitimate goods across the border. Of course, I don't remember all of the details, but what I do remember was listening to many taped phone calls as a result of Federal wire-tapping of the defendant's calls. When it came time for the jury to deliberate on the innocence or quilt of the parties involved, I was chosen by the other jurors to be the jury foreman. I will never forget when the judge asked me to stand and read the jury's verdict. We fried him.

Did you know that the basis for our court system dates back to the days of Moses when he was in the desert? Moses was overwhelmed by the judicial needs of the two million people he was leading. When his father-in-law, Jethro, saw what was happening he suggested that Moses lessen his load. "Listen now to me and I will give you some advice, and may God be with you. You must be the people's representative before God and bring their disputes to him. Teach them the decrees and laws, and show them the way to live and the duties they are to perform. But select capable men from all the people—men who fear God, trustworthy men who hate dishonest gain—and appoint them as officials over thousands, hundreds, fifties and tens. Have them serve as judges for the people at all times, but have them bring every difficult case to you; the simple cases they can decide themselves…If you do this and God so commands, you will be able to stand the strain, and all these people will go home satisfied." (Exodus 18:19-23)

By the way, if you are ever called to serve on a jury, do it! You will be happy that you did.

See you tomorrow, God willing!

June 10 — The Wedding Feast

My Dad came from a very large family – eleven children. Several of the family still lived in Southern Illinois where they grew up and where we lived for several years when I was a small boy. Howard was the youngest of his brothers and Dad seemed to have a close relationship with him. So, when it came time for Howard to get married, who did Howard and Eleanor chose to be their ring bearer? You guessed it; it was wee little me. I think I was about four or five years old at the time. Truthfully, I only remember one part of the ceremony. Just about the time it came for me to hand over the rings, I had to go to the bathroom.

The Roberts' clan was good about having family reunions every five years. When we lived in Cincinnati, we went back to Southern Illinois to attend one of those reunions with Mother and Dad. While we were there, we learned that Howard's daughter was getting married in the not to distant future, and they invited our daughter to be the flower girl. She was about the same age that I had been when I was the ring bearer for Howard and Eleanor. I knew she would not let me down and she didn't. She was the perfect picture of what a flower girl should be! It may have taken two generations, but my family was finally redeemed.

Had we not gone to the family reunion we would have missed the opportunity to wipe the slate clean from my trespass of twenty-five years earlier. There was a wedding feast in the Bible that some maidens missed because they were not ready. The story is told in Matthew 25. "At that time the kingdom of heaven will be like ten virgins who took their lamps and went out to meet the bridegroom. Five of them were foolish and five were wise. The foolish ones took their lamps but did not take any oil with them. The wise, however, took oil in jars along with their lamps... "At midnight the cry rang out: 'Here's the bridegroom! Come out to meet him! "Then all the virgins woke up and trimmed their lamps. The foolish ones said to the wise, 'Give us some of your oil...'"No,' they replied, 'there may not be enough for both us and you. Instead, go... buy some for yourselves. "But while they were on their way..., the bridegroom arrived. The virgins who were ready went in with him to the wedding banquet. And the door was shut." (Matthew 25:1-10) The door was shut and the opportunity was lost.

During my life, I have made many mistakes and left many opportunities on the table. However, one mistake I have not made. My oil jar is full and when the bridegroom comes I will be ready. How about you?

See you tomorrow, God willing!

June 11   Mrs. Malaprop

One of my favorite electives during my undergraduate work in college was a speech class. Given my personality, I knew it would not be overly difficult if I would simply do the required work. The first class assignment was a two-minute speech on a word in the English language. Before giving the speech to the class, we were to provide the professor with the word we were using and a brief outline of the speech. When the speech ended, someone in the class was then asked to critique the overall delivery and content.

It was a snap. I chose just the right word for the speech and then carefully crafted the content. As I handed the written outline to the professor, I watched his eyes to see if there was any reaction. There was no reaction; he was playing coy. Okay, now it was time for me to stand before the class and deliver the speech.

I began; "traditional grammar classifies words based on eight parts of speech. These parts are nouns, pronouns, verbs, adjectives, adverbs, conjectures, propositions, and rejections. The word I am featuring in my speech is a noun which was derived from a play that ran on Broad Street in New York for many years." By now the professor who was sitting in the back of the class was in stitches. It was all he could do to keep from laughing out loud. The reaction from the class members was quite another story, because they did not know what was going on. Some felt sorry for me while others had a look of disdain – if they had talked they would have said "get this hillbilly out of here."

After a little more mangling of the English language, I revealed the word – malaprop. It is a word derived from a 1775 play by Richard Sheridan, "The Rivals," in which one of the main characters, a Mrs. Malaprop, frequently misspoke with great comic effect. The cat was out of the bag and I had secured an "A" for the entire class even though we had had only one session.

In the four Gospels, the phrase "they did not understand" appears nine times. For example, Luke 9:45 says, "But they did not understand what this meant. It was hidden from them, so that they did not grasp it, and they were afraid to ask him about it." It wasn't time for God to reveal the hidden message. Again in Luke 18:34 we see the same content, "The disciples did not understand any of this. Its meaning was hidden from them, and they did not know what he was talking about."

You can miss out on a lot of life if the Word hasn't been revealed to you.

See you tomorrow, God willing!

June 12 — Gag Gifts

Gag gifts are always showing up around us. When my wife turned thirty in Cincinnati, a group of our friends invited us over for a casual dinner. To no one's surprise there were gifts. The first gift was a large bouquet of flowers wrapped beautifully in florist paper. As she unwrapped the florist paper, she was stunned. Her friends had gone to the florist and purchased all of their dead flowers; it was a sad sight, but very funny.

I am an avid eater of ice cream and I do not like a small bowl. If you are going to eat ice cream, then you need to eat enough to get satisfied, don't just whet your appetite. Knowing my desires, one of our friends in Pennsylvania gave me a one-cup ice cream maker as a Christmas gift. It was never used for making ice cream because of its small size, but it became the annual "who got the ice cream maker" Christmas gift. The year after I received the gift, I re-gifted it to a family member of the couple who gave it to me who then re-gifted it to my daughter the next year. Even though it has been twenty years since I received the original gift, it would not surprise me to find it under the Christmas tree some year when I least expect it.

There was one gag gift that backfired. Rush Limbaugh had a line of men's ties that were a bit gaudy. Knowing that I was not a big fan of Rush, I received one of these ties as a Christmas present. However, the tie turned out to be one of my all-time favorites because it was a black tie with beautiful stained glass windows as the focal point. And, they were stained glass windows that you might see in an elegant old church. What my friend meant for a joke, turned out to be a wonderful gift.

The story of Jacob's son, Joseph, in Genesis ends with a similar twist. If you recall, Joseph's brothers had sold him into slavery when he was a teenager, because of their jealousy towards him. Over a decade later, these same brothers would unknowingly stand before Joseph seeking food to save their family from starvation. It took a while before Joseph revealed himself to them, but when he did, all the brothers feared retaliation. Joseph did the unexpected; he forgave them and gave them this bit of wisdom, "Don't be afraid. Am I in the place of God? You intended to harm me, but God intended it for good to accomplish what is now being done, the saving of many lives.'" (Genesis 50:19-20)

The next time something bad happens to you, just consider this–Satan may desire to harm you, but God can turn it into a blessing. My stained glass window tie is an excellent example.

See you tomorrow, God willing!

June 13 — A Little Change

"There is a little change on my dresser. Didn't I see some loose change by the couch? I remember finding it under the cushions. Do you have any money in your purse? What about the washer? Sometimes I leave some change in my pockets when I put my pants in the laundry basket."

Believe it or not, that was a conversation my wife and I had the first week we lived in Cincinnati. I had not gotten my first paycheck and the cupboard was bare. We scrounged up every penny we could find, went to the grocery store, and had enough money to purchase a loaf of bread, a small jar of peanut butter, and a half dozen eggs. To make matters worse, the needle on the gas tank of the car was already in the red. Would I be able to make it to work the next day to pick up that paycheck?

I did make it to work the next day and got that paycheck and things slowly got better. We moved out of the furnished apartment that was our first residence and, with a little support from our families, we purchased some inexpensive furniture and moved into a two-room apartment where we lived for a couple of years.

The first few years of marriage are filled with change and I learned to adjust to a multitude of circumstances. As the years have gone by, I learned some valuable lessons.

"I know what it is to be in need, and I know what it is to have plenty. I have learned the secret of being content in any and every situation, whether well fed or hungry, whether living in plenty or in want. *I can do everything through him who gives me stre*ngth." (Philippians 4:12-13) Those words were written nearly two thousand years ago, but they are as true today as when they were first written, particularly the words I have placed in italics.

See you tomorrow, God willing!

June 14 — A Hundred Dollar Bill

The Boys and Girls Club of Pitt County holds an annual dinner auction to raise operating funds for the five locations that they operate. It is always a well run affair with many exceptional values to be auctioned off to the highest bidder. Most of the items are displayed at the site of the dinner and bidding is mostly of the silent auction mode. For several years, we bought a table at the auction and took along friends to enjoy the evening with us and, perhaps, spend some money for a good cause.

There were nearly always two items at the auction that interested me. One was a trip by private plane to Ford's Colony Country Club in Williamsburg, VA and the other was a weekend at a very nice home at the Country Club of North Carolina in Pinehurst. On several occasions, I was the successful bidder on one or both of these items. And, nearly always there were people at the table with me who were more than willing to split the cost of the item four ways.

On the year in question, I was fortunate enough to have my son-in-law and two other friends at the auction. We were the high bidder on the Williamsburg trip and we made the appropriate plans to enjoy our win. All went well on the day of the trip. Our host and pilot was on time and the weather was beautiful. We arrived at the course and began the round with eager anticipation. We were playing well despite the heat, but we were thrilled to see the drink cart approach us about the fourth hole. As we were paying for our drinks, my son-in-law discovered that he only had a $100 bill in his wallet. Needless to say I bought his drink. I am probably exaggerating, but the drink cart must have come by at least ten times during the round. I can still hear him saying, "All I have is a $100 bill."

By the time the round was finished we had hounded him to death about his $100 bill. He couldn't wait to buy me lunch just to shut me up. It was the perfect ending to a perfect day.

I wonder if he knew he was following Biblical principles when he bought my lunch. "Let no debt remain outstanding, except the continuing debt to love one another, for he who loves his fellowman has fulfilled the law." (Romans 13:8)

See you tomorrow, God willing!

June 15 — Double Your Blessing

"Bobby Lee is going through a mid-life crisis when he turns 40; he's dreaming of faster, more exciting times. But when his father dies, he is suddenly the family patriarch and shoulder to lean on. After an affair and a new sports car he finally feels free, but is freedom what he really wants?"

That is the description of a motion picture released in 1980. I first saw the movie in 1986 the year I turned forty and the year my dad died. So, I could relate to some of the feelings that Bobby Lee was having. Fortunately, I was not going through a mid-life crisis nor did I have an affair. By the spring of the following year, my wife was also turning forty so we decided to buy a new sports car, a 1986 Alfa Romeo. During the fourteen years we owned the car in Pennsylvania, it never saw the road in the winter and it was always housed in the garage.

Once we moved to North Carolina, the Alfa became a year round car. After we got down to three cars following Mother's death in 2009, I drove the Alfa as my main vehicle. As luck would have it, the computer gave out in 2010 and I took it to a foreign auto specialist to have it repaired. It has been at that garage for well over a year. Repeated attempts on my part to find out the status of the car have been fruitless. There was always a good excuse. "The computer had to be sent to California for repair." "There are major problems with the car's wiring." "It's too hot to work today." You get the point.

I was finally able to catch the owner of the auto repair company at the site. He acknowledged that he had been going through serious personal problems that involved his health, his marriage, and his business. I talked with him for about fifteen minutes and then prayed with him about his situation. With tears in his eyes, he thanked me for my patience and my concern. I promised to follow up with him about his personal needs and the car.

There was a time in my life when I was too insecure in my faith to pray with a person at the very point of their need. It was so much easier for me to say, "I'll pray for you, and postpone the actual prayer for a later time, if I remembered. I still miss opportunities, but I try to make it a habit of praying with the person, right on the spot. "Share with God's people who are in need. Practice hospitality." (Romans 12:13) I'd like to add the phrase right then and there. If you are insecure like I was, allow the Holy Spirit to remove your doubt and enjoy the double blessing of praying with your friend or acquaintance.

See you tomorrow, God willing!

June 16   The Riddler

When my grandsons were younger, I liked to tell them riddles that were really brain-teasers. Here are some examples. If a plane crashes in the middle of the Ohio River that separates Ohio and Kentucky, which state is responsible for burying the survivors? The answer – no one buries the survivors. Here is another. If it takes a man an hour to dig a hole, how long will it take two men to dig a half a hole? The answer – you can't dig a half a hole. Once the shovel removes any dirt, you have a hole. One last example. How do you pronounce the name MacDonald? How about MacNamara? How about MacIntosh? How about MacReynolds? One last chance – how about MacHinery? If you pronounced the last one machinery, you win the prize.

We had a lot of good laughs with these riddles and I tried to come up with fresh ones whenever we visited them from Pennsylvania or when they came to see us. It has been a long time since I have been able to stump them.

The Bible is full of mysteries and Jesus used parables, which are somewhat like riddles to teach His disciples important life lessons. However, there is at least one specific riddle in the Bible and you can find it in the Book of Judges. It involves Samson and his interaction with some Gentiles. "Let me tell you a riddle," Samson said to them. "If you can give me the answer within the seven days of the feast, I will give you thirty linen garments and thirty sets of clothes...."Out of the eater, something to eat; out of the strong, something sweet." (Judges 14:12-14) Before meeting these men, Samson had torn a lion apart with his bare hands. Several days later as he passed by the dead lion, a swarm of bees had made honey in the carcass of the lion, thus the background for the riddle. Samson's wife begged him to tell her the answer to the riddle. When he finally relented, she passed on the answer to the Gentiles. After they gave him the correct answer, Samson went berserk and " the Spirit of the Lord came upon him in power. He went down to Ashkelon, struck down thirty of their men, stripped them of their belongings and gave their clothes to those who had explained the riddle." (Judges 14:19)

Here is one last riddle. "On one occasion an expert in the law stood up to test Jesus. 'Teacher,' he asked, 'what must I do to inherit eternal life?' 'What is written in the Law?' he replied. 'How do you read it?' He answered: 'Love the Lord your God with all your heart and with all your soul and with all your strength and with all your mind; and, 'Love your neighbor as yourself.'" (Luke 10:25-27) If you have to remember just one riddle, that is the best one.

See you tomorrow, God willing!

June 17   Do It for the Lord

Business travel is rarely enjoyable and is sometimes downright unbearable. This particular day of travel had the potential to be in the unbearable category. I was leaving Allentown early in the morning on the way to Minneapolis with a stopover in Pittsburgh. Later, the same day, I would reverse the trip arriving home around midnight. I don't know how many times I had told myself not to make one-day trips like that one, but it seemed like the most cost-effective way to get my business done and be able to sleep in my own bed.

Around seven a.m. in the morning, I was on the plane headed for Pittsburgh. It was a beautiful morning and the flight was proceeding in a routine fashion. I had already gotten my Bible out of my briefcase and was deep into my morning devotions. When the flight attendant walked by my seat she said, "Colossians 3:17." As she walked on down the aisle, I quickly flipped to Colossians and read that verse, "And whatever you do, whether in word or deed, do it all in the name of the Lord Jesus, giving thanks to God the Father through Him." It was a nice way to start the day.

I don't remember much about the business I conducted that day, but I do remember sitting at the gate in the Pittsburgh airport about ten p.m. that same evening waiting for the plane to take me back to Allentown. As I sat there wearily, I noticed the same flight attendant who had spoken to me on the plane that morning walking towards me. As she approached, I said to her, "Colossians 3:18." She replied, "No, Colossians 3:17." I replied, "No, Colossians 3:18." With that, she sat down in the seat beside me; got out her Bible; and proceeded to look up Colossians 3:18. "Wives submit to your husbands, as is fitting in the Lord." She laughed and then I asked her how she happened to be on the morning flight from Allentown and the night flight back to Allentown? She explained that she had small children and that she flew on two flights each day. By spending the night in Allentown and returning to Pittsburgh each morning, she could spend almost the entire day with her family. It was clear to me that she already understood the essence of both Colossians 3:17 and 18.

As we travel through life, God puts some very interesting people in our paths to help guide and direct us. It could be a flight attendant; it could be your cleaner; it could be your next-door neighbor; it could be your brother or sister; it could be your children; or it could be a clerk at your favorite store. Keep your eyes and ears open.

See you tomorrow, God willing!

June 18 — To My Daughter

Tomorrow is Father's Day so I want to take this occasion to write a two-part letter to the two people in the whole world who have the right to call me by that name. Today, my daughter, this letter is for you. Before you were ever born, you stole my heart, and then when you finally arrived I was hopelessly lost. As a little girl you loved to sit in my lap and let me read to you, but better yet, you actually enjoyed my singing.

Do you remember all of the Glenn Campbell songs that I used to sing to you? (Wichita Lineman, By the Time I Get to Phoenix, Everything a Man Could Ever Need) They were like Brahms Lullaby in their ability to encourage you to fall asleep. Do you remember going to see the Glenn Campbell concert at the old Cincinnati Gardens? He was a big star at that time and even though you were very little at the time, you squealed through the whole performance. Mom also remembers you watching his variety show on television and dancing and squealing through every show.

As you got older you developed new techniques for controlling your Dad. When my friend and I got together, there were sure to be jokes flying around a mile a minute and you laughed whether they were funny or not. I can remember those times as if it were yesterday. I told you that if I ever became a comedian, I was going to take you along to sit in the front row of the audience. I have always wanted to ask you – were the jokes really funny or were you just being a good daughter?

When you were in college you used to call home to talk to us. If I answered the phone, I would ask how you were and then quickly turn the phone over to your mom since I figured that was who you wanted to talk to. After one of those calls ended, my wife told me that you asked her, "I wonder if Dad would talk longer on the phone with me if I were a boy?" That was a wake up call. I hope you noticed that I never again passed along the phone to your mom quite so quickly.

Only because I don't want to make this letter too long, I want to thank you for one last gift – a wonderful family complete with a loving, caring husband and two bright, handsome grandsons. My prayer for them is that one day they too will have a daughter as beautiful as you are! "Charm is deceptive, and beauty is fleeting; but a woman who fears the Lord is to be praised." (Proverbs 31:30) Man sees only the outside; God judges by what He sees on the inside. Father's can see that beauty as well.

See you tomorrow, God willing!

June 19   To Chris

Yesterday, I wrote the first part of a two-part letter to the two people in the whole world who have the right to call me Father. Yesterday's letter was to my daughter; today's letter is to you, my son. I am not sure I have told you this story before, but if I have, it bears repeating. Before you were born there was a man where I worked who thought he was funny and he would frequently ask me "how many sons do you have?" It was his twisted way of telling me that I was not a man because I had no sons at the time. The day you were born, I called him on the phone and asked him, "How many sons do you have?" He answered – "one." I responded –"that's how many I have!" It was a proud day in my life.

Since the athletic genes ran in my family, I couldn't wait until you were old enough to play sports. Do you remember me pitching tennis balls for you to hit with a baseball bat in our backyard in Cincinnati? You could really swing a bat at a very early age. At first, I would pitch the ball to the area you were swinging and you would crash them over the fence. Occasionally I would pitch a ball away from the bat to see if your hand-to-eye coordination was improving. In no time, you were smashing the ball no matter where I pitched them.

Our tenure in Cincinnati coincided with the era of the Big Red Machine and you were a big Joe Morgan fan. My job at the time gave me ready access to Cincinnati Reds games and you went with me several times, generally dressed in a Joe Morgan tee-shirt and a lefty glove on your hand. We had a great time.

As you got older, football became you sport of choice, but there was another sport that was always lingering for attention and it has stayed with you into adulthood – fishing. I think you must have gotten the outdoors genes from your grandfather. Whether it is fishing or riding on your four-wheeler, you derive a great deal of pleasure from being in the open air. And, I must say, God's creation is a good place to be.

Now, you have a new love of your life, your daughter. She is such a treasure and we love her as much as you do. She will grow into a wonderful young lady before you know it, so don't miss a single thing. Remember, she is the one who calls you "Father."

"Sons are a heritage from the LORD, children a reward from him." (Psalm 127:3) Son, you are a part of my heritage from the Lord and your daughter is a reward from Him to all of us.

See you tomorrow, God willing!

June 20 — Sound the Alarm

Last fall our pastor delivered a series of sermons about the loss of the next generation from the church in North America. The sermon series was called, *Sound the Alarm*. Depending on which statistics you believe, approximately 75% of our children are lost to the church by the time they are freshmen in college or leave the nest. It is an alarming statistic. Further compounding the situation is the birth rate in the United States, which has fallen below two per family. That means couples are not having enough children to replace themselves.

In his series, he gave us instructions on how each of us could contribute to reversing this unacceptable trend. One of the key pieces of advice was to let our children and our grandchildren see first hand how important God is in our lives. And, he added, it is not enough to talk about it; we must live it, breathe it, and demonstrate it.

In a recent Charles Stanley devotion, he said, "At any time, we are just one generation away from being a pagan nation. Consider what could happen to our country if we stopped sharing the truth about Jesus with our children: the next generation would exist with no Biblical foundation." Mr. Stanley then pointed to Psalm 78 and said, "We have been given divine instruction to teach the truth to our children. We do this by modeling a godly life, teaching the Word, and sharing our testimony of the Father's provision and leading. Our obedience concerning the training of children will determine the future moral character of our nation." And, I might add the future of God's church.

Here are the first four verses of Psalm 78. "O my people, hear my teaching; listen to the words of my mouth. I will open my mouth in parables, I will utter hidden things, things from old – what we have heard and known, what our fathers have told us. We will not hide them from their children; we will tell the next generation the praiseworthy deeds of the Lord, his power, and the wonders He has done."

Reread that last verse. "We will tell the next generation the praiseworthy deeds of the Lord, his power, and the wonders He has done." If you are taking that obligation seriously, praise the Lord. If you are not, it is never too late to start.

See you tomorrow, God willing!

June 21 — Wimbledon

If a tennis player had a "bucket list," attendance at the U. S. Open at Flushing Meadows, New York and Wimbledon in London, England would be two of the items on the list. Since our home in Pennsylvania was only about two hours from New York City, my wife and I were able to attend several U. S. Opens and see many of the best tennis players in the world on both the men's and women's side of the game.

In the summer of 1985, our family was temporarily living in London while I was on a six-month work assignment. While I didn't get to Wimbledon, my wife and daughter did and they told me that it was quite an experience. Although I didn't get to the tournament, I did go to an event where I had my picture taken with Martina Navratilova, one of greatest women players of all time. The picture is a little out of focus, but I am sitting right there with her for all posterity to see. There is only one problem with the picture; it was taken at Madame Tussauds' Wax Museum in London, and the fact that the photo is a little out of focus hides the fact that Martina is not real; she is a wax replica.

In today's world it is often hard to tell the real from an imitation. When we were in New York City a few weeks ago we were walking through Chinatown and you couldn't go a block without someone offering to sell you designer pocketbooks, Rolex watches, Channel sunglasses or a plethora of other high-quality "knock-offs." Or, better yet, listen to your favorite politician and discern the truth from the rhetoric.

Can you imagine how difficult it was in ancient times to determine what was true and what was false? "But there were also false prophets among the people, just as there will be false teachers among you. They will secretly introduce destructive heresies, even denying the sovereign Lord who bought them—bringing swift destruction on themselves." (2 Peter 2:1). Fittingly, the book that follows 2nd Peter in the Bible, 1st John, gives further instruction, "Dear friends, do not believe every spirit, but test the spirits to see whether they are from God, because many false prophets have gone out into the world." (1 John 4:1) How do we test the words of false prophets? By comparing what false prophets say versus what the Bible says.

If your spirit tells you it is wrong, listen.

See you tomorrow, God willing!

June 22 — Homemade Ice Cream

In the early 1950's, my family lived in Southern Illinois on a small farm that was just large enough to make a living. My dad loved to farm, but he realized that the one hundred acres he farmed needed to be enlarged significantly or he would need to find a new vocation. No one else in the family liked living on the farm so we moved to Virginia in 1956.

There was one part of living in Illinois that I really liked. We lived in the land of relatives. Within twenty miles of where we lived, we had more aunts, uncles and cousins than you can imagine. Dad came from a family of eleven and many of them had been raised in that part of the world and had stayed around. Not only were the relatives close in proximity, they were also close emotionally. My memory probably fails me, but it seemed to me that we were at someone's house every weekend. For the kids, it was great because there were always cousins of my age to play with.

Summers were the best time to be around family. One of the relatives had a large cabin on Lake Benton near the place we lived. Every Sunday afternoon, part of the Roberts' clan would descend on the cabin with swimming suits, playing cards, and food to feed a king. . However, the coup de grace was homemade ice cream. Each family had a machine to hand crank a batch of its own special flavor. Some liked vanilla; some liked chocolate; some liked fresh pineapple; but my favorite was always fresh peach. If you have never eaten hand cranked, homemade ice cream, you have lived a sheltered life. I can't begin to tell you how good it is. Late in the afternoon, as the children completed the task of hand cranking the ice cream, we would begin the feast. I might be exaggerating (a trait I learned at an early age), but it was not unusual for us to consume at least three gallons of this liquid gold every Sunday afternoon. As I think back, this is probably the genesis of my addiction to ice cream.

All of us have a tendency to look back on days gone by and relive some of our pleasant experiences. However, as pleasant at those Sunday afternoons were and as good as the ice cream was, they pale in comparison to the goodness of my Lord and Savior. "One thing I ask of the Lord, this is what I seek: that I may dwell in the house of the Lord all the days of my life, to gaze upon the beauty of the Lord and to seek him in his temple." (Psalm 27:4) We can never go back, but we can sure look forward to things more beautiful than our tiny minds can imagine.

See you tomorrow, God willing!

June 23   Two Simple Verses

The Trans-Alaska pipeline was built between 1974 and 1977 after the 1973 oil crisis caused a sharp rise in oil prices. The task of building the pipeline had to address a wide range of difficulties, stemming mainly from the extreme cold and the difficult, isolated terrain. During that timeframe, I worked at a company that manufactured synthetic lubricants for jet engines. Synthetic lubricants have much lower freezing points than a natural crankcase oil or hydraulic fluid and much higher boiling points which makes them useful in extreme operating conditions. With a little reformulation, these oils were a natural fit for the extremely cold conditions that construction equipment faced while working on the pipeline.

In order to market the new lubricant, I was sent to the North Slope of Alaska in the dead of winter to interview on camera the men who operated large equipment that was in daily use. The day that I arrived in Fairbanks a sign on one of the bank thermometers read minus sixty-three degrees.

All of the interviews were shot outdoors and filming was a challenge. First, the emulsion on the film would freeze after about ten minutes, so we had to shoot quickly and then go back inside to let the camera warm up. The second challenge was holding a metal microphone in your hand while doing the interviews. Even with very heavy gloves, the coldness of the metal would penetrate very rapidly adding to the overall discomfort.

To make a long story short, I was able to get all of the information I needed plus a classic line from a grizzled veteran of the project. I asked the man how they had coped before they were able to obtain our synthetic lubricants. He answered very matter of factly, "We wouldn't have been able to work; the oil would have been frozen solid as a brick." He had summed up our selling point in one simple sentence, in words we could all understand.

The Bible has 1188 chapters so it would be difficult to sum up its message in one simple sentence. However, if I were forced to do so, I might boil it down to two verses in the Gospel of John. First, John 3:16 "For God so loved the world that he gave his one and only Son, that whoever believes in him shall not perish but have eternal life." He loved us so much that He gave His only Son that we might have life eternal. The second verse is a follow on; John 14:6, "I am the way and the truth and the life. No one comes to the Father except through me." Jesus is THE way and He is the only way. Two simple verses out of 1188 chapters in the Bible. To paraphrase the construction worker from Alaska, "We wouldn't have been able to get to heaven; our sins would have been as heavy as a brick."

See you tomorrow, God willing!

June 24 — Whitewashed Tombs

Sightseeing in Europe is dramatically different than sightseeing in the United States. Here we tend to visit locations to see natural wonders such as the Grand Canyon, Niagara Falls, the rugged coastline of the Pacific Coast or the beauty of the Painted Desert. In Europe, the places of interest tend to be locations dripping with history. There are museums galore and we had the opportunity in 1985 to spend time at two of the most famous – The Louvre in Paris and The National Gallery in London.

While we loved to visit the museums and other historical sites, it was the ancient churches that really caught our fancy. In London, there was St. Paul's Cathedral. The current cathedral – the fourth to occupy this site – was designed by the court architect Sir Christopher Wren and built between 1675 and 1710 after its predecessor was destroyed in the Great Fire of London

A second famous church in London is Westminster Abbey–one of the most famous churches in Europe. Dating back to the 11th century this church is the traditional site of royal weddings, coronations, and funerals, many royals are buried in the abbey's tombs, including Elizabeth I and Mary Queen of Scots.

In Paris, we visited Notre Dame, the site of the Victor Hugo novel known to many of us as "The Hunchback of Notre Dame." Because of its location on the Ile de la Cité in the historic centre of Paris and the famous movie, this is one of the most famous cathedrals in the world. We also spent some time at Sacre Coeur, another Parisian church with magnificent architecture.

Among our other favorites were Canterbury Cathedral, der Kölner Dome in Cologne, Germany, and Winchester Cathedral in Winchester, England. All of the churches and cathedrals that we visited, and there were many more, were beautiful on the outside. They had beautiful domes and spires; they had magnificent stained glass windows; they had incredible monuments and statues; and they were all cold and dark. Western Europe, the cradle of modern Christianity, has become a "post-Christian society" in which the ruling class and cultural leaders are anti-religious. "Woe to you, teachers of the law and Pharisees, you hypocrites! You are like whitewashed tombs, which look beautiful on the outside, but on the inside are full of dead men's bones and everything unclean." (Matthew 23:27) This is very likely the comment Jesus would have made concerning many of these churches. Even Jesus is not present in these churches, they are simply whitewashed tombs.

Since our bodies are holy temples, we can say the same thing about ourselves; if Jesus is not present in us, we are simply whitewashed tombs, just like the Pharisees. I fear that I spent too much of my own life as a whitewashed tomb. I am now working on the inside. How about you?

See you tomorrow, God willing!

June 25 — Chef Bill

My mother was a good cook. Even though we didn't have a lot of money when I was growing up, we never went hungry. Mom could make a good meal out of about anything. Decades ago, the main meal of the week in virtually very family was Sunday dinner. One of our main dishes was pot roast with carrots, potatoes, onions and gravy. The only bad thing about pot roast was leftovers. Usually, we ate on that same roast until Wednesday. In our house, no meal was complete without dessert and that is where Mother really shined. She made pies, cakes, cookies, brownies, puddings, and all types of candies; some of her recipes are still being used in the family today. None of the desserts, however, matched her cast-ironed skillet cherry cobbler.

I suppose it was natural that I would inherit the cooking genes. Mother told me that I got it naturally because her father was also an accomplished chef. My first memories of cooking were around the Christmas holidays. When my sister was in high school, she would let me help her make Christmas cookies. After I got married, my wife would let me help her in the kitchen and she taught me how to cook other things. It didn't take long before my curiosity was piqued.

One night when we lived in Pennsylvania after a not-so-good meal at a local restaurant, my best friend and I decided that we could do a better job of cooking than most restaurants and we could save some money to boot. Not long thereafter, we began a regular pattern of cooking gourmet meals for our wives. We would look up classic recipes, shop at the farmer's market for just the right ingredients and then prepare the entire feast for our beautiful brides. Most of the time, the meals were superb, if I do say so myself. However, my friend's wife was not always quite as lavish with her praise. Even if the meal had been perfect, there was no way she would acknowledge our efforts. My wife was much smarter; she knew not to look a gift horse in the mouth. She must have been reading from Proverbs 14:1, "The wise woman builds her house, but with her own hands the foolish one tears hers down." My wife wanted more of a good thing, but my friend's wife was too foolish to see what she was receiving, so she unwittingly tried to tear it down.

I have learned a valuable lesson from that experience. Accept gifts with grace; build up the giver; and, never tear them down.

See you tomorrow, God willing!

June 26 — Oh Happy Day

I am not a boater, nor have I ever owned a boat. Therefore, I cannot verify the truth of a statement that I have heard concerning boat ownership. "The two happiest days in the life of a boat owner are the day he buys the boat and the day he sells it."

My sister's husband owned a boat that he kept at a marina near Occoquan, Virginia. One summer when our daughter was around two years old, we visited my sister and spent an afternoon on their boat. Her husband was a great captain and my sister was an excellent hostess. I think one of the reasons the afternoon sticks in my mind is the eight-millimeter moving pictures we took while riding on the Chesapeake Bay.

Another boating expedition that I remember took place in the early 1990's. On one of our summer vacations to Emerald Isle, we rented a sailboat and sailed to Shackleford Island for shelling and swimming. One of the things I learned during the trip was the difference between Jellyfish and a Portuguese Man O' War. While we were anchored just off the island, several of us decided to take a swim around the boat. As we were swimming, we noticed a number of Jellyfish in the water and became alarmed. The captain told us that the Jellyfish we saw were relatively harmless; the real culprits were Portuguese Man O' War, which is not technically a Jellyfish, but rather a slightly different fish with a much more dangerous sting.

While my boating experiences have all been positive, I have heard many horror stories of people being caught on the ocean when a storm came up quickly. Small boats are no match for the incredible power of the sea. Can you imagine how Jesus' disciples must have felt when an unexpected storm caused them to fear for their lives? "One day Jesus said to his disciples, 'Let's go over to the other side of the lake.' So they got into a boat and set out. As they sailed, He fell asleep. A squall came down on the lake, so that the boat was being swamped, and they were in great danger. The disciples went and woke him, saying, 'Master, Master, we're going to drown!' He got up and rebuked the wind and the raging waters; the storm subsided, and all was calm." (Luke 8:22-25) After seeing the wind listen to Jesus' command, the disciples asked themselves a pointed question, "Who is this? He commands even the winds and the water, and they obey him."

The next time you are on a boat, no matter how big or how small; no matter if you are on the ocean or a river; no matter if the captain is inexperienced or a crusty veteran; here is my advice – invite Jesus to go along with you and you will have no reason to worry.

See you tomorrow, God willing!

June 27 — The Horse with Striped Pajamas

Look there daddy do you see, the horse with striped pajamas on,
Nope, that's not what it is at all,
That's an animal people call a zebra, I see.
But it still looks like a horse with striped pajamas on to me.

Look there daddy do you see, the bird with his tuxedo on,
Nope, that's not what it is at all,
That's an animal people call a penguin, I see.
But it still looks like a bird with his tuxedo on to me.

Look there daddy do you see, the man with his fur coat on,
Nope, that's not what it is at all,
That's an animal people call a gorilla, I see.
But it still looks like a man with his fur coat on to me on to me.

Every time I visit a zoo, the words to this childhood song come racing through my mind. Last week when we were visiting our son in Columbia, South Carolina, we took our granddaughter to the Riverbanks Zoo. She saw the horse with striped pajamas; she saw the bird with his tuxedo on; she saw the man with the fur coat on; and she fed the giraffes and the goats. But, her favorite animals were two large brown bears that playfully fought each other and then took a swim in their pool right in front of her.

When you are three years old, everything is new and exciting. Following our trip to the zoo, it was back to the hotel for a dip in the pool. It was the perfect, cool way to end an otherwise, hot, but exciting day with our granddaughter.

I have always been amazed at how easy it is for me to remember the words to hundreds of songs when I often forget the five items on the grocery list when my wife sends me out for supplies. In Biblical times, the ability to memorize words with music was well known. The entire book of Psalms is a good example. Many were originally incorporated in Israel's temple worship as songs that were sung antiphonally. And Psalms 125 through 134 were short Psalms that were called "Songs of Ascents," written to be sung on the ascent up the temple stairs as Hebrews made their pilgrimage to Jerusalem. You may recognize the first verse of Psalm 133. "How good and pleasant it is when we live together in unity." Listening to Christian music is a really good way to memorize scripture. And, going to the zoo with your granddaughter is an excellent way to enjoy one of God's blessings.

See you tomorrow, God willing!

June 28   Three Cheers for Bill

Since I was a young boy, sports have always been an important part of my life. In the previous one hundred seventh-eight letters, I have talked about football, baseball, tennis, running, kayaking, fishing, and golf. Before the year is over, I may also bore you with stories about basketball, biking, water polo, platform tennis, and who knows what else. Today's story, however, is not about the sports per se, but a wonderful group of young people who support student athletes – the cheerleaders.

My favorite cheerleader was a young lady at my high school. I think she was about fifteen or sixteen years old when she first earned her spot on the cheerleading squad. She was so energetic, beautiful, and, I might add, athletic. During my senior year in high school, I was the captain of the football team and this young lady was the captain of the cheerleading team. She was such a good cheerleader that I asked her to be my life long cheerleader, a position she accepted. She has been cheering me on for nearly five decades.

My second favorite cheerleader was another young lady. She was also beautiful, energetic, and athletic. Even though the high school she attended had over two thousand students, there was only one cheerleading squad for all sports. Those young ladies and young men cheered for football, boys and girls basketball, and wrestling. Their entire school year was filled with so many cheerleading assignments that there was not time for any other extracurricular activities. By the way, the second cheerleader was my daughter.

Have you ever wondered why there are cheerleaders? I know the answer and it is not limited to athletic endeavors. There are times in all of our lives when we need someone to "cheer us on." Life gets very difficult at times and it would be easy to quit if someone weren't standing beside us and telling us "you can do it." Would you believe the book of Proverbs knew that as well? It's not too surprising because human nature hasn't changed in over three thousand years. "An anxious heart weighs a man down, but a kind word cheers him up." (Proverbs 12:25)

If you think you don't have a cheerleader in your life, you are wrong. "You hear, O Lord, the desire of the afflicted; you encourage them, and you listen to their cry." (Psalms 10:17). It is comforting, isn't it?

See you tomorrow, God willing!

June 29 — Ink Blot Tests

My undergraduate degree is in chemistry with a minor in mathematics, so I suppose it should surprise no one that my first job after we got married was in a research laboratory. I liked the job and it was nice to use some of the things I had learned in college. I particularly liked the synthesis of new chemicals and then testing the performance characteristics of the new chemicals in practical applications. Most of the experimental chemicals are no better than the one's currently being used in the marketplace.

After about two years, I began to realize that the working environment in a research lab didn't fit my personality. To really succeed, I would have needed to return to school at night and get a PhD in Chemistry. Frankly, I had had all the chemistry education I wanted. Since I liked the company and we liked living in Cincinnati, I went to my boss and asked him if there might be other opportunities that fit my skill set. Apparently, I had shown enough potential and before long I was scheduled for a day long set of aptitude tests. My favorite parts of the tests were the Rorschach Ink Blot Tests which some psychologists use to examine a person's personality characteristics and emotional functioning. Since I have always liked to look at cloud formations and find images in the clouds, the ink blots were a snap. To make a long story short, that day of psychological testing uncovered two compelling results. One, I had the lowest mechanical aptitude that they had ever measured and, two, I had a very strong creative aptitude.

Since I had proven myself to be a good writer on my research reports, I was asked to transfer to the advertising department as a technical writer. Reluctantly, I made the move and forty years later I am still working in advertising. Go figure.

In the Old Testament, God called on Moses to step out of his comfort zone and lead the Israelites out of Egypt. After many excuses, "Moses said to the LORD, 'O Lord, I have never been eloquent, neither in the past nor since you have spoken to your servant. I am slow of speech and tongue." The LORD said to him, 'Who gave man his mouth? Who makes him deaf or mute? Who gives him sight or makes him blind? Is it not I, the Lord? Now go; I will help you speak and will teach you what to say.'" (Exodus 4:10-12)

As each of us move through life, there are times that we must listen for God's call in our lives. Sometimes we have to listen very carefully and wait for God to respond to our prayers. If it is in His will for us, He will make our paths straight.

See you tomorrow, God willing!

June 30 — Washed Away

As you walk up and down the beach, you see many things. There is a wide selection of seashells; there is driftwood; there are dead fish; there is litter; there are people all over the place with towels, beach chairs, and umbrellas; and there is artistry that flees with the incoming tide.

Of course, sand castles are one of the favorite things that are constructed in the sand. If you take your small children or grandchildren to the beach and do not make a sand castle, you are definitely in the minority. Some sand castles are simple, while others can be somewhat elaborate. One step up in the category of sand construction is sand sculptures. I have seen mermaids, crocodiles, whales, sharks, and many other designs that are far beyond my capabilities. God gives each of us different skills, and artistic ability was not in my toolbox.

A simpler form of expression that you see on the beach is writing in the sand. How many times have you seen a heart with an arrow piercing the middle with words that say "I love you" sprawled through it? Although somewhat less frequent, I have also seen scripture written in the sand. The ocean can be overwhelming and I am sure it moves people to give God the glory for His creation. Of all the things I have seen written in the sand, I can only remember one that I am truly grateful that the tide has washed away.

In 1985, I was walking along the beach with my wife and daughter. The beach was not my favorite place to be, but they loved to be there so I was being a good father and husband, outwardly. Inside, I was bored, so bored in fact, that I began to scribble in the sand with my toe the word "boring." While it was a true expression of my feelings at the time, it did not go over very well with the two most important ladies in my life. They were offended, and rightfully so.

Over the years, my attitude towards the beach has changed. I have learned to spend time looking for shells; to swim in the ocean and enjoy body surfing; and to take a beach chair and a good book to the beach and relax. I am so glad that my indiscretion has been washed away.

"Let us draw near to God with a sincere heart in full assurance of faith, having our hearts sprinkled to cleanse us from a guilty conscience and having our bodies washed with pure water." (Hebrews 10:22) Through the blood of Jesus Christ, all of our sins have been washed away. All of our evil deeds, our evil thoughts and our evil words are gone once we accept Jesus as our Lord and Savior. Just think about those sins as words scribbled on the sand washed away daily by the rising and setting tide,

See you tomorrow, God willing!

July

July 1 — Sanibel Island

Sanibel Island lies off the West Coast of Florida and is one of our favorite beaches. Although we have only been there twice, we have very fond memories. Sanibel is attractive to us for two reasons. One is the shells that wash up on the island. This happen as a result of Sanibel being a barrier island with an unusual layout having an east-west orientation when most islands are north-south. Hence, the island is gifted with great sandy beaches and an abundance of shells. It is also due to the fact that Sanibel is part of a large plateau that extends out into the Gulf of Mexico for miles. It is this plateau that acts like a shelf for seashells to gather.

On our first trip to Sanibel we experienced the full blast of shelling. During that trip, there were so many wonderful shells coming up in the surf that I simply sorted through hands full of shells in the breakers and threw the best ones to my daughter on the beach. On that same trip, we had invited both sets of our parents to spend the week with us. We had a glorious vacation enjoying the time with our family and the weather was sparkling. It was so sunny that our daughter overdid it one day and got a bad sunburn. She wasn't the only one. While my wife's dad was pretty well covered from head to foot, he managed to let his feet get sunburned. He probably did it so his granddaughter would not feel alone.

Our second trip to Sanibel was in 2006 and that reminds me of the second reason that we enjoy Sanibel Island. Because of its location on the West Coast of Florida, it is a spectacular place to watch the sun set in the ocean. The only place I have seen a sunset that compares to the ones you see at Sanibel are those that you see from a cruise ship. While on Sanibel, we made a special effort to be on the beach as often as we could in the evening so we could see the sun as it went down.

Both sunrises and sunsets are one of the gifts God gives us to remind us of His spectacular glory. Yet, in the New Jerusalem there will be no need for the sun, "The city does not need the sun or the moon to shine on it, for the glory of God gives it light, and the Lamb is its lamp. The nations will walk by its light, and the kings of the earth will bring their splendor into it." (Revelations 21:23-24)

Next time you see a beautiful sunrise or sunset, think about Revelations 21:23-24. You don't want to miss that sight.

See you tomorrow, God willing!

July 2 — Wrestling with God

In Eastern Pennsylvania, where we lived for nearly twenty-five years, high school and college wrestling is nearly as fanatical as football. Once the football season is over, it is quite common for the football players to participate in wrestling as a means of keeping in shape for the next season. Therefore, it was not surprising that our son should take up wrestling even as a young man of about ten years old. Personally, I never liked the sport very much. My own high school was too small to have a wrestling team so I had no experience to rely on.

Our son was a pretty good wrestler so we enjoyed attending his meets. While I had no appreciation for the finer points of wrestling, I did understand the physical requirements of the sport and the athletic prowess needed to succeed. The part of wrestling that I abhorred was the never-ending pressure to meet the weight requirements in order to wrestle at the lowest possible weight. I understood the concept, I just didn't like the fact that kids went to extremes to lose weight prior to the weigh-in. If you have ever been around wrestling, you know what I mean – spitting, forced sweating, no eating, and other unmentionable techniques. I suppose the theory behind the weight loss is a good one – make sure you wrestle in the lowest weight class possible.

The first recorded wrestling match in history took place in the book of Genesis when Jacob took on a wrestler way out of his weight class. "So Jacob was left alone, and a man wrestled with him till daybreak. When the man saw that he could not overpower him, he touched the socket of Jacob's hip so that his hip was wrenched as he wrestled with the man. Then the man said, 'Let me go, for it is daybreak.' But Jacob replied, 'I will not let you go unless you bless me.' The man asked him, 'What is your name?' 'Jacob,' he answered. Then the man said, 'Your name will no longer be Jacob, but Israel, because you have struggled with God and with men and have overcome.'" (Genesis 32:24-28)

There have been times in my own life when I have tried to wrestle with God. However, unlike Jacob, I have not won any matches. As I have grown older and wiser, I have discovered it is much better to be on His team and simply be a good cheerleader.

See you tomorrow, God willing!

July 3 — Now That's Real History

History was never one of my favorite subjects. About the only detail I remember from my college course was an incorrect answer on an exam for which I received bonus points. The question was "what was the most significant event in U. S. history in 1892?" My answer was "that was the year Pabst won the Blue Ribbon for brewing excellence." It wasn't the answer the professor wanted, but he gave my full credit for my ingenuity.

I suppose if the study of history weren't so dry, it would be more interesting. For example, we know the details of what happened on July 4, 1776. What if we had been able to study the feelings of the colonists on July 3, 1776 as they anticipated the importance of the following day? The raw emotion of each person would have been incredibly interesting. Were they afraid? Were they jubilant? Were they anxious? Did they think they would be able to make it as an independent nation? Why didn't they tell us and make the history books compelling?

Here is another date that we know about the details, but not much about the emotional trials of the day. The day was July 3, 1963. On that day, the first and only child was born to a young couple in Eastern North Carolina. What were they thinking that day? Were those new parents nervous? Remember in those days there was no ultrasound so they didn't know the sex of the baby that would arrive that day. I'm sure they were elated when their son came out healthy and screaming. That son is now my daughter's husband.

The Bible does a little better job of teaching us the history of ancient times, and including the emotional story as well. On the day before Good Friday, we know what the disciples were doing and what they were feeling. While they were eating the Last Supper, they learned that one of their own would betray Jesus. They were very sad and began to say, "Surely not I, Lord?" (Matthew 26:21-22) Afterwards, when Jesus went to the Garden to pray the disciples could not stay awake. "Could you men not keep watch with me for one hour?' When he came back, he again found them sleeping, because their eyes were heavy...Then he returned to the disciples and said to them, 'Are you still sleeping and resting?'" (Matthew 26:40-45) The emotional impact of the day had taken its toll on the disciples and they were unable to give Jesus the support He needed.

God sure knows how to write so that we can remember not just the details but the spiritual impact of history. Why can't the history of the most important day in U. S. history be as interesting as the most important day in Christian history?

See you tomorrow, God willing!

July 4 — Handy Man

Poor Richard's Almanac was published by Benjamin Franklin, who adopted the pseudonym of "Poor Richard." Franklin, American inventor, statesman, and publisher, achieved success with *Poor Richard's Almanac*. Almanacs were very popular in colonial America, with people using them for a mixture of seasonal weather forecasts, practical household hints, puzzles, and other amusements. Like Proverbs in the Bible, Franklin's almanac contained many sayings that were profound and have stood the test of time. My favorite from his almanac is "fish and visitors smell after three days."

Even the best of profound sayings have their exceptions. My wife's mom and dad would often visit us when we lived in Cincinnati and later in Allentown. We were thrilled when they came to visit, happy to have them stay as long as they wanted. When they came, I had extra reason to be excited. Her dad was the ultimate "Handy Man." He could fix anything and he loved to help me out. Sometimes, it was something simple like a doorknob or a light switch. Other times, it was a little more complicated like taking down a door and planing it so it didn't get hung up on the carpet. To him, all projects were simple. To me, they were all like nuclear physics.

His most amazing feat came when we lived in Allentown. We lived in the country and our house had a fireplace that we frequently used out of necessity when thunderstorms knocked out our heating system. Since we lived on an acre lot that was covered with hardwood trees, we had ready access to firewood. Despite the fact that he was nearly eighty years old, he managed to split an entire cord of wood in one afternoon. I was amazed and impressed.

While there are several men in the Bible who achieved some pretty marvelous feats, two come to mind for me. The first is Abraham who fathered Isaac at the age of one hundred. When God told Abraham that he would father a child at that age, his reaction was predictable, "Abraham fell facedown; he laughed and said to himself, 'Will a son be born to a man a hundred years old? (Genesis 17:17) The second senior citizen of note was Moses who was asked by God to lead the Israelites out of Egypt at the age of eighty. "The LORD said, 'I have indeed seen the misery of my people in Egypt. I have heard them crying... So now, go. I am sending you to bring my people the Israelites out of Egypt.'" (Exodus 3:7, 9-10)

As a youngster of sixty-four years old, I gain real confidence from my father-in-law, Abraham and Moses. It seems that I have quite a few good years ahead of me. As my grandson says, if you still got it, you can still play with it.

See you tomorrow, God willing!

July 5 — Contagious Christian

Several years ago, we took a course at church called "The Contagious Christian." The purpose was to teach us how to share our faith with others in a manner that was personal and non-theological. While I don't remember too many of the details of the course, I do remember the key premise – tell people what you were like before Jesus came into your life and what you are like now that He is your Lord and Savior. Since we took the course, I have learned to share that message in a very brief time with people who are seeking or lost.

Does my testimony make a difference? Do people change immediately? Do all of their troubles disappear once they know about Jesus? I can only say that the answer to each of those questions is as varying as the weather. I would love to say that my testimony changed lives in an instant, but it just doesn't work that way. In fact, it can be very disheartening to see people seemingly ignore your best efforts to help them. That brings me to a second principle we learned in the "Contagious Christian" class – helping bring someone to Jesus is a process not an event. If you view the process as a chain, then our effort is simply one link in that chain. If we are fortunate, we may someday be the last link in someone's chain so we will see the conversion. Unfortunately, we are often a link that is earlier in the process. We must trust that we are planting seeds that God will make grow in the future.

Not too long ago, I had invited an acquaintance of mine to attend church with us. He told me that he had been raised in the church but had not gone since he was married because his wife felt that there were too many hypocrites in the church. I assured him that her opinion was correct and that the church was also chock full of sinners. I shared my story with him and somewhat later he and his wife began to attend the church on a regular basis.

I shared this story at lunch a short time ago and one of my friends shared a great line with me. He said, "If you let a hypocrite stand between you and God, who is closer to God?" How true!

At a time in our country God is being forced out of our everyday activities, it is time for each of us to learn how to share our faith. "After this the Lord appointed seventy-two others and sent them two by two ahead of him to every town and place where he was about to go. He told them, 'The harvest is plentiful, but the workers are few. Ask the Lord of the harvest, therefore, to send out workers into his harvest field.'" (Luke 10:1-2)

Be a contagious Christian.

See you tomorrow, God willing!

July 6 — Fresh Lobster

When we moved to Pennsylvania in 1977, our kids were nine and six, respectively. Since we lived a few miles from town, we decided to buy a rather large metal above ground swimming pool for the kids to enjoy. It was a great idea, but it had a few flaws. We discovered the first flaw when we filled the pool with water. Being in the country, we did not have "city water." Our water came from a well that was over two hundred feet deep. Do you know what the temperature of well water is? If you said fifty-five degrees, you win the prize. So, problem number one could be solved if we waited a few days for the water to warm up.

Our second problem was where to put the pool to have some semblance of privacy. To achieve that goal we had to have the pool close to the house which meant no sunshine because of all the trees around the house. That exacerbated problem one because the sun did not directly hit the water to warm it up. To make a long story short, the kids rarely swam in the pool so our investment was a disaster – almost.

We did find two uses for the pool. The first use was discovered by our son. He found out that it was a good place to keep snakes and turtles that he would find. Once they were in the pool, there was no way out. Neither my wife nor I liked this particular application. The second use was more comical. On one of my sister's visits, I bought some live lobsters to serve for dinner her husband was particularly fond of them. I brought them home and put them in the pool to keep them fresh until evening when we would boil them. Little did I know that lobsters could not survive in fresh water. By the time we cooked them they were already dead. So much for storage.

"Folly delights a man who lacks judgment, but a man of understanding keeps a straight course." (Proverbs 15:21) My backyard, metal, above-ground swimming pool was folly from the very beginning. I did not think through the issues of having the pool and then I made matters worse by trying to use the pool for other things. Isn't it great that we are allowed to make stupid mistakes in our lives and move on? In fact, it is at our point of greatest weakness that God can work in us. "But he said to me, 'My grace is sufficient for you, for my power is made perfect in weakness.' Therefore I will boast all the more gladly about my weaknesses, so that Christ's power may rest on me." (2 Corinthians 12:9)

See you tomorrow, God willing!

July 7 — Equipping the Saints

In many cities across the United States once prosperous neighborhoods have declined and become a blight. The elegant homes that once stood proudly have fallen into disrepair and the manicured lawns are now patches of grass and litter. Children riding bicycles and playing in the streets have been replaced by prostitution and drug dealing.

There are certain parts of West Greenville that fall into this picture. A couple of years ago, our church heard God's call to plant His flag in an eighteen square block portion of West Greenville to help reclaim the area from Satan. First, the church bought a rundown two-story house in the midst of the area and began restoration. While there are plans for the house at some point in the future, the house gave us a reason to be in the neighborhood and gave us a chance to interact with our new neighbors. About a year later, we purchased a second house two blocks away, which was in better shape, and rapidly restored it. That house became our "office" and again gave us access to the neighborhood.

That second house became our meeting place for Sunday afternoon strolls. On a nice Sunday afternoon, many people still sit on their porches in that part of town so we didn't hesitate to initiate conversation them. Over a period of a year, we got to know many of the families, especially the children. On my first few walks, I noticed an amazing amount of litter on the streets and in the yards. A significant portion of the litter was beer, wine and liquor bottles along with plenty of soft drink cans and fast food bags.

On one Sunday last summer there were probably eight to ten of us making the Sunday stroll. I asked if it was okay to take along a large trash bag to pick up some of the trash. I was told that it was okay, so away we went. Within the first two blocks, we had filled the trash bag to overflowing. I had not come prepared. Just as I announced that we would have to stop because the bag was full, another one of our team found a roll of large black garbage bags in the street gutter. God had put a punctuation mark on the work we were doing that day.

While we don't always pray before we begin our walks, we should. We should pray these words from Hebrews 13:20-21, "May the God of peace, who through the blood of the eternal covenant brought back from the dead our Lord Jesus, that great Shepherd of the sheep, equip you with everything good for doing his will, and may he work in us what is pleasing to him, through Jesus Christ, to whom be glory for ever and ever. Amen."

He can even equip us with garbage bags if that is what we need at the time.

See you tomorrow, God willing!

July 8 — Tour de France

Cycling is certainly not one of the major sports in the United States, but in other parts of the world, particularly Europe, it is. The most famous bicycle race in the world is an annual affair held in France and nearby countries. It was first staged in 1903 and the race covers more than 2,200 mile over a period of about three weeks. For years, the winners of the Tour de France were typically Europeans until Lance Armstrong came along in the early 1990's. Armstrong won more Tour de France's than any other ride with a total of seven. Doping controversy involving unproven allegations have surrounded Lance Armstrong for years, although he has never tested positive nor been formally accused of doping.

Enough about Lance Armstrong. When I lived in Pennsylvania, I rode bicycles on a regular basis. My buddy and I used to take long rides every weekend. While the mountains that we climbed were not as extreme as those in the Alps and Pyrenees, they were steep enough for me. I always enjoyed the work out and it was a good complement to my regular running regime. My friend loved to cycle with me because it was the one sport he could beat me with relative ease. On the hills, he buried me and would often come back to see where I was.

Unlike the doping that has occurred in the Tour de France, there was another type of doping that I experienced on one of my weekend rides. As I came flying around one of the many curves on the country roads where we took our rides, I inadvertently left the pedal down on the same side as I was leaning. If you have ever ridden a bike, you know what happens. The dope on the bicycle goes down in a heap; that is exactly what happened. Fortunately, I was wearing a helmet which protected me from serious injury. Unfortunately, I landed squarely on my right shoulder and incurred a second degree shoulder separation. To make matters worse, my wife was in Virginia at the time visiting our parents with the kids so I was forced to fend for myself. A couple of days later when she got home I went to the doctor who confirmed the shoulder separation and put my shoulder into a sling. I truly felt like a dope.

"Even as he walks along the road, the fool lacks sense and shows everyone how stupid he is." (Ecclesiastes 10:3) Isn't this an appropriate Bible verse? If it had just said, "Even as he rides his bicycle along the road …" That would have been a little too much.

See you tomorrow, God willing!

July 9 — Competitive or Zealous?

My brother was, is, and will always be a competitor. It is that competitive nature that made him successful in many athletic endeavors and I suppose in the ultimate game of life. He and I learned to hone those competitive juices when we were young. When we lived on the farm in Southern Illinois, we were only eight and eleven, but I can recall baseball games between the two of us. Since we had no fielders, the only way to get an out was to catch the ball on the fly or hit the runner with the ball as he rounded the bases. I should clarify that we did not play with a hard ball. Nevertheless the sting of being hit with a rubber ball caused several minor disagreements.

Several years later when we lived in Virginia our one-on-one competitiveness switched to basketball. We had a backboard and goal nailed to a tree in our backyard and we spent many hours duking it out in basketball. By this time, we were teenagers so the intensity had increased several degrees. Still later, the competition between us switched to the golf course. My brother started out playing golf right handed and before long he was shooting in the high seventies. He decided that he didn't like playing right handed so he switched to playing left handed and he rapidly progressed to that same level of proficiency. How many people do you know who can play that well from either side of the ball?

We had a lot of fun playing golf together, but we also enjoyed playing together on the same high school football, basketball, and baseball teams. He was the ultimate team player and his competitive attitude never failed to bring out the best in other players on the team. I believe his best sport was basketball where he was the team's leading scorer and fiery playmaker.

There is a companion word used in the Bible to describe a competitive person. The Bible uses the word zealous. "Do not let your heart envy sinners, but always be zealous for the fear of the Lord." (Proverbs 23:17) "It is fine to be zealous, provided the purpose is good, and to be so always and not just when I am with you." (Galatians 4:18) Over the years, both my brother and I have learned to change the focus of our competitiveness. I like the word zealous. It seems to be a lot more positive.

See you tomorrow, God willing!

July 10 — Down at Your Feet

While my wife and I had both been on a mission trip before, we were excited about our upcoming trip to Bulgaria in the summer of 2008. We had been through most of Western Europe years ago but had never been into any of the countries in the old Eastern Bloc. This trip would also be vastly different from our trip to Honduras because the needs of the people in the two countries were vastly different. From a more selfish standpoint, we were looking forward to the trip as a time to deepen friendships with a number of people from our church that we knew well.

Our entry point into Bulgaria was through the capital city of Sofia. From there we travelled by car to Lovech, a city about an hour due north of Sofia. Our appointed task was to help convert an old "Roman bath house" into a church. Since it was very early in the process, our specific job was to help create new concrete floors. That meant mixing concrete by hand and transporting the mix by wheelbarrow to skilled laborers who poured and smoothed the concrete in place. It was hard labor, but we sang, smiled, hummed, and joyfully performed physical labor by day while visiting orphanages, soup kitchens, church services and other places during the late afternoons and evenings.

By the end of our week, we were physically drained but spiritually charged. On Friday afternoon, we were taken back to Sofia to start the first leg of our trip back to the United States. One of our Bulgarian hosts gave us a walking tour of Sofia before dinner. As we walked the streets, I sang at the rear of the group and another member hummed another tune, as she was prone to do. By this time in the trip, one member of our team had heard all of the singing and humming she could take so she commented to her friend about our annoying habits. No sooner had the negative words come out of her mouth when she tripped over some broken concrete on the sidewalk and feel hard to her knees. In an instant, her friend began to sing to her "Down at your feet, oh Amy, is the most High Place; in your Presence Lord, I seek your face!" Once we realized that she was not hurt, we laughed until our sides hurt.

It was truly a God moment, "all the holy ones are in your hand. At your feet they all bow down, and from you receive instruction..." (Deuteronomy 33:3) We had received our instructions and carried them out to the best of our abilities. It was time to bow down to our Maker and praise Him for all He had done!

See you tomorrow, God willing!

July 11   Landscape Lackey

My wife is the gardener in the family; I am just a landscape lackey. She tells me where to dig and plant and that is what I do. I am very obedient, just a little slow. When it comes to digging holes, I love Eastern North Carolina. The soil in our yard is rich and sandy and you can dig a hole in no time. I can use a shovel, a posthole digger, or a trowel with very little effort. I can make the hole as big as I want and adjust as I go.

You may be wondering why I would bother to tell you this seemingly boring information. Here is why. We lived in Eastern Pennsylvania for nearly twenty-five years and you cannot stick your shovel in the ground an inch without hitting a rock. No hole of any size was easy to dig, and when you started, you never knew how big the hole would get before you were finished removing the rocks that you uncovered. If you happened to hit a very large rock, you got a very large hole. Digging the hole required more than a shovel. Typically, you needed a shovel, a pickax, and a large steel pry bar. It sounds ridiculous, but those tools were needed if you were going to dig a hole.

There were so many rocks on our property that I built several rock walls around the yard to provide a natural separation between woods and grass. In the rock wall directly behind the house, chipmunks made their home and were always running around causing our Cocker Spaniel to go crazy. Quite often, we would let the dog out the back door to chase the chipmunks into hiding. In all of our years living there, she never caught a chipmunk, but she had a great time trying.

No matter where we live, as long as God is present, we are at home. "For the LORD your God is bringing you into a good land—a land with streams and pools of water, with springs flowing in the valleys and hills; a land with wheat and barley, vines and fig trees, pomegranates, olive oil and honey; a land where bread will not be scarce and you will lack nothing; a land where the rocks are iron and you can dig copper out of the hills. When you have eaten and are satisfied, praise the LORD your God for the good land He has given you." (Deuteronomy 8:7-10) As the old saying goes, "if God gives you lemons, make lemonade. If he gives you rocks, make rock walls."

See you tomorrow, God willing!

July 12   Broken Bones

As we were preparing to leave for a visit to help our granddaughter celebrate her third birthday, we received a text message that she had fallen down the stairs and hurt her wrist or arm. My son and his wife took her to the emergency center to get x-rays and told us that they would let us know the extent of her injury. An hour or so later, we received a photo of her with her forearm and wrist bandaged. The x-rays showed no damage, but the doctor wrapped the arm because she said it hurt. It was a perfect placebo. When we arrived in Columbia on Sunday afternoon for our visit, she was fine. She favored the wrist a little bit, but was no worse for the wear. By Monday afternoon, she had forgotten that her arm was even injured.

When I was twelve years old, I was not so lucky. My friend was the son of the president of Clinchfield Coal Company so he had a few things in life that I didn't have; one of them was a pony. One afternoon, we saddled up his pony and went for a ride in the meadows. As the two of us rode the pony, the saddle slipped and we tumbled to the ground. My wrist snapped; there was no doubt that it was broken and x-rays taken at the hospital confirmed what we already knew. They put a plaster cast on my wrist that stretched all the way to my elbow. During the night, the arm swelled so much that the cast was too small and I was experiencing not only the pain from the broken bone, but also the pressure from the swelling. The next morning it was back to the doctor who split the cast with a medical saw and retaped it to relieve the pressure.

As a sidebar to the broken wrist story, it was that spring that I played my very first round of golf. I recall vividly playing those first few rounds with that cast on my left arm. Some people say that the cast was a natural aid to my early play. It forced me to keep my left arm and wrist straight as I took my backswing. I guess I will never really know if it helped me or not.

Within about six weeks, the doctor removed the cast and the wrist was as good as new. I could then hold the golf club properly and my swing was just right. Pharaoh, king of Egypt was not so lucky. "Son of man, I have broken the arm of Pharaoh King of Egypt. It has not been bound up for healing or put in a splint so as to become strong enough to hold a sword." (Ezekiel 30:22) It is not good to be on the bad side of the Most High God. God healed my wrist, Pharaoh wasn't so fortunate.

See you tomorrow, God willing!

July 13 — Read the Owner's Manual

I am not very mechanically inclined and I am not very good at following the lousy owner's manuals that supposedly tell you how to put something together. You need to know this about me to fully appreciate the difficulty I experienced one Christmas about thirty-five years ago. There were two Christmas presents that year that Santa had left ahead of time for me to assemble. One of those presents was a set of kitchen appliances that little girls loved to play with. These appliances were not the wonderful plastic toys of today; they were made of sheet metal. The other was a bicycle with training wheels.

Since I didn't have to follow the instructions for the assembly of the bicycle, I was in pretty good shape. I managed to get the bike together with few glitches. I can't remember any glitches, but I'm sure there were some given my ability.

When it came time to assemble the sheet metal stove and refrigerator, I was in trouble. There were far too many parts and the instructions assumed that I knew far more than I actually did. To make matters worse, the sheet metal edges of the toys were very sharp. I don't know how long it took me to complete the assembly that Christmas Eve, but I do remember that my poor hands were a bloody mess by the time I finished.

In one of Charles Stanley's monthly devotions he said. "The Bible is the most remarkable book ever written. It is not only the complete owner's manual to life but also a personal love letter to each of us from our Father." He is correct. When I first starting reading the Bible on a regular basis, it was too much like the owner's manuals I mentioned in the first part of this story. It was hard to understand and I would rather have done the assembly without the manual if at all possible. However, the more I read, the more God revealed His instructions and the easier it has been to follow them. "My son, do not forget my teaching, but keep my commands in your heart, for they will prolong your life many years and bring you prosperity. Let love and faithfulness never leave you; bind them around your neck, write them on the tablet of your heart. Then you will win favor and a good name in the sight of God and man." (Proverbs 3:1-4)

Don't forget to read the instruction manual. Some assembly may be required.

See you tomorrow, God willing!

July 14 — Lightning Show

On the evening of the fourth of July, my wife and I were sitting on our back porch watching some of the neighbors shoot off fireworks. Just as one of the rockets exploded in the air, there was a magnificent bolt of lightning in the sky. I couldn't help but think that God was just reminding us that there is nothing that man can make that approaches the wonder of His creation.

During the hot humid moths of July and August, there are many thunder storms that roll through our area and I am always drawn to the porch to watch the aerial display. Sometimes the lightning bolts are perpendicular with the ground while at other times they seem to stretch across the sky as if they are touching each other to join in the party.

The most spectacular lightning shows that I have seen are at the beach. There must be incredible energy that flows from the ocean to the sky because no where else do these light shows match the intensity of a beach storm. As far as pure beauty, there is nothing like watching a thunderstorm from an airplane flying at thirty-five thousand feet. All you can see are explosions of light below you as you fly comfortably above the storm.

While scientists are able to explain what causes lightning to occur, can they explain who creates the right conditions? When Job finally realized that he was wrong to question God's sovereignty, God talked to him about His majesty and he used lightning several times to make His point. "He fills his hands with lightning and commands it to strike its mark." (Job 36:32) "He unleashes his lightning beneath the whole heaven and sends it to the ends of the earth." (Job 37:3) He loads the clouds with moisture; he scatters his lightning through them." (Job 37:11) "What is the way to the place where the lightning is dispersed, or the place where the east winds are scattered over the earth?" (Job 38:24) "Do you send the lightning bolts on their way? Do they report to you, 'Here we are'?" (Job 38:35)

The next time you are watching the splendor of a summer lightning show, just think about the Creator. And, remember how patient He was with Job. He has the same patience with us, and I need it.

See you tomorrow, God willing!

July 15   Times to Remember

My youngest grandson had outpatient surgery to repair some cartilage damage to his knee. He is at home now and resting comfortably. Football for the coming season is out, but healing is expected to be one hundred percent so if he desires, he will be able to play again during his senior season.

My own football career ended with a knee injury near the end of my senior season in high school. On the very last play of a thirteen-thirteen tie with rival Lebanon, I was tackled before I could get off a "Hail Mary" pass for a possible winning touchdown. I went down awkwardly and did not get up. I tried to play in the next game, but the knee simply would not hold up. My football career was over and my dreams of playing on the college level were over, probably a blessing in disguise.

By November, it was surgery time. I had the surgery to remove torn cartilage in my left knee the third week of November, which I recall because I was in the hospital the day President Kennedy was assassinated. I also happened to be watching the television when Jack Ruby shot Lee Harvey Oswald as he was entering the police station. It's probably a safe bet to assume that everyone over sixty years old remembers right where they were when they got the news that the president had been killed. To the present generation, it will be the memory of the planes flying into the World Trade Center on September 11, 2001. For an earlier generation, it was likely the day that Pearl Harbor was bombed.

Can you even begin to imagine the impact of Jesus' crucifixion on those people who were His followers or who had been touched by His life? Here is a little of what they had to remember. "And when Jesus had cried out again in a loud voice, he gave up his spirit. At that moment the curtain of the temple was torn in two from top to bottom. The earth shook and the rocks split. The tombs broke open and the bodies of many holy people who had died were raised to life. They came out of the tombs, and after Jesus' resurrection they went into the holy city and appeared to many people." (Matthew 27:50-53) I think it is safe to say that it was a day that would stick in their minds forever. In fact that event was so profound that it has stuck in the minds of billions of people for over two thousand years.

See you tomorrow, God willing!

July 16   Coin Collector

Numismatist is a word that is hard to spell and even harder to pronounce. It is defined as one who collects coins, paper currency or medals. The term is one of many positive images you could assign to my wife's father. He was a coin collector extraordinaire. Both the large safe in his bedroom and the smaller safe in the kitchen cupboard were filled with valuable coins. Even more of his collection was stored in safety deposit boxes at the local bank.

He had gold coins of many shapes and sizes. The most valuable was an octagonal shaped $50 gold piece. He had quite an array of gold coins of virtually every denomination that had ever been minted. He also had a collection of silver dollars that was the envy of any collector. Over the years, he had obtained every year and mint mark and had slowly upgraded each of these available coins so that his collection was top notch. It would take far too long for me to cover the breadth and depth of the remaining parts of his collection.

As any avid coin collector knows, the United States Mint sells sets of special quality coins each year. Each set contains one of each variety of coin that is being placed into circulation that particular year – one of each denomination and one of each mintmark. Through the government, you can purchase either "proof" coins or "uncirculated coins."

The proof coins are specially made for collectors and have a mirror like finish with absolutely no scratches. The uncirculated coins, which cost somewhat less, receive no special handling, but because they do not go into circulation, they will have higher value as they age. These coins are also placed in special wrapping to protect them from wear.

Jesus did not carry any coins and was obviously not a collector. Twice when he was confronted with issues surrounding coins, he had to ask someone else to get a coin for him to answer his critics. "Bring me a denarius and let me look at it. They brought the coin, and he asked them, 'Whose portrait is this? And whose inscription?' 'Caesar's,' they replied. Then Jesus said to them, 'Give to Caesar what is Caesar's and to God what is God's.' And they were amazed at him." (Mark 12:15-17) "After Jesus and his disciples arrived in Capernaum, the collectors of the two-drachma tax came to Peter and asked, 'Doesn't your teacher pay the temple tax?... But so that we may not offend them, go to the lake and throw out your line. Take the first fish you catch; open its mouth and you will find a four-drachma coin. Take it and give it to them for my tax and yours.'" (Matthew 17:24, 27)

Jesus knew the value of coins; He simply chose to collect something far more valuable – our salvation.

See you tomorrow, God willing!

July 17   Our Granddaughter's Birthday

On this day, three years ago, our son became a dad for the first time. At age thirty-seven, he was a little older than most first-time dads, but that fact made no difference to him and, in fact, it probably made the day even more special. His wife had carried her baby all the way until her due date, so the doctor had advised her to check into the hospital so he could induce labor. That was perfect for us, so we jumped in the car and made the trek to Virginia so we could be there when she was born.

When the blessed baby arrived, the mother's first question was "does she have red hair?" Since both of her boys from previous marriages had red hair, she assumed that her newborn would also have red hair. Much to her surprise, she told her that the hair was brown like our son's hair. It didn't matter. What mattered most was that she had arrived into this world safely and healthy. A very special day had ended on a happy note.

In the next few months following her birth, we drove to Virginia on a number of occasions to enjoy our new granddaughter. On her first birthday, we drove back to Virginia to help her celebrate. While she had a great time at her party, she was too little to appreciate all of the presents, people, and food. For her second birthday, we rented a cabin in Boone, North Carolina and celebrated her birthday there. We have fond memories of that weekend, but all she remembers is "mooing" at the cows and all of the balloons we blew up for her. Last week, we helped her celebrate birthday number three a few days early in Columbia, South Carolina. For her, the highlight of the visit was time spent in the hotel pool with us,

Next weekend, our son's family will be back in Virginia celebrating his daughter's birthday with her mother's side of the family. Would you believe there is a Bible verse that talks about what is going on in St. Paul today? "No one could distinguish the sound of the shouts of joy from the sound of weeping because the people made so much noise. And the sound was heard far away." (Ezra 3:13) We'll probably hear the laughter all in the way in North Carolina.

On some days, it is hard for us to see all of the blessings that God has poured over us. On a day like today, it is incredibly easy. "The LORD has done great things for us, and we are filled with joy." (Psalms 126:3) All of us need to stop and smell the roses, every day!

See you tomorrow, God willing!

July 18   On the Move

When we moved from Pennsylvania to North Carolina in 2001, we had to go through the trials and tribulations of what to do with twenty-five years of accumulated stuff. Some junk got thrown away; some stuff got sold in a big yard sale; and the rest of the treasures got packed into a moving van to be used in our new home. Little did I know that during the next tree years, we would go through the same process three more times.

First, my aunt died in 2002 and the task of taking care of her worldly goods fell on us. While my sister took the lead, there was plenty of work for all of us. The first step was to determine if there were items that any of the family wanted to keep, again that was the treasures. We then packed up a bunch of stuff and called one of the charitable organizations and donated those items to them; then the junk was put in the garbage.

Our next major house cleaning involved the sale of mother's house and the redistribution of all of her keepsakes. Mother had lived in her house for over forty years and, while she was not a hoarder, she had kept a lot more things than she needed. By now, I think you are getting the picture. First, you keep all of the treasures. Then you have a yard sale and sell the stuff along with some items from Fran's house; then you call the garbage man to haul away the junk.

Our fourth major move of the period was the easiest. When we moved from our rental house in Greenville to the new house we had built, we were able to skip the yard sale and garbage steps. Since we had lived in the rental house for only a year, we didn't have time to accumulate any extraneous goods. In fact, we hadn't even unpacked many of the boxes we had moved from Pennsylvania.

By the time we move again, we will have learned some very valuable lessons. There will be far fewer treasures and far more stuff. "Do not store up for yourselves treasures on earth, where moth and rust destroy, and where thieves break in and steal. But store up for yourselves treasures in heaven, where moth and rust do not destroy, and where thieves do not break in and steal. For where your treasure is, there your heart will be also." (Matthew 6:19-21)

As we grow older, we realize how little material things matter in our lives. Houses come and go. Treasures tarnish and become broken or lost. However, the love of our Father and our loved one's lasts forever. Where are your treasures?

See you tomorrow, God willing!

July 19 — Where to Look for Jesus

Last Sunday, Pastor Isidro from La Romano, Dominican Republic was visiting our church to bring us up-to-date on all that we have contributed to their well being. When he spoke of contributions, he meant love first and everything else second. In the last five years, our church has sent forty mission teams to La Romano. Pastor Isidro painted an incredible picture of the many people whose lives had been changed as a direct result of help in his ministry.

In his sermon, there were two messages that jumped out. His first message was simple, "you are not poor unless you have absolutely nothing to give to someone else." If you have two shirts and your friend needs one, you can give him one. By that definition, few of us will ever fit the poor category. His second message was also simple, but elegant. If you want to look for Jesus, you will find Him where there are people in need.

There was a community prayer walk in West Greenville that was organized by our church but at least three other Greenville churches participated. Around three hundred people showed up, enough to break into six teams and literally cover every block of West Greenville. Pastor Isidro walked with one group and they came upon a group of young boys playing basketball with a badly deflated, worn out ball. During his sermon on Sunday, he said that it was a good example of finding out that Jesus needed a basketball and on Sunday afternoon he returned to West Greenville and delivered a new one to the young folks. I was impressed.

On Monday morning as I was completing my morning prayers, I closed by asking Jesus to show me where He was on that day. I went to work in the morning and as I was driving home, I saw a man I know walking along the street. I rolled down my window at a stop light and asked him if he needed a ride. He jumped in the car and I drove him about a mile to his destination. I wished him a good day and proceeded on my way home, and then it struck me. God had indeed answered my morning prayer. Jesus needed a ride and unknowingly I had provided just what he needed.

Jesus was pretty clear about our need to serve the needy. "For I was hungry and you gave me something to eat, I was thirsty and you gave me something to drink, I was a stranger and you invited me in, I needed clothes and you clothed me, I was sick and you looked after me, I was in prison and you came to visit me." (Matthew 25:35-36) He could just as easily have said when I need a basketball or a ride. Look for Jesus. My bet is you will find him right where He said He would be.

See you tomorrow, God willing!

July 20 — Food Fellowship Hospitality

Food, fellowship, and hospitality have always been critical elements of our culture dating back to Biblical times. Jesus told a story about a man who went to his neighbor to borrow some food late at night because he had a surprise visitor who was in need of something to eat. Although the neighbor had been awakened and was in no mood to provide him with food, he obliged him anyway because the culture demanded it.

In our church in Pennsylvania, there was a group that consisted of five couples with ages ranging from the early thirties to the early seventies. The oldest couple in the group was the ring leader. He was a Southern gentleman who had been raised in Southern aristocracy. He told us stories of riding his bicycle down the halls of his house and also told us that he was taught how to cook by the family's resident chef. She had quite a different story. She had been in the Woman's Army Corp. (WAC's) during World War II and had danced with Eisenhower at the end of the war. They were quite a pair.

Our small group of couples met several times a year to share a gourmet meal that was always prepared in collaboration by all couples. It was his job to call a meeting of the ladies in the group to plan the menu. His name was Earl, so the planned group was called "Earl's Pearls." He was the elder statesman, and the ladies were his ladies in waiting.

While the food was always superb, it was the fellowship that made the meals memorable. One evening we were eating at our house where the dining room was very small. In fact, it was so small that once ten people were seated around the table, there was no getting out until the meal was over. Toward the end of the meal, Earl was telling a story that brought convulsive laughter to the whole group. As the pitch of the laughter hit its peak, a nearly empty wine glass shattered, just like you see on television. It was a moment for the ages. You simply had to see it to believe it.

While Jesus walked the earth, He performed many miracles and did other things that were hard to believe because of their magnitude. In the closing verse of John's Gospel he says, "Jesus did many other things as well. If every one of them were written down, I suppose that even the whole world would not have room for the books that would be written." (John 21:25). He is still performing miracles in people's life.

See you tomorrow, God willing!

July 21 — Showers of Blessings

When you get to be my age, it is hard to remember much about any particular day. There are exceptions, however, and this date in 1990 is one of them. That was the day my daughter got married at Emerald Isle, North Carolina.

It started out to be a gorgeous summer day. That morning I played tennis with some friends who had made the trip from Pennsylvania to attend the wedding. I recall vividly that I was virtually incapable of hitting the ball despite the fact that I was a pretty good player at the time. My mind was clearly on the ceremony that was scheduled to take place at four in the afternoon.

By mid-afternoon storm clouds began to form in the southwest and we knew we were in for some rain. It turns out that it was more than some rain; it was a lot of rain. The deluge started about 3:30 and it rained so hard that none of the out of town guests who were staying less than two miles from the church could get to the ceremony. The groom's family from Greenville had left plenty early so they arrived at the church before the brunt of the storm hit. To make a long story short, the ceremony was delayed until almost 4:30 to give our Pennsylvania friends time to get to the church.

Finally, the wedding ceremony was completed and we made our way to the clubhouse at Pebble Beach where we held the reception. It started raining again and we had to run back and forth with umbrellas to the arriving cars to keep people from getting soaked. We had placed wooden hearts about three feet high around the clubhouse for decorations. By the time the rain finally stopped, they were submerged and you could only see the top of the hearts as you crossed over the walkway to the reception. One of our friends commented that the submerged hearts were symbolic of a marriage that could survive even the toughest challenges.

The rain, however, did nothing to dampen the spirits of the married couple or any of our friends and family in attendance. When we received the photographer's proofs of the day, we could not find a single picture of our daughter without a smile as big as the sky. It was a glorious day.

Rain on your wedding day is a superstition said to bring good luck to the marriage. According to the old wives' tale, the knot in "tying the knot" becomes wet and is harder to break, thus making the marriage stronger. I think there is a better explanation in the Bible in Ezekiel 34:26 where it says, "I will bless them and the places surrounding my hill. I will send down showers in season; there will be showers of blessing." If He rains on your parade, it is probably showers of blessings.

See you tomorrow, God willing!

July 22 — Bill – The English Teacher

I don't know for sure how I got the habit of helping my children and grandchildren with their spoken English. I probably mimicked similar behavior from my sister and mother. Both of them had a habit of correcting my English as I was growing up. I don't know how many times my sister would say "He doesn't" to me when she heard me say "He don't." I have to admit, she was effective because I did learn from her corrective tone.

There are three specific examples of bad grammar that I have been known to correct. See if you can recognize them. Number one – "Can I have this last piece of pie?" My answer will always be "I don't know, can you?" There is a difference in asking permission to do something or asking if one has the capability of doing it. Number two is my all-time favorite, the dangling participle. Here is an example. "I saw a bear going to the beach the other day." My response would be – "how did you know the bear was going to the beach?" Perhaps I am a little too hard on people, but this particular grammatical error makes for good humor. Number three is the misuse of a word by converting it from one part of speech to another. For example, I had a friend in Pennsylvania who routinely asked me "do you golf?" I would respond as politely as possible "yes, I do play golf." Golf is a noun not a verb.

I had to learn the hard way that there are gray areas in grammar, particularly when it comes to the pronunciation of words. When we moved from Pennsylvania to North Carolina, I found a host of words that have more than one acceptable pronunciation.

Pecan is at the top. My Southern friends prefer "pee can", while I always say "pee con."

A second good example is the word caramel. Some say "care a mel" while I prefer "car a mel." Again, both are acceptable. Last, but not least is the word that we use to describe the relationship of one of us has to the sister of one's mother or father. Some people say ant. I prefer to pronounce the "au" to get the long sound "awe nt."

I often tell myself not to be pedantic, but I never say it out loud or someone will think that I am using big words to impress people. Jesus didn't use big words or complicated messages to communicate with people. The most important statements were always very clear. Perhaps the most quoted verse in the Bible is the best example, "For God so loved the world that He gave His one and only Son, that whoever believes in Him shall not perish but have eternal life." (John 3:16) It doesn't get any clearer than that.

See you tomorrow, God willing!

July 23 — Breakfast Club

Habits are a hard thing to break and that also applies to good habits. For example, when we are at Emerald Isle, I still have a strong desire to go for a run up and down Coast Guard Road. Even though my synthetic hip doesn't allow me to run, I still have the urge. Another good example is the "breakfast club" which met for years on Saturday mornings when we lived in Pennsylvania.

The breakfast club was composed of several regular couples and a multitude of guests. It was our practice to meet for breakfast every Saturday morning at eight o'clock at the restaurant or diner of choice of the host for the morning. Getting to choose the eating establishment on a Saturday morning was not a good thing because the person who was hosting for the morning was also the person who paid for breakfast that day. When you happened to be hosting, you were also wondering how many guests might be brought along on that day. It was normally not abused, but it happened with some regularity.

There were two places that dominated our eating venue. Emmaus Diner, located in a suburb of Allentown, was where we ate most often. It was a diner owned by a Greek family which insured that you could get a good, filling breakfast for around five dollars a person. My favorite location was The Powderbourne, a restaurant associated with a gun club. This restaurant was located out in the boondocks, but the food was excellent. Their Canadian bacon was out of this world. It was thick and crispy, just like I liked it

There were several things we liked about the breakfast club. First, we spent many an hour laughing and cutting up with good friends. When we needed to be serious, we were, but it was always good fellowship. Two, by meeting for breakfast at eight in the morning, we got the weekend off to an early start. It was our normal practice to run errands after breakfast which would get us home between ten and eleven with plenty of time to take care of weekend chores. Three, since breakfast is the most important meal of the day, we fed our bodies in a proper fashion.

Looking back on the breakfast club, there was one person who was missing that should have been invited every Saturday morning, Jesus. Had we spent every Saturday morning discussing God's Word and His place in our lives, there may have been people whose lives would have been changed. We missed a great opportunity. "In vain you rise early and stay up late, toiling for food to eat—for he grants sleep to those He loves." (Psalms 127:2) When God is at the center of your life He grants you peace. When He is not at the center, you work in vain.

See you tomorrow, God willing!

July 24   Fish Ponds

In our backyard in Pennsylvania, we had a small fish pond installed and populated mostly with Koi. While it was very small, we enjoyed the soothing effect of the waterfall that was the result of recirculating the water in the pond and we also enjoyed watching the fish lazily swimming in their limited space. In fact, we liked the first pond so much that it was not too long before we added a second pond just below the first one. It was probably three times the size of the original pond and was linked to the first pond by an overflow stream.

There was only one problem with the location of the two pools. Our backyard was at the base of a wooded hill that was entirely trees and rocks. Whenever we got a torrential rain, the water would run off the hill and into the fish ponds. On one occasion, the torrent of water into the ponds was so heavy that it carried debris into the ponds. Our solution was to remove all of the fish from the ponds and drain each pond in order to clean out the dirt and other junk. We had a small plastic swimming pool and a couple of five-gallon buckets that we used to house the fish during the cleaning process. After cleaning the ponds and waiting for the water to refill them, we left the fish in their temporary home while we went to church. When we came home, one of our large Koi was missing. We later found the carcass in the woods; the victim of a neighbor's cat.

When we moved to North Carolina we had a small fishpond installed in the backyard just in back of the house. Because of its proximity to the house, we didn't have to worry about flooding. The only threats to the fish this time were snakes, raccoons, and cats; or so we thought. One Saturday afternoon we were watching a college football game on the television and it wasn't going too well. Our son-in-law walked over to my prayer bench which sits in front of a window overlooking the fishpond. When he looked out the window, he saw a Blue Herron having lunch from our pond. Before the day was over we placed a net over the pond and have left in place ever since. When we returned from church the next morning, we saw the same Blue Herron on top of our house, apparently waiting for his next meal. We had foiled his plans.

Although we had taken away the Herron's dinner, we were not worried. "Look at the birds of the air, they do no sow or reap or store away in barns, and yet your heavenly Father feeds them." (Matthew 6:26)

See you tomorrow, God willing!

July 25 — Snakes, Snakes and More Snakes

The blazing one hundred degree heat has had an impact on the critters that frequent our yard. On a daily basis, you can watch the birds drinking and bathing in one of the bird baths that we have in our backyard. Even the squirrels have been seen chasing away the birds to get their chance to wet their whistle. We love to watch these creatures; it is another species that has been seeking water that is a bit more annoying.

Snakes have shown up. First, I accidentally uncovered a "smooth earth snake" while I was working in a mulch bed around the front of the house. It is a small snake, about eight inches long, that lives in moist leaves and mulch and feeds on earthworms. After I killed the harmless reptile, I had to go on a website to identify the species.

One evening I came home from running errands and my wife couldn't wait to tell me she had killed another small snake in the garage. Finding a snake in the yard is one thing, finding one in the garage is quite another. She had done exactly as I did; she quickly got an axe and cut off the snakes head. It was back to the website to identify this intruder. The snake she killed was a rat snake. Unlike the small earth snake, the rate snake can grow to a length of six feet long

Our fishponds always attracted snakes. On several occasions over the last two or three years we have been forced to chase "Red-Bellied Water Snakes" out of the pond. My wife's concern for our Koi far outweighs her fear of snakes so she has become quite adept at chasing them down and cutting off their heads. While we know there are good snakes and bad snakes, we live by the motto "the only good snake is a dead snake."

From the beginning of time, the serpent has been a symbol of evil. "Now the serpent was more crafty than any of the wild animals the LORD God had made. He said to the woman, 'Did God really say, 'You must not eat from any tree in the garden'?'" (Genesis 3:1) After the serpent successfully lured Eve into eating from the apple, God cursed the serpent for all time. "So the LORD God said to the serpent, 'Because you have done this…You will crawl on your belly and you will eat dust all the days of your life. And I will put enmity between you and the woman… he will crush your head, and you will strike his heel.'" (Genesis 3:14-15)

God said man would crush the head of the serpent, and we do. By the way, in this severe heat, if you hear a snake talking to you, it's time to go inside a get a drink of cool water.

See you tomorrow, God willing!

July 26   What's Behind Bedroom Four

We have only owned three houses in our entire life. The first two houses were previously owned homes that were five to ten years old when we bought them. The first house in Cincinnati was a nice starter home that we occupied for about six years. Our house in Pennsylvania was our place of residence for early twenty-five years. It was larger, and had many more features. Its real bonus was its location. Instead of wall-to-wall houses like we experienced in Cincinnati, the Pennsylvania house was out in the country on a nice one-acre wooded lot.

By the time we moved to Greenville in 2001, our housing needs were evolving. It looked like we could have both of our aging mothers living with us for some period of time. As we looked for houses, our main concern was to find a house with three bedrooms on the first floor. Surprisingly, that proved to be more difficult that we thought. After having no success for an extended period of time, we made the decision to build. It was probably in the back of our minds all along since we had never built a house for our own specifications. Once we decided to build, we were not over the hump. We had a hard time finding a house plan that met our needs. Finally, we settled on a house plan that had three bedrooms on the first floor. The plan included two bedrooms on one side of the house with a single bathroom serving those two bedrooms. Our bedroom was to be on the other side of the house to give us some privacy.

We had already bought our lot for the house and our new house plan did not meet the covenants of the neighborhood. Our lot required a house of twenty-five hundred square feet. Our new house plan was only twenty-three hundred square feet. Our builder told us he could very easily add a second floor to the plan giving us extra space and allow us to meet the HOA requirements. On the second floor, we have a fourth bedroom, a large den and office for me and a bonus room where we have exercise equipment.

By the way, we never did have both of our mothers living with us, my wife's mom did spend some time with us and my mother lived with us for over three years. The house has served us well, but is now much too large for our needs. God led us before and He will lead us again. "The Lord foils the plans of the nations; he thwarts the purposes of the peoples. But the plans of the Lord stand firm forever, the purposes of his heart through all generations." (Psalms 33:10-11)

See you tomorrow, God willing!

July 27　　　　　　　　　　　　　　　　　　　　　Fraley Room

The Fraley Room is the extra bedroom upstairs in our house. We had quests from Pennsylvania coming to visit recently so I was in the room making sure that everything was ready for guests. As I completed my assigned tasks, I was drawn to many of the items in the room which brought back a flood of memories.

We call the upstairs bedroom the "Fraley Room" because it is full of antiques and keepsakes from my wife's side of the family. The room is more like a room you would see in a museum than a guest room. As you enter the room, the first thing you will see is an ornate full-sized bed that was in my wife's bedroom when she was growing up. The bedroom set consists of the bed, a table, a large dresser, and a small dresser. The dressers and the table have granite tops that provide a touch of elegance. At the end of the bed is an old floor model Singer Sewing Machine. It hasn't been used in years, but my wife tells me that her mother sewed on it for many years.

The floor and the walls are also covered with memories. The pictures on the wall tell some interesting stories. There is a photo of a young lady who was my wife's great grandmother, a full-blooded Cherokee Indian. There is a sepia toned photo of her dad, his three brothers, and his mother that appears to be taken somewhere on a farm. In the picture, her dad is holding some apples; one brother is holding a small pig in his arms; another brother has his arms around a cow's neck; and the other brother is shown with a dog standing upright with its paws on his arms. I can't tell what the mother was holding, but I suspect she was holding in her laughter at the hilarity of the scene. A discussion of the room would not be complete without mentioning a few of the knick-knacks lying around. Her dad loved to smoke a pipe and we have one from his collection along with an empty can of Prince Albert pipe tobacco. Right beside the pipe is one of the many ornate belt buckles that he possessed. This particular belt buckle commemorates his days as a bus driver and owner of Clinchfield Coach Lines. Her dad was a wonderful storyteller and we heard many stories about his bus line. I only wish I remembered them well enough to share those stories with you.

There are rare treasures in the "Fraley Room," but there is no monetary value to speak of. The value lies in the memories that we are able to recall as we remember our loved ones. "By wisdom a house is built, and through understanding it is established; through knowledge its rooms are filled with rare and beautiful treasures." (Proverbs 23: 3-4)

See you tomorrow, God willing!

July 28   The Marriage Certificate

On one of the walls of the "Fraley Room" is a recessed set of shelves that house some of the pictures that I mentioned in yesterday's story. In addition to pictures on those shelves, there are a few other items. The most precious is a small wooden chest about eight inches long, five inches wide, and four inches deep. In that chest is a collection of memories that my wife's mom saved over the years. In the box are letters that she received from her husband-to-be when he was working in Norton. My wife's dad's social security card was in the box, and there are many greeting cards from various anniversaries and birthdays. There are two war ration books from World War II, one was her mom's and one was her grandmother's. Also included in the box is the original copy of their "Marriage Certificate" dated May 13th, 1943.

Much of the shelf space is covered with small tea cups and saucers that my mother collected over the years. The tea cups were brought to Mother from all over the place. She collected them during her own travels and whenever, any of the kids would travel to some out-of-the way location we would bring her back a special tea cup. When we were in Europe we brought her cups from Germany, Holland, France, Belgium and England. Although the names on the cups were not familiar to me, I found out later that brands such as Waterford, Limoges, Tirschenreuth, and Royal Worcester are quite well known among serious collectors of fine china. I also found out that until the 1700's virtually all porcelain in the world came from the Far East. It was not until the mid-1700's that Europeans developed the skills to make fine porcelain.

In the corner of the room sits one more blast from the past. On a mannequin, my wife's wedding dress is displayed. Although it has slightly faded over the years, it is still as beautiful as the day she wore it. And the bride who wore it is still as beautiful in my eyes as the day we were married.

As I finished this story, I realized that I had begun with a mention of my wife's parents' wedding certificate and ended with the description of my wife's wedding gown. It is not a coincidence. To God, marriage is sacred and He wanted me and you to be reminded of that fact. "But at the beginning of creation God made them male and female. For this reason a man will leave his father and mother and be united to his wife, and the two will become one flesh. So they are no longer two, but one. Therefore what God has joined together, let man not separate." (Mark 10:6-9)

Tomorrow, I have one more little story to tell you about items in the room of memories.

See you tomorrow, God willing!

July 29 — Mirror, Mirror on the Wall

Would you believe there is one more story in the "Fraley Room?" There was a hat rack/mirror that hung in the entrance hall at my wife's family's house. It was always filled with a number of hats. That hat rack now hangs on the wall of the "Fraley Room."

The first hat on the rack is my father-in-law's bus driver hat. On the hat is the medallion of Clinchfield Coach Lines for driver number seven. The only story I remember about the bus line was one that was told at the annual Lion's Club Minstrel. It seems that a woman gave birth to a bouncing new baby on one of the bus routes from St. Paul to Dante, a distance of eight miles. When the woman was asked why she got on the bus in her state of pregnancy she replied: "I wasn't pregnant when I got on the bus." The bus might have been slow, but it wasn't that slow.

The second hat also belonged to my wife's dad and it was one of his dress hats. He never went anywhere without a hat. At one time I thought he wore the hat to protect his balding head, but now I realize it was just part of being fully dressed as becoming a man of his stature.

Hats three and four belonged to my mother-in-law and they represented different parts of her life. The first hat was one of her church hats. It had the appearance of leopard skin and it was of the old pill box design. It looked good on her and it was deemed to be necessary whenever she went to church. The second hat was the straw bonnet she wore to the beach. Unlike much of our family, she was not inclined to get sunburned on her face or anywhere else for that matter. So, whenever she went to the beach with us, she covered herself well.

There is one other hat on the rack that belongs to me and it has been part of the family for years. It is my reindeer hat that comes out every Christmas. When our grandsons were small, it was just as much a part of the Christmas decorations as a Christmas tree.

Stories from the "Fraley Room" bring back fond memories of our loved ones who have gone to be with the Lord. The mirror on the hat rack is like a window that allows us to see images of the past. Unfortunately, we cannot see the future. We can only imagine.

"Now we see but a poor reflection as in a mirror; then we shall see face to face. Now I know in part; then I shall know fully, even as I am fully known." (1 Corinthians 13:12) Heaven is real and one day we will see clearly and be seen once again by those who have gone before us.

See you tomorrow, God willing!

July 30   Piano Man – Not Me

I have a confession to make. All of my life I have wished that I could play the piano, but I never did anything about it and now I am content to admire those who can play. I suppose it was natural that I would have a desire to play; my sister took piano lessons for years so she knew how to play. Mother loved to play, although I don't know if she ever had a lesson in her life. After we had all grown up, Mother bought herself a small organ/piano and she would sit and teach herself to play music for herself and her cats and dogs.

When my wife's grandmother died, we inherited her piano and my wife started our daughter on piano lessons. She took lessons in Cincinnati and when we moved to Allentown, she continued to take lessons. It wasn't her favorite pastime, but she reluctantly took lessons and practiced to keep peace in the family. My wife loves to tell stories about our daughter's daily practices – to say she watched the clock would be a drastic understatement. Once she got into high school, the piano lessons were a thing of the past. I guess it just never did take.

Once she got married and our son-in-law came into the picture, our piano sang as it never sang before. Despite the fact that he never had a lesson in his life, he can make the piano sing. He plays by ear and it is amazing the sound that he could coax from our piano. No one enjoyed his piano playing more than my wife's mother. When she was at our house and he came to visit, it was a real treat for her to hear him play.

My wife's grandmother's piano stayed in the family from about 1973 until we moved to North Carolina in 2001. We were going to sell it until a friend of ours mentioned that she would be interested in buying it from us. Before my wife knew what was happening, God spoke through her and gave the piano to her friend as a response to the question–how much do you want for it?

At this point in my life, I am content to listen to those who can play the piano, key board or organ. We are blessed at our church to have many people who use these instruments to help us praise God. In the very last verse of the Minor Prophet Habakkuk we see these words – "The Sovereign Lord is my strength; he makes my feet like the feet of a deer, he enables me to go on the heights. For the director of music. On my stringed instruments." When I am praising God along with the stringed instruments that is exactly how I feel. I hope you feel the same way.

See you tomorrow, God willing!

July 31 — Uncle Tommy–Not

For the second time in a couple of months, I have received feedback from one of the letters that has enriched the original story. This particular feedback is about Thomas E. Fraley – no, not the Thomas E. Fraley that is my wife's brother, but the Thomas E. Fraley that was my wife's grandfather. After reading about the picture of my wife's dad dressed as a girl and displaying long hair with curls, my wife's brother may have shed some light on the picture. Here was his response; "I think the picture of dad in girl's clothes was a picture that his mom had sent to her husband Thomas E. Fraley saying "I need help raising these boys, as boys not as girls." At that time, Thomas was working for a steel mill in Ohio and would come back to Virginia to visit with her and the boys. Thomas E. Fraley later went to the Panama Canal and died there of malaria."

After his Dad died, as the oldest son, my wife's dad was forced to quit school at the age of twelve and go to work to help support the family. His first job was a shooter's helper in the coal mines. It was a tough job for a small boy, but he stuck with it to provide the needed income for the family. Finally, he saved enough money to buy a car and that kick-started his entire future career. He used his car as a taxi service. He would drive kids to college or take people on short trips wherever they needed to go. After the taxi service, he got a job driving a meat delivery truck. Staying in the transportation business, he was soon selling cars during the Great Depression. When his supervisor cheated him out of a sale and commensurate commission, he moved on. It wasn't too long before he was driving buses between Southwest Virginia and Eastern Kentucky. The rest of his career as an owner of Clinchfield Coach Lines is well documented.

During those early years, he learned a valuable lesson – he learned that people can be pretty unkind and ornery, but you still needed to be nice to them. He once told my wife's brother that "you don't have to like people to be nice to them." Funny thing, the Bible says almost the exact words. Jesus spoke these words in the Gospel of Matthew: "You have heard that it was said, 'Love your neighbor and hate your enemy.' But I tell you: Love your enemies and pray for those who persecute you, that you may be sons of your Father in heaven." (Matthew 5:43-45a) Sometimes that advice is hard to do, but if we are to be Holy as He is Holy that is just what we are called to do. If you have people in your life who is bugging you, pray for them right now.

See you tomorrow, God willing!

August

August 1 — Navigator

A few weeks ago, we made a trip to South Carolina to visit my son and his family. We didn't need directions on how to get there, we simply needed a street address to enter into our Garmin Navigation System and the lady who resides inside that little box would tell us how to get there. We followed her instructions all the way and ended up at the campground where they are living while he is on this assignment.

It's a shame that the new generations will grow up and not get lost. They will never experience the bravado of a male driver refusing to stop and ask directions no matter how badly he is lost. Technology has yet again removed a source of life's experiences from us.

When we moved to Pennsylvania in 1977, our son was only six years old, yet he had a remarkable sense of direction. During the first summer in our new home, he went with the family of one of his friends to a dairy that sold many flavors of homemade ice cream. When he got home he raved about the ice cream and the selection of flavors. We couldn't wait to try it for ourselves. He told us where the place was, but it was so far out in the country that we were unable to find it. On the following weekend, we took our son along to show us the way. While he had been there only one time, he navigated us through turn after turn of country roads until we arrived at the dairy. He was right about the ice cream; it was delicious. Hoffman's Diary is still the only place I have ever seen where milk is sold in bags rather than bottles. We made our way back to that spot many times during our years in Pennsylvania and we finally learned how to get there without him in the car.

In the Book of Jude, there are some wonderful verses that talk about lost souls. "They are godless men, who change the grace of our God into a license for immorality and deny Jesus Christ our only Sovereign and Lord… They are wild waves of the sea, foaming up their shame; wandering stars, for whom blackest darkness has been reserved forever." (Jude 1:3, 13) Wandering stars! Lost forever in the blackest darkness. Imagine what it would be like just driving around for eternity with no one to show you the way. All of us have access to the best map that will ever be published – The Bible. When you feel lost, check it out. It will help you find your way.

See you tomorrow, God willing!

August 2   Visiting the High Places

One of my favorite movies of all time is "The Sound of Music" which starred Julie Andrews and Christopher Plummer. For those of you who are too young to remember this movie, it was about a musical family trapped inside Nazi Germany who escaped through the Alps by conveniently disappearing after one of their performances. The music in the movie was unforgettable and so was the scenery from atop the Alps.

Can you imagine my excitement in the summer of 1965 when I stood on a glacier atop one of those Alpine mountains and saw the same scenery with my very own eyes? It was a moment I will never forget. I happened to be in Germany that summer with some fellow students from the University of Virginia. UVA paid my way over and back and got me a job for the summer working at a resort on the island of Wangerooge, which sits on the North Sea on the northern border of Germany. While our group scattered for the summer to different jobs, we reunited later and traveled across Western Europe. One of the stops we made was Innsbruck, Austria, which is where I saw the majesty of the Alps.

In ancient times, it was common for people to set up their places of worship on the "high places." It was there that they sensed that they were closer to their gods. The Bible talks about this phenomenon in many places. For example, God warned the Israelites what He would do if they worshipped false gods. Leviticus 26:30 says, "I will destroy your high places, cut down your incense altars and pile your dead bodies on the lifeless forms of your idols, and I will abhor you."

Conversely, God told the Israelites where He could be found. "Now Moses was tending the flock of … and he led the flock to the far side of the desert and came to Horeb, the mountain of God." (Exodus 3:1). It was on Mount Horeb that God appeared to Moses in the burning bush and it was there where Moses received the Ten Commandments. The prophet Malachi reminded the Hebrew nation many years later, "Remember the law of my servant Moses, the decrees and laws I gave him at Horeb for all Israel." (Malachi 4:4)

It is wonderful to stand atop a high mountain to see God's beauty all around us. While I have never been at the rim of the Grand Canyon or the top of Mt. Everest, I have seen pictures and the scenery is breathtaking. Lucky for us, we don't have to go to the Grand Canyon, Mt. Everest or Mount Horeb to find God. He lives in us in that empty spot in our heart that only He can fill.

See you tomorrow, God willing!

August 3 — Kids Say the Darndest Things

Did you ever notice that kids have no tact? They say exactly what is on their mind, and it doesn't matter whether the words that come from their mouths are positive or negative. I bring this up because I got off the scale the other day and my weight is a few pounds over what I would like for it to be. When our oldest grandson was about five years old, he told me exactly what the scale would have told me if it could talk – "Bopbo, your stomach is as big as Santa Claus." At that time, he was right. The words stung, but how could I do anything but laugh. In fact, everyone around the dinner table found the comment quite funny.

Several Christmases later, it was my other grandson's turn to add his funny statement. Their great grandmother had given our grandsons $50 each to spend on Christmas presents when we went into New York City to see the Radio City Music Hall Christmas Show. As part of the trip, we went shopping at the world famous toy store, FAO Schwarz, where the boys wanted to spend their money. The youngest found what he wanted, a GI Joe Jeep, but since it was $90, he was not allowed to purchase that item. Little did he know that on Christmas Day he would find out that we had already purchased that item as one of our gifts for him. When he opened the gift on Christmas morning, the first excited words out of his mouth were "it's the ninety dollar one!" He was really impressed.

To complete the round of grandchildren, I have an equally embarrassing comment from our granddaughter. She has a tiny stuffed rabbit that she loves to carry with her. I asked her if the rabbit had a name. Since she didn't give me a name, I suggested Hare-y as a clever name. She liked the name and a little while later she told me the full name of the rabbit – Hare-y Butt Cheek. We were rolling on the floor with laughter. I'm sure somewhere along the line, someone had inadvertently exposed his or her butt cheeks and our son had taught her that particular expression. No matter where it came from, it gave us a good laugh.

Jesus knew all about little children and He never wanted to hinder what they might say. "'Do you hear what these children are saying?' they asked him. 'Yes,' replied Jesus, 'have you never read, from the lips of children and infants you have ordained praise?'" (Matthew 21:16) When they are little, we get the good with the bad. Whatever their little minds think, their mouths will let if flow forth. Sometimes it is funny and loveable, while other times it can be embarrassing. I wouldn't have it any other way.

See you tomorrow, God willing!

August 4   Summer Vacation

From the summer of 1968 until 1976, our entire clan vacationed in Myrtle Beach, South Carolina. It was an annual event that coincided with miner's vacation, the first two weeks in July. We drove from Cincinnati to St. Paul after work on a Friday and caravanned with Mother and Dad that same night, generally arriving in Myrtle Beach around sunrise. When my brother lived in Johnson City, Tennessee, he was part of the caravan.

In the first couple of years, we stayed at the Buccaneer Motel in South Myrtle Beach. It was a cozy, two-story motel that had seen better days. However, it fit our needs very well so we came back more than once. It was at that location that our daughter gave my dad his real name, Zappy. None of us have any idea where she came up with the name, it just blurted out one evening when Dad was asking her his name. She responded, "No anybody, just Zappy." The name stuck and as long as I can remember, that is what our children called my Dad.

It wasn't too many summers later that we moved up to the *Myrtle Beach Travel Lodge*. It was a newer motel with swimming pools on both sides of Ocean Boulevard. One of the pools had slides for the kids so we spent more time at that pool than the other. One of the nicest features of the Travel Lodge was their children's program. Children under a certain age, perhaps ten years old, could spend the morning participating in supervised activities managed by the staff at the motel. The club was called the "Sandy Sea Turtle Club," and it was well organized and well promoted as an attraction for families with small children. Our daughter really enjoyed the activities and to our dismay when we received a promotional postcard the next year from the Travel Lodge, there was our daughter, the central character on their post card. She was famous.

Our family times at Myrtle Beach were filled with time on the beach, late night small change poker games, and trips to the amusement park. After the rides, it was off to Painter's for some homemade ice cream. It was our policy to allow the big winner from the previous evening's poker game to purchase the ice cream for the kids the following day. It never failed; if you won at poker, you always spent more than you won on ice cream the next day. Of course, winning is not always about money. "Let love and faithfulness never leave you; bind them around your neck, write them on the tablet of your heart. Then you will win favor and a good name in the sight of God and man." (Proverbs 3:3-4) Winning favor and a good name in the sight of God sounds like a much better result to me.

See you tomorrow, God willing!

August 5 — Left Behind

July and August are the prime months for family vacations for most families in the United States. Yesterday I wrote about the family vacations that we took for nearly ten years in Myrtle Beach, South Carolina. Today I have another family vacation story to tell you. There is only one problem with the story – I don't know where the family went; I don't know if they had any fun; and, I don't know if they went with any other extended family members. Now that I have told you what I don't know, I well tell you what I do know – I was left behind!

I was six or seven years old at the time and Mother and Dad packed up the car with my siblings and me for parts unknown. Our first stop was West Frankfurt, a town about ten miles away from our home. The stop was to drop me off at my aunt and uncle's house to spend the week while the rest of the family went off without me. I was surprised and crushed.

Once I got over the shock of being left behind, I made the best of the situation. After all, my aunt and uncle were always wonderful to me, and their daughter was only a year younger than I was. We got along very well and we had a great time playing all kinds of games.

Every now and then I ponder why I was left behind. I should have asked mother while she was still alive. I suppose I could ask my siblings, but I'm not sure they will remember or know the real reason. I thought about writing a book with the title "Left Behind", but I found out the title was already taken. The topic of that book is far more important. It's about the rapture that is described in 1st Thessalonians. "For the Lord himself will come down from heaven, with a loud command, with the voice of the archangel and with the trumpet call of God, and the dead in Christ will rise first. After that, we who are still alive and are left will be caught up together with them in the clouds to meet the Lord in the air. And so we will be with the Lord forever." (1 Thessalonians 4:16-17) I don't want to be "left behind' when that day comes. How about you?

See you tomorrow, God willing!

August 6 — South Pacific

For as long as I can remember, music has been a part of my life. While I do not have any particular skills, I can carry a tune and I love to sing. Unfortunately, my first entry into organized music was for all of the wrong reasons. The year was 1963 and I had just begun my senior year in high school. As fate would have it, our high school got a new music teacher and choir director that year and she just happened to be about twenty-three years old and the reigning Miss Southwest Virginia. When the call went out for some male voices to join the St. Paul Chorus, several of my friends and me heard the call. The fact that each of us enjoyed singing simply added to the overall pleasure.

Miss Jessee's objective was to have us perform the music to South Pacific for the community. I would love to tell you that we worked hard at learning the music, but to tell you the truth, we worked harder at goofing off. We were obnoxious to everyone else in the chorus and downright rude to an aspiring young teacher. Nevertheless, in between goofing off, we managed to learn the music and the show moved on. For a reason I will never understand, I had a lead vocal role in the song "There is Nothing Like a Dame." Once the community performance was over, Miss Jessee had had enough. She got tired of our impudence and misbehavior and gave us poor marks for our lack of effort. She put up with more than she deserved.

Here is what I should have learned from that overall experience.

1. There is no excuse for bad behavior.
2. When you sing, you should not be singing for your own glory, but for the one who gave you the voice to sing.
3. There is nothing like a dame. I did learn that part.
4. Never be bigger than the team.

The psalmist knew why we were given voices to sing and instruments to play. "Sing joyfully to the LORD, you righteous; it is fitting for the upright to praise him. Praise the Lord with the harp; make music to him on the ten-stringed lyre. Sing to him a new song; play skillfully, and shout for joy." (Psalms 33:1-3) It would be a few years later that I would experience my next foray into music. I'll tell you about it tomorrow.

See you tomorrow, God willing!

August 7 — Scoffers?

After my experience in the high school chorus my senior year in high school, it would be over twenty years before I became involved with any organized music. We had been members of our church for well over ten years when the Spirit moved me to join the choir. It was a very small choir, only eight members on a typical Sunday, and most of the members were over sixty. Since I am in that category today, I now realize how young the choir members were. It was not the most talented group of singers, but we had a lot of fun and we effectively led the congregation in singing.

Our choir director and organist was a talented musician, but her life was not filled with joy and her choice of music and the speed at which she played reflected her attitude. Perhaps that is why God had me join the choir. The bad behavior that I demonstrated in the high school chorus was still there, but slightly refined. Two of the other men in the choir joined me in mischief and there was never a choir practice that was dull. We laughed a lot and the poor organist and choir director could not help but smile at our behavior. In a loving way, we were given the title of scoffers. The dictionary defines the word as follows–to mock at or treat with derision or to show or express derision or scorn. That might have been a little severe, but the name stuck. In the Book of Jude, God warns His followers about scoffers. "In the last times there will be scoffers who will follow their own ungodly desires." (Jude 1:18).

During the ten or so years that I was in the choir, there was very little turnover so I got to know the other choir members very well. Several of them became good friends and brothers and sisters in Christ. Here is what my friends taught me. "Dear friend, do not imitate what is evil but what is good. Anyone who does what is good is from God. Anyone who does what is evil has not seen God." (3 John 1:11). Good friends are a real treasure.

Yesterday, I talked about some things I should have learned while in the high school chorus. Twenty years later I had made some progress, but being a "scoffer" meant that I still needed work on my behavior. While my friends helped me, I still had a way to go. I did learn not to sing for my own glory. However, I was now singing to the congregation so I was still not there. Thankfully, I had learned about teamwork so I had made progress.

Fortunately, my musical journey still had a long way to go.

See you tomorrow, God willing!

August 8   Bill and the Multicolored Sweaters

When we moved to North Carolina in 2001, I was thrilled to sing in the choir at our new church. It inspired me and put me around a bunch of other people who really love Jesus. Because I am short, I was placed in the front row of the choir and the bass section was in the center so I was visible to the whole congregation. During my first Christmas, I wore several sweaters that my wife had bought me over the years; she bought me another beautiful multicolored sweater after Christmas that I wore just after the first of the year. To make a long story short, many people came up to me and commented that they had seen me in the choir and they loved my array of sweaters. It sure fed my pride.

The very next Sunday I dug deep into my reservoir of sweaters to find another bright one that would draw yet more attention to me. Just as I was getting ready to go out the door for church clothed in my beautiful multicolored sweater, God tapped me on the shoulder and questioned my motives. Why did I need to be noticed? What was my purpose of being in the choir? Was I in the choir to praise Him or draw attention to myself? I turned around, took off the bright sweater, and replaced it with a plain dark grey sweater that would keep me warm and yet would draw no attention to me.

As I looked back over the days leading up to my conflict around pride, I should have seen the handwriting on the wall (Suddenly the fingers of a human hand appeared and wrote on the plaster of the wall...Daniel 5:5). Just three days earlier my wife and I had attended a midweek service at another church to hear a friend of ours preach. Two scripture verses that he used that night caught my attention. In Isaiah 6:5, the prophet comes face-to-face with God, ""Woe to me!" I cried. "I am ruined! For I am a man of unclean lips, and I live among a people of unclean lips, and my eyes have seen the King, the Lord Almighty." It was a humbling experience. The second verse was from 2nd Chronicles 26:16 and it said, "But after Uzziah became powerful, his pride led to his downfall." When we let pride lead our lives, we too soon forget the One who really leads our lives.

In my journal where I captured the details of this experience, I had written a prayer that I want to share with you.

Lord, in my human frailty, help me to look in the mirror and see you, not me. Help me to remember that everything I have comes from you. How can I be prideful, I am nothing without you!

My musical walk is not over; I am still learning.

See you tomorrow, God willing!

August 9 — Total Praise

After spending thirty-five years worshipping in the Episcopal Church, we had developed a pattern of worship that was reserved at best. Our first experience in a church that did not seem to be quite so reserved was, oddly enough, a non-denominational church in Palmas, Puerto Rica. While on vacation with some friends, we attended two services in a casino that had been damaged when one of the hurricanes hit the island. The music was lively and, you guessed it, the words were displayed on a screen. It seemed very odd to us, but it would begin an evolution in our worship style that has been morphing for over ten years.

When we returned home to Pennsylvania, those same friends invited us to attend their church, which was about thirty miles from where we lived. That church was another non-denominational church with a similar worship style as we had experienced in Puerto Rico. However, unlike the small, satellite church in PR, this one was huge. The style of worship was so different that I felt like I was being entertained rather than going to church. How wrong I was!

When we moved to North Carolina, we couldn't wait to attend the church that my daughter and her family had chosen. It had a wonderful style of music and a grand choir. We have now been attending that church for ten years and I can honestly say that our personal style of worship continues to evolve. I have recently been participating in a twelve-week learning experience with all members of our Creative Arts Team, which is essentially the choir, musicians, and sound technicians. Here is just one nugget I want to share with you. Praise is defined as an expression of approval or admiration, an expression of deepest respect or gratitude as an act of worship. The key is "an expression." You cannot just praise in your heart, there must be an external expression. Continuing this line of thought, an expression is defined as the process of making known, conveying, or putting into words, one's thoughts, feelings, emotions or opinions. In other words, some one must see your feelings before an expression of praise takes place.

Let me tell you how important external praise is to our worship experience. "From the lips of children and infants you have ordained praise because of your enemies, to silence the foe and the avenger." (Psalms 8:2) Look at those words carefully – our praise silences Satan. Praise causes panic and confusion in Satan's ranks. That's reason enough for me. Check out 2 Chronicles 20:1-30 for a story that demonstrates this principle in great detail. It will only take you a few minutes and it is well worth your investment in time.

See you tomorrow, God willing!

August 10   The Washtub

There is an old black and white photo in one of our picture albums that shows my mother giving me a bath in a washtub outside an old farmhouse. My brother is in the foreground and he appears to be five or six years old at the time. That would make me two or three years old. Until a couple of weeks ago, I did not know the significance of the photo, but after talking to my sister, I now understand where the picture was taken and why I was being bathed outside.

When I was born in 1946 in Logan, West Virginia, my dad had a very good job with a mining company and my sister told me that we lived in a very nice house with a maid and a cook. She also told me she had very pretty clothes and life was good. However, a short time later in Southern Illinois, my grandfather died and my dad returned to Illinois because he always wanted to be a farmer. Together with his younger brother, dad purchased the farm from the other nine brothers and sisters and went into farming. According to my uncle, their first investment was a two hundred dollar white-faced breeding bull–a sizeable amount to pay in 1949. As dad's luck would have it, the homesick bull drowned in a flooded pond trying to get back to its original home.

The picture mentioned in the first paragraph was taken on that farm and there was no running water or indoor plumbing in the house. If the weather was good, as it apparently was on the day in question, it made sense to bath outdoors. In my sister's eight-year old mind, we had moved from the penthouse to the outhouse.

Although I have no memories of that homestead, I do remember that we lived in Illinois until 1955 when we moved to Virginia and my dad once again worked in the mines. I won't find out the whole story of dad's first venture into farming until I see him again in heaven.

The Bible tells us a lot about our heavenly Father, things we will not know or understand if we don't spend time in His Word. In Deuteronomy, for example, we are told about the connection between obedience to our Father and blessings. "See, I am setting before you today a blessing and a curse— the blessing if you obey the commands of the Lord your God that I am giving you today; the curse if you disobey the commands of the Lord your God and turn from the way that I command you today by following other gods, which you have not known." (Deuteronomy 11:26-28) Every morning as I spend quiet time with God, I learn something about my Father. He is truly amazing.

See you tomorrow, God willing!

August 11 — Custom Jewelry

For several years when we lived in Pennsylvania, my wife worked in a jewelry store. The store had been previously owned by our next door neighbor, but when he moved to Florida, he sold the store to one of his previous employees. The young lady who bought the store was a talented designer of custom jewelry and her husband helped run the business side of things. For several reasons, this job was a good fit for everyone. First, because my wife was more mature and a Christian, she added a sense of stability for the business. Second, since our children were grown and out of the house, it gave my wife a nice diversion while allowing her to make a little spending money. And, last but not least, it gave her a chance to purchase some really neat custom jewelry.

While I don't know too much about how to make custom rings, necklaces, bracelets, and ear rings, I am going to tell you a little bit about the process. Obviously, the first step is the sketching of the item to be made. Once the sketch is approved, a wax mold is carved in which the molten metal is poured to form the ring, ear ring, etc. Where, you might ask, does the metal come from? A very good question. In many cases, a customer might bring to the store an old piece of gold or silver jewelry that could be used to make the new piece. That metal is melted and purified to remove dirt and grime as well as any impurities that may have been in the initial metal. Once the dross is removed, the melted metal is poured into the mold, cooled, and then polished. If the item contains any stones, these are set in the molded product just prior to completion. Finally, just before the item is given to the customer, it is tested for strength. That is my layman's description of how custom jewelry is made.

For several decades the scientific community has known that each person has a unique DNA. That fact is simply proof of what we as Christians have known all along – each of us are custom jewelry in God's eyes. And, just like custom jewelry, we need to have our impurities removed before God can use us properly. "Remove the dross from the silver, and out comes material for the silversmith; (Proverbs 25:4) First, God refines us through the process of life. Our trials and tribulations help prepare us and strengthen us. "The crucible for silver and the furnace for gold, but the Lord tests the heart. (Proverbs 17:3) Before completion, God tests our heart. That is where our strength resides. Matthew 12:34b says it best, "For out of the overflow of the heart the mouth speaks."

Let me assure you, God doesn't make any costume jewelry, only custom jewelry. He doesn't make any junk.

See you tomorrow, God willing!

August 12 — An Unbirthday Party

Before I retired, our normal vacation month at Emerald Isle was August. When my wife's mother was with us, the timing was such that we could help her celebrate her birthday at the beach. If I recall correctly the date was August 12th. Since my mother had a permanent site for her camper at the beach, she was always there as well to wish my wife's mother a "Happy Birthday." However, it was not unusual for mother to tell us that she wished her birthday wasn't in January when there was no one around to help her celebrate.

After hearing this comment for a couple of years, my wife came up with a brilliant idea; we would have a "Happy Unbirthday Party" for my mother in August complete with cake, candles, presents, and, most importantly, lots of people. When the next year rolled around, we were ready. It so happened that the year we had mother's party, my wife's was staying with her son in Virginia so there was no conflict with her regular party.

We did not tell mother that a party was coming. We simply invited her for dinner and waited to see her reaction when she realized we were celebrating her birthday in August instead of January. To no one's surprise, she was touched. After she blew out the candles on her unbirthday cake, she was allowed to open her presents, but the best present of all wasn't wrapped in a box. It was the opportunity to share her birthday with so many friends and family members.

As Christians, there is another birthday of our own that we should celebrate every day; I suppose in some respects we could call it our unbirthday. It is the day we are born again; the day we say good-bye to our past life and are born again in the Spirit. For many Christians, it is a hard concept to get their hands around. If you are in that category, don't despair. Even Nicodemus, one of the most learned Pharisees of Jesus' day was dismayed. "How can a man be born when he is old?" Nicodemus asked. "Surely he cannot enter a second time into his mother's womb to be born!" Jesus answered, "I tell you the truth, no one can enter the kingdom of God unless he is born of water and the Spirit. Flesh gives birth to flesh, but the Spirit gives birth to spirit." (John 3:4-6)

Celebrate the day you were born of water and the Spirit. It's okay if you want to call it your unbirthday.

See you tomorrow, God willing!

August 13 — Gentle Giants

Owning a Great Dane can be quite an experience. Josh was a male harlequin who was as gentle as he was big. As with most Great Danes, they are just overgrown puppies. They love to lean against you and their enormous size will pin you against a wall if you aren't careful. Great Danes also love to sit on your lap; they simply plop their hind quarters on your lap with their two front legs planted firmly on the ground. You have to see it to appreciate the sight.

It was bad enough that we had one Great Dane as a house dog; we had to have two. Here is how it happened. We got a telephone call from a friend of ours who ran a dog kennel. He was calling to tell her that they had just received a female Great Dane from the Great Dane Rescue League and she was brindle colored dog. Since we already had a harlequin, black and white, it made since to add a brindle, black and brown to our household. We went to the kennel to take a look and our son talked us into bringing her home. We were now the owners of two Great Danes, both of whom lived entirely inside. What were we thinking?

Like two kids, the personalities of the two dogs were as different as day and night. Josh was low-key and well behaved under all circumstances while Brindle was high strung. They were quite a pair. Just before Josh died after Christmas in 1994, my wife commissioned a painting of the two dogs for me as a Christmas present. Long after both dogs have been gone, the picture hangs in our family as a reminder of the two gentle giants who turned out to be the last dogs we would ever own.

Both of our Great Danes had been rescued. Both lived to a ripe old age for Great Danes and both enjoyed their adopted family. One of the most interesting rescue stories in the Bible involved Shadrach, Meshach, and Abednego. When confronted by Nebuchadnezzar for failing to bow down and worship him, these three faced the perils of the fiery furnace. However, they responded with great faith: "If we are thrown into the blazing furnace, the God we serve is able to save us from it, and he will rescue us from your hand, O king. But even if he does not, we want you to know, O king, that we will not serve your gods or worship the image of gold you have set up." (Daniel 3:17-18) Perhaps you recall what happened. They were thrown into the furnace and not a hair on their heads was singed. God had indeed rescued them. As I look back on my own life, I can recall many times that He has rescued me. He loves me just like He did the Hebrew children.

See you tomorrow, God willing!

August 14 — The Pool Hall

If I say pool, what image comes to your mind? For many of us in the family, we picture a pool table in the basement of my father-in-law's house. It was there that we spent many an hour shooting pool and listening to stories. According to my wife, her dad obtained the regulation pool table from the bus depot in Dante when it ceased operation. Although it was in a slightly crowded spot, we learned to contort our bodies when an adjoining storage table or a support beam happened to block the natural path of the pool cue. Her dad had also installed a traditional pool table light over the table so the lighting was very even and conducive to great play. The way I shot, it might as well have been dark.

Frankly, I was never a very good pool player. Both her father and brother were better than I was, but it didn't matter. Our favorite time to play pool was just after a big meal. Here was our logic. We needed to get out of the ladies way while they cleaned the kitchen. I'm sure the ladies saw through our ploy, but since her dad was with us, we were free to go. He was king of the castle.

The original pool table that was in his basement will make its way to Lebanon before too long. When it does, it will sit proudly in my brother-in-law's family room and new generations will roll balls across the table and into the fine leather pockets. Or perhaps when they are very small they will simply get a kick out of just smashing balls together. No matter what they do, my wife's dad will be looking down on them with that wry smile only he could project.

Oddly enough, when you say the word pool, not everyone thinks about billiards. Some people think about small bodies of water, i.e. the Pool of Bethesda. In the Gospel of John, Jesus heals an invalid who had been lying on his mat at the pool for thirty-eight years waiting for someone to carry him into the pool when the water stirred. When Jesus saw the man lying there, He asked him a very odd question–"Do you want to get well?" (John 5:6b) As I pondered that question, I wondered – why would he ask him that question? Of course he wanted to get well, he had been waiting thirty-eight years. How many of us would rather stay in our pity pot than make the bold moves we need to take in order to free ourselves from whatever burden is haunting us? Jesus knows, that is why He asks us the question – do we want to get well? If we do, He is the answer. Do you want to get well?

See you tomorrow, God willing!

August 15 — Sleeping with Bears

By 1998, my daughter's family had moved to their current residence in Greenville. It had plenty of space for us when we came to visit. There was a guest bedroom that provided privacy and allowed us to get up in the morning at the hour of our choosing without worrying about disturbing anyone else in the house. When we came to visit after Christmas that year we had planned to stay in the guest room. We just didn't follow that plan.

When we arrived, my grandsons wanted to sleep with me. How could I refuse? Instead of sleeping in the upstairs guest room, we pulled out the sleeper sofa in the family room and prepared to spend the night there. It is a large enough bed to handle a grown up and two young children – in theory. I have never slept with a bear cub, but I suspect if it didn't claw you to death it would have provided a better night's sleep than trying to sleep with my young grandsons.

Here are some things I learned about sleeping that night. One, it is not necessary for everyone in the bed to sleep perpendicular to the head of the bed. It is okay to sleep at any angle you so desire. Two, there are no assigned spaces for the inhabitants of the bed. It is perfectly okay to roam the entire area of the bed during the night. Three, the covers do not belong to anyone. There is only one person who cannot possess the covers – the poor sucker who sleeps in the middle of the bed. Four, if you want to get a good night's sleep, don't sleep with two cub bears. Five, if you love you grandchildren like I do, never miss the opportunity to be kicked, punched, jabbed, pushed, or hugged – it's more like sleeping with angels than bears.

Please realize that I am not making fun of my grandsons. There is a story in the Old Testament about some youths who were making fun of Elisha for being bald headed. "He turned around, looked at them and called down a curse on them in the name of the Lord. Then two bears came out of the woods and mauled forty-two of the youths." (2 Kings 2:24) If those two bears could maul forty-two of the youths, just think what two bear cubs could do to one "old" man.

My advice to all of you, get as close to your children and grandchildren as you can, even if it costs you a good night's sleep.

See you tomorrow, God willing!

August 16 — Saturday Morning Pancakes

Early in our marriage when we lived in Cincinnati, I was burning the candle at both ends. I was working at least forty hours a week and taking nearly a full schedule at night pursuing my Masters in Business Administration degree. Many nights I would get home from school as late as 10 pm and my kids would already be in the bed. I knew my schedule was full, but I also realized that my wife's schedule was full as well. Caring for two young children is tough enough with two parents, but it is even tougher when one of the parents is rarely at home.

One of the ways I could help out and show my appreciation was to make pancakes for the kids on Saturday morning. It was a nice family ritual. My wife told me that I should make the pancakes for them because my pancakes were much better than hers. I knew her ploy, but it didn't matter, the kids enjoyed my attention and I enjoyed making the pancakes.

Over the many years of our marriage, my wife has used the same line many times. Christmas cookies are a good example. "I just can't make Christmas cookies as good as you can. You cookies turn out so much better," that is what she says. I have tried the same technique on her, but it doesn't work. There is only one thing she will not let me do. She tells me to stay away from the washing machine. I just can't seem to separate the clothes properly, so everything coming out of the wash becomes the same color, particularly if I happen to wash something red.

In the book of Leviticus, God instructs the Israelites about all types of offerings to God. One of them was called a "thank offering." Looking back on the Saturday morning pancake tradition, I now realize that the pancakes were actually "thank offerings." For our children, they were my way of saying thank you for being my children and thank you for putting up with my absentee role as a father. For my wife, those pancake breakfasts were my way of saying thanks for filling in for so many hours. Letting you sleep a little longer on Saturday mornings was just one way I could say "thank you."

"'If he offers it as an expression of thankfulness, then along with this thank offering he is to offer cakes of bread made without yeast and mixed with oil, wafers made without yeast and spread with oil, and cakes of fine flour well-kneaded and mixed with oil." (Leviticus 7:12) Doesn't that sound like pancakes to you?

See you tomorrow, God willing!

August 17 — Two Marthas

As we were talking about my mother-in-law's birthday a few days ago, my wife recalled one of the years when she happened to be with us in Pennsylvania on her birthday. My wife planned a very special day for her. Early in the morning, they boarded bus in Allentown for New York City. While her mom had been with us to New York City before, my wife made sure that the birthday visit to the Big Apple would be a new experience.

When the bus arrived in New York City, they boarded another bus for a tour of The City. By the time the bus had finished its route, it had completely circled Manhattan. The tour guide, as you might expect, was well versed on the historical spots of interest to the general public. For example, he pointed out the location where John Lennon was shot and the luxury apartment where Jackie Onassis once lived. Of course, there were several stops on the route to allow the tourists to stretch their legs and see some sites up close and personal.

The lunch stop was at Southport at the southern tip of the island. From Southport, you can see the Statue of Liberty and the ferries that leave regularly for Staten Island. The Southport stop also included enough time to do a little shopping. While my wife's mom was not up to too much walking, she did enjoy seeing all that the shops in New York City had to offer.

By the time, they returned to Allentown by late afternoon, they were exhausted. However, spending the day together was a priceless experience. You see, both of them spent much of their lives attending to other people and insuring that the household was operating smoothly. For one day, nothing got in the way of spending special time together. The Bible would have called them "Marathas."

"As Jesus and his disciples were on their way, He came to a village where a woman named Martha opened her home to him. She had a sister called Mary, who sat at the Lord's feet listening to what He said. But Martha was distracted by all the preparations that had to be made. She came to him and asked, 'Lord, don't you care that my sister has left me to do the work by myself? Tell her to help me!' 'Martha, Martha,' the Lord answered, 'you are worried and upset about many things, but only one thing is needed. Mary has chosen what is better, and it will not be taken away from her.'" (Luke 10:38-42) Make sure you take the time to spend with your loved ones. Mary chose to spend time at the feet of Jesus, she chose better.

See you tomorrow, God willing!

August 18 — To A Friend

I am going to dedicate this story to a high school friend. I last saw him about fifteen years ago at the restaurant that he and his wife owned and ran. My friend was the best football player in the region in the early sixties when we played. Together with another friend, and me, we had a powerful backfield that could run with power and elusiveness. One friend went on to play college football, but neither my restaurant owner friend nor I played any more football after our high school careers were over.

Let me tell you about some of his great games. In one game against a very strong opponent, he scored five touchdowns, the shortest of which was sixty-six yards. He scored on a punt return; he scored on a pass interception; he scored on a running play; and he scored on a pass reception. By the time the game ended, our opponent had seen enough of him.

In another game against a school much larger than ours, he took a sideline pass that I threw him and went ninety-eight yards for a touchdown. At the time, it put both of us in the record books with the longest touchdown pass in the history of Virginia high school football. As a result of that play, we were able to play this much larger school to stand-off – the game ended in a twenty to twenty tie.

After high school, he went to Viet Nam. When he got back, I lost track of him for many years. At one time in the mid-eighties, he owned and ran a nursery business in Washington D.C. called the Wise Guys, referring to Wise County Virginia, our boyhood home. Throughout his life from his high school days forward, he struggled with alcohol addiction. For a while, he would get the disease in check and then it would rear its ugly head again. In the end, it was a burden he simply could not carry and he passed away a couple of years ago.

All of us carry some burden through our lives. When we find Jesus, He helps us carry that burden and life is good. If we try to carry the burden by ourselves, the weight is just too heavy. Even the Apostle Paul, had to cope with a heavy burden. "To keep me from becoming conceited because of these surpassingly great revelations, there was given me a thorn in my flesh, a messenger of Satan, to torment me. Three times I pleaded with the Lord to take it away from me. But he said to me, 'My grace is sufficient for you, for my power is made perfect in weakness.' Therefore I will boast all the more gladly about my weaknesses, so that Christ's power may rest on me." (2 Corinthians 12:7-9) If any of you are carrying a heavy burden, share it with your heavenly Father. His grace is sufficient.

See you tomorrow, God willing!

August 19   Spelunking

The Boy Scouts of America is a wonderful organization to help young men learn life skills. My favorite part of being a scout was the hikes that the troop would take on weekends. We would go out into the woods and learn about different trees; how to make camp; and how to clean up after ourselves to insure that we left nature just as we had found it. If the hike turned into an overnight stay in our tents, it was a super event. There is nothing like a group of young men with their leader spending the night in the woods and cooking our evening meal over a campfire.

On one of our weekend hikes, we were to explore a well-known cave that was close to our town. First, I remember that it was the darkest place I had ever been to in my life. If everyone turned off his flashlight, you could not see the person standing right beside you. Two, it was very damp and cool. Little did I know at the time, but as soon as you go down into the bowels of the earth a little ways, the temperature quickly becomes in the fifties. While that is not too cool, it seems very cold on a hot summer day. Three, I remember the beauty of the rock formations. The fourth thing I remember about being in a cave is that they are a little scary. Footing is slippery; you can't see where you are going, even with a flashlight; and there seem to be bats everywhere. I guess when you are eleven or twelve years old, scary is fun!

In Biblical times, caves were often a place of refuge because it was one way of getting out of the weather and into an "air conditioned" environment. When Elijah was fleeing from Jezebel, he took cover in a cave. "There he went into a cave and spent the night. And the word of the LORD came to him: "What are you doing here, Elijah?" (1 Kings 19:9). When Saul pursued David to try to take his life, David and his men also hid in a cave. When Saul "came to the sheep pens along the way; a cave was there, and Saul went in to relieve himself. David and his men were far back in the cave." (1 Samuel 24:3) It was so dark in the cave that as Saul was standing there David was able to cut off the corner of his robe without attracting any attention. Of course, the most famous cave in history is the tomb in which Jesus was laid for burial.

If you have never experienced the thrill of spelunking, I would suggest you do so at some point in your life. It has been very popular for centuries.

See you tomorrow, God willing!

August 20   Trip from Hades

Everyone who travels on a regular basis has a story like the one I am preparing to tell you. The trips are called the "trips from Hades" because only the evil one could go to all the trouble to make a routine business trip so unpleasant.

A business companion and I were on our way to Fayetteville, Arkansas. My secretary had made all the arrangements and it was a trip I had made several times before so I did not anticipate any problems. Most of the flights out of Allentown were USAir so I was not surprised that we were headed for Charlotte, NC, a major hub for that airline. My secretary had mistakenly booked our trip to Fayetteville, NC and the mistake had been caught by our sales representative in Arkansas who was going to meet our flight when we arrived. He discovered the error when the flight number that he was given did not coincide with any flights coming to the Fayetteville, Arkansas airport.

When we got off the plane in Charlotte, we were met by USAir personnel who had been alerted of our problem. Our first option was to grab our carry-on luggage and head for an American Airlines flight headed for Nashville, TN and then continuing to Fayetteville. As fate would have it, we just missed that connection. The next option was to take a USAir flight to Dallas, TX and then a connecting flight. While those flights would not get us to our hotel until after midnight, we had no other alternatives so we hopped on the Dallas flight.

The trip to Dallas was uneventful and we boarded the plane for Fayetteville when we got the bad news. The Fayetteville airport was closed because an incoming flight had gone off the runway. As we got off the plane, we were asked if we would like to fly to Tulsa and grab a rental car for the one and a half hour drive to Fayetteville. We were now grasping for straws so it was off to Tulsa. By the time we arrived in Tulsa it was after one a.m. and only one rental car company was still open and they only had one car available. We were second in line. Much to our dismay, the person in front of us could not get the car because it had to be returned to the Tulsa airport. We quickly offered the person a ride and we were able to get the car and drive to Fayetteville arriving about 3 a.m. By the way, the plane that went off the runway closing the Fayetteville airport was the Nashville connection that we missed from Charlotte.

"But the Lord is faithful, and He will strengthen and protect you from the evil one." (2 Thessalonians 3:3) The "trip from Hades" could have been much worse. God's hand was at work behind the scenes. Sometimes it is easier to see than others.

See you tomorrow, God willing!

August 21 — Climbing Higher

For two years when I was around eleven years old, we lived in a small mining town in Virginia. The house was a very small three-bedroom model that was barely large enough for our family of five, plus my Collie, Prince. The thing I remember most about the house was the basement, which was mostly dirt, but it did have a furnace room with a coal-fired heater that fed hot water to radiators throughout the house. The best thing about the house was its ready access to miles of forest.

Every day when I came home from school, Prince would greet me with wild enthusiasm because he knew his day had just begun. For the last few hours of each day, Prince and I would roam the woods looking for adventure. He was my best friend; he was Tonto and I was the Lone Ranger.

On our daily trips, we saw an abundance of wild life. It was not unusual to see deer, raccoons, possums, squirrels, many types of birds, and, of course, an occasional snake. The only time I was actually a little scared was the time we ran into a rattlesnake. Fortunately, Prince scared the snake away with no harm to us or the snake.

The most exciting part of our trips to the woods was climbing trees. My favorite "climbing tree" was at the summit of one of the highest ridges. I would climb to the very top of that tree in order to survey the land. Since Prince couldn't climb with me, he barked the entire time. I don't know whether he was trying to tell me to be careful or to come back down and play with him.

God talked about just such a tree in the book of Daniel, "The tree grew large and strong and its top touched the sky… Its leaves were beautiful, its fruit abundant…Under it the beasts of the field found shelter, and the birds of the air lived in its branches; from it every creature was fed." (Daniel 4:11-12) That tree, however, was a symbolic tree that represented Nebuchadnezzar's kingdom at the peak of his reign. Shortly after Daniel interpreted the dream about this great tree, Nebuchadnezzar's kingdom was torn from him until he realized the source of all of his blessings.

When I was eleven years old climbing trees, I didn't think much about the Creator of those trees. As I have grown older, and a little bit wiser, I am drawn to other Bible verses about trees. Psalms 92:12-15, "The righteous will flourish like a palm tree, they will grow like a cedar of Lebanon; planted in the house of the Lord, they will flourish in the courts of our God. They will still bear fruit in old age, they will stay fresh and green, proclaiming, 'The Lord is upright; he is my Rock, and there is no wickedness in him.'" That's my kind of tree.

See you tomorrow, God willing!

August 22   Let Go

Little children are often apprehensive about leaving their parents to spend time with their grandparents or other family members. Every time we go to visit our granddaughter she is reluctant to stay with us until she has had a little time to remember who we are. Even then, she is torn between staying with "Mom and Dad" or enjoying the play time she experiences with us. It is almost comical to see the difficult time she has in letting go of the parental cords to let us enjoy the pleasure of her company.

I can recall when our niece was little. When she would come to visit my wife's mom and dad when we were there, she refused to leave the protection of her mother's arms. Of course, she eventually loosened up to play with our children, but she was always a little leery of us.

There was one little one in the family who had no such fears. The year our oldest grandson started grade school, we were visiting with my daughter and we asked our other grandson, who was three at the time, if he would like to go back to Pennsylvania and stay with us for a few days. Before you could blink an eye, he was packed and ready to go. He loved to play in the woods with our grown son and he also enjoyed playing in the dirt with a large collection of Tonka trucks that were left over from our son's childhood.

There is a picture on the front of our refrigerator today that shows our youngest grandson in a blue camouflage outfit that we bought him on that visit. He and our son would wear their "camo" outfits and hide from us in the trees surrounding the house. He stayed busy the entire week and I think he simply refused to think about his parents for fear of getting homesick. On one occasion when his mom called to talk with him, he simply refused to get on the phone. He was having a great time and he didn't want homesickness to ruin it.

In many ways, we are like little children in our fear of reaching out to God for the blessings He has in store for us. Yet that is what He requires if we are to know Him. "For the kingdom of God belongs to such as these. I tell you the truth; anyone who will not receive the kingdom of God like a little child will never enter it." (Luke 18:16-17) As the old AA saying goes, "Let go, and let God."

See you tomorrow, God willing!

August 23 — Don't Believe Satan

I was flying high in 1985. My boss was sending me to Europe for six months to organize a marketing effort for our European operations that were headquartered just outside of London. During my time there, I was to visit each of our countries in Western Europe and recommend a course of action to maximize the impact of all of their marketing efforts. It was a big job, but I felt well prepared to take on the task. Because most of the work was over the summer months, my family was able to live with me before departing in mid-August so our daughter could begin her college life. With a few minor glitches, the summer was fabulous and I successfully completed my assignment.

When I returned home in the fall, more doors opened for me. The Public Affairs Department in which I worked had four sections – Advertising and Public Relations (my responsibility); Corporate, Financial and Employee Communications; State and Community Relations; and Federal Government Relations. Just after my return to work in the United States, the manager of the second section died suddenly of a heart attack at age forty-three. His areas of responsibility were assigned to me and I received a big promotion. I was soaring higher and higher.

God was truly blessing me, but I was too blind to see it. My pride was telling me how good I was; how smart I was; how hard working I was; how fine a family I had; and, the trouble was – I believed every word Satan was telling me. I should have known better, "When he lies, he speaks his native language, for he is a liar and the father of lies." (John 8:44b)

By early 1986, I was on overload and a number of things happened that brought be down from the heights I had achieved during the previous year. God was now trying to get my attention and He was successful. In a not so gentle way, He was reminding me that He was the source of all my blessings and He could take them away just as quickly as He provided them. Fortunately, I heard Him and began to give Him credit for what He deserved all along. It doesn't always happen that way. "'The pride of your heart has deceived you, you who live in the clefts of the rocks and make your home on the heights, you who say to yourself, 'Who can bring me down to the ground?' Though you soar like the eagle and make your nest among the stars, from there I will bring you down,' declares the Lord." (Obadiah 1:3-4) Though the Edomites were descendants of Isaac, they did not worship God, but instead they counted on their own invincibility to save them. It was not enough for them, and it is not enough for any of us.

See you tomorrow, God willing!

August 24   He's Hushed

My wife's granddad was nearing his ninety-fifth birthday when we went to visit him. DaDo was in relatively good health and was still living by himself at that time. Since it was around the Christmas holidays, we took him a Christmas present and sang some Christmas carols with him. Perhaps one of our children had gotten a portable tape recorder for Christmas that year; it is the only explanation I can give as to why we happened to have a tape recorder with us when we were with DaDo. Nevertheless, the tape recorder was on when we began to sing Silent Night. Right in the middle of the song, Dado stopped singing and exclaimed, "I can't sing, and he's hushed." It seems that when my son stopped singing, DaDo refused to continue. As long as he had a partner, he would continue. When his partner stopped, so did he, or so it seemed at the time.

We kept that precious recording and we listen to it on occasion. We will never forget the joy on his face when he made his famous comment. He may have become quiet and stopped singing, but he did not stop smiling. It was a Christmas treasure of major proportions.

"The LORD your God is with you, he is mighty to save. He will take great delight in you, he will quiet you with his love, he will rejoice over you with singing." (Zephaniah 3:17) It is quite amazing that this verse from the minor prophet Zephaniah would capture our episode with DaDo. He had not stopped singing because our son stopped; we had quieted him with our love. Furthermore, God had taken delight in us and rejoiced over DaDo with our singing. "My soul will be satisfied as with the richest of foods; with singing lips my mouth will praise you." (Psalm 63:5) God rests in the praises of His people and so did DaDo.

See you tomorrow, God willing!

August 25 — Earthquakes

The earthquake that occurred on Tuesday, August 23, 2011, was centered around Richmond, Virginia. According to the Associated Press, it was the most powerful earthquake to strike the East Coast in 67 years. It shook buildings and rattled nerves from South Carolina to Maine. Television news coverage showed frightened office workers spilling into the streets in New York, and parts of the White House, Capitol and Pentagon being evacuated." I am sorry to report; neither my wife nor I felt any of the tremors.

That was not the case in 1974 when we lived in Cincinnati. On June 5 of that year, a small earthquake (magnitude 3.2) hit the Cincinnati area. Not only did we feel the effects of the earthquake, we saw some effects as well. Despite the small magnitude of the quake, we were in a perfect location to see what happens when the earth shakes. Believe it or not, we were on the fifth floor of one of the major department stores in downtown Cincinnati. We happened to be in the china department looking for monogrammed glasses. When the tremor occurred, you could feel the building sway and you could see and hear the china dance and tremble. While nothing actually fell off a shelf, the sound of trembling china was a unique sound.

In the Bible, there are many references to earthquakes with respect to the end times - "the LORD Almighty will come with thunder and earthquake and great noise, with windstorm and tempest and flames of a devouring fire." (Isaiah 29:6) "Then there came flashes of lightning, rumblings, peals of thunder and a severe earthquake. No earthquake like it has ever occurred since man has been on earth, so tremendous was the quake." (Revelations 16:18) I don't mind the small earthquakes that we have experienced. However, I hope I am not around for the big one.

See you tomorrow, God willing!

August 26 — Playing in the Waves

On Friday, August 19, my wife and I drove from Greenville to Columbia, South Carolina to pick up our granddaughter who had decided that she wanted to visit us and go to the beach. We arrived in Columbia by mid-afternoon, went straight to our son's temporary residence, and picked her up before we checked into the hotel where we normally stayed. She likes the swimming pool there so we quickly changed into bathing suits and spent a couple of hours in the pool before having dinner that evening with our son and his wife.

By late morning on Saturday, it was off to Greenville. Because of bad weather, we stayed in Greenville until Tuesday when we headed to our condo on Emerald Isle. Our granddaughter was so excited; she couldn't wait to get to the beach and she had waited so patiently for nearly three days. Once she got to the ocean, she wasn't disappointed. Much to our surprise, she had no fear of the waves slapping on the shore. We held her hands as the waves crashed against her legs and on occasion caused her to lose her balance. However, despite the water in her face and the sand in her swimsuit, she was not deterred. In fact, she wanted to inch farther and farther into the waves and she squealed every time a big wave hit her. On Wednesday, my daughter came down to the beach to spend the day with us. At one point, a wave hit our granddaughter and knocked her off her feet and she got her head in the water. She bounced up like a ball and declared, "I'm tough."

It was our son all over again. I remember our first trips to Myrtle Beach when he was her age. He was fearless when it came to the ocean. He wanted to be knocked down so he could get up again and show how tough he was. We had to watch him like a hawk to keep him from going out too deep in the ocean.

As I finish writing this story, we are anticipating the arrival of Hurricane Irene. We will not be at the beach to watch the power of the storm. The waves will be large and dangerous, unlike the small waves that children love to play in. One cannot help but marvel at the mystery and power of the ocean. For me, it always reminds me of my God. Speaking through the prophet Isaiah, here is what God had to say about the ocean -

"For I am the Lord your God, who churns up the sea so that its waves roar—the Lord Almighty is his name." (Isaiah 51:15). Over the next few days as we watch the path of Irene as it passes our shores, remember that it is God who churns up the sea and it is God who protects us in the storm.

See you tomorrow, God willing!

August 27   Summer of 1965

By the summer of 1965, my siblings and I had graduated from high school or college and were independent. So independent that we all took off for parts unknown that summer. My sister went to Hawaii with three friends that were elementary teachers. My brother went to Florida with one of his friends, and I headed to Europe to work in Germany for the whole summer. We had really flown the coup.

In my sister's case, each of the travelers got jobs in the restaurant industry. Unlike her friends, she didn't want to serve dinners or lunches. She got a job serving drinks at the Royal Hawaiian Sheraton on Waikiki Beach where you could see the waves rolling in each evening. She told me that she served several famous movie stars but Billy Casper (a famous golfer) is the person she remembers most. When he told her that he was Billy Casper she told him she was little Red Riding Hood and laughed. He called the matri d' over to prove who he was. While she was there, they had a tidal wave alert that was very scary.

My brother's trip to Florida was far less memorable. However, he did recall that a man from Texas drowned in rough surf not too far from the shore. I wonder if it was the same time they had the tidal wave alert in Hawaii – just kidding.

Like my sister's trip to Hawaii, my experience in Germany was extraordinary. For six weeks, I had a job washing dishes in a resort hotel. I washed pots and pans that were almost large enough for me to crawl into them to wash them properly. What I remember most about my work experience was the diversity of the young people who were employed for the summer in the kitchen. There were two girls from Finland, a boy from Canada, another girl from Spain, and several German teens. Our dinner table was like a United Nations meal. After my six weeks of work were completed, I had the opportunity to travel across Western Europe sightseeing. By the time I left from the port of LeHavre, France, I was exhausted and dead flat broke, so broke that I had to spend my last night sleeping on a park bench.

Despite the fact that we had been scattered all over the globe, we all came back home safe and sound. God had looked after us, even though I didn't understand the concept at the time. "Although I sent them far away among the nations and scattered them among the countries, yet for a little while I have been a sanctuary for them in the countries where they have gone." (Ezekiel 11:16) God has been looking after His children for years and He will never stop no matter where we are.

See you tomorrow, God willing!

August 28 — California Dreamin'

Yesterday, I told you about trips that my siblings and I made in the summer of 1965. I should also mention that my wife had taken off for California that same summer. While I crossed the Atlantic on a coal barge from Norfolk to Bremerhaven, Germany, a trip that took fourteen days, she climbed on a train for the cross country trip to Los Angeles to visit her mother's sister and her family. She had hoped to see the sights of America; instead, she saw a lot of open land and the dirtiest parts of every city that the train passed through. At least it didn't take fourteen days. Her mother's sister had two daughters that were close to her age so she expected to have a nice summer vacation.

In fact, she had such a good time that she decided to stay longer and enrolled at Chaffey Junior College to begin her college years. When I got her letter while I was in Germany telling me that she would not be home when I returned, I was devastated. It was okay for me to leave for the summer; it wasn't okay for her to leave for the fall and possibly longer. The good news was that she only stayed for one semester and then returned home to Virginia.

While she was there, Chaffey Junior College played the freshman basketball team at UCLA the year Lew Alcindor was a freshman. That was in the days when freshmen were not eligible to play on the varsity. Some of you may not remember that Lew Alcindor later changed his name to Kareem Abdul Jabbar, who later became the all-time leading scorer in the NBA. Chaffey was demolished that night, but my wife got to see the greatest scorer in the NBA play before he even played his first varsity intercollegiate game.

While attendance figures for that game are not known to me, I suppose there were a lot of spectators there that night. The largest crowd to see Jesus was very likely the day he fed the crowd who had come to see Him heal and perform other miracles. "And he directed the people to sit down on the grass. Taking the five loaves and the two fish and looking up to heaven, he gave thanks and broke the loaves. Then he gave them to the disciples, and the disciples gave them to the people. They all ate and were satisfied... The number of those who ate was about five thousand men, besides women and children." (Matthew 14:19-21) There were probably over ten thousand people in the crowd counting the women and children; and, He fed them all with five loaves and two fish. I'd say that was a record performance. After all He was the greatest scorer of all time, only His scores were not meaningless baskets, but saved souls.

See you tomorrow, God willing!

August 29   Hurricanes and Ice Storms

As I look out my bedroom window into the backyard of our house and our nearest neighbor, I can see presents that Irene left behind. Our backyards are full of broken limbs and a tree about three feet in diameter is down next door. We were fortunate that none of the limbs or the tree fell in the direction of our houses. We lost power for only an hour and there was no flooding in our part of town. God had certainly placed His hedge of protection around us.

As I looked at all the limbs in the backyard, it reminded be of a different type of storm that we experienced our first winter in Pennsylvania. The temperature that day was right at the freezing point and light rain began to fall. It wasn't too long before the water began to freeze as it hit the trees or anything else above the ground. By evening, we knew we were in trouble. Our house was surrounded by large hardwood trees, and it wasn't long before we began to see what happens when a limb becomes laden with ice. Limbs began to break off, often hitting the roof of the house as they fell. These weren't small limbs, but limbs large enough the knock off gutters and damage the roof. Before long, we had lost power. We survived the night and arose the next morning to a winter wonderland. The sun shining on the ice covered trees reflected the morning light giving the appearance of trees full of diamonds. However, the sight of a yard filled with broken limbs was not so beautiful. It looked like a war zone.

When Jesus performed His first miracle at the wedding in Cana, it must have left a similar indelible mark on the memory of those who witnessed the event. "Jesus said to the servants, '"Fill the jars with water'... Then he told them, 'Now draw some out and take it to the master of the banquet'...and the master of the banquet tasted the water that had been turned into wine. He did not realize where it had come from, though the servants who had drawn the water knew... This, the first of his miraculous signs, Jesus performed in Cana of Galilee. He thus revealed his glory, and his disciples put their faith in him." (John2: 7-9, 11)

Can you imagine what it must have been like to witness miracle after miracle? Yet, for each disciple there must have been one or two which really stuck in their minds. "Jesus did many other things as well. If every one of them were written down, I suppose that even the whole world would not have room for the books that would be written." (John 21:25)

From North Carolina to Vermont people will have memories of Hurricane Irene. However, Jesus miracles will be remembered around the world for all generations to come.

See you tomorrow, God willing!

August 30   The Mansion in Norton

On a recent trip to Virginia, we decided to take a short trip to the house where my wife's grandmother had lived for many years. What had been an elegant home in the nicest part of town was now in horrible disrepair. The front door was wide open so we went in the house to look around. I could see my wife close her eyes and try to recall memories of the house from another era.

Since the house was only about twenty-five miles from the town where she grew up, my wife and her brother would visit their grandmother often and she has many fond memories of those visits. To a little girl, her grandmother's house was a mansion. The house was clustered with many other fine homes in the city. Like many homes of that era, it had some charming features. For example, the entry door was a wide wooden door with glass inserts. To either side of the door were additional glass panels. Once you came in the door, there was a formal entryway. Leading into a bedroom on the immediate left were elegant wooden doors with multiple glass panels. There was also a huge staircase with wooden banisters that both my wife and her brother used as their own personal sliding board. As was common back in the fifties, there was a wooden swing on the front porch that was the site of many evening story telling sessions.

The mansion was also full of antiques. When her grandmother died in 1967, her antiques were widely dispersed among many family members. Two of the items we received are still part of our home décor. The first treasure is an oak kitchen cabinet, complete with a porcelain pull out shelf for baking. The Hoosier cabinet, which is still in excellent condition, also has the traditional flour storage container that swings out for ease of use. The second item in our house also sits in the kitchen. It is a small kitchen table with pop up sides. Because it also has a drawer to store silverware, the table makes a perfect worktable in the center of the working space of the kitchen. I suspect the best thing about the two items is their connection to my wife's heritage and memories.

During the early fifties, the three-story, five-bedroom house served as a boarding house. It was also used by weary travelers who became so comfortable with the excellent hospitality that they returned year after year not only to sleep and have a good meal, but also to reconnect with their wonderful hostess. My wife inherited her grandmother's gift of hospitality, a gift that Paul spoke about in his letter to the Romans. "Share with God's people who are in need. Practice hospitality." (Romans 12:13)

See you tomorrow, God willing!

August 31 — Burned Hands

Close your eyes for a moment. Visualize something for me before you read this story. I want you to picture a small boy, perhaps two or three years old. Now, I want you to see in your mind that same little boy with his hands covered in white gauze. It is a sad picture. You want to pick him up and give him a big hug because you know he must be in pain. Good job!

For my daughter and the rest of the immediate family, we don't have to use our imagination, just our memory. When our youngest grandson was a year old, he made the mistake of putting his hands against a hot opened oven door after our daughter had finished cooking dinner. He had been warned many times not to touch the hot surface, but he had never really understood why he was instructed to stay away. He had to find out for himself, and as a result, he ended up with very bad burns on both hands. Fortunately, the healing took place with no complications and he had learned a very valuable lesson.

When I was a youngster, I can remember learning some tough lessons myself. One of those lessons stands out in my mind just like it was yesterday. In 1956 we lived in a small apartment. Near our apartment was a railroad line with a spur that often had boxcars temporarily parked there. With some of my friends, we decided to climb onto the boxcars and jump from the top to the ground. We found some materials to soften the landing and dared each other to make the leap. When I reached the top and looked down, I realized it was much higher than I thought. However, it was too late to back out, so I made the leap. As I hit the ground, my knee smashed into my face, splitting my eye wide open. The blood running down my face was my red badge of courage for the moment. However, when I went home a little later, mother was not too happy with the stupid decision I had made. Like my grandson, I had learned a valuable lesson.

Both he and I had good excuses for our mistakes; we were too young to know better. We hadn't listened to the advice of our parents and we had paid a price. As I have grown older, I know where to seek instruction about all things–"I will instruct you and teach you in the way you should go; I will counsel you and watch over you. Do not be like the horse or the mule, which have no understanding but must be controlled by bit and bridle or they will not come to you. Many are the woes of the wicked, but the Lord's unfailing love surrounds the man who trusts in him." (Psalms 32:8-10) To whom do you listen?

See you tomorrow, God willing!

SEPTEMBER

September 1 — God's Presence

In September of 1995, our friends were about to celebrate their fiftieth birthdays and they invited us to go with them to Bermuda for the special occasion. Since we had never visited Bermuda, it sounded like a wonderful way to spend a long weekend. We made our travel plans, which included an all-inclusive three nights at the Hamilton Princess Hotel.

Whenever we go to any resort that involves an ocean, we always plan to go snorkeling. Unfortunately, when we got to Bermuda, Hurricane Luis was in the area and the ocean was rough to say the least. The water had so much suspended sand in it that visibility was virtually zero – so much for snorkeling. Our next best option was to visit Horseshoe Bay, one of the most famous beaches on the island. Bermuda's pink sand beaches look as if they have been dyed with iridescent paints. The soft rose color of Bermuda's beaches perfectly contrasts with the aquamarine ocean waters, creating a beautiful place to relax.

As we sat on the beach, we could see the powerful edges of the impending hurricane. Waves were at least fifteen feet high as they hit the breakers offshore. Later that same evening we saw a more comical sight at the Princess Hotel after we had completed dinner. As we were walking around the hotel, the wind was gaining strength, creating waves on the swimming pool that were large enough to slap against the sides of the pool sending sprays of water into the air.

The hurricane never did hit us with any measurable strength, but we felt its presence the whole time we were there. At the end of the trip, my wife purchased a nice photo book of Bermuda to give to our friends as a remembrance of the trip. She wrote a nice note on the inside cover and gave them the book as we were leaving the airport. Much to our dismay, Judy had done exactly the same thing for us – the identical book. I guess you can say great minds think alike.

We have fond memories of our excursion of Bermuda. While the threat of a hurricane was always there, its presence turned out to be a reminder of the power of our God. "Where can I go from your Spirit? Where can I flee from your presence? If I go up to the heavens, you are there; if I make my bed in the depths, you are there. If I rise on the wings of the dawn, if I settle on the far side of the sea, even there your hand will guide me, your right hand will hold me fast." (Psalms 139:7-10) God's presence is everywhere if we have eyes to see.

See you tomorrow, God willing!

September 2 — Build on the Rock

While we had a very large wooded lot at our home in Pennsylvania, the back yard was practically useless. Between the rocks, an old stump, and the fishponds, there wasn't too much room for a useable yard. I finally decided to build a large deck that would make the space more usable. Since our son was living with us at the time, I had a good carpenter to help me through the rough patches.

The first step that we took was to lay out a plan. We knew that as we dug out the foundation for the deck we would run into many limestone rocks, both large and small. Since there was a gentle slope to the terrain, we decided to build a two-level deck to minimize the amount of earth (and rocks) we would have to move. We also decided that the upper deck should have an arbor that would serve as a climbing source for the Wisteria that grew near the back of the yard.

Since we were in no particular hurry to complete the project, we worked on the deck as time permitted. Early on, it was much more digging and too little building. As I said before, there is no shortage of rocks in the ground in Eastern Pennsylvania. Digging the foundation for the lower deck was slow, but not too difficult. Digging the foundation for the upper level was quite another story. To minimize the amount of work we had to do, we decided to build the outside frame first and then dig out enough space for the individual two by eight floor boards. It seemed like a good idea at the time. All went well until we hit "grandfather rock." We uncovered a boulder the size of a small refrigerator. Since the outside frame was already built, we not only had to fully uncover the rock, we had to devise a plan for getting it outside the frame. Somehow or another, using two by eights as fulcrums, we managed to succeed.

My son and I built that deck in 1991. We were back in Pennsylvania some fifteen years later and we drove by our old home. To no one's surprise, the deck was still standing and ready to serve its owners for another twenty years. It was built on a solid foundation. "He is like a man building a house, who dug down deep and laid the foundation on rock. When a flood came, the torrent struck that house but could not shake it, because it was well built. But the one who hears my words and does not put them into practice is like a man who built a house on the ground without a foundation. The moment the torrent struck that house, it collapsed and its destruction was complete." (Luke 6:48-49) Build your life on the Rock and it will prosper under any circumstance.

See you tomorrow, God willing!

September 3 — Failing the Test

All through my years of education, I never had any problems with taking tests. In fact, I did very well and I was very fast. I remember one of my exams in graduate school very well. I finished the entire exam in about a half an hour, turned in my Blue Book, and made my way out the door. Since I was the first to finish, I noticed a lot of the other students look at me as I left. However, the look that I received was not one of admiration; they were looking at me with eyes that said "poor guy, he must have given up and quit." They never knew that I had scored an "A" on the exam and for the course.

The reason I am telling you this story is to set the stage for another story that is not quite so positive. When we moved to Pennsylvania in 1977, I had to get a Pennsylvania driver's license. I had been driving for nearly fifteen years so I did not anticipate any trouble with the examination. That was problem number one, don't take anything for granted. Problem number two was my appearance. I went to the location for the exam dressed in a suit and tie. The examiner, who was quite a bit older than I was, looked at me with a quite different look than I got from the graduate students who saw me leave early. The examiner's look said, "This guy thinks he is pretty smart, I think I will show him he is not as smart as he thinks he is." Problem number three was another oversight; make sure you know what form the test takes. I expected a written exam, but to my surprise the examiner caught me off guard and starting throwing questions at me. When I missed for the third time, he said, "strike three, you are out. Come back when you are better prepared." I left with my tail tucked between my legs and just a little more humble than when I had arrived. The next day I went back to the site and passed the test with flying colors. I was really happy that I didn't get the same examiner the second time even though I was much better prepared.

I received a valuable lesson that day from an older gentleman I had never met. "Young men, in the same way be submissive to those who are older. All of you, clothe yourselves with humility toward one another, because, 'God opposes the proud but gives grace to the humble. Humble yourselves, therefore, under God's mighty hand, that he may lift you up in due time.'" (1 Peter 5:5-6) It's too bad that God has had to teach me the humility lesson so many times since then. For some of us, it is a hard lesson to learn. How many times has He had to teach you?

See you tomorrow, God willing!

September 4 — Rites of Passage

As young men grow to maturity, there are certain rites of passage that must take place before they become a man. Oddly enough, shaving is one of those rites. Men, can you remember watching your father shave? Wasn't there some point in that experience that your father let you put some lather on your face and swipe it off with something less hazardous than a real razor? I remember those times with my Dad and I remember my son doing the same thing with me. It is a rite of passage.

Things are different in today's society. For one thing, beards are back in vogue so fewer young men are shaving. My oldest grandson has a nice beard as do many of his peers. Number two; more people today use electric razors than in my day. I tried electric razors a time or two, but just couldn't get used to the feel. Number three, shaving creams have changed immensely. I actually starting used a shaving gel when they first came out in the early 1970's. I started using Edge Gel when it first came out because I got as many free samples as I wanted. My company at the time supplied the key chemical ingredient that made the gel work.

The older foaming shaving creams are still used my many people, but no one found a better use for these foams than my daughter. She would buy a can of shaving cream and let her boys empty the foam all over the top of her wooden kitchen table and play in the foam. As I type this letter, I can see two 8 x 10 photos, one of the boys, ages six and three, with their faces, hands, arms and bare chests covered in foam and a smile on their faces that reflects the great time they were having.

In Old Testament times, if a man made the vow of a Nazirite, to separate himself for God, he was not allowed to shave. "All the days of his vow of separation, no razor shall touch his head. Until the time is completed for which he separates himself to the Lord, he shall be holy. He shall let the locks of hair of his head grow long." (Numbers 6:5) When his time of separation from the people was complete, he was then allowed to shave. "And the Nazirite shall shave his consecrated head at the entrance of the tent of meeting and shall take the hair from his consecrated head and put it on the fire that is under the sacrifice of the peace offering." (Numbers 6:18) Wouldn't it be great if all the people we see on an every day basis were allowing their beards to grow because they had separated themselves for the Lord? Perhaps some of them are.

See you tomorrow, God willing!

September 5   Labor Day Victory

Labor Day has always been one of my favorite holidays. My first fond memory of Labor Day was in 1963. In Virginia, high school football games are not allowed until Labor Day weekend and in 1963 we opened our season with a game against Mountain City, Tennessee at home. We beat them by several touchdowns, but for me the season got off to a rocky start. I sprained my left ankle badly on the opening kick off, but managed to play the entire game without too much trouble. However, when I got up the next morning, I could hardly walk. Here is where the story takes a twist.

Labor Day weekend was also the traditional ending of the Club Championship at Lake Bonaventure Country Club where I spent all of my spare time in the summer. I had made it through all of the match play rounds and was to compete for the championship on Labor Day. Not being able to walk presented a slight challenge. I never considered forfeiting the match; it would be better to lose in pain than to give up. Although I never road a cart at the tender age of sixteen, I did that day. Since my left ankle was too sore to bear any weight, my golf swing on Labor Day was modified to keep all my weight on the right side. It isn't a great way to play, but that day it worked. Somehow or another I managed to swing easily, keep the ball in play; and defeat a very worthy opponent. I think at first my opponent felt sorry for me, but by the end of the match he knew he had made a mistake. At sixteen, I was the youngest club champion in the history of the club.

I can't begin to tell you how excited I was about my surprising triumph -"Then will the lame leap like a deer, and the mute tongue shout for joy. Water will gush forth in the wilderness and streams in the desert." (Isaiah 35:6) I may not have been leaping like a deer, but I was certainly gushing forth with joy.

Many years later, I had returned to Lake Bonaventure to play in a Member Guest tournament with my brother-in-law. As we teed it up to play in the Friday evening kick-off round, one of the competitors commented – "I heard that I would be playing with the Club Champion from 1963, I expected you to be eighty years old."

See you tomorrow, God willing!

September 6 — Refrigerator Art

When our granddaughter was with us for a week in August, we had the opportunity to take her to church with us. Since she thought it was too loud in the sanctuary, my wife took her to one of the Sunday school classes for three year olds. While she was slightly concerned that our granddaughter would not want to stay without her, the teacher of the class assured my wife that she would be fine. So, my wife came back to the sanctuary for the remainder of the service. The teacher was correct; our granddaughter had a great time and she proudly gave us a construction paper piece of art that she had made while she was in the class. I don't have to tell any parent or grandparent where the art now resides – of course; it is on the front of the refrigerator.

For over forty years, my wife has used the front of our refrigerators as an art gallery of sorts. First, it was the art that our children brought home from either school or church. Then along came the next generation and the front of the refrigerator had art from our grandchildren. I suspect it won't be too many years that we will be placing art from a third generation of our family on the front of another refrigerator.

As I was riding along in the car a few days ago, I heard a sermon on Christian radio that talked about refrigerator art. The preacher compared all Christians to refrigerator art, imperfect yet loved dearly by the ultimate parent. Sometimes it is hard to decipher whether a drawing is of a horse or a dinosaur. Yet, we don't care; we love the drawing because our child or grandchild had made it just for us. That is how God feels when we give Him attention, no matter how imperfect the attention is.

God knows that we are incapable of perfection that is why we need Jesus. "Although he was a son, he learned obedience from what he suffered and, once made perfect, he became the source of eternal salvation for all who obey him…" (Hebrews 5:8-9) Through His perfection we obtain salvation, but not on our own merits. "We all stumble in many ways. If anyone is never at fault in what he says, he is a perfect man, able to keep his whole body in check." (James 3:2) Look at those two terms "never at fault" and "keep whole body in check." That certainly doesn't describe me or anyone else I know, except Jesus. The next time you pass by the refrigerator and look at some refrigerator art, thank God that He loves us in our imperfection.

See you tomorrow, God willing!

September 7 — Buried Alive

When you watch males and females playing in the sand, there is usually one big difference. Men and boys like to get the sand all over them while the ladies prefer to be a little more pristine. While I distinctly remember my dad being buried in the sand, I can never remember burying my mother. Likewise, I can remember my kids burying me, but not their mom. And, when our grandsons came around, both of them loved to bury their dad in the sand and be buried themselves. You ladies will have to forgive me if I forgot that you were buried.

When my wife and I went to Honduras on a mission trip, I had a bad experience that involved a minor version of being buried alive. Part of the work that I was doing on the trip was digging a large trench in front of the church. The trench was being dug to pour the concrete for the entry way and steeple. Since there was no heavy equipment, the trench was being dug by hand, and I was one of the "hands." As the trench got deeper, it got harder and harder to throw the dirt out of the trench so it began to build up on the top side of the trench. Finally, the weight on the edge of the trench got too heavy and the sidewalls gave in burying me all the way up to my thighs. It took a few minutes to dig me out and fortunately, I was not harmed. As I looked back on the experience, I realized how stupid I had been to throw the dirt in a location that would add too much weight to the edge of the trench. I also laughed when I thought about how OHSA would have viewed this particular work site.

There is a scene in the Bible that, in a way, talks about someone being buried alive. It seems Lazarus had died and been buried. When Jesus heard the news, He commented, "Our friend Lazarus has fallen asleep; but I am going there to wake him up." (John 11:11) In Jesus' mind, Lazarus was still alive. "On his arrival, Jesus found that Lazarus had already been in the tomb for four days… Jesus called in a loud voice, 'Lazarus, come out!' The dead man came out, his hands and feet wrapped with strips of linen, and a cloth around his face. Jesus said to them, 'Take off the grave clothes and let him go.'" (John 11:17, 44) The first thing we do when we are uncovered after being buried in the sand is wash off all the excess sand on our bodies. For Lazarus it was the same thing, his friends who watched in amazement were told to remove his grave clothes and let him go. The next time you see someone buried in the sand, think about the miracle Jesus performed with Lazarus.

See you tomorrow, God willing!

September 8 — The Hair Cut

My wife's mother loved nothing more than to please her husband in every way. If he got up at 4 am in the morning to go hunting, she was up making breakfast for him. If he brought some of the other bus drivers home with him for breakfast or lunch, she was happy to oblige. She even let her hair grow long because that was the way he liked her hair. Her mom's hair was really long – according to my wife her hair was at least half way down her back and a real inconvenience to care for. My wife remembers her mother washing and drying her hair, a process that took quite a while in the days before hair dryers and no frizz hair products. She also recalled how much time it took for her mother to braid her hair and then stack it on top of her head. Her mom was a beautiful lady and she wanted to look good for "her man" so she went through the necessary rituals to please him.

By 1960, she was being encouraged by her sister-in-law to get her hair cut and ease her daily burden of caring for such long hair. She finally succumbed to the advice and got her hair cut. My wife was a freshman in high school at the time and she remembers the day her mom got her locks cut. It was a bold move for someone who lived to please her husband. While her husband was not totally pleased with her decision, he did not make a big deal of it and he grew to like the shorter hair over the years.

Little did my wife's father know at the time, but that little excursion to the hairdresser in 1960 would become as much a part of her life as breathing and eating. Every week, with few exceptions, for the next forty-plus years, her mom would make her way to the beauty parlor for a shampoo, set and trim. It was a nice way to treat herself and make her feel beautiful.

"Wives, in the same way be submissive to your husbands so that, if any of them do not believe the word, they may be won over without words by the behavior of their wives, when they see the purity and reverence of your lives. Your beauty should not come from outward adornment, such as braided hair and the wearing of gold jewelry and fine clothes. Instead, it should be that of your inner self, the unfading beauty of a gentle and quiet spirit, which is of great worth in God's sight." (1 Peter 3:1-4) Could it be that my wife's mother had just finished reading from Peter's first letter when she decided to get her hair cut?

See you tomorrow, God willing!

September 9 — Taking Bear Island

One of my mother's favorite day trips was an excursion to Bear Island. Mother always gave very strict instructions for the outing. Her instructions made it seem more like we were Marines from Camp Lejeune taking possession of an island rather than a family going on a shelling expedition. The first instruction was to pick her up no later than eight o'clock in the morning so we could get the very first ferry to the island. We did not have time to stop and eat because it was imperative that we be first in line for the first ferry that left at nine o'clock. If you were first in line, it meant that you would also be first off the ferry and in a position to "take" the beach on the far side of the island from where the ferry dropped us off. Once the ferry dropped us off, there was about a ten to fifteen minute walk to get to the beach on the ocean side of the island. That walk was not for the faint of heart. It was the fastest you would ever see mother walk. You had to be the first on the beach in order to get the first shot at whatever had washed up the night before.

The path that crossed the island was just about dead center in terms of the beach which awaited us on the ocean side. While the best shelling was almost always to the left towards Emerald Isle, we would often deploy the team left and right so we could cover the entire beach. Although I don't specifically remember how many good shells we actually found on Bear Island, I do remember the enthusiasm that mother showed in taking the beach. My wife did tell me that she found her first sand dollar on Bear Island and the only Lion's Paw that she has ever found in over forty years of shelling.

Mother's instructions were very explicit and we always listened and were obedient. Before the Israelites conquered Jericho, an angel of the Lord appeared to Joshua to give him some very strange, yet strict instructions for his mission. "March around the city… Do this for six days. Have seven priests carry trumpets of rams' horns…On the seventh day, march around the city seven times, with the priests blowing the trumpets. When you hear them sound a long blast on the trumpets, have all the people give a loud shout; then the wall of the city will collapse and the people will go up, every man straight in." (Joshua 6:3-5)

Despite the odd instructions, the Bible tells us that Joshua and the Israelites got up early each morning and carried out God's plan – and the walls came tumbling down. I suppose the moral to this story is this – listen to your mother and Father and your missions will succeed, no matter how high the walls.

See you tomorrow, God willing!

September 10 — The Great Physician

During my last couple of years in high school, my dad worked the night shift at a coal mine near Appalachia. He was fond of that shift because there were no other bosses around to interfere with his crew. The men who worked for dad liked to work for him because he was fair and he didn't kiss up to any of the big bosses.

Since he was not home in the evenings, my mother and I would often go to some friend's house to play cards. We always played at their house because they had two children and an elderly mother who stayed with them. I will never forget one evening when we had just arrived at their house and we were holding a conversation with the elderly mother. The conversation turned to current movies that were coming to the Lyric Theater. Since St. Paul never got a movie until somewhat late in the distribution cycle, the quality of a movie was well-known before it reached the Lyric. As we talked about "Dr. Zhivago" coming to town, the mother commented, "It's about time; we could sure use a good doctor in this little town." It was all we could do to keep from bursting at the seams with laughter.

The most famous doctor in the Bible was Luke – "Our dear friend Luke, the doctor…" (Colossians 4:14). Luke was the author of the Gospel of Luke and the Book of Acts. While Luke was not an eyewitness of the events he recorded in his Gospel or in Acts, he carefully collected and investigated many written and oral eyewitness accounts. His material was written essentially for a Greek audience unlike Matthew's Gospel, which was aimed primarily at a Jewish audience. "Therefore, since I myself have carefully investigated everything from the beginning, it seemed good also to me to write an orderly account for you, most excellent Theophilus, so that you may know the certainty of the things you have been taught." (Luke 1:3-4) I can hear Theophilus saying, "It's about time we got a good doctor/writer in this country." Collectively, the Gospels of Matthew, Mark, Luke and John give us a clear picture of the Good News of Jesus Christ so that we may know the certainty of His life. I need to correct the first sentence of this paragraph; Jesus was really the most famous doctor in the Bible and I'm glad He came to my town.

See you tomorrow, God willing!

September 11 — Je Me Souviens

For the first eighteen years of working in Pennsylvania, I was responsible for the company's communications activities. In 1995, I was pulled from my full-time job and put on a team of individuals who were to spend six months "reengineering" the largest division in the company. It was incredibly challenging, but full of land mines because we were to question the way everything had been done for decades and make recommendations on how to improve customer focus and reduce costs.

At the end of the six months, the "reengineering" team met with the key decision makers in Quebec City, Quebec to help communicate the new business processes. It was a stressful meeting made more pleasant by our surrounding. The meeting was held at Le Chateau Frontenac, which stands high on a bluff overlooking the mighty St. Lawrence River. Le Château Frontenac was a memorable and inspiring place to stay in one of the most beautiful cities in the world. Frontenac is not merely a hotel located in the heart of Old Québec—it is the heart of it. Since the meeting was held in late summer, we were able to walk the streets of downtown Quebec and enjoy the carnival atmosphere of an old European city. The highlight of the meeting actually began on Friday when my wife arrived to spend the weekend with me.

One of the highlights of the weekend was our trip on the funicular, which links the Haute-Ville (Upper Town) to the Basse-Ville (Lower Town). The funicular is a type of railway that was opened on November 17, 1879, as a means of easy transport of people and goods from the St. Lawrence River up the steep cliff to the Upper Town. The Lower Town by the river is the oldest part of Quebec City and is home to historic architecture, cobblestone streets, interesting shops and restaurants.

Every spring I am reminded of our trip to Quebec City when I see license plates on cars from that region headed south for spring golf outings. The reason the plate is so memorable is the slogan that appears prominently on each tag – "Je me souviens." The English translation of the phrase is "I remember." For residents of Quebec it means much more. "We remember the past and its lessons, the past and its misfortunes, the past and its glories."

Throughout the Old Testament, God calls on His people to remember the past and its lessons. "Remember that you were slaves in Egypt and the LORD your God redeemed you." (Deuteronomy 15:15) Remember the wonders he has done, his miracles, and the judgments he pronounced. (1Chronicles 16:12) "Remember the former things, those of long ago; I am God, and there is no other; I am God, and there is none like me." (Isaiah 46:9) Perhaps we should look more closely at the currency that we carry around with us all the time – "In God we trust."

See you tomorrow, God willing!

September 12 — Empty Nesters

There is a wonderful group of people that we have had the privilege to know since we first came to North Carolina. It is a group of "empty nesters" that form a small group at our church. Since its inception, the group has served as "greeters" at the church. To get to know each other a little better, we developed a pattern of meeting the second Tuesday of every month to have a group dinner. At each meeting, the host was also responsible for the devotion for the evening. Closing prayers allowed members to share their individual concerns and bring the members closer to one another, like a family.

Several years ago, around 2003, our pastor encouraged all of its members to go through a study of Rick Warren's "The Purpose Driven Life." With the book came a forty-day study guide that small groups used to move through the material. Each small group, including our Connections Group, met weekly to study and discuss the material. There was one very special thing about our study – we finished the study on a Caribbean cruise aboard the cruise ship "Norwegian Majesty." It was a beautiful ending to a most thought provoking spiritual experience.

Over the nine years that the family has been together, we have had our share of ups and downs. We have lost some members to relocation; some have left the church; and three of our members are waiting for us at the feet of Jesus. We have also added members and each time a new couple comes on board they add a special set of gifts that other members do not possess. Just like the church, our family is made up of many disparate parts, each required to strengthen the family. We have people who love to pray; we have people who love to teach; we have people who have the gift of hospitality; we have people who love to serve; and we have others who have the gift of compassion.

Our Connections Group is just a microcosm of the church that Paul talked about in his letter to the Corinthians. "The body is a unit, though it is made up of many parts; and though all its parts are many, they form one body. So it is with Christ. If the whole body were an eye, where would the sense of hearing be? If the whole body were an ear, where would the sense of smell be? But in fact God has arranged the parts in the body, every one of them, just as he wanted them to be." (1 Corinthians 12:12, 17-18)

Be a part of God's family and become an heir to the throne.

See you tomorrow, God willing!

September 13 — Scuba Diving

My wife and I have been snorkeling all over the Caribbean – in Mexico, St. Johns, St. Maarten, Puerto Rico, Bermuda, and the Grand Caymans – and we love to look at the beautiful fish and aquatic life. I knew if I ever had the chance to go SCUBA diving, I would jump at the chance. On one of our trips to Akumal on the Yucatan Peninsula of Mexico, I got my chance.

When we visited the beach at Akumal one day, we noticed that they offered a short-course in SCUBA diving that would enable me to take a couple of training courses and then go on a real dive. The first day was spent in a swimming pool at the resort. The next day we graduated to the shallow water just off the beach. I didn't get in water over my head that day, but I did get used to swimming around in a little larger area than a swimming pool.

On the third day I was off to the ocean. We boarded a small boat to take us just off the beach in an area where the water was about seventy feet deep. When we first got off the boat and into the water, we had to go through one more training stage before we could descend. We had to be shown how to control the air in our life vests in order to reduce our buoyancy and we were also instructed to go down slowly to reduce the pressure on our inner ears. Finally, we were on our way to the bottom. The experience was awesome. The highlight of the trip was seeing a nurse shark. According to our guide, that particular species of shark is harmless. Fortunately, on that day he was correct.

Did you know that the first scuba diving equipment was described in the Bible nearly three centuries ago? It's true! Just look in the Book of Jonah, Chapter One. "But the Lord provided a great fish to swallow Jonah, and Jonah was inside the fish three days and three nights." (Jonah 1:17) "To the roots of the mountains I sank down; the earth beneath barred me in forever. But you brought my life up from the pit, O Lord my God. 'When my life was ebbing away, I remembered you, Lord, and my prayer rose to you, to your holy temple.'" (Jonah 2:6-7) I don't think Jonah had any training and I think he dived deeper than seventy feet. Nevertheless, he survived because God had an important job for him to do in Nineveh. The tasks that God calls each of us to do may not be as important as the one Jonah was called to perform, but it doesn't matter. What matters is this – God wants to use you and He will help you every step of the way.

See you tomorrow, God willing!

September 14 — Deer Hunters

My wife left for Emerald Isle on Thursday morning and I had planned to join her the next day, if I could get some items completed at work. When she called me that night, I could tell by the tone of her voice that she was excited. Then she told me – "I saw three deer on the way to the beach today." I couldn't wait to respond – "how did you know they were on the way to the beach?" Her answer put me in my place – "because they were already in the sand dunes. Gotcha!" Indeed, it was not a dangling participle; the deer were really on their way to the beach. It wasn't the first time this summer that we have seen deer close to the beach. On two occasions, we have seen a single deer near the walkways to the beach so we know that they must have been getting very close.

Deer on Emerald Isle are plentiful. It is unusual to go down Coast Guard Road in the evening without seeing at least one deer. Last summer, my wife was hosting her "Threads of Comfort" small group and one of the ladies was up early one morning and saw a doe with three fawns a short distance from our deck. As luck would have it, she had her camera ready and was able to get a very sweet picture of the scene.

I am not a hunter so shooting a deer would never be on my bucket list. While I do not have any issue with those who do hunt our four-legged friends, there is no way I could ever shoot one myself. When we lived in Pennsylvania, we were far more likely to take a high-intensity spotlight to look for deer at night in the many cornfields that were near our house. It was a real treat to catch the shining eyes of a herd of deer on their nightly strolls to feed.

When God created the earth, He did not originally intend for the deer to be food for man. "And God said, Behold, I have given you every herb bearing seed, which [is] upon the face of all the earth, and every tree, in the which [is] the fruit of a tree yielding seed; to you it shall be for meat." (Genesis 1:29) Later after the great flood, He amended the instructions–"Every moving thing that liveth shall be meat for you; even as the green herb have I given you all things." (Genesis 9:3) I must admit that I do enjoy a little venison every now and then, but someone else is going to have to shoot it. I just can't get that picture of Bambi out of my mind.

See you tomorrow, God willing!

September 15 Broken Wrist but Not Broken Spirit

Back in 2002, my mother was still able to live alone for short periods of time at her camper on Emerald Isle. At that time she lived with us in Greenville, but she liked to stay at her camper when we went to the beach for a short stay. One evening when we returned from our evening dinner, I asked our grandson to open the door to the camper to let mom's dog out to greet us. As mother approached the stairs to the deck of her camper the dog jumped up at mother because she was so happy to see her. Unfortunately, mother had just put her foot on the top stair and the dog knocked her backwards to the ground. As she tried to break her fall with her hands she broke her right wrist.

Since it was obvious that her wrist was broken, we drove her to the emergency room to get medical care for her broken wrist. The rest of the night was a blur, but we did get the wrist set. What I remember most about the subsequent weeks was the time I would spend with her every day helping her go through the rehabilitation exercises the doctor had assigned her to make sure the wrist healed properly. Two times a day, we would go to the screened porch and I would force her to do all sorts of exercises that she did not like. Many times, she was unhappy with me, but she complied. By the time we made our last trip to the doctor for a final check up, the wrist had healed perfectly and mother had not lost any range of motion in her wrist. Although she didn't like it, she had been obedient to the doctor's orders for her own well being.

Obedience is defined as "compliance with someone's wishes or orders or acknowledgment of their authority." Most of us are not thrilled with the implications that the word implies. Yet, obedience to God's will is our most essential act of worship.

"If you are willing and obedient, you will eat the best from the land; but if you resist and rebel, you will be devoured by the sword. For the mouth of the Lord has spoken." (Isaiah 1:19-20) The prophet Isaiah says it very succinctly. If you are obedient you will eat the best of the land; if you are not, you will be devoured by the sword. Is that too hard to understand?

See you tomorrow, God willing!

September 16   The Resemblance is Scary

When children are born, one of the first things people is "doesn't he (or she) look just like his father (or mother). It is a natural thing to do and generally the statement holds a lot of truth. There is no denying that every child carries some of the genes of the father and the mother. Whether we like it or not, many of us do look a lot like either our father or mother or some other close relative.

Our granddaughter, for example, carries a lot of genes from my wife's side of the family. If you compare our granddaughter's current pictures with my wife's childhood pictures you cannot help but see the resemblance.

Our daughter brought us a photograph one day that showed a picture of a boy about ten years old who was holding a sharp knife and appeared to be helping the family at a hog killing. We asked her what her son was doing in the photo because we were surprised that they had let him have such a large knife in his hand. That is when we learned the truth. It was not a photo of her son; rather it was a photo of her husband when he was a boy. The resemblance is scary.

A few years ago when my mother was living with us, she always went to church with us on Sunday morning. On one of her first visits, we happened to be sitting just across the aisle from dear friends. When the service was over, I went over to say "Hi" to them and to introduce them to my mother. The comment back to me was hilarious, "You didn't have to tell me she was your mother; I could see it from a mile away." Then he proceeded to rub his hand gently over his nose and chin as if to tell me where the resemblance lied. Yes, I do have a protruding chin and a slightly long, hook nose, but then again, so did mother.

There is a moral to this story. We look like some other member of our family because we have inherited their genes. Once we accept Christ into our lives, we have a new inheritance. "And you also were included in Christ when you heard the word of truth, the gospel of your salvation. Having believed, you were marked in him with a seal, the promised Holy Spirit, who is a deposit guaranteeing our inheritance until the redemption of those who are God's possession—to the praise of His glory." (Ephesians 1:13-14) From that point on, we look different. "For of this you can be sure: No immoral, impure or greedy person—such a man is an idolater—has any inheritance in the kingdom of Christ and of God." (Ephesians 5:5) In other words, if you are a Christian, it should show and if you are not, it will also show.

See you tomorrow, God willing!

September 17 — Feet of Clay

For a couple of years in the late nineties, we vacationed in Palmas del Mar on the southeastern corner of Puerto Rica. Since I had worked for the same company for over twenty years, I had earned five weeks of vacation each year and I had also learned that two weeks gives you enough time to really disengage from your job and truly relax. My wife discovered after the first year that the condominium we rented cost the same thing for a month as it did for two weeks so she went two weeks before I did.

On our trip to Puerto Rica the prior year, we had become familiar with a small church so we got involved with a Bible study group that was beginning a multi-week journey through the book of Daniel. She alerted me about the study so I tried to keep up back in Pennsylvania so I could join the study when I finally arrived. If you have never read nor studied the book of Daniel, I highly recommend it. It is chock full of dreams and their interpretation, prophecy, wonderful stories and characters, and evidence of God's power and grace.

My favorite story in the Book of Daniel is told in Chapter Two when Nebuchadnezzar had a dream which none of the wise men of Babylon could interpret. Finally, Daniel came forward to interpret the dream. "You looked, O king, and there before you stood a large statue—an enormous, dazzling statue, awesome in appearance. The head of the statue was made of pure gold, its chest and arms of silver, its belly and thighs of bronze, its legs of iron, its feet partly of iron and partly of baked clay. While you were watching, a rock was cut out, but not by human hands. It struck the statue on its feet of iron and clay and smashed them." (Daniel 2:31-34) Notice that last expression, the statue was destroyed because it had feet of clay. That expression has been part of our vocabulary for centuries and its root goes back to the book of Daniel.

As I have travelled my own path of life, I have admired many people only to discover at a later date that they had feet of clay. Just like me, they had faults that became more apparent the more I got to know them. It didn't make them bad people, it only exposed a universal truth – we all have feet of clay. Only Jesus has feet that are perfect. In Him there are no flaws, no clay feet. If He isn't your friend, perhaps He should be; you will never find any flaws in Him.

See you tomorrow, God willing!

September 18 — On Eagle's Wings

After we moved my mom to an assisted living facility where she could receive better care, all of the family members who lived in Greenville made regular trips to see her and play "Kings Around the Corner." Mother loved to play cards and as her Alzheimer's disease progressed, it was one card game that she could still enjoy. Several days a week, I would make the short trip to see her and play cards. She was always glad to see me.

Sunday afternoons, however, were a special treat. Typically, on Sunday afternoons we would go for a ride. I think it was her favorite activity. It didn't matter where we went or how long we stayed out. She loved to sit in the front seat and look at the unfamiliar countryside. She also learned to anticipate the end of each trip. Unless the weather was awful, we would end each drive with a trip to McDonald's to get an ice cream. Like many of us in the family, it was her favorite dessert.

There was one special Sunday afternoon that the trip took on new dimensions. My wife was with me the day we decided to take my mom on a drive to see an eagle's nest. It was about a thirty-minute drive and we knew she would love to see the Bald Headed Eagle's nest that we had seen on previous trips. We picked mother up in the early afternoon and headed on our expedition. Once we reached our destination, we got out of the car and pointed out the eagles to mother. Having been an avid bird watcher all her life, she was thrilled. After we left the eagle's nest, we headed for a Dairy Queen to get mother her Sunday afternoon ice cream treat.

It was a glorious day that I will not soon forget. Michael Crawford, a well-known Broadway vocalist, recorded a CD called "On Eagle's Wings" that included the 91st Psalm. I can't help but think of Mother every time I hear or read the words. Here are the first six verses of that Psalm.

"He who dwells in the shelter of the Most High will rest in the shadow of the Almighty.
I will say of the LORD, 'He is my refuge and my fortress, my God, in whom I trust.'
Surely, he will save you from the fowler's snare and from the deadly pestilence.
He will cover you with his feathers, and under his wings, you will find refuge; his faithfulness will be your shield and rampart.
You will not fear the terror of night, nor the arrow that flies by day,
nor the pestilence that stalks in the darkness, nor the plague that destroys at midday." (Psalms 91:1-6)

As we watched the eagles on that Sunday afternoon, God reminded me that despite mother's condition, she was still under the wings of her God and mine. It was a memorable day.

See you tomorrow, God willing!

September 19 — Muffin

Before our daughter was old enough to go to school, she had regular bouts of tonsillitis. After yet another visit to the doctor, we were advised to have her tonsils removed before she got any older since the recovery from the operation is much easier the younger the patient. We took the doctor's advice and scheduled her for the surgery a little before her fifth birthday. As predicted by the doctor, her recovery was quite rapid and before too long she was up and about.

Shortly after the surgery, we visited our parents in Virginia. For a late birthday present, my mother and my wife took our daughter to see a black Cocker Spaniel puppy that was advertised in the paper. Since mother had always had Cocker Spaniels, she wanted our daughter to have one as well. As fate would have it, the dog was predestined to be hers. How do I know that? First, the place that they went to see the dog was called "Shirley's Place," my wife's name. That was the first clue. The second clue was even stronger. The dog had been born on my daughter's birthday, September 20. That was all the evidence that my mother needed so she purchased the dog for her. She named her new puppy "Muffin" and she became a dear member of our family.

Like all of our dogs over the years, Muffin was a house dog although she did have a tendency to run away every chance she got. We would often let her go out in the backyard with us if we were going to be outside for a while. She was so sneaky. She would slowly walk toward the corner of the house to make sure no one was suspicious. However, once she got just out of sight, she would take off like a proverbial bat out of %&$*. If she got away, which she often did, she would come home stinking to high heaven with the hair on her body full of burrs. At times he was so badly covered that we had to resort to a haircut to get her clean. She did not like to be clean shaven; she was a beautiful dog and she knew it and cutting her hair took away her persona.

Looking back on the chain of events that led Muffin to our household, we know God's hand was in it. "But the plans of the LORD stand firm forever, the purposes of his heart through all generations." (Psalms 33:11). God wants us to be happy and He is always doing little things for us that too often go unnoticed. Keep your eyes open. "Taste and see that the Lord is good." (Psalms 34:8)

See you tomorrow, God willing!

September 20 — The Rocking Chair

There is an old, black, wooden rocker that sits in the attic of our home in Greenville. Today, that rocking chair will have been in the family for forty-four years. If I could read your minds, I think I would hear two questions. One question would be how do you know it has been in the family exactly forty-four years on this particular date? And the second question would probably be who cares?

I'll answer the second question first. Who cares? The answer is we do. Here is why we care. That rocking chair was used by my wife and me as well as both sets of our parents, to rock two little babies to sleep and if they didn't want to sleep, at least we could settle the babies down and cuddle a little with them. Of course, the two babies were our two children and both of them were rocking chair babies. Yes, my wife and I both spent many days and nights rocking in it. Maybe one day we can pass it on, after we get it refinished to the point of removing all of our daughter's leg brace scratches and dog's teeth marks.

You might think that the second question is a little harder to answer with any degree of certainly. How do I know that the rocking chair has been in the family for forty-four years on this exact date? The answer is very simple. The delivery of the rocking chair to our small one-bedroom apartment in Cincinnati was made the day our daughter was born. Since we were at the hospital when the delivery was made, it didn't even go directly to our apartment, but Mrs. Cooley received it on our behalf along with a giant stuffed Panda bear that was also delivered that day. As you might expect, the Panda bear is no longer with us. It lost its stuffing years ago.

You have no doubt figured out that the rocking chair story is my sneaky way of wishing my daughter a happy birthday today.

p.s. I sent this letter to my daughter ahead of time to make sure it was alright to send it to other people. She said yes, on one condition. I said okay, what is the condition? She said that I needed to use a verse from Proverbs to accompany the story. I said okay, what is the verse? She said use Proverbs 26:25, which reads, "Though his speech is charming, do not believe him..."

See you tomorrow, God willing!

September 21 — Chicken Wire

When I lived on a farm as a young boy, we had lots of chickens. Of course, the chickens provide both eggs and wonderful meat. Just the other day, I had a discussion with someone about the gory details of cutting off a chicken's head and then removing its feathers after dipping the dead bird in scalding water. It wasn't a pretty sight, but it was part of life on the farm.

Another part of life on the farm that also related to chickens was the special wire used in a chicken house. Poultry netting, or chicken wire, was invented in 1844 by a Charles Barnard who was the son of a farmer. The wire was specially invented to fence poultry livestock. It is a very thin mesh so it is not too expensive and it does not need to be extra strong to keep chickens caged. Over the years, chicken wire has been used for many other things, particularly making inexpensive cages for other small animals.

That is actually where this story begins. When my wife's brother was a small boy, he was hard to keep in tow. On one occasion, he went down the back walkway where his uncle's Jeep was parked and proceeded to get into the unattended vehicle. As luck would have it, he accidentally released the emergency brake and the car rolled down the bank. Luckily, there was no damage to the car, but her brother did receive a small amount of damage from the liberal use of a branch on his posterior.

On yet another occasion, there was a police car that was parked in the same place as the Jeep. Again, her brother went down the walkway and entered the unattended car. This time he found a loaded gun in the front seat and proceeded to play with it. Since he was too little at the time to generate enough pressure on the trigger to fire the gun, no shots were fired. My wife's dad had had enough. He went to the hardware store and bought enough chicken wire to fence off the entire walkway to make it more difficult for her brother to get off the walkway. Another use for chicken wire had been invented.

In a way, we all have invisible chicken wire that impedes our ability to live a life that is dedicated to our Father in heaven. However, eventually we learn how get around the chicken wire and be free. "You have been set free from sin and have become slaves to righteousness... When you were slaves to sin, you were free from the control of righteousness... But now that you have been set free from sin and have become slaves to God, the benefit you reap leads to holiness, and the result is eternal life." (Romans 6:18, 20, 22) If you haven't learned how to get around the chicken wire in your life, you are missing out.

See you tomorrow, God willing!

September 22   A Baby Changes Everything

"They are having a little girl on 2/2/12." That is the reply my wife's brother sent me after he read the recent letter titled – The Resemblance is Scary. If you change the names and the date, it could be the same message that goes out to untold numbers of people around the world on a daily basis foretelling the arrival of a new baby. The message is so short, yet so profound. If it happens to be a first child and a first grandchild, you cannot begin to measure the impact it will have on the parents and grandparents, not to mention the legion of other relatives who will also be affected.

For new parents to be, they must get tired of being told that once the baby arrives, their lives will never be the same. Yet, once the baby does arrive, they very quickly realize the truth in the statement. There is a Christian song sung by Faith Hill that is titled "A Baby Changes Everything" and the words are so true. Despite the fact that a baby steals all of your time, all of you resources and all of your energy, they also steal your heart, forever. Grown up children finally learn the meaning of unconditional love.

Then there are the grandparents. When you become a grandparent, you join the least exclusive, most enjoyable club in the world. You get to enjoy all the benefits of a baby without all of the work. While you watch your child do most of the work, you also get a little sense of payback, not in a bad way. I think you just feel like your child will have a better appreciation of the attention we gave them when they were babies. I have heard grandparents say on many occasions, "If we knew grandchildren were so wonderful, we would have skipped the children and gone straight to grandchildren." There is no bond quite like the bond that develops between grandparents and grandchildren. That bond starts early when you receive a new name, often invented by the grandchild. My daughter gave my Dad the moniker, Zappy; my first grandson gave me the name, Bopbo; and who knows what name my brother-in-law will receive.

The message my brother-in-law received foretold an event that will happen about four months from now. How about this message that was sent out nearly seven hundred years before Jesus was born! "For to us a child is born, to us a son is given, and the government will be on his shoulders. And he will be called Wonderful Counselor, Mighty God, Everlasting Father, Prince of Peace." (Isaiah 9:6) You talk about a baby that would change lives. Remember, "A Baby Changes Everything."

See you tomorrow, God willing!

September 23 — Everything We Need

I sell the morning paper, sir.
My name is Jimmy Brown.
Everybody knows that I'm the newsboy of this town.
You can hear me holler "Morning Star" up and down the street,
No hat upon my head, sir, no shoes upon my feet.

Those are some of the words to an old country music song from the sixties. I always liked the song because I was a newsboy. While I didn't sell newspapers on the street, I did have a morning newspaper route and I delivered the paper all over town. Unlike the newspaper delivery of today, my clients got their newspapers on their porch or inside the screen door if that is what they requested. Every morning I had to get up by six a.m. to make sure that the papers were delivered in time to be read before people headed off to work. If I remember correctly, I made about five dollars a week.

As a teenager, I had other jobs that helped keep me in spending money. I routinely baby sat for the family who lived right next door to us. They had two young girls who were very easy to watch. It was a snap. I also mowed several lawns in the neighborhood for those people who either had no lawn mower or no desire to be out in the heat during the summer.

My very first money earning venture was on the farm in Illinois. During the summer the wild blackberries were abundant along fence rows and along the railroad tracks. If I had nothing better to do, I would pick the berries and sell them for twenty-five cents a quart. God provided the inventory; I simply had to provide the labor and initiative.

Throughout my life, God has provided me with every thing I need to be joyful in Him – from wild blackberries to a beautiful family and friends. What more could I ever want? "Command those who are rich in this present world not to be arrogant nor to put their hope in wealth, which is so uncertain, but to put their hope in God, who richly provides us with everything for our enjoyment." (1 Peter 6:17) Did you see that? He richly provides us with everything for our enjoyment. He is an awesome God, isn't He?

See you tomorrow, God willing!

September 24   Coffee or Tea?

My mother always had a pot of coffee ready. If there was anything left in the pot at the end of the day, it was not unusual for her to warm it up the next morning and finish the pot before making a fresh one. She liked to drink her coffee with cream and sugar and my dad drank his the same way.

Frankly, I didn't like the taste of coffee so when we got married we only made coffee when we had visitors. After I moved out of my job in the research laboratories and into an office job, I was often in meetings where everyone was drinking coffee. Not to be the odd one, I poured myself a cup of coffee and loaded it up with cream and sugar so I could stomach the taste. Over a short period of time, I began to develop a taste for coffee. For quite a while, I drank my coffee loaded with cream and sugar until I went on a diet and decided to try the coffee black to eliminate some calories. Much to my dismay, I learned to like the coffee without the cream and sugar and have drunk it black for the last forty years.

On a regular day, I drink two or three cups before leaving for work or the golf course. If I go to work, I drink another cup or two before lunch. Am I hooked on caffeine? A couple of times a year, we go on a fast. During the fasts, I give up coffee and all other drinks except fruit juice and water. On the first day of every fast, I get a headache. After this happened a few times, I learned that the headache was caused by caffeine withdrawal. I suppose that means I do have a physical addiction to caffeine. Fortunately, I do not have a mental craving so I have no problem getting through the one day of discomfort.

Fasting is a natural part of our worship of God. Throughout the Old and New Testament, fasting is mentioned as a means of getting closer to God and getting a clearer picture of what God wants us to do with our lives. "'Even now,' declares the Lord, 'return to me with all your heart, with fasting and weeping and mourning.' Rend your heart and not your garments. Return to the Lord your God, for he is gracious and compassionate, slow to anger and abounding in love, and he relents from sending calamity. Who knows? He may turn and have pity and leave behind a blessing—grain offerings and drink offerings for the Lord your God." (Joel 2:12-14) I love the final verse – "who knows? He may turn and have pity and leave behind a blessing." Anytime we walk along the path God has ordained for us, He will leave behind a blessing.

See you tomorrow, God willing!

September 25 — Short and Stocky

Wales is a country that is part of the United Kingdom, bordered by England to its east and the Atlantic Ocean and Irish Sea to its west. Wales has over 700 miles of coastline but is generally very mountainous. If you visit Wales, one of the first things you will notice is how wonderfully green the country seems to be. Not surprisingly, Wales was an agricultural society for most of its early history, the country's terrain making arable farming secondary to pastoral farming, the primary source of Wales' wealth. In the 18th century, the introduction of the slate and metallurgical industries, added another primary vocation for the residents of Wales – mining. The mountains of Wales have abundant seams of both copper and coal so it was natural for these resources to be utilized.

In 1985, on one of my trips to Europe, I had the opportunity to visit the small town of Acrefair in southern Wales. Our company had a manufacturing plant in that town so I was there to visit the site. When I arrived in the town, I could not believe my eyes. Every man that I saw in the town looked just like my dad. They were all short and stocky with heads that were slightly large compared to their bodies. I knew that dad's ancestry was Welsh, but in my wildest dreams, I would never have believed what my eyes were seeing. Not only were the men of similar appearance and build, their vocations were identical to the two vocations that dad had worked his entire life – farming and mining.

That evening as I was lying in my bed trying to fall asleep, I thought about the events of the day. We are but clay in the hands of the master potter. He molds us in ways that we can never imagine, and He gives us the physical, mental, and spiritual gifts that we need to perform the tasks He assigns us here on this planet earth. Why do we not gladly perform the work He gives us to do? "Woe to him who quarrels with his Maker, to him who is but a potsherd among the potsherds on the ground. Does the clay say to the potter, 'What are you making?' Does your work say, 'He has no hands'?" (Isaiah 45:9) The very God who created us has the right to use us for whatever purpose He has placed us here. "Does not the potter have the right to make out of the same lump of clay some pottery for noble purposes and some for common use?" (Romans 9:21)

All of us who have accepted Christ as our savior are being used for noble purposes, no matter how trivial our efforts may look to others. God sees us just like I saw the men of Wales; we are all created in His likeness.

See you tomorrow, God willing!

...nber 26 — Poison Ivy

...letter is written for the males in the family. Some of it may apply to the female gender, but ...cainly not to the degree that the infirmity affects us. As men, we do not like for other people ...to tell us what to do. Early this year, I wrote a note about my grandson that was entitled "Who is Your Boss?" Here are the key words from that story. "You're not the boss of me." Eventually, we have to decide, who is the boss? "I am the Lord your God, who teaches you what is best for you, who directs you in the way you should go." (Isaiah 48:17).

On May 9th, I wrote a story about myself titled "Know It All." It was not a very flattering title, but it described me pretty well. "The ways of the Lord are right; the righteous walk in them, but the rebellious stumble in them" (Hosea 14:9). That verse caused me to pause and think back on my life and recall how obstinate I have been over many things. It seems that I always had to be right.

I haven't specifically written stories about some other males in the family that deal with this particular subject, but if I did, the content would not differ very much. All this having been said, why am I bringing up all of this negative stuff? Here is why. I was recently working in my backyard and the next day I noticed that I had gotten into some poison ivy. Fortunately, I do not get a bad rash from contact with the plant so it is more a nuisance to me rather than a problem. I couldn't help but think of a time when the son of one of our friends coupled his male hard-headedness with poison ivy. The young man and his dad were working in their yard when his dad spotted some poison ivy and warned his son to avoid it. Being all knowing, he told his dad that it was not poison ivy and proceeded to rub it all over his face to prove his point. He did prove a point, just not his. When he woke up the next morning he could not open his eyes because of the swelling. His face was covered with a poison ivy rash.

Here is what the Psalmist tells us about people who do not listen. "But my people would not listen to me... So I gave them over to their stubborn hearts to follow their own devices. If my people would but listen to me... how quickly would I subdue their enemies and turn my hand against their foes... you would be fed with the finest of wheat; with honey from the rock I would satisfy you." (Psalms 81:11-16) It is a hard lesson for us to learn. I am getting better. How about the rest of you?

See you tomorrow, God willing!

September 27

Last week, we went the Outer Banks to spend some leisure time with members of my wife's side of the family. The week was our first opportunity to spend any extended time with my wife's niece and her husband. On the very first evening, we learned that they love to play games. Our first experience was playing the game, "Taboo." The object of the game is to get your partner to say a designated word. You may use other words and phrases to give your partner clues. However, on the card showing the designated word are five other words that are taboo. You cannot use any of those words or you lose that entire round. Of course, the five words that are "taboo" are the ones that you would like to use. Each team is given one minute to get as many designated words as possible until someone reaches the winning score of thirty. I will tell you right now, we did not win. Her brother and his wife did not win. To make matters worse, if you combined their score with ours, we still would not have beaten her niece and husband.

The word "taboo" actually comes from Polynesian society. It described a sacred prohibition put upon certain people, things, or acts which makes them untouchable, unmentionable. In our own culture, the word is used to describe any social prohibition or restriction that results from convention or tradition.

When the Israelites were wandering in the desert for forty years, God sent Moses down from Mount Sinai with Ten Commandments that became their guides for living for the rest of their lives and ours. The first two commandments described actions that were really "taboo" for God. "I am the Lord your God, who brought you out of Egypt, out of the land of slavery. You shall have no other gods before me. You shall not make for yourself an idol in the form of anything in heaven above or on the earth beneath or in the waters below. You shall not bow down to them or worship them; for I, the Lord your God, am a jealous God, punishing the children for the sin of the fathers to the third and fourth generation of those who hate me, but showing love to a thousand generations of those who love me and keep my commandments." (Exodus 20:2-6) Those are just a couple of the rules for the real game of life. While the game of life has many, many rules, it is any easy game to win. All you have to do is accept Jesus as your Lord and Savior and you win. It also makes the game so much easier.

See you tomorrow, God willing!

September 26   Poison Ivy

September 28   Change

When we lived on a farm in 1953, we did not own a television. In fact, at that point in history most families did not own televisions. Believe it or not, the radio was our source of recreation. I can remember listening to the Red Skelton Show on the radio and enjoying his humor. I also remember listening to Amos and Andy on the radio. Again, it was also hilarious, but far superior once it became a regular television show. One year for Christmas, sometime in the mid-nineties, my son gave me a set of six video cassettes with the entire Amos and Andy series on them. Those shows are even funnier today than they were fifty years ago. Two other radio shows that I listened to on a regular basis were Sky King and The Shadow. Even after we got our first television set in 1954, there were only one or two channels.

Another evolution in technology that deserves to be mentioned is the telephone. When we lived on the farm, we had a "party line." In simple terms, a party line meant that multiple families shared one telephone line. While you had a special ring if someone were calling you, that did not keep someone in a completely different household from answering the phone or listening to your conversation, if they so desired. If you wanted to make a call, you often had to wait until the line was not being used by one of the other families who shared the "party line." As an aside, when we first moved to Pennsylvania in 1977, we shared a party line for a few months until a private line could be installed.

Looking back over the past fifty years it is amazing how much change we have seen – phones and television are just two small examples. Can you imagine what changes will take place in the next fifty years? Adapting to change can be a challenge. For many people of my generation, the computer is just too much change to warrant the effort to learn. Therefore, they ignore the possibilities. Sometimes, we just want a little stability in our lives. Perhaps it would be better if we had a little less change. I have something very important to tell all of you. The most important thing in your life will never change.

The minor prophet Malachi tells us – "'I the Lord do not change. So you, O descendants of Jacob, are not destroyed. Ever since the time of your forefathers you have turned away from my decrees and have not kept them. Return to me, and I will return to you,' says the Lord Almighty." (Malachi 3:6-7) If it seems like God has abandoned you, think again. It is you who have turned away. Return to him. He will never change.

See you tomorrow, God willing!

September 29 — Financial Peace University

Stressed about your finances? Do you want to learn the best strategies for managing your money? In this 13-week class taught by Dave Ramsey, you'll learn about saving, eliminating debt, setting up a budget and planning for the future. Given the state of our economy, it isn't too surprising to see a course like this being offered to help people manage their finances. Here is something that may be a little surprising to some of you; the course is being sponsored by several churches in Greenville right now and is largely a Christian-based effort across the United States.

My daughter and her husband signed up for the course to get a better feel for where there money was going; they have been blessed financially so their objective for taking the course was to improve their stewardship of the money they have. Their son and his wife-to-be are taking the course with them and I can't think of a better way to start off a marriage than to get on the same page financially. Money problems are the single largest cause of divorce in the United States.

My wife and I took a similar course when we moved to North Carolina in 2001 and it has had a major impact on our money management for the last ten years. For us, there were two major outcomes. One, we began to keep close track of every dollar that we spent in order to see exactly where our money goes. Once we had a realistic picture of where we were spending our money we began the process of annual budgeting in critical categories ranging from food to entertainment to gasoline to utilities. We now know where our money goes and we do not let any category get out of control. The second major outcome of the course was a different perspective on debt. Without debt, you can have financial freedom.

The Bible has a lot to say about money and its use. The first thing to know is that it all belongs to God. "I have no need of a bull from your stall or of goats from your pens, for every animal of the forest is mine, and the cattle on a thousand hills." (Psalms 50:9-10) Secondly, it never says that money per se is bad. However, it does say in many places that it can become a snare. "People who want to get rich fall into temptation and a trap and into many foolish and harmful desires that plunge men into ruin and destruction. For the love of money is a root of all kinds of evil. Some people, eager for money, have wandered from the faith and pierced themselves with many griefs. But you, man of God, flee from all this, and pursue righteousness, godliness, faith, love, endurance and gentleness." (1 Timothy 6:9-11) Pursue righteousness and the fruit of the Spirit and you will succeed in life.

See you tomorrow, God willing!

September 30 — Shattered Dreams

What do you want to be when you grow up? That is a question you often hear posed to children and teenagers as they consider their life ambition. A poll taken in 2009 listed the following professions as the top five: writer, pop star, pro athlete, doctor and movie star. I am surprised that "writer" is number one, but the other four professions are as expected.

When I was growing up, I did not have a career aspiration, but I did have one dream and that was to play football at the college level. I started playing football on an organized level in the eighth grade and continued to play all the way through high school. Although I am short of height, I was big enough to play major college football back in the days when most linebackers weighed slightly over two hundred pounds. As a senior in high school, I weighed one hundred ninety five pounds and I'm sure with a little weight training I would have been heavy enough to play. A better question might have been – was I good enough?

In retrospect, my dream of playing college football was shattered by a serious injury to my left knee only three games from the completion of my high school career. There is a great book by Larry Crabb entitled "Shattered Dreams" that I read in the past year that really helped me understand events in my life. Here is a great quote from the book – "God is always working to make His children aware of a dream that remains alive beneath the rubble of every shattered dream, a new dream that when realized will release a new song, sung with tears, till God wipes them away and we sing with nothing but joy in our hearts."

It took me awhile to get over my shattered dream, but now I know that God had something much better for me. In the book of Genesis, Joseph shared dreams about his future with his brothers that ultimately led to his shattered life in Egypt. He eventually became second in command to the Pharaoh. When Joseph's family came to Egypt for food, it was all he could do to keep his identity from them. Finally, he said, 'I am Joseph! 'Come close to me'... 'I am your brother Joseph, the one you sold into Egypt … it was to save lives that God sent me ahead of you.'" (Genesis 45:1-5) Little did Joseph know that his original dream was not really shattered, it simply did not pan out as he had envisioned it. I suppose all of our shattered dreams are that way. God's plans are always better anyway.

See you tomorrow, God willing!

OCTOBER

365 love letters

October 1 — Jet Lag

Nearly all of us have had the opportunity to fly long distances and traverse many time zones in the process. If the number of time zones you pass through happens to be small, one or two, it is not likely to cause you trouble with your sleeping patterns. However, if you fly from the East Coast of the United States to the West Coast, you will absolutely have trouble going to bed and getting up at your normal hours. The phenomenon is called "jet lag," and it may last several days. A recovery rate of one day per time zone crossed is a fair guideline.

In the spring of 1985, I was going to England for a two-week business trip. My normal pattern for dealing with the five-hour time difference was to take the late night flight from Newark to London that left on Sunday evening and arrived at Heathrow around six a.m. on Monday morning. I found that if I could sleep for a while on the plane, I could go straight to work on Monday morning and try to get on London time as fast as possible. The week was jammed with meetings during the day and dinners in the evening. I managed to get through the week with no apparent jet lag. I suppose the adrenaline kept me going. On Friday after work, I declined another group meal and told my colleagues that I would see them on Monday morning. When I went back to my hotel, I decided to lie down for a short nap before I went out for dinner. My short nap turned out to be a fourteen-hour night of sleep. I did not wake up from my nap until eight o'clock the next morning. I had not avoided jet lag, I had just postponed it.

One of my favorite stories in the Bible is told in 1 Kings, Chapters 17-19. It is the story of Elijah and his run-ins with Ahab and Jezebel. After his ordeal, Elijah fled from Jezebel and by the time he reached his destination, he was exhausted. "'I have had enough, LORD,' he said. 'Take my life; I am no better than my ancestors.' Then he lay down under the tree and fell asleep.'"(1 Kings 19:4-5) It doesn't say how long Elijah slept, but it does lead us to believe that he fell asleep due to exhaustion. To make a long story short, an angel of the lord appeared to Elijah and fed his physical and spiritual spirit. There is the lesson. No matter how tired we are; no matter how downtrodden; no matter how much sleep we have lost; God will care for His children. I feel better knowing that. How about you?

See you tomorrow, God willing!

October 2 — Opening Night

My mom always had a dog to keep her company sometimes more than one. Most of the time, she had Cocker Spaniels, but occasionally another breed would creep into the mix by mistake. Mother's last dog was not Cocker Spaniel, although it was supposed to be. Jill was given to Mother by her veterinarian when her Cocker Spaniel died. He told her it was a mixed breed Cocker Spaniel, but it turned out he was wrong. By the time you could tell it wasn't what it was supposed to be, mother had fallen in love again. It turned out that Jill was a Schipperke. They are about the same size as a Cocker Spaniel, but have longer hair and a long cork-screw tail. Their worst feature is this, they shed constantly. You could almost see a trail of black hair following Jill as she walked through the house.

Jill was a very good companion for mother, but also a problem. The dog psychiatrist called Jill's condition, "separation syndrome." In layman's terms, that means the dog went wacko every time it was left alone. If Jill were left alone in a car, she would eat seat belts, rip the cushions, or chew on anything else to calm herself. She did the same thing if she were left alone in a house.

In October 2002, my wife and I completed the building of our current home here in North Carolina. Mother and Jill were living with us at the time and when we built the house; it was designed to have space for my mother or my wife's mother if the situation arose. The very first evening we were in the house, we went out for about an hour to get a bite to eat. We were tired from moving, so cooking that evening was out of the question. We left Jill in Mother's room knowing we wouldn't be gone very long. When we returned from dinner, we were aghast. Jill had demolished the carpet in front of the door and ruined the paint on the bedroom door by violent scratching. As my wife viewed the destruction, she turned white and walked away. I knew she was about to pop, but she said nothing.

I saw a lot of forgiveness that night and I have a better feel for what Jesus meant when Peter asked Him about forgiving. "Then Peter came to Jesus and asked, 'Lord, how many times shall I forgive my brother when he sins against me? Up to seven times?' Jesus answered, 'I tell you, not seven times, but seventy-seven times" (Matthew 18:21-22). How long does it take to forgive someone seventy-seven times? In my wife's case, it was about two seconds. I should also add that God doesn't really worry about seventy times seven for Himself; the number of times He forgives us is infinite and it's a good thing, because that is just what I need.

See you tomorrow, God willing!

October 3 — Colorful Sayings

As I was reading my Bible the other morning I finished the story of Samson in the book of Judges. Most people are more familiar with the story of Samson and Delilah; however, Samson had another wife before Delilah that also caused him much consternation. Samson had posed a riddle to thirty Philistines and promised them a reward if they could solve the riddle. When his wife pried the answer to the riddle from him and gave the answer to her Philistine brothers, Samson was forced to pay off his promise. In anger he responded to the "winners," "If you had not plowed with my heifer, you would not have solved my riddle." (Judges 14:18) What a colorful expression!

Samson's remark reminded me of my father-in-law and his colorful expressions. Here are some of my all-time favorites. That man is "busier than a one-armed wall paper hanger." "Is that you spoke or a fence rail broke?" Or, try this one, "nervous as a long-tailed cat in a room full of rocking chairs." He was a great story teller and I loved his use of colorful language to enhance a story.

My dad also had a few favorite sayings, which had a barnyard flavor since they were likely derived from his early years on the farm. When we got a heavy rain, Dad would always say "it is raining like a cow peeing on a flat rock." When he talked about money, he would say it was "scarce as hen's teeth." And finally, when we couldn't get anywhere no matter how hard we tried, dad would say "we were running around like a blind dog in a meat shop."

I have a few sayings of my own. One of my favorites relates to trying to get one over on me – "It's like trying to sneak the rising sun by a rooster." I am also quite fond of the phrase from an old country song – "Lights are on, but nobody is home" – an expression that is used to describe someone who is not playing with a full deck. You get the idea.

D. L. Moody is a well known evangelist and publisher who founded the Moody Institute. He published a number of sayings related to our Christian walk. Here are a few.

"Law tells me how crooked I am; grace comes along and straightens me out."
"Excuses are the cradle ... that Satan rocks men off to sleep in."
"God never made a promise that was too good to be true."

In closing, I'd like to leave you with one more colorful expression that speaks to our desire for natural things rather than our desire for God. It is a verse from the minor prophet Micah, Chapter 2 verse 11 – "If a liar and deceiver comes and says, 'I will prophesy for you plenty of wine and beer,' he would be just the prophet for this people!" Now that is colorful language.

See you tomorrow, God willing!

October 4 — Winding Roads

In the southwestern corner of Virginia where I was raised the scenery is absolutely gorgeous. The region is part of the Appalachian Mountain Range that extends from southeastern Canada to Central Alabama in the United States. The highest peaks of the mountains running through Virginia soar to heights of nearly five thousand feet often providing panoramas that have to be seen to be fully appreciated. This time of year when the leaves are changing, you will not see more beautiful colors anywhere.

When we moved from Illinois to Virginia in 1955 when I was nine years old, I was not used to the mountains. Southern Illinois is flat country and the view consists of miles and miles of corn, wheat, and soybean fields. The roads are flat with few turns in the road. All of that changed when we moved. When you are crossing over a mountain, travel is very slow. There are "S" curves after "S" curves and it seems as if you are traveling in circles to get where you want to go. For some people, riding in a car under these conditions causes one to become sick to his or her stomach. For quite a while, I was one of those people. The family liked to go for rides on Sunday afternoon to see the new scenery. While everyone else in the car was enjoying the ride, I was doing all I could to keep from getting sick. It was no fun, to say the least. I finally grew out of the impairment or we finally quit going on Sunday afternoon drives; I don't remember which it was.

As I think back on my life, I know that I have travelled on many crooked roads. I have not followed the straight road that Jesus calls on us to walk. After all, why should I be different? It took the Israelites forty years to get out of the wilderness because they kept going in circles. Had I followed the straight path, life would have been filled with less nausea! "Listen, my son, accept what I say, and the years of your life will be many. I guide you in the way of wisdom and lead you along straight paths. When you walk, your steps will not be hampered; when you run, you will not stumble. Do not set foot on the path of the wicked or walk in the way of evil men. Avoid it, do not travel on it; turn from it and go on your way." (Proverbs 4:10-15) These words from the book of Proverbs are pretty clear. It's a shame that is so hard to follow them on our own.

See you tomorrow, God willing!

October 5 — Death of a Friend

Yesterday, I attended a funeral at our church for a friend of mine who died of a heart attack at the age of sixty-one. I know his wife much better than I knew him because she has been a member of our choir for many years, and I served with her on a worship arts committee that met regularly for over a year. She is a woman of great spiritual depth and maturity so I know she will handle his death as well as anyone could be expected.

While I didn't know her husband too well, here is what I did know about him. He was always smiling and always in good spirits. Even though he had had health problems during the last few months, you would never have known it by looking at him or talking to him. There is one other thing I know about him; I know where he is right now.

When someone I know dies at an age that is younger than I am, it causes me to think about my own mortality and to think about myself in a different light. One thing that I would like for you to know is why I smile all the time. I smile because I:

- grew up knowing I was loved
- have been blessed with good health all my life
- have a wonderful wife who loves me despite all my faults
- have two beautiful children who have great spouses
- am blessed with five magnificent grandchildren
- have more material goods than I could ever need
- am blessed with a keen mind and an ability to relate well with people
- know Jesus and have a personal relationship with Him

It would not be hard for me to make the aforementioned list much longer, because I have truly been blessed. As I near my sixty-fifth birthday, I am confident that my life has had meaning and I pray that I will continue to be a blessing to others. In a couple of weeks, my wife and I will be going on our third mission trip, this one to the Dominican Republic, to share our blessings with underprivileged people in that part of the world. If it is anything like our last two mission trips, to Honduras and Bulgaria, we are in for wonderful blessings.

Earlier, I said I knew where my friend is today, and furthermore, I know where I will be when my life is finished on this earth. God's word is very clear. "I tell you the truth, whoever hears my word and believes him who sent me has eternal life and will not be condemned; he has crossed over from death to life." (John 5:24) My friend has crossed over from death to life and those who loved him here will see him again. Praise be to God.

See you tomorrow, God willing!

October 6 — Yet I will Rejoice

Yesterday I wrote about a funeral at our church and I mentioned that the man's wife is a woman of great spiritual depth and maturity. After reflecting on the funeral for an evening, I couldn't help but share with you what I saw of her deep faith at the funeral. First, the music that was sung at the funeral was spirit-filled and she didn't miss the opportunity to demonstrate her passion for God in her personal worship. Having worshipped with her for years I can tell you without a shadow of a doubt that her husband's death has done nothing to challenge her faith. As our lead singer offered his gift of music with the singing of "Midnight Cry," she was on her feet with her arms raised to her Mighty God who has held her hand during this time of grief.

Tears rolled down my face as I marveled at her courage and her acknowledgement that God had not deserted her. I know that she will face times when she will miss her best friend. I know there will be moments when she will ask "why?" I know she will be lonely when her extended family returns to home. I know because she is human.

There is something else I know about her. She will not let anything separate her from the love of God. "For I am convinced that neither death nor life, neither angels nor demons, neither the present nor the future, nor any powers, neither height nor depth, nor anything else in all creation, will be able to separate us from the love of God that is in Christ Jesus our Lord." (Romans 8:38-39) The prophet Habakkuk knew about people like my friend. "Though the fig tree does not bud and there are no grapes on the vines, though the olive crop fails and the fields produce no food, though there are no sheep in the pen and no cattle in the stalls, yet I will rejoice in the Lord, I will be joyful in God my Savior." (Habakkuk 3:17-18) No matter what happens, she will be joyful in God her Savior. I have nothing more to add.

See you tomorrow, God willing!

October 7 — Not All That Glitters Is Gold

My father-in-law was a great storyteller. One of my favorite stories was about a small revolver that he kept in the safe in his bedroom. He told us that he bought the brand new revolver from an acquaintance who had won the revolver in a game of chance. The game of chance happened to be a "tip board" that my father-in-law had run. A "tip board" was a piece of cardboard that had a ten by ten matrix (or larger) of slips of paper (called tips) mounted on the board. You purchased as many tips as you liked. Most of the tips were blank but some contained a number. If you purchased a tip and happened to get a blank, you knew you had no chance to win the item being raffled. If you happened to get a number, you knew you had a good chance of winning. The purpose of having blank tips was to encourage people to buy as many tips as it took to have some chance of winning. To make a long story short, he sold all of his tips and made a nice profit on his raffle. The aforementioned acquaintance won the revolver, which he did not want, so my father-in-law bought it back from him for half of the price he had paid for it.

After hearing many of his stories, I was convinced that he had the "Midas Touch." King Midas is popularly remembered in Greek mythology for his ability to turn everything he touched into gold. Of all the stories I heard from my father-in-law, none involved losing money.

My father-in-law also knew that gold and silver were not really important, but family was. He knew what Job proclaimed after losing all that he had. ""If I have put my trust in gold or said to pure gold, 'You are my security,' if I have rejoiced over my great wealth, the fortune my hands had gained... then these also would be sins to be judged, for I would have been unfaithful to God on high." (Job 31:24-28) Although he did indeed have a Midas touch, he never let it consume him. He was generous to all of us and that is how we remember him.

See you tomorrow, God willing!

October 8 — Early to Bed

God has blessed me with good health all of my life. During the twenty-five years that I worked in Pennsylvania I did not miss a single day of work because of illness. When the flu ran through the community, it missed me, as did every other ailment that seemed to hit everyone else. While I do eat properly (by and large) and I generally get enough exercise, I can't attribute my good health to my own actions. Clearly, God has blessed me with good health. There is, however, one thing that I do that helps more than anything else; I generally get a good night's sleep.

When I was in college, I was amazed by the number of "smart" people who would stay up all night cramming for final exams. As for me, it was more important to get a good night's sleep so my mind would be sharp for the exam.

From my earliest days, I have always been an early riser. It is rare for me to sleep past six a.m. no matter what time I go to bed. I generally wake up around five-thirty and I now go to bed around eleven in the evening. On an average night, I get about seven hours of sleep and that seems to work well for me. During my working career, my wife will tell you that I was never up past ten o'clock in the evening and I was generally in bed by nine. Until I retired, I needed eight or nine hours of sleep to keep me going.

There is one other secret component of my sleep; it is called the afternoon nap. God told us that the Sabbath was to be a day of rest and I took Him seriously. "Remember the Sabbath day by keeping it holy. Six days you shall labor and do all your work, but the seventh day is a Sabbath to the Lord your God. On it you shall not do any work, neither you, nor your son or daughter, nor your manservant or maidservant, nor your animals, nor the alien within your gates. For in six days the Lord made the heavens and the earth, the sea, and all that is in them, but *he rested on the seventh day.*" (Exodus 20:8-11) Sunday afternoon's were made for napping. Nothing refreshes you more than a short nap. My favorite birthday card of all time was given to me by daughter many years ago and I can still remember the verses inside the card. "My dad told me to learn from yesterday; plan for tomorrow; and nap this afternoon." I don't know if I ever gave her that advice, but if I didn't I could have. Remember the old adage, "Early to bed, early to rise, makes a man healthy, wealthy and wise." It is still true.

See you tomorrow, God willing!

October 9   Are You Equipped?

I have always been a big football fan. As I watch the game today, there is a huge difference in the equipment that players wear. Let me give you a few examples. When dad played high school football in the early 1930's, they wore leather helmets. There are some wise guys in the family who have suggested that when I played there were leather helmets; while that may be funny, it isn't true. By the time I played the game in the mid-sixties, the helmets were plastic, but many of the players had a single-bar facemask like the one's you see worn today by place kickers. Although the helmets were plastic, they were nowhere near the quality of construction that they are today.

By the time my son played football, equipment had evolved yet another step. All of the shoulder pads, hip pads, and other equipment had gotten much lighter, more durable, and provided better protection. When my grandson became the fourth generation of football players in the family, you could see another step in the evolution. Helmets now provide much better protection and the facemask is almost impenetrable. There are extra pads for ribs, and other vulnerable parts of the body. Even the shoes are better.

While injury is still possible with the best equipment, the chance of being hurt greatly increases if you happen to use the wrong equipment. Believe it or not, there are good examples in the Bible. Let's take Goliath for example. "A champion named Goliath, who was from Gath, came out of the Philistine camp. He was over nine feet tall. He had a bronze helmet on his head and wore a coat of scale armor of bronze weighing five thousand shekels; on his legs he wore bronze greaves, and a bronze javelin was slung on his back." (1 Samuel 17:4-6) He had the best equipment available and he was huge, but it didn't do him any good.

The Bible also tells us that there is much better equipment available. "Therefore put on the full armor of God, so that when the day of evil comes, you may be able to stand your ground, and after you have done everything, to stand. Stand firm then, with the belt of truth buckled around your waist, with the breastplate of righteousness in place, and with your feet fitted with the readiness that comes from the gospel of peace. In addition to all this, take up the shield of faith, with which you can extinguish all the flaming arrows of the evil one. Take the helmet of salvation and the sword of the Spirit, which is the word of God." Ephesians 6:13-17) No matter what game we play, the equipment described in Ephesians will protect us because it is the armor of God.

See you tomorrow, God willing!

October 10 — Coming Home!

Two little boys, ages four and seven, are kicking a walnut around their yard in the days way before soccer was even thought about in the United States. The youngest of the two boys kicks at the walnut, slips, and goes down in a heap. To his brother's dismay, he cannot get up. His thigh bone has snapped and the game is over. For the next six weeks, the little boy will spend twenty-four hours a day with his leg in traction in the hospital. By now I am sure you have guessed that the little boy was I. It was a freak accident and I have not suffered any on-going problems from the break.

As fate would have it, another member of my family would suffer more than I did. The day I came out of the hospital after my six-week stay happened to be my sister's birthday. I think that I got more presents than she did and she could not have been very happy. As a ten year old, I am sure she didn't want to share her special day with a clumsy brother who had broken his leg and was so thoughtless as to come home on her birthday. Shame on me! Over the years, we have joked about that day, and to my knowledge she has not held a grudge.

In the book of Genesis, there is a well known story of two siblings who had let the events of life get in the way of their relationship. Jacob had stolen Esau's birthright and then fled to another country to save his life. Years later, with his wives and children, he returned home to face his brother. Jacob feared for his life and he prayed to God for protection. "Save me, I pray, from the hand of my brother Esau, for I am afraid he will come and attack me, and also the mothers with their children." (Genesis 32:11) God had already gone before him and softened Esau's heart. "But Esau ran to meet Jacob and embraced him; he threw his arms around his neck and kissed him. And they wept." (Genesis 33:4)

How many of us carry old scars from the past? Many of these scars have been inflicted on us by family members, and those were the deepest wounds. The next time you are in your "pity pot," just think about the story of Jacob and Esau and how God made sure this story had a happy ending.

See you tomorrow, God willing!

October 11 — Moving On

We had lived in Cincinnati for ten years when it came time to move on. I had accepted a new job in Pennsylvania that offered more opportunity. We had roots in Cincinnati; we had a close church family; we had a small group of couples our age that had developed very strong friendships; and I had friends at work that helped me become a more mature businessperson. Let's face it, moving took its emotional toll on all of us.

Twenty-five years later, it was time for me to take early retirement and move from to Greenville, NC. Our daughter had left in 1985 to go to college and when she got married in 1990, we knew she had settled into a new life. Our son was also gone. The number of friends we had made in Pennsylvania was exponentially larger than our group of friends in Ohio. We had an even larger group of friends from our church; we had a larger group of couples who shared common interests; I had a group of golfing buddies; and I had new friends where I worked and many business associates I had met during my working career. However, time marches on and we had to leave them behind, just as we left our friends behind in Ohio.

At the time one moves, there is an expectation that friends will always be friends. While that might be true philosophically, it rarely turns out to be true in practice. Of all of our friends in Ohio, we only talk regularly with one. Among our friends in Pennsylvania, we do keep in close contact with several people, but we remain close friends with only a few.

I suppose our experience in moving around is the norm, not the exception. Unfortunately, staying in the same place all of your life is not always possible. Staying in Cincinnati was not an option for me. Staying in Pennsylvania was not an option for my daughter if she wanted to start life in a more favorable climate. And, staying in North Carolina was not an option for our son if he wanted to start life fresh in a place where he felt more at home. Until we get to heaven, we will not see God's hand in all of these moves, but rest assured His hand has been there all the time. When God called Abram to pull up stakes, it was an early indication that God moves people where He wants them to be. "The LORD had said to Abram, "Leave your country, your people and your father's household and go to the land I will show you." (Genesis 12:1) He has been moving people around for centuries and He will never stop. At this point in my own life, I am trying to be more aware of where He wants me to be.

See you tomorrow, God willing!

October 12 — Hole-in-One

A few days ago, I received a response from one of my letters. The reply simply said "Hole-in-One." As a golfer, I knew immediately what the intent of the message was and I responded to the individual. My response was just about as short – "That, my brother, is a supreme compliment!"

For all of you golfers out there or "wanna be" golfers, the hole in one is a lifetime aspiration of every golfer. It is that one perfect shot. You do not have to be a professional to achieve the goal, nor do you even have to be any good at the game. Some people achieve the goal very early in their golfing life. Other people may play the game their entire life and never make a hole-in-one. Personally, I thought for many years that I was going to fall into the latter category. For the first forty plus years of my golfing career, I flirted with making a hole-in-one many many times. Hardly a year went by without a close call. On one occasion, the friends who were playing with me congratulated me on my first hole-in-one only to reach the green and find the ball directly behind the pin hanging on the lip of the hole.

Finally on October 19th, 2004, I made my first, and probably last, hole-in-one. I had kidded with my grandsons that they might beat me to the punch. Both of them had near misses when they were playing regularly. Since my daughter was "home schooling" them at the time, I pulled out my cell phone on the next tee and called my oldest grandson to let him know that he had missed his chance.

For years I had chased my goal of making a hole-in-one and I had finally arrived. How had my life changed? What had I really achieved? Was the world a better place? For all King Solomon achieved and for all his worldly possessions, he knew those achievements and possessions were meaningless, "Yet when I surveyed all that my hands had done and what I had toiled to achieve, everything was meaningless, a chasing after the wind; nothing was gained under the sun." (Ecclesiastes 2:11) Later in the same chapter of Ecclesiastes, Solomon provided this profound wisdom. "A man can do nothing better than to eat and drink and find satisfaction in his work. This too, I see, is from the hand of God, for without him, who can eat or find enjoyment? To the man who pleases him, God gives wisdom, knowledge and happiness, but to the sinner he gives the task of gathering and storing up wealth to hand it over to the one who pleases God." (Ecclesiastes 2:24-26) If you are unfamiliar with these words, I encourage you to read them again and ponder their meaning. It could change your life.

See you tomorrow, God willing!

October 13 — Learning to Swim

Learning to swim is not like learning to walk. It is not compulsory and to many people it is altogether unnecessary. Some people learn to swim when they are children and some never learn.

Personally, I taught myself how to swim along the edge of Lake Benton in Southern Illinois. Our family had a small cabin on the lake and we spent a great deal of time at the cabin in the summer. Dad was working as a salesman at the time and he was apparently doing well enough for us to have a second home, modest as it was. I can remember swimming in water that was only inches deep as I learned the proper strokes. Eventually, I moved into slightly deeper water and repeated the motions until I was in even deeper water. It sounds strange, but that is how I remember it.

There is another technique that other people use to encourage people to learn how to swim. You simply throw the person in deep water and let their natural instincts take over. Sometimes it works; and sometimes it does not work. During the first year of their marriage, my brother-in-law and his wife went on a vacation to Myrtle Beach with another couple. She could swim as long as her face was in the water. However, she could not swim if she tried to swim any other way. My brother-in-law convinced her that if she would just jump into the deep part of the pool, she would overcome the mental block. When she tried it, she nearly drowned while her husband stood on the edge trying to encourage her. Finally, someone jumped into the pool and helped her out. To this day, she can still swim with her face in the water, but not otherwise.

Let's face it, some people are just not meant to learn how to swim. There is a story in the Bible that relates to swimming, but has a little different twist. Jesus could walk on water, and so could Peter for a short time. However, when he took his eyes off Jesus he began to sink. "'Lord, if it's you,' Peter replied, 'tell me to come to you on the water.' 'Come,' he said. Then Peter got down out of the boat, walked on the water.... But when he saw the wind, he was afraid and, beginning to sink, cried out, 'Lord, save me!' Immediately Jesus reached out his hand and caught him. 'You of little faith,' he said, 'why did you doubt?'" (Matthew 14:25, 28-31) In my sister-in-law's case, it was not lack of faith that caused her to sink; it was simply lack of proper swimming technique. For many of us, we fail at many endeavors for the same reason Peter sank, lack of faith. Where in you life is lack of faith causing you to sink?

See you tomorrow, God willing!

October 14 — Give Proper Recognition

Mother was going to be turning eighty in January of 2002 and we were planning on having an eightieth birthday party for her at her church in St. Paul. We had been talking about mother's health for some time. The question that we faced was not complicated, but the answer was difficult. How long could she keep living by herself and where would she go? Her memory had been getting worse and worse and the last time I had been to visit her, I had found quite a number of uncashed insurance checks in her desk.

When her birthday finally rolled around we all showed up. We invited many of her friends from the church as well as other friends in the small town. We fed them well and even provided them with some entertainment. My son-in-law played the guitar and my sister and I sang "Knowing You Jesus" and "In the Morning When I Rise." I am sure that we weren't very good, but our hearts were in the right place.

Within just a few weeks of her birthday, our worst fears were realized. Mother had not been seen for a couple of days so one of her friends went by the house to check on her. She was deathly ill and was rushed to the hospital where she was diagnosed with double pneumonia. While she was in the hospital she had a mild stroke. After being in the hospital for a few days she was ready to be released. However, the hospital would not release her to go home by herself. She had to have somewhere to go. My wife and I decided to take her back to Greenville with us until she recouped. After being with us for a few weeks, it was apparent that she could never live alone again.

Many "Baby Boomers" are also part of another generation known as the "sandwich generation" because we are caught in the middle of caring for aged parents and maturing adult children. For my wife and me, we have had the good fortune of caring for both of our mothers. There was never a doubt in our minds about what we would do. In fact, God gave us some pretty clear directions. "Give proper recognition to those widows who are really in need. But if a widow has children or grandchildren, these should learn first of all to put their religion into practice by caring for their own family and so repaying their parents and grandparents, for this is pleasing to God." (1 Timothy 5:3-4) Paul gave these instructions to Timothy two thousand years ago, and the words still ring true today.

See you tomorrow, God willing.

October 15 — What Is This?

Children are picky eaters and it is hard to change them. Parents will do almost anything to encourage their children to try new foods and clean up their plate. When I was growing up, I was taught to clean my plate because there would be no more food until the next meal. As a growing boy, the tactic worked well and I learned to eat everything, even food that may not have tasted too good at first bite.

When our kids were growing up, we tried to get them to clean their plates and try new foods. Our son would eat almost anything. Our daughter, however, would try some foods, but her appetite was not as good so it was hard to get her to clean her plate. She developed her own special technique to make it look like she had eaten a large portion of her food. As she ate, she would make sure that the remaining food was spread across the whole plate giving the allusion that there was only a small amount remaining.

A story about picky eaters would not be complete without mention of two other folks in the family. When our son-in-law first came into the family, he could not even look at a banana without having a gag reflex. Although we encouraged him to try, he simply could not take more than a small bite without getting sick. Years later, he overcame this mental block and eats bananas and other fruit on a regular basis.

Our youngest grandson's story is much funnier. He does not like mushrooms. Everyone else in the family likes mushrooms both cooked and raw. Several dishes that my wife makes include mushrooms but she leaves out the mushrooms for his sake. However, there was one occasion that she used cream of mushroom soup in one of her casseroles thinking she might be able to sneak it by him. As he was eating, he stopped and pulled a very tiny bit of mushroom from his mouth; held it on the tip of his finger; and then he proclaimed in a very loud voice to all around the table, "What is this?" As I said in another story, it was like trying to sneak a sunrise by a rooster.

In Biblical days there were many regulations concerning the food that people were allowed to eat, lest they become unclean. Over the years, I'm sure it had a major impact over the types of foods people got used to eating and the types of foods they liked.

"Don't you see that whatever enters the mouth goes into the stomach and then out of the body? But the things that come out of the mouth come from the heart, and these make a man 'unclean.'" (Matthew 15:17-18) The moral of the story is this – "eat, drink, and be happy. But, watch what comes out of your mouth.

See you tomorrow, God willing!

October 16   Use Your Gifts Wisely

At our first training session for our upcoming mission trip to the Dominican Republic, each member of the team was asked to volunteer for a specific duty while we are there. I volunteered to be the historian for the trip since journaling is an activity that I would be doing anyway. Would you believe that my wife looked at the list of options and chose hospitality? When God was handing out gifts, she got enough hospitality to last her a lifetime.

When anyone comes to our house to visit or to have dinner, she will leave no stone unturned to insure that our guests have a memorable experience. Let me take a dinner party or a family holiday meal as an example. After the house is thoroughly cleaned, she starts decorating. If it happens to be the Christmas season, the entire house is decorated and she does a beautiful job. On other occasions, the focus of the decorating is likely to be on the dining room table. Her table decorations are out of this world, ranging from ice skating figurines on mirrors during the winter to myriads of unique seas shells in the summer time.

At many of our dinner parties, particularly the family gatherings, it is not enough to decorate the table, she also includes small toys that even the so-called grown ups will use for entertainment between courses. There are spinning tops and flashing lights, not to mention the small puppet-like characters that collapse at the push of a button. It is all about increasing the quality of the overall experience.

Of course, the hospitality would be useless if the quality and quantity of food failed to measure up. There must be hot hors d'oeuvres, cold hors d'oeuvres, plenty of meat and potatoes, and scrumptious vegetable dishes, all capped off with homemade dessert, ice cream and coffee. The meals are fit for a king and that is the way she chooses to treat her guests, like royalty. She truly has the gift of hospitality.

In Paul's first letter to Timothy, there is a reference to her, "and (she) is well known for her good deeds, such as bringing up children, showing hospitality, washing the feet of the saints, helping those in trouble and devoting herself to all kinds of good deeds." (1 Timothy 5:10) No one does it any better than she does. Paul gave my wife her first instructions in his letter to the Romans. "Share with God's people who are in need. Practice hospitality." (Romans 12:13) She has practiced hospitality for as long as I have known her, and she is good at it. Make sure you use the gifts God has given you.

See you tomorrow, God willing!

October 17   Stolen Crackers?

For the last several years I have had the good fortune to go the Myrtle Beach to play golf with three other golfers who are regulars with me at Brook Valley. Since we have been going for several years, there are a handful of courses that have become part of our "tour." One of those courses is named "Crow's Creek" for a reason that will become apparent as the story unfolds.

Three years ago as we were playing at Crow's Creek, one of the guys had a pack of crackers disappear from the golf cart at some point during the round. He accused the person who was riding with him in the cart of taking the crackers since he didn't know what happened to them. He told him that the crackers had been stolen by one of the crows that are always around the course. Unfortunately, the "cracker" man didn't believe the story and continued to think that his buddy had pulled a trick on him.

The following year, we were once again playing at Crow's Creek. This time, I had a pack of opened crackers in the golf cart and as I walked off of the green after finishing a hole, a crow flew out of the golf cart with my pack of crackers in its beak. The crows had struck again, but this time I caught them in the act. Now, over a year later, the "accuser" of the previous year finally conceded that his riding partner had been telling the truth – an oddity in itself.

Crows and their cousins, the raven, are notorious scavengers. They will steal food from other birds or any other source available to them. That is one of the reasons why the story of Elijah in 1st Kings is so amazing. God had Elijah fed by ravens for several years. "Then the word of the LORD came to Elijah: ... You will drink from the brook, and I have ordered the ravens to feed you there." ... The ravens brought him bread and meat in the morning and bread and meat in the evening, and he drank from the brook." (1 Kings 17:2, 4, 6)

There are two lessons to learn from this story. One, if you are ever playing golf at Crow's Creek, don't leave any food around for the crows to snatch. Two, if God wants to use you for some purpose, He will do so; it doesn't matter if the job fits your particular skill set. He uses whomever he chooses. Just ask Moses, Gideon, Jonah, Noah, Isaiah, or even ravens. They will tell you.

See you tomorrow, God willing!

October 18 — Travel by Train

My first real experience with trains as a source of transportation took place in the summer of 1965 when I went to Germany to work for the summer. Since the train system throughout Europe is quite extensive and trains tickets are economical, that was my primary mode of transportation. Unlike the United States where the train station is often located in some undesirable part of a town or city, that is not the case in Europe. Der Bahnhoff is usually located near the center of a city convenient to hotels and sights of interest. Since my first real experience with train stations was in Germany, I still think of train stations as "Bahnhoff" because that is where the association in my mind is strongest.

Twenty years later when the whole family went to live in London for the summer, our teenage children got their first experience riding on trains. The train station in Epson was within walking distance of our flat so it was not unusual for the family to grab a train and go somewhere interesting during the day while I was working. My favorite spot in London was Trafalgar Square –the location of The National Gallery of Art, one of the foremost art museums in the world. While my wife also enjoyed the museum, she also liked to travel to Kensington to visit another world famous location, Harrods's Department Store.

Over the last century, man's ability to get from place to place in a short period has changed dramatically. Trains in Japan and the Far East travel at speeds approaching two hundred miles per hour and airplanes carry passengers around the world at speeds approaching the speed of sound. Travel just isn't what it used to be. However, there is one thing about travel that has not changed, you still have to be careful where you go, not everywhere is safe. "Do not set foot on the path of the wicked or walk in the way of evil men. Avoid it, do not travel on it; turn from it and go on your way. For they cannot sleep till they do evil…They eat the bread of wickedness and drink the wine of violence. The path of the righteous is like the first gleam of dawn, shining ever brighter till the full light of day. But the way of the wicked is like deep darkness; they do not know what makes them stumble." (Proverbs 4:14-19) If you simply remember one other verse from the Bible, you can be assured of walking on the right path – "Your Word is a lamp to my feet and a light for my path." (Psalms 119:105) If He isn't lighting the path, don't go there.

See you tomorrow, God willing!

October 19   World Series Memories

As the World Series comes around each year, my mind wanders back to the years when we lived in Cincinnati. Our kids were both born there, so there are many priceless memories from their early years. Of course the World Series reminds me of Cincinnati because our tenure there happened to coincide with the era of the "Big Red Machine." It seemed as if they were perennially in the World Series and playoffs.

My office in downtown Cincinnati was within walking distance of the stadium. An even bigger bonus was access to the games that was made available to me from many vendors that I routinely used in executing the day-to-day activities of my work. On one particular sunny afternoon, my wife and I took our son to one of the games. The plan was for my wife and son, who was three or four at the time, to meet me at my office. My wife had decked him out in a Joe Morgan sweatshirt, Cincinnati Reds baseball cap, and allowed him to bring along his baseball glove so he could be in full regalia. When she brought him into the office to show him off to my colleagues, he was not a happy camper. While she was holding him and talking to one of the folks in the office, I will never forget his stealth move. He slowly moved his baseball glove over the lower part of his face and stuck his tongue out at the person we were talking to. Fortunately, that individual could not see what he had done, but we did. It wasn't funny at the time, but it sure does make for a good story nearly forty years later. I believe the Reds won their game that day and went on to win the World Series.

Chris's actions were that of a small boy who was in a place he didn't want to be, around people he didn't know, and it was delaying his departure for the ballpark. When he hid his face and his tongue, he meant no offence and the person who was the target of his protruding tongue had done nothing to deserve his unseen affront. However, there are times in our own lives when our own actions may cause God to hide his face from us. There are many verses in the Bible when people in distress call out to God and plead for Him not to hide His face. "A prayer of an afflicted man. When he is faint and pours out his lament before the Lord. Hear my prayer, O Lord; let my cry for help come to you. Do not hide your face from me when I am in distress. Turn your ear to me; when I call, answer me quickly." (Psalms 102:1-2) If you come to God with a contrite heart, let me assure you, He will not hide His face.

See you tomorrow, God willing!

October 20 — The Alarm Clock

Getting children to go to bed at night is a chore most parents do not like to undertake. When our kids were babies, either my wife or I would rock them to sleep and that particular approach was good for them and for us. There is nothing quite like having a little one fall asleep in your arms. They are so cuddly and dependent and you wish at times that they had stayed at that age. I can also remember that there were times that nothing seemed to work. They didn't want to go to sleep and I didn't have the patience to rock them all night. If that happened, it was necessary to simply put them in their bed and let them cry themselves to sleep. It wasn't much fun to listen to them cry, but it was better than allowing them to stay up too late.

When our youngest grandson was just a toddler, our daughter came up with an ingenious way to get him to go to bed. She would set an alarm clock for a certain time and tell him that when the alarm clock went off it was time for bed. Although he didn't like the concept very much, it seemed to work. Whenever the alarm clock went off, he made his way to bed making pouting faces as he made his trek to the bedroom. My wife remembers when they would be at our house in Pennsylvania and the alarm would go off. He often got to stay up a little longer, but the tears would still start as soon as it went off. He was having so much fun with everyone and didn't want to go to bed.

There is a story in the Bible that talks about time in a very strange way. God, in all His power, made time retreat to prove His awesome power. The story can be found in 2nd Kings. Hezekiah had asked Isaiah, "'What will be the sign that the Lord will heal me and that I will go up to the temple of the Lord on the third day from now?' Isaiah answered, 'This is the Lord's sign to you that the Lord will do what he has promised: Shall the shadow go forward ten steps, or shall it go back ten steps?' 'It is a simple matter for the shadow to go forward ten steps,' said Hezekiah. 'Rather, have it go back ten steps.' Then the prophet Isaiah called upon the Lord, and the Lord made the shadow go back the ten steps it had gone down on the stairway of Ahaz." (2 Kings 20:8-11) If our grandson had had that kind of power that alarm clock would never have gone off and our poor daughter would have had to come up with another ingenious method to get him to bed.

See you tomorrow, God willing!

October 21 — Happy or Cheerful

You know that with a maiden name like Coffman, my mom was very likely of German descent. Many German surnames were given to the bearer of the name because of their trade. The actual German spelling of mother's name is Kaufman and the English meaning is "merchant." Somewhere in mother's genealogy there was obviously a storekeeper. Thus, the derivation of the surname. It is hard to tell when the spelling of the name changed from the Kaufmann to Coffman, but I will take a guess based on another similar story.

I had always assumed that my wife's father's was English since the name Fraley has an English type spelling. One time when I was talking to him about the name, I got a story that really surprised me. When his ancestors came over from Europe to the United States, they happen to come through Ellis Island. As they came through immigration, they were asked to provide their last name. With a heavy accent they said "Fröelich." I can tell you with no fear of contradiction that the surname "Fröelich" is not an English name. In fact, the surname "Fröelich" belongs to the category of surnames that were derived from nicknames, usually based on the "personal", or "physical" characteristics of the initial bearer of the name. In this instance, the name is derived from the Middle High German word "vraelich," which means "happy" or "cheerful." Thus, this surname evolved from a nickname for a merry or cheerful person. That would have suited my father-in-law just fine. Nevertheless, to the official, it sounded like Fraley, so that is what he wrote down and that became the family's new name in America.

In the Bible, names quite often bore significant meaning. For example, Jacob's eighth son was named Asher "Then Leah said, 'How happy I am! The women will call me happy.' So she named him Asher." (Genesis 30:13) Too bad my father-in-law wasn't named Asher, then he could have been Asher Vraelich or Happy Happy.

Of course, there is another person in the Bible whose name carries special significance – "an angel of the Lord appeared to him in a dream and said, 'Joseph son of David, do not be afraid to take Mary home as your wife, because what is conceived in her is from the Holy Spirit. She will give birth to a son, and you are to give him the name Jesus, because he will save his people from their sins.' All this took place to fulfill what the Lord had said through the prophet: 'The virgin will be with child and will give birth to a son, and they will call him Immanuel' —which means, 'God with us.'" (Matthew 1:20-23) Next time you say the name Jesus, remember that it means – God with us.

See you tomorrow, God willing!

October 22 — Transformation

When I was at work the other day at the advertising agency where I spend some spare time, one of our clients came into our office with his three year old daughter. She was very sweet and very shy, but I managed to engage her in a short conversation. I could tell that the man was smitten with his little girl as all men are with their daughters. As I talked to our client about his daughter, I was reminded of another time over thirty years ago when I had had a similar conversation with business associates.

In my job in Pennsylvania, it was not unusual to have dinner with business associates. One evening, while I was having dinner with three other men about my age, the polite conversation turned to our families. Of course, a natural question is "how many children do you have and what are their ages?" As luck would have it, three of us at the table had teenage daughters and one of the men had a daughter who had passed through the teenage years and now was married with small children. The man who had the "older" daughter proceeded to tell the rest of us a story that I will never forget and one that should be passed on to all men who have daughters.

Here is what he told us. "When your daughter gets to the age of about twelve or thirteen, God comes and takes away your daughter and leaves you a substitute that looks exactly like your own daughter. When your daughter reaches the age of about nineteen or twenty, God brings back your daughter and takes away the substitute." We all laughed, but we realized the truth in his proclamation. The teenage years can be very difficult for all children, but I think girls have a much more difficult time. My daughter and I made it through those tough years and we have a very special father-daughter relationship to this very day.

We all go through periods of transformation in our lives, some very subtle and some brutally apparent. For teenage girls, it is a major transformation. Yet, when we finally accept Jesus Christ as our Lord and Savior, the transformation is even more dramatic. "And we, who with unveiled faces all reflect the Lord's glory, are being transformed into his likeness with ever-increasing glory, which comes from the Lord, who is the Spirit." (2 Corinthians 3:18) When the Holy Spirit comes alive in us, we begin to reflect the ever increasing glory of God. I am still a work in progress, how about you?

See you tomorrow, God willing!

October 23 — Modern Manna

For forty years the Israelites roamed the desert living off their daily ration of manna. Only two generations of people in the history of the world have seen manna or know what it tastes like. Let that sink in for a moment – only two generations in the history of the world have tasted manna. I suppose the Israelites learned to use the manna in creative ways to make the meals more interesting, but perhaps not.

If there were modern day manna, it would be peanut butter. For people of my generation and perhaps one or two more generations, peanut butter was a staple. When I was a child, I can vividly remember eating peanut butter right out of the jar with a spoon when I needed a snack. At other times, I would spoon it out of the jar into a bowl and mix either jelly or syrup with the peanut butter to make it sweeter and less sticky. During my high school years, my lunch bag always included a peanut butter and sweet pickle sandwich. How does that sound? Believe it or not, it was good. The sliced sweet gherkins really enhanced the overall flavor. There was also a small ice cream shop in St. Paul, the Frostie Bossie, that had peanut butter milk shakes. Again, they may sound awful, but to a peanut butter aficionado, they were awesome.

By the time I moved on to college, peanut butter was no longer just a food, it was my life line. Money was a little scarce so there was always a large jar of peanut butter in my room and an equally large box of crackers. If it hadn't been for peanut butter and pizza, I would probably have starved.

Now that I am a senior citizen, you would think that peanut butter no longer has a place in my eating habits. That would be wrong. Where would Christmas cookies be without Buckeyes? Or Peanut Butter Blossoms? Or Peanut Butter Fudge? And, you have never lived until you have had a piece of Peanut Butter Pie.

For the Israelites who roamed the desert for forty years, manna was their only source of food. However, when Jesus came He opened their eyes to a new reality, "Our forefathers ate the manna in the desert; as it is written: 'He gave them bread from heaven to eat. For the bread of God is he who comes down from heaven and gives life to the world.' 'Sir,' they said, 'from now on give us this bread.' Then Jesus declared, 'I am the bread of life. He who comes to me will never go hungry, and he who believes in me will never be thirsty.'" Even without peanut butter, there is no better Bread than this.

See you tomorrow, God willing!

October 24 — Honduras Revisited

In a few days, we will be leaving to go to the Dominican Republic on a mission trip. It will be our third mission trip, having gone to Bulgaria in 2008 and Honduras in 2001. Although we never know what to expect when we go on such a trip, we do know that God will show up and bless us even more than we bless the people we are going to serve.

I will never forget the circumstances of our first mission trip. Like so many other people, I had the attitude that there were plenty of people in the United States who needed our help so we didn't need to go to a foreign land to serve others. Despite the fact that Jesus said "go and make disciples of all nations" (Matthew 28:19), I figured that someone else could do "all nations" and I would stick to home. In January of 2001, we had returned from Puerto Rica and enjoyed a two-week vacation with too much food, wonderful accommodations, and plenty of sun and fun. On some of our day trips, we had also seen the poverty that exists in virtually all Caribbean nations.

God knew we were ripe for the picking. The very week we returned home, there was an invitation from the Episcopalian Diocese of Bethlehem for churches to consider mission trips to Honduras to help rebuild the country following the devastation of Hurricane Mitch in 1998. Despite the fact that our church was very small, we decided to send a team.

We have so many fond memories of that trip. The children, despite their poverty, were incredible. They were always laughing and smiling and their interaction with us was beautiful even though there was a language barrier. Each day, as we completed our physical labor, we would provide wheel barrow rides to the children as we took all of the tools back to the shed where they were stored. My wife carried bubbles with her every day and never hesitated to stop her own work to spend a few moments with an eager child.

Who knows what awaits us in the Dominican Republic? The answer is – God does, and it is likely to include children just like we saw in Honduras. "Sitting down, Jesus called the Twelve and said, 'If anyone wants to be first, he must be the very last, and the servant of all.' He took a little child and had him stand among them. Taking him in his arms, he said to them, 'Whoever welcomes one of these little children in my name welcomes me; and whoever welcomes me does not welcome me but the one who sent me.'" (Mark 9:35-37)

See you tomorrow, God willing!

October 25 — Thieves Come to Steal

I have always been a law-abiding citizen. Except for a few parking tickets my slate is pretty clean. However, I have been on the receiving end of criminal behavior on more than one occasion. When we lived in a one-bedroom apartment in Cincinnati, our apartment was robbed. I am sure that the robber was disappointed with his take; we had no money and very few items of any value. We did, however, lose both of our class rings and an antique gold ring that my wife had gotten from her grandmother. There was little monetary loss, but there was sentimental loss.

My second run in with criminals was an episode at the University of Cincinnati. The criminal who broke into my car got nothing, but I almost lost my life when he stabbed me several times trying to escape after I caught him in my car. Had it not been for a Good Samaritan, I may not have been around to tell all the stories I have shared with you in the last year.

My cars must have had a "rob me" sign on them because there was another incident in Cincinnati that involved theft from my parked vehicle. When I worked in downtown Cincinnati, I discovered that if I came to work before eight a.m. I could find free parking on the street within eight to ten blocks of my office. Since funds were still scarce in the family, it was worth the walk. Like an idiot, I had left my tennis racquet and some other items in the back seat in plain view of anyone walking by the car. For a thief, it was like taking candy from a baby.

In the last year, my wife had her first experience with a thief. She had gone to participate in the water aerobics and parked her car in a parking lot by the pool area. When she returned to the car after the session was over, her leather purse containing some cash, several credit cards, her driver's license, and precious pictures was stolen. A car thief had struck again.

In the grand scheme of things, thieves have not really taken too much monetary value from us. The losses have been more inconvenient than catastrophic. In the end, possessions such as those we have lost to thieves didn't mean much. As it says in the Gospel of John, "The thief comes only to steal and kill and destroy; I have come that they may have life, and have it to the full." (John 10:10) We have not let the devil destroy us. Because we have Jesus in our lives we have abundant life. My prayer for you is that you realize all that God has in store for you and that you don't allow the thief to steal, kill and destroy.

See you tomorrow, God willing!

October 26   Bridge or Life

My mother was a card player extraordinaire. I think everyone in the whole family has memories of playing "Kings Around the Corner" with her. While that was the only card game she played in her later years, it was not her game of choice. Mother loved to play Bridge.

Before the days that mother started to work full-time, she belonged to two bridge clubs that had luncheon meetings weekly. She was also a substitute in other Bridge clubs because she was a very good player and a lovely cheerful person to be around. My dad also played, and many of their friends were Bridge players. When they played in the evenings with their friends they allowed me to watch as long as I wasn't too much of a nuisance. Watching them play is how I learned the game.

I once asked mother why she liked to this particular card game. Her first response was no surprise. She said, "I love to play because it challenges my mind. You have to play with the cards you are dealt, sometimes the cards are running for you and sometimes the cards run against you. It doesn't matter; all you can do is get the most out of the hand you are dealt." That pretty much summed up her life. She didn't quit with that one answer. She went on to say, "Bridge is a team game. You cannot possibly win on your own. You must communicate with your partner through the bidding process and you must always trust your partner to carry his or her load." That was another glimpse of mother's personality. Commenting even further, she said, "You also have to be very aware of the rules of the game, which are somewhat complex, and you have to stick to the rules. Trying to play Bridge with someone who either doesn't know the rules or refuses to play by them is an uncomfortable experience. Part of the rules is knowing how to keep score. If you are playing a complicated game and you don't know how to keep score, you are in real trouble."

Bridge is a challenging and the rules of the game, particularly scoring, are complicated. You would think that the rules of life should be even more complicated, particularly the scoring. Not so. On one occasion an expert in the law asked Jesus, "What must I do to inherit eternal life?" In other words, what do I have to do to win in the game of life?" Jesus asked the man, "What is written in the law?" "He answered: 'Love the Lord your God with all your heart and with all your soul and with all your strength and with all your mind'; and, 'Love your neighbor as yourself.' 'You have answered correctly,' Jesus replied. 'Do this and you will live.'" (Luke 10:27-28) Are you winning? Or do you even know how to keep score?

See you tomorrow, God willing!

October 27 — A Sight for Sore Eyes

While I was on a temporary assignment in Europe during the summer of 1985, we had the opportunity to see some incredible sites. On one of the trips from England to the mainland of Europe, we took a car ferry from England to Holland and drove our English car (with the steering wheel on the wrong side) from the Dutch port down to Brussels. It was a great experience for all of us and we each have fond memories of that escapade. Oddly enough, one of the memories that sticks in my mind is seeing all of the Mercedes-Benz taxis on the streets of Brussels.

On another occasion, my wife and I flew to Paris for a couple of days and left our children in Epsom. Paris is one of the foremost cities in the world for sightseeing. Within one square mile, you can see some of the world's most famous sights. The Eiffel Tower, built in 1889, is both a global icon of France and one of the most recognizable structures in the world. The tower is the tallest building in Paris and the most-visited paid monument in the world. Located on the Right Bank of the Seine River is Le Louvre, a central landmark of Paris. Like the Eiffel Tower, it is world renowned and one of the world's most visited museums. We spent an entire day there looking at the magnificent art masterpieces and sculptures housed there. Moving west from Le Louvre you come to the Place de la Concorde, the largest public square in Paris. The square sits at the east end of the Avenue des Champs-Élysées, the most prestigious avenue in Paris. At the other end of the Champs-Elysees sits the Arc de Triomphe, which honors those who fought and died for France in the French Revolutionary and the Napoleonic Wars.

There are two reasons I am giving you this tour of Paris. One, the sights are unbeatable. Two, as we were walking up the Champs-Elysees, we ran into a couple from our church in Allentown. They did not know we were in Europe and, likewise, we did not know they were there. They were a sight for sore eyes.

It was on Resurrection Sunday that the disciples discovered that Jesus was missing from the tomb. "Now that same day two of them were going to a village called Emmaus, about seven miles from Jerusalem. They were talking with each other about everything that had happened. As they talked and discussed these things with each other, Jesus himself came up and walked along with them; but they were kept from recognizing him.... Then their eyes were opened and they recognized him, and he disappeared from their sight." (Luke 24:13-16, 31) Truly this was a sight for sore eyes. Their Lord and Savior, and ours, had defeated the grave.

See you tomorrow, God willing!

October 28 — Celebration of the Potter

When I walked over to the trash can this morning to dump out the old coffee grounds, I saw the November issue of Carolina Country on the counter and the headline on the front cover caught my attention. The headline read – "*Celebration of Potters.*" I knew that God wanted me to get something from that article so I opened the magazine and searched for it. First, I looked through the table of contents with no success. I glanced through the entire magazine looking for the article that I knew must be there. Still no success. Finally, I looked on the inside front cover to see if there might be a caption that would give me the information I was seeking. There it was – "On the Cover; Blaine Avery at work in his Seagrove Pottery & Tileworks will be among those at the Celebration of Potters." Why should I care about the Celebration of Seagrove Potters?

God was very quick to set my mind at ease. Yesterday evening, my wife and I went to church to join the rest of our mission team to be commissioned for our trip. During the time we spent together, one of the ladies showed us a beautiful communion set that had been made for our team to take to the DR. She had been working on the set for quite a while, but it seemed as if every time she put her newly made pottery in her kiln, it either cracked or the colors faded so much that the pottery was not the quality she desired. Now it was ready to go and my wife volunteered to be the carrier for this precious cargo.

We left the church and headed to a friend's house to deliver a meal and some presents for a newborn baby and his big sister. It was another reminder of the great potter. When you see a newborn baby you know beyond a shadow of a doubt that God has molded that bundle of joy in the mother's womb.

I looked at the cover of that magazine again to see if my eyes had tricked me. I blinked a couple of times and I saw a new headline that read "Celebration of The Potter", not "The Celebration of Potters." Here is what the unwritten article in Carolina Country said, "Yet, O Lord, you are our Father. We are the clay, you are the potter; we are all the work of your hand." (Isaiah 64:8) It was just His way of getting my spirit ready for our mission trip.

See you tomorrow, God willing!

October 29 — The Fourth Watch

"Meanwhile, the disciples were in trouble far away from land, for a strong wind had risen, and they were fighting heavy waves. About three o'clock in the morning Jesus came toward them, walking on the water. When the disciples saw him walking on the water, they were terrified. In their fear, they cried out, 'It's a ghost!' But Jesus spoke to them at once. 'Don't be afraid,' he said. 'Take courage. I am here!'" (Matthew 14:24-25 NLT)

Our mission team for the Dominican Republic is leaving at 3 a.m. this morning and heading for Raleigh/Durham airport to begin our journey. The Bible verse from Matthew struck me as being incredibly poignant with respect to our trip. On that evening in Jesus' time, His disciples were terrified because a storm had arisen on the lake and Jesus was not in the boat with them to protect them.

When we get in the van this morning on the fourth watch, the disciples in the van will have varying levels of fear concerning the trip. Some of the disciples have never been on a mission trip and wonder just what they have gotten themselves into and fear of the unknown is gnawing at them. One couple has traveled a lot and is comfortable with the journey, but they aren't comfortable with the uncertainty that lies ahead. Yet another couple has been with Jesus across other lakes and knows what awaits them, but they have never crossed this lake before so there is also fear of the unknown for them. Five other disciples have already crossed this particular lake with Jesus and know what lies on the other side, but deep down they fear that they may not be up to the test. Yet, all the disciples are filled with wondrous anticipation knowing full well that Jesus will show up.

Before we arrive in the Dominican Republic late today, I am absolutely sure that we will see Jesus. Perhaps we will not see Him walking on the water, but we will see Him in our spirit. Once that happens, our fears will disappear and we will be ready to serve Him just as His disciples did two thousand years ago.

See you tomorrow, God willing!

Vamos a buscar Jesus en Barrio George.

October 30 — Honor Those Before

After a long journey from Greenville to La Romano, the team arrived at the Mission House around 3 pm. We spent the next hour settling into our quarters and then we began a tour of the facilities that have been finished in the last five years.

Our first tour was of the newly completed building where we are staying. All I can say is "Wow". It is more than a place for missionaries to sleep and eat. There is also a free clinic for people in need of medical care and a ministry aimed at helping young women through unwanted pregnancies and mentoring them and teaching them how to care for their new infants.

From the mission house we went to the church. Again, it was impressive with a striking mural painted on the wall behind the pulpit. The mural was painted by a lady from our church with special assistance from many children in the church. As you entered the front door you could see the reflection of the mural on the shiny tile floor. Words cannot express the surreal effect.

From the church we walked across the street to a small school that houses over 450 students on a daily basis. It isn't just a secular education; it is so much more.

Starting on Monday, we will begin work on the next phase of development on the 40-acre site–a much larger school. As we stopped at each location on the campus, our hosts shared stories of God's amazing presence in Barrio George; all of this in the last five years.

I couldn't help but be thankful for the dedication, commitment, and generosity of all the people from our church, other churches, and the people of La Romano who have tilled the soil and watched the harvest of an abundant crop.

Matthew 4:36 assures us that we are not the first to witness the harvest of work done by others. "I sent you to reap what you have not worked for. Others have done the hard work and you have reaped the benefits of their labor." Praise God for His awesome power and His amazing work. Our team will also plow that others may reap an even larger harvest.

See you tomorrow, God willing!

October 31 — How Big Is Your God?

There was a time in my life when I used to hear about mighty things that God had done and proclaim that I was surprised at the miracle He had pulled off. Now, I never use the word "surprised" when I hear about something He has done; I now say that I am amazed.

Today, our mission team visited four barrios in La Romano, and I was quite surprised to find out that our reach in La Romano goes much deeper that Barrio George. Since the early 2000's, our ministry teams have been involved with the building of six churches, three schools, two churches in the Haitian bateys, and a medical clinic.

One of our visits was to one of the poorest barrios in La Romano. It is a mixed Haitian and Dominican barrio that had been ruled by gangs. A team from our church went into the barrio and helped build a church and the nature of the barrio began to change. First, the ring leader of the ruling gang found Jesus. He then helped convert two other gang members and before long the gang headquarters became a general store for the barrio.

At another barrio, our host told us the story of a barrio that had been totally filled with hate. Through the power of the Holy Spirit, the building of a church in that barrio led to the overnight destruction of Satan's power that had resided there. Today, the small church is splitting at the seams with regular services four to five days a week. The people in that barrio know how big their God is.

My favorite stop was to an undeveloped piece of land in a barrio known as Brizas del Mar. The piece of land belonged to our host's father-in-law. When he died, he requested that the land be developed into a community garden. When we arrived at the spot, it was still truly undeveloped, yet as we stood on the ground we already knew how big our God is. Having seen what had taken place in the 40-acre site in Barrio George in only five years, we knew God would have no trouble with this piece of land.

There is a story in 2nd Kings that tells you a little bit about how big God is. When Hezekiah was king, the Assyrians were threatening to destroy Jerusalem unless Hezekiah surrendered. Hezekiah did the smart thing, he invoked the power of the Most High God. God delivered a message through the prophet Isaiah and he got a promise from God that he had nothing to fear. "That night the angel of the Lord went out and put to death a hundred and eighty-five thousand men in the Assyrian camp. When the people got up the next morning, there were all dead bodies." (2 Kings 19:35) Do you think the Israelites knew how big their God was? Do you know how big your God is?

See you tomorrow, God willing!

November

November 1 — Love One Another

Each of our days here in La Romano begins with a morning devotional. It is a time to read God's Word and share what He might be saying to us through His Word or through our brothers and sisters. One morning, we used John 13:34-35 as the centerpiece of our devotion. "A new command I give you, that you love one another. Just as I have loved you, you are to love one another. By this, all people will know that you are my disciples, if you love one another."

How are we doing? When one team member shared his own personal testimony at the church service on Sunday morning, everyone was there to give him hugs of encouragement after he completed his brave assignment. Another miracle of love that Jesus displayed at the service was a small boy, perhaps two years old, who was overly friendly. When one of our team picked him up to love on him, he wanted to touch the person's head, and ultimately, the head's of each team member. Each time he laid his hands on head, it was as if he were praying over each of us. God was honoring us in a way that we couldn't fully understand, but we could certainly feel His love.

Another story was about an experience that one of our team had while we were on one of our walks. As we walked through one of the poorest of the barrios, he noticed a dead tarantula in the dirt road. Later he discovered that the tarantula had been killed in a nearby home and thrown in the road. Was it God's way of telling the team that we were sent to the Dominican Republic to stomp on Satan every chance we get. Satan doesn't like the love that we show each other and the remarkable people we see and touch at every opportunity.

Yesterday, we finally went to work. Alongside our brothers from the DR, we all helped transport cement into the trenches that will form the foundation for the new school. It was hard labor, and by day's end we were exhausted. At the first work break of the day, we were all invited to share a comment with the entire group. One by one there were comments of gratitude, especially coming from our hosts about our contribution to their new school. We weren't just working, we loved on them, and they on us. Since I started this story with a verse from the Gospel of John, I suppose I should complete the story with another verse from John. "My command is this: Love each other as I have loved you. Greater love has no one than this that he lay down his life for his friends." (John 15:12-13) This week, we are indeed laying down our life for our friends here in the DR.

Guess who is getting the most blessings?

See you tomorrow, God willing!

November 2 — A Firm Foundation

For the second straight day, we literally worked in the trenches. By days end we had completed the pouring of concrete for the entire foundation of the school. Once we finished the foundation, we began pouring the concrete for the pillars on which the walls and roof will get their support. The term pouring concrete is a bit of a misnomer for the work that was done. At the worksite, the concrete is mixed on the ground and moved by bucket to where it is needed. If the proximity of the pour is close to the mixing spot, the buckets are moved along a bucket brigade. If, however, the distance is too far for a bucket brigade, it is simply a matter of carrying heavy buckets of concrete to where they are needed.

Both men and women participated fully in the work at the site, not just in the bucket brigade, but also in carrying the concrete and filling the buckets to be carried. By mid-afternoon on Monday, the ladies opted to spend their time at the mission house interrelating with the children. Some of the women did face painting while others did fingernails.

In many ways, it was symbolic that our team was given the privilege of helping pour the foundation for the school. The foundation must be solid if the school is to stand firm. The Bible tells us a lot about a solid foundation. "He will be the sure foundation for your times, a rich store of salvation and wisdom and knowledge; the fear of the Lord is the key to this treasure." (Isaiah 33:6) Without a doubt the foundation of the new school is built on a solid foundation of love from the Dominican Republic to North Carolina.

At the morning break on Monday, we sang a song about that very thing.

Dios es bueno, alabrala (God is good, worship and praise)
Yo plue mi pie, en la roache firme. (You put my feet on the solid rock)

As the song was being sung, I recognized the phrase "Dios es bueno," so I made it a point to learn the rest of the words for later in the week. "Therefore everyone who hears these words of mine and puts them into practice is like a wise man who built his house on the rock. The rains came down, the streams rose, and the wind blew and beat against that house; yet id did not fall because it had its foundation the rock." (Matthew 7:24-25) Jesus is that rock, the very cornerstone of our foundation.

"By the grace God has given me, I laid a foundation as an expert builder and someone else is building on it. But each should be careful how he builds. For no one can lay any foundation other than the one already laid, which is Jesus Christ. (1 Corinthians 3:10-11)

There is nothing left to say.

See you tomorrow, God willing!

November 3   A Perfect Day

I knew it was going to be a glorious day, but in my wildest dreams I would never have imagined how much of Himself God could pack into a single day. As we did our individual morning devotions on the roof of the Mission House, we saw several members of the Dominican community gathering at a tree near the church. Each person picked up seven rocks and threw a rock on the pile each of the seven times the entourage circled the tree. Each of the seven rocks that a person carried and ultimately threw on the pile represented a burden that the individual was placing at the feet of Jesus. The seven trips around the tree represented the Israelites circling of Jericho that brought down the walls and victory over the city.

Around 9:15, we boarded our church bus for a visit to one of the many Haitian bateys around La Ramano. On our way our host told us that this batey was one of the smallest, which fit the vision cast by Jesus when He called on His disciples to serve the "Least, Lost and Last." When we arrived we unloaded some clothes and shoes we had brought for the thirty families who live there. Just after that, the fireworks began. As we arrived, my wife was handed a baby to hold while the mother of the baby helped with one of the school classes. It turned out that baby was the child of a mother who had been loved on by a previous mission team while she was pregnant. The mother had breast cancer in both breasts and had prayed that she would live long enough to deliver her newborn. Not only had the mother delivered a healthy baby, she was now cancer free. Praise God!

It would take pages to tell you about all of the stories of love and hope from Batey Anon. When a pouring rain came, it was time to leave the batey and return to the Mission House. "Come to me, all you who are weary and burdened, and I will give you rest. Take my yoke upon you and learn from me, for I am gentle and humble in heart and you will find rest for your souls. For my yoke is easy and my burden is light." (Matthew 11:28-30)

At the beginning of the day, we had cast our burdens on Jesus at the prayer tree. We had then carried the burdens of the "Lost, the Least, and the Last" as we served the people in Batey Anon. As the team sat on the roof of the Mission House at day's end and went through our debriefing session, we agreed that it was the perfect ending to a perfect day.

See you tomorrow, God willing!

November 4 — He Calls Me Friend

As the sun rose on another day here in Barrio George, we knew we were in for a hard day's work. Although we had completed the pouring of the concrete foundations for the school, there were a total of twenty-four concrete columns yet to be poured. We had completed pouring seven of the twenty four on Tuesday and the carpenters had spent all day on Wednesday completing the construction of the forms around each column. When we arrived on the site on Thursday, we discovered that the Dominican workers had already completed pouring another five columns, so we were off to a good start. Before 1 p.m. we had completed our job. It was an exciting moment as the last bucket approached the concrete form. As the concrete was poured, a loud yell went up from everyone there and we all celebrated "with high fives" and hugs. We had not only finished our job of pouring the foundation and columns for the school, we had symbolically completed the development of personal relationships with the other workers and school age children who had helped with the construction of a school that would be theirs.

After Pastor Isidro had all of us join hands and circle for prayer, God sealed our friendships. Spontaneously, each member of our team began to take off their shoes, gloves, hats, and sometimes their socks and give them to one of the workers with whom they had developed relationships. It was quite a stirring moment. When we arrived at the construction site on Monday morning, we were just a bunch of American's that had come to Barrio George to provide them with a little labor. Little did they know, we had come "looking for Jesus in Barrio George" (Vamos a buscar Jesus en Barrio George). Among many other places, we had found him amidst our Christian brothers on the construction site. We know that all of the workers there have not yet received Jesus as their Lord and Savior, but it is my guess that these particular men also met Jesus again and each time you meet Him, it is harder to stay away.

Our morning devotional on Wednesday morning was from the Gospel of John, 15:1-17. Here is what verses 13 and 14 say, "Greater love has no one than to lay down his life for his friends. You are my friends if you do what I command." During our week here in La Romano, we have heard Jesus' call.

See you tomorrow, God willing!

November 5   Loving the Least, Lost and Last

Can you imagine a large room at the Mission House crowded with about seventy-five women? The women are either pregnant or have one or more children under three years of age. These women are part of a pilot program being run by Compassion International. The program, called "The Child Survival Program," focuses its attention on young women who are dealing with unwanted pregnancies and who are being taught how to take care of themselves and their children. The women in the program are required to attend two meetings a month at the Mission House and they receive two visits a month at their homes.

The ladies on our team helped make the session on Thursday a success. Their only real responsibility was to help love on each and every one of the women. Step one was to help those ladies with small babies by holding each baby to give the mother a much needed break.

For the women with slightly older children, it could have been as simple as playing with the child while the mother watched on. Speaking of special attention, each of the women who had a child with her was photographed with her child or children. After seeing the image on a digital camera, each woman was assured that she would receive a print of her own. In all likelihood, it would be the first photograph any of the women would have of their beautiful offspring.

For all of our team members who worked at the Compassion International session, it was a day to show love and affection to a group of women in bad need of a loving hand. It was yet another example of the team loving the "Least, the Last and the Lost." And each of them performed his or her duties with mercy, grace and love.

At our final evening debriefing session last night, each individual shared his or her most compelling image of the week. Not one single person mentioned the completion of the work on the school foundation. Each highlight was about an encounter with an individual who needed us as much as we needed them or about an overall feeling of deepened relationships with members of our team or members of our host team. "Woe to you, teachers of the law and Pharisees, you hypocrites! You give a tenth of your spices – mint, dill and cummin. But you have neglected the more important matters of the law – justice, mercy and faithfulness. You should have practiced the latter without neglecting the former. (Matthew 23:23) In a very powerful way, this verse summed up the entire philosophy of our mission trip to the Dominican Republic. We had heard Jesus' instructions and lived them out. And guess what, He had allowed us to see him every step of the way.

We came looking for Jesus in Barrio George and we had found Him around every corner.

See you tomorrow, God willing!

November 6 — A Wonderful Mentor

Although we were fairly mature when we moved to Cincinnati, we were very young and wet behind the ears. However, we were fortunate that one of my early bosses took us under his wings and helped us immensely in many ways. My boss and his wife had been married before, but each of their spouses had died. They were a beautiful couple about fifteen to twenty years older than we were.

He had gotten into the advertising business from the same route as I had. He had been a chemical engineer before he switched careers and I had been a research chemist. He knew a lot about advertising and I knew nothing. He patiently shared all he knew with me, and over time he was able to entrust all of the work to me without concern.

However, it wasn't the work mentoring that was so invaluable to my wife and me. They loved to entertain and they often included us in their events, especially if it involved work-related people such as individuals from out of town who were representatives of major chemical magazines. She took the time to share her hors d'oeuvres recipes with my wife and we watched the way they made everyone feel welcome. I truly believe that my wife's gift of hospitality was honed during those years. I should also add that my boss was not a spectator in these parties. He also did some of the cooking and he was certainly an active participant in every event.

During the eight years I worked with him, he provided me with exactly what I needed to mature in a number of areas of my life. He did what any good mentor should do, and I am eternally grateful. There are many examples in the Bible of individuals who had wonderful mentors. The story of Elijah and Elisha is one of the best. Just before Elijah was taken to heaven, Elijah asked Elisha what last thing he could do for him. "When they had crossed, Elijah said to Elisha, 'Tell me, what can I do for you before I am taken from you?' 'Let me inherit a double portion of your spirit,' Elisha replied.'" (2 Kings 2:9) If you have a really great mentor like I had, that is what you will receive – "a double portion." Everyone needs a good mentor to help him or her along many fronts. Do you have one?

See you tomorrow, Gods willing!

November 7   Spiritual Mentor

Yesterday I wrote about my boss and his wife in Cincinnati who proved to be wonderful mentors to my wife and me during the eight years I worked for him. His influence was work and play related, but did not include a spiritual component. Many years later, when I was ready, God brought another person into my life who helped me greatly in terms of my spiritual walk.

My friend was a lawyer by education, but he had become a real estate developer in Eastern Pennsylvania. We had met the he and his wife through some other good friends and developed a friendship from that meeting. He was a sharp businessman and I always enjoyed spending time with him. However, it wasn't his business acumen that impressed me; it was his dedication to time in the Word. He started every day with the Bible. He arose early, around 5:30 a.m., to make sure that time with God was his first priority of the day. At that time in my life, that was not one of my priorities, but it wasn't long before I realized how important that commitment was. It has been part of my daily routine now for nearly twenty years, no matter where I am or how busy I may be.

In another story, I mentioned the influence that he and his wife had on our worship life. They attended a church that was non-denominational in a town, about twenty miles from us. Once we visited their church, we knew that our time of worship in the Episcopal Church would soon be coming to an end. We never knew what it was like to worship God in such an exuberant manner. There is nothing wrong with the Episcopalian style of worship; however, it is fair to say that it is somewhat staid. As my wife has said on more than one occasion, "I never knew that the music would stay in my heart all week long." Once we moved to North Carolina, we didn't have to look for a church. Our daughter and her family had taken us to their church on more than one occasion and it offered the same spirit-filled worship experience that we had come to love.

One of the favorite songs sung by the choir at that church sums up my attitude toward worship. The song is called "Total Praise" and the song is based on the 150th Psalm. In the NIV version of the Bible, the word "praise" appears thirteen times and there are only six verses in the entire psalm. "Praise the Lord. Praise God in his sanctuary; praise him in his mighty heavens. Praise him for his acts of power; praise him for his surpassing greatness...Let everything that has breath, praise the Lord. Praise the Lord." (Psalm 150:1-2, 6) Here is my recommendation to you, give Him your "Total Praise."

See you tomorrow, God willing!

November 8 — God Won't Hang Up

When our daughter was in school at East Carolina University, she had a 1971 Volkswagen convertible that was starting to lose its usefulness. Because of the run down condition of the car, it made it difficult for her to come home for visits. One weekend she called and told us that she would drive as far as Washington D.C. to my sister's house if we would be able to meet her there and bring her the rest of the way home. Of course we responded in a positive manner since we were always anxious to see her and see how she was doing. All was going very smoothly until we got within an hour of home. It was about one a.m. in the morning and we were on the four-lane highway that approaches Reading, PA. My wife was driving when a deer ran out in front of the car and she hit it head on. Through God's protection no one was hurt but the deer and the car. The impact of the large deer hitting the car smashed in the front and punctured the radiator.

It wasn't too long a wait before the state police arrived and called a tow truck to take the car to a GM dealer in Ephrata. After the tow truck came, the policeman drove us to an all-night diner where we called a friend in Allentown to pick us up and take us home. That is where the fun really began.

One of the definitions of a friend is someone you can call at 3 a.m. in the morning and expect them to help you in a moment of crisis. So, I called my best friend of ten years to see if he would get out of bed and come and take us home. From the diner, we placed the call. The phone rang a couple of times before he answered. Without a word being said, they hung up the phone before we could say a word. Not knowing what was going on, we tried again and they answered and hung up again. Not to be dissuaded, we tried a third time and finally they reluctantly spoke to us and agreed to come and pick us up. As we rode home in his car he explained to us that for several nights, they had been receiving annoying calls in the middle of the night. Frankly, they had gotten very tired of a ringing phone in the middle of the night.

The Psalms are full of man's pleading to God for answers to his troubles. Psalm 102:2 seems to be very appropriate for this story. "Do not hide your face from me when I am in distress. Turn your ear to me; when I call, answer me quickly." God is in the delivery business. He will deliver you from you trials and tribulations when you call on His Name.

See you tomorrow, God willing!

November 9 — Senor Juan

Senor Juan is one of my new friends in La Romano. He is a man of very small stature, but his smile is as large as anyone's. That comment would probably surprise many of the missionaries who have been to La Romano on previous trips. Why the change? Senor Juan met Jesus a few months ago and accepted Him as his Lord and Savior and his whole demeanor has changed.

Senor Juan is in charge of security at the Mission House. When we would return from one of our bus excursions, Senor Juan was the first to greet us and he never backed away from a big hug. He was also the last to bed at night and one of the first to rise in the morning. Since he was used to being last to bed and first to rise, Senor Juan could not figure out why I was always seemed to be up when he went to bed and still up when he got up the next morning. In fact, I am told that Senor Juan asked one of our team members if I ever went to bed. Those wee hours of the morning were the quiet time that I needed to compose the team updates that went back to Greenville each day.

My favorite mental image of Senor Juan took place early Friday morning. We had completed the pouring of the concrete for all of the support columns the day before and had gathered at the school site to pray. As the combined Dominican and American team prayed, Senor Juan could be seen on the roof of the Mission House about a hundred yards away with his arms raised to the heavens praising God with us. He was an important part of our team and he wanted to thank Jesus for helping us lay a proper foundation for the new school.

Senor Juan is a new man; he was once blind to the wonders of our Mighty God. In the Gospel of John there is a wonderful story about a man who had been blind from birth. Jesus restored his sight and created great controversy among the Pharisees. "'Give glory to God,' they said. 'We know this man is a sinner.' He replied, 'Whether he is a sinner or not, I don't know. One thing I do know. I was blind but now I see!' Then they asked him, 'What did he do to you? How did he open your eyes? He answered, 'I have told you already and you did not listen. Why do you want to hear it again? Do you want to become his disciples, too?'" (John 9:24-27) When God takes away our blindness, He shows us the world in a brand new light. That is exactly what happened to Senor Juan and me. My prayer is that He has taken away your blindness as well.

See you tomorrow, God willing!

November 10 — Just A Memory

St. Paul High School is no more. At the beginning of this school year all of the students who would have attended the high school in the 2011-2012 school year were transferred to the nearest Wise County High School about twelve miles away. Many of the students opted not to go to Coeburn but to attend the nearest high school at Castlewood in Russell County. That high school is only about three miles away, but has been the biggest sports rival of the high school in St. Paul for as long as I can remember.

As you might expect, my wife and I have many fond memories of our high school days. Although we didn't actually start dating until her senior year in high school, we had known each other for years. She was the captain of the cheerleading team and I was captain of the football team. It was classic Americana.

My brother, my wife's brother and I had played football, basketball, and baseball together. Despite the fact that we played against much larger high schools, our sports teams rarely had losing seasons. The only real challenge was in football. We had so few players on the team that we couldn't hold scrimmages in a traditional manner. We could only scrimmage to one side of the line because we had less than twenty-two able bodied boys on the team. Just about everybody played both offense and defense.

Despite the small enrollment in the high school the academic results of students going on to college were impressive. A high percentage of kids went on to college and most did very well. I suspect it had a lot to do with the small class sizes. My graduating class in 1964 was the smallest in the history of the school with a whopping twenty-three students. Think about it, to finish in the top ten percentage of the class you had to be the salutatorian. My wife's graduating class one year later was one of the largest in school history with over thirty kids in her class.

The closing of the high school is the end of an era. They can close the school, but they can't take away our fond memories of football games, misbehaving in class, proms, or graduation days. All of those memories are locked in our minds forever.

There will be no more graduating classes from St. Paul High School. Some who have graduated in the past are still in Southwest Virginia, but many more have been scattered around the United States. The prophet Zechariah had this to say about the Israelites who had been scattered about after their deportation to Babylon. "Though I scatter them among the peoples, yet in distant lands they will remember me." (Zechariah 10:9)

The physical school we prized still stands, but the high school portion has been eliminated. It is just a fond memory.

See you tomorrow, God willing!

November 11 — Veteran's Day

When our parents were alive and living in Virginia, we made a special point to visit them on a regular basis. In the early years of our marriage, we drove from Cincinnati to St. Paul virtually every holiday. My wife even quipped on one occasion that we even came to visit them on Ground Hog's Day. We loved and respected both sets of parents and we wanted our children to grow up knowing and loving them as we did.

When we moved to Pennsylvania, the drive went from five hours to ten hours so we made the trips a little less frequently, but we still never missed a major holiday. When we drove from Allentown, it so happened that Harrisburg, Virginia was exactly half way. There was a Howard Johnson's Motor Lodge and restaurant at one of the exits that became our refueling and eating place. On one of our stops in the restaurant, our son noticed some men in uniform and asked us "are those some of the soldiers that got killed in the war?" We laughed at his question and told him "no, they weren't killed in the war, but they certainly were serving their country."

Over the years, I have thought about his question. I suppose, if he asked me the same question today, I might answer him a little differently. I would say that every person in uniform represents men and women who have died for his or her country to defend the rights that we have here. Foremost among those rights is our freedom of religion. At no time in the history of the world have Christians been more persecuted than they are right now. We take our freedoms for granted and do not do a good job of showing our appreciation for those who defend our liberties.

On this Veteran's Day, I want to thank every man and woman, past and present, who has served this country on my behalf. "The Lord bless you and keep you; the Lord make his face shine upon you and be gracious to you; the Lord turn his face toward you and give you peace." (Numbers 6:24-26)

See you tomorrow, God willing!

November 12 — Time, Talent and Treasure

The church we attended for over twenty years in Pennsylvania had its financial challenges. Occasionally, someone would bequeath some funds to the church and there would be short-term relief, but by-and-large, operation was nearly always on a month-to-month basis. I believe God likes it that way because it forces us to depend on Him.

Our church had an annual pledge drive to enable members of the church to make a financial commitment. From those commitments, an annual budget would be developed. One year, ahead of the canvas, one of our members suggested we conduct an auction and title it a "Talent Auction" to stress the time, talent, and treasure that God gives to each of us. The items to be auctioned would all be derived from our talents. It could be baked goods; it could be gardening; it could be tax consulting; it could be baby sitting. The items could be as broad as anyone's imagination. The first auction was held and to our great surprise, not only did we have good attendance and lots of fun, we also made a big contribution to the church's financial pool.

Every year, the auction grew in size and attendance. By the fifth or sixth year, we had 75 – 100 items to be auctioned, plus a whole table of baked goods for a silent auction. On the Sunday afternoon of the auction, a group of us would spend the afternoon preparing an index card for each auction item describing the item and naming the donor. The auctioneer would use this card during the auction. When I saw an item from an anonymous donor, I knew what I had to do. I described the item as required and then named the donor as Ann Onymous. Since the particular item was well into the auctioned items, the auctioneer fell right into the trap. No sooner had the supposed donor's name gotten out of his mouth when he realized he had been had. He was a good sport and the attendees had a good laugh.

I had used one of my talents, the gift of laughter, to make the evening more successful, but the evening was really about calling attention to all our gifts. In Matthew 25, Jesus tells the parable of the talents. He tells us that we are given different talents and each should use what we have to further His kingdom. However, He also tells us what happens when we don't use our talents in the proper way. "For everyone who has will be given more, and he will have an abundance. Whoever does not have, even what he has will be taken from him." (Matthew 25:29) Earlier in the Gospel of Matthew, Jesus had warned us about our treasure, "For where your treasure is, there your heart will be also." (Matthew 6:21) How are you using your talents?

See you tomorrow, God willing!

November 13 — Birthday in New York

When I worked in Pennsylvania, the company where I worked sponsored bus trips to New York City on a few Saturdays during the year. One year, one of these bus trips happened to fall on my birthday, so my wife thought it would be a good idea to invite some friends and celebrate my birthday the entire day in New York.

Well, as the line from a famous Robert Burns poem says, "the best laid plans of mice and men often go astray." Our plans for the Saturday in New York began to fall apart in a hurry. The two men who were going to accompany me decided at the last minute that a Penn State football game that afternoon was more important than keeping their commitment to go to New York City to help me celebrate my birthday.

I was not deterred. I continued with my plans and headed to New York with five ladies in waiting. Upon arriving in NY, our first stop was at Dean & Deluca and things immediately got weird. First, one lady picked up a few choice mushrooms to use in her Thanksgiving stuffing. When she checked out, the clerk told her that the mushrooms she had picked out were thirty-two dollars. She had seen eight dollars a pound on the sign so she couldn't figure out why she was being charged so much. She had not looked closely enough; the mushrooms were eight dollars *per quarter pound*. One of the other ladies made sure that her purchase wouldn't be too expensive; she just walked out the door without paying for her small loaf of bread.

An hour or so later when we were enjoying lunch in a small Italian Café in the Village, the mushroom lady asked the other lady how much she had paid for her loaf of bread (she had seen her walk out without paying). It wasn't until that moment that she realized what she had done. She was aghast.

We all had a good laugh over both of the Dean & Deluca incidents as well as many other things that happened that day. Despite the fact that my two male friends abandoned me at the last minute, I had a glorious day.

In the book of Ecclesiastes, Solomon displayed some of the incredible wisdom. As the verses say, there is a time for everything. "There is a time for everything, and a season for every activity under heaven… a time to weep and a time to laugh, a time to mourn and a time to dance… a time to be silent and a time to speak…" (Ecclesiastes 3:1, 4, 7) On that Saturday in New York City, it was not time for me to spend it with my male buddies. It was time, however, for me to spend the day laughing out loud with my wife and her friends of the gentler sex. It was a birthday I will never forget.

See you tomorrow, God willing!

November 14 — Our First Home

When we moved into our first home in Cincinnati, we were thrilled. It was a small, three-bedroom ranch with a large fenced-in yard. It was the perfect first home for a family with a new born baby boy and his soon to be four year old sister.

The first room to be redecorated was our daughter's bedroom. Just before our son was born, we had purchased a new bedroom set for her. It was light gray with a blue accent color. The set consisted of a four-corner bed, a dresser with mirror and another small chest with a book case on top. My wife chose a light blue paint for the room and we set some of her doll collection on the shelves of the bookcase to make the room fit for the princess that would occupy the room for the next six years.

Our son's room was my responsibility. Using masking tape, I laid out a football field on one of the bare white walls and a baseball diamond on another. I painted the walls green and then removed the masking tape to leave behind the white lines that mark the boundaries of the two playing fields. I then stuck a Cincinnati Reds pennant on the wall with the baseball field and a Cincinnati Bengals pennant on the other wall and I had a room appropriately decorated for our little athlete.

Would you believe that I don't remember much about the decoration in the rest of the house? Here is what I do remember. If you had come into our house and looked around, you would not have known that we were Christians. There were no crosses; there were no pictures on the walls; there were no Bibles in prominent places; and sadly to say it would not likely have been a part of our everyday conversation. We knew God, but you certainly couldn't tell it by looking around our house.

"Fix these words of mine in your hearts and minds; tie them as symbols on your hands and bind them on your foreheads. Teach them to your children, talking about them when you sit at home and when you walk along the road, when you lie down and when you get up. Write them on the doorframes of your houses and on your gates, so that your days and the days of your children may be many in the land that the Lord swore to give your forefathers..." (Deuteronomy 11:18-21)

As I look back on my life, I can readily see the many mistakes of commission and omission that I made. Re-read a few of the phrases in these verses from Deuteronomy. Had I been a regular reader of the Bible, I would have understood these directions. I suppose that the letters I write every day are trying to make up for lost time.

See you tomorrow, God willing!

November 15 — Wall of Crosses

At our home in North Carolina, there is a very large wall at the foot of the stairs outside our bedroom. The wall is about ten feet wide and about twelve feet high. That wall is covered with crosses of many colors, shapes, materials of construction, and sizes. On the wall are crosses from Bulgaria, the Dominican Republic, Canada, Israel, Mexico, and parts unknown. Despite the fact that there are about seventy-five individual crosses on the wall, if you stand back a little, you will also notice that the crosses also work together to form a large cross. Make no mistake; we are reminded every time we enter our bedroom that Jesus gave His life for us on the cross.

Some of the crosses come with stories.

Mexico – The Mexican cross is fittingly the first one I need to discuss. It was brought to us by our daughter when she returned from a tenth anniversary trip to Cancun. The story depicted by that cross actually begins at the beginning of time and the ceramic cross she brought us has a big red apple at the center and snakes' heads coming out of the tree along the horizontal beams of the cross. Our need for the cross started in the Garden of Eden.

Israel – One of my wife's friends brought her this cross when she returned from her trip to the Holy Land. The Jerusalem cross, also known as Crusaders' cross, is a heraldic cross or Christian symbol consisting of a large Greek cross surrounded by four smaller Greek crosses, one in each quadrant. The four smaller crosses are said to symbolize either the four books of the Gospel or the four directions in which the Word of Christ spread from Jerusalem.

Bulgaria – We picked up the Bulgarian cross on our mission trip Bulgaria. The cross is actually an intricately carved square with a cross in the center. The cross in the center of the square is composed of six etched scenes depicting stories from Jesus' life. Three scenes form the horizontal beam and four scenes run vertically with one scene shared. Those six scenes are replicas of a medieval icon featuring those scenes.

Dominican Republic – These crosses are hand made and painted by young boys. The crosses are made to help make money for their families. It seems very fitting that the cross is still being used to help the Least, the Lost, and the Last.

For all who believe in Jesus Christ as our Lord and Savior, the cross is a symbol of His love for us. For those who do not believe, "For the message of the cross is foolishness to those who are perishing, but to us who are being saved it is the power of God." (1 Corinthians 1:18) It is foolishness to those who are perishing! If you are perishing in any way, look to the cross.

See you tomorrow, God willing!

November 16 — Amazing Grace

For nearly twenty-five years, we attended a small Episcopal Church in Pennsylvania. The church was named after Queen Margaret of Scotland who was canonized in 1250 by Pope Innocent IV. To recognize its Scottish heritage, the church held an annual St. Margaret's Day celebration on the second Sunday of November. Attendance on that particular Sunday rivaled Easter and Christmas because of the festivities.

First of all, we had several members of the church who were of Scottish heritage who wore their kilts on that Sunday. Other people were content to wear a plaid tie or a Scottish head piece. If you happened to walk in the church as a visitor on that particular day, you would have wondered exactly what was going on.

The highlight of St. Margaret's day was the inclusion of bagpipes at the processional and the playing of *Amazing Grace* at the end of the service. Most of you have heard *Amazing Grace* played on bagpipes at some point in your life so you know how penetrating it can be. I'm not sure why that hymn is the music of choice for bagpipes, but I do know it is incredibly effective.

Here is what Wikipedia has to say about the hymn. "Amazing Grace" is a Christian hymn with words written by the English poet and clergyman John Newton (1725–1807) and is one of the most recognizable songs in the English-speaking world. Newton wrote the words from personal experience. He grew up without any particular religious conviction but his life's path was formed by a variety of twists and coincidences that were often put into motion by his recalcitrant insubordination. He was pressed into the Royal Navy and became a sailor, eventually participating in the slave trade. One night a terrible storm battered his vessel so severely that he became frightened enough to call out to God for mercy, a moment that marked the beginning of his spiritual conversion. His career in slave trading lasted a few years more until he quit going to sea altogether and began studying theology. "Amazing Grace" was written to illustrate a sermon on New Year's Day of 1773.

"Let us then approach the throne of grace with confidence, so that we may receive mercy and find grace to help us in our time of need." (Hebrew 4:16) John Newton received mercy in his time of need and he wrote the most famous hymn ever written about God's amazing grace. God's grace is available to all who seek Him and it is truly amazing.

See you tomorrow, God willing!

November 17 — Just Love on Them

Beginning in the early part of 2002 and ending with my mother's death in late 2009, my wife and I had a great deal of time to learn how to deal with aging parents. As Alzheimer's disease progressed in both of our mother's lives we learned that the best thing we could do for them was to love on them and keep them as comfortable as possible. Today, we routinely see our friends caring for their aging parents and we always give them the same advice "just love on them every chance you get."

God likes that advice and He reminds us to practice it daily. When we returned from the Dominican Republic in early November, all of us on the team brought back images of poverty that are difficult to shake as we returned to our blessed life styles. One young lady helped us put things in the proper perspective when she told her mother "the people in Barrio George and other parts of the Dominican Republic will always be poor. All we can do is love on them while we are there, pray for them at all times, and support them financially to the best of our abilities." That is pretty sage advice coming from such a young lady.

Throughout Jesus' earthly ministry He served the poor and there is not one place in scripture where He took away their earthly poverty. Jesus always dealt with their spiritual poverty. In fact, Jesus had more to say to people who had money than vice versa. When a rich young man came to Jesus to ask what he must do to inherit the kingdom of God, Jesus ultimately told him, "'If you want to be perfect, go, sell your possessions and give to the poor, and you will have treasure in heaven. Then come, follow me.' When the young man heard this, he went away sad, because he had great wealth." (Matthew 19:21-22) In the story about the pouring of expensive perfume over Jesus' feet, Judas Iscariot was incensed because so much money was wasted on this act of love. Jesus rebuked him saying, "You will always have the poor among you, but you will not always have me." (John 12:8) Sounds familiar doesn't it? You will always have the poor among you. Don't let your material things get in the way of loving on those whose greatest need is to be loved back.

See you tomorrow, God willing!

November 18 — Is God Nudging You?

When our daughter was about to graduate from high school in 1985, she knew that college was the next step in her life. First, she needed to identify where she would go to school. The first criterion for choosing a college was "it must be south of the Mason-Dixon Line." She loved the warm weather in the south and had had enough of cold winters. She was also looking for a college where she could use her creative talents. Since East Carolina had a good fashion design major and it met the "go south" criterion, ECU became her college of choice. She applied, was accepted, and began her college journey in August of 1985.

By her third year at ECU she was an accounting major with a gnawing concern – why was she really in college? Had she gone to college because that was what she was supposed to do? Now, she wondered if it was really what she was supposed to do. She decided to take a break after her junior year and see what life had to offer. She got a job and it wasn't too long before she met her husband –to-be and got married in July of 1990.

When she became pregnant with their first son in the summer of 1991, she received a nudging from God about a brand new educational path. As she had ultrasound pictures taken of her developing baby, she was enthralled by the work performed by the people who were caring for her. After her son was born, she knew that she needed to go back to school and prepare herself to be an ultrasound technologist. She enrolled at Pitt Community College and on August 20, 1996 she officially received her degree in medical sonography.

I am telling this story at this point in time because I received a nudge from God to do so. I had finished my devotions one morning and prayed for God to give me a relevant story. In my spirit he said, "go take a look at the photo albums about ten feet away from you, in one of those books, you will find the story I want you to tell. Write the story and I will tell you what it means!"

"If you are willing and obedient, you will eat the best from the land..." (Isaiah 1:19) The baby boy that my daughter delivered in 1992 is now in his second year at East Carolina. Next spring, he will be marrying his soul mate. My daughter was obedient to God's nudging and she and her family have been blessed. She has eaten from the best of the land. That is the message God wanted me to deliver; God wants to bless us, but He also wants us to be obedient to His call on our lives.

See you tomorrow, God willing!

November 19   Love Letters

Back before the days of cell phones and email, it was difficult to stay in touch with friends or loved ones. Can you believe, we actually sat down and wrote letters and sent them by "snail mail?"

During the summer of 1965, I was in Germany and the lady who is now my wife was in California. We wrote letters to each other almost every day. These letters weren't the length of a text message or an email, they were long letters that expressed deep emotions and described in detail the events of our lives. We still have many of those letters and they are a wonderful keepsake. Have any of you written long text messages or emails that bare your soul and become keepsakes for the rest of your life? Today, you are lucky if you get a hand written thank you note that expresses appreciation for something nice that you have done. When you do get a personal thank you note or letter of appreciation, it is a blast from the past. The written word has power.

Remember when I wrote the series of letters about the Fraley Room? In my wife's mother's keepsake box, she had letters from her dad that were over seventy-years old. One day, my wife began to read one of those letters, but quickly decided that they were not for her eyes. Perhaps some day she will feel differently, but not now. Do you have any emails or text messages over a month old?

I suppose you could say that I am guilty as well. After all, I have sent out 322 email letters over the last year and no "snail mails." However, there is a difference. First, I have poured out my soul and allowed God to speak through me even though the letters have been distributed electronically. Second, the letters are being printing out as a keepsake for the future. And, last but not least, the electronic media has enabled me to reach many people and has made it simple for them to reply to me when they feel so moved.

The renowned Christian writer, Larry Crabb wrote a book about the Bible that he called "66 Love Letters." The premise of the book was that the Bible was a collection of 66 letters from God to His people that give us the full picture of His love for us.

"In the beginning was the Word, and the Word was with God, and the Word was God." (John 1:1) "That which was from the beginning, which we have heard, which we have seen with our eyes, which we have looked at and our hands have touched—this we proclaim concerning the Word of life." (1John 1:1)

I read these love letters from God every day to remind me of how much God loves me. He made sure His love would last forever.

See you tomorrow, God willing!

November 20 — Christmas Cookies

Some people call them "bulls-eyes." Others call them "black-eyes." But everyone calls them delicious. They are really called "Buckeyes" and they are one of my favorite Christmas cookies. The base of the unbaked cookie is a mixture of butter, peanut butter, confectioner's sugar and crushed Rice Krispies. The dough is then rolled into small balls, which are dipped in chocolate, but not completely covered. Because the ball is not completely covered the cookie has the appearance of a buckeye. For those of you who have never seen a buckeye, they look somewhat like a chestnut only they are more round. There are quite a few different varieties of the small trees which bear the buckeye nut and you may not be surprised to learn that one of them is in Ohio, i.e. The Ohio State Buckeyes.

I started making Buckeyes at Christmas when we lived in Ohio and I suspect that I have made them every Christmas for nearly forty years. A double batch makes about one hundred cookies, but it is not unusual for me to make three to four batches during the Christmas season. When I say, "I make them," I should clarify that I do not always make them by myself. Over the years I have had plenty of help from my wife, my daughter and my grand kids. They all like to eat them so they don't mind helping on occasion. It is always a treat for me to have others get their hands all sticky in the peanut butter mixture.

Although my Christmas baking started with Buckeyes, it has grown significantly over the years. In addition to the Buckeyes, I make sure that I bake some other cookies that are favorites of one or more other people in the family. For example, my daughter loves Peppermint Pinwheels, but my wife prefers Danish Wedding Cookies. My son and son-in-law both like Peanut Butter Blossoms while I like to pig out on peppermint brownies. My two grandsons like a variety of the cookies but tend to favor the one's I have already mentioned.

I do love to bake and eat Christmas cookies and between my wife and me we probably bake between twelve hundred and fifteen hundred cookies every season. Our neighbors have grown accustomed to getting their annual cookie plate as have our family members and other friends.

No matter how good the cookies are, they are nothing compared to the sweetness of the Christmas season as we are reminded of the birth of our Lord and Savior. There is a wonderful verse in Colossians that puts the cookies into perspective. "Therefore do not let anyone judge you by what you eat or drink, or with regard to a religious festival… These are a shadow of the things that were to come; the reality, however, is found in Christ." (Colossians 2:16-17) "Taste and see that the Lord is good." (Psalms 34:8)

See you tomorrow, God willing!

November 21   Cook's Helpers

I walked by the refrigerator in our kitchen the other day. For some reason, I stopped to look at a photo of my granddaughter that shows her helping my wife mix up the batter for some brownies. With a precious smile on her face, she is holding a large spoon and preparing to assist with the mixing of the batter in a large yellow bowl.

For an instant, another picture flashed through my brain and I had to blink my eyes to see if there was another picture on the front of the refrigerator that I had not seen before. It was just my mind playing tricks on me; there was no other picture there. However, the picture I saw in my mind was real. It was an identical scene that occurred over forty years ago. One Thanksgiving when my daughter was two or three years old, we were visiting my mother in Virginia and my brother was also there with his son. Mother was preparing apple pies for the Thanksgiving feast and she had invited her grandchildren to assist her. We took a picture of my daughter in a pose very similar to the picture of our granddaughter I had just seen. In the picture of our daughter, she was caught chewing on some of the cut up apples, and she had a similar precious smile on her face.

Does history repeat itself? The answer is a resounding yes. One day, God willing, my daughter and granddaughter will be seen with their own granddaughters assisting them with the preparation of some delicious dessert.

I have come to realize that human nature has not changed since the beginning of time. When times are tough we look to God for help. However, once the trouble has passed we often fall back and forget what God has done for us. Here is just one example and it partially retells the story of the Israelites escape from bondage in Egypt and their settlement in a land dripping with milk and honey. "So I have come down to rescue them from the hand of the Egyptians and to bring them up out of that land into a good and spacious land, a land flowing with milk and honey."(Exodus 3:8). However, it didn't take them too long to take God's provision for granted. Before they even reached the Promised Land, they had again fallen away from God. "Go up to the land flowing with milk and honey. But I will not go with you, because you are a stiff-necked people and I might destroy you on the way." (Exodus 33:3).

I don't know about you, but I'd like a little milk and honey. It would sure be good in some cake that a grandma and her granddaughter might be mixing up.

See you tomorrow, God willing!

November 22   The Carcass

The Great Dane is a very old breed, known as the "Apollo of all dogs." Dogs resembling the Great Dane have appeared on Greek money dating back to 36 B.C. There are also drawings of these dogs on Egyptian monuments from roughly 3000 B.C. The earliest writings of dogs that sounded like Great Danes were in Chinese literature dating back to 1121 B.C.

There is another thing about Great Danes that some people don't appreciate – they are really big. The tallest recorded dog was a Great Dane that stood forty-four inches at the shoulder. Males, which are generally larger than females are normally thirty to thirty-four inches at the shoulder, and our Harlequin Great Dane was thirty-six inches at the shoulder. Let me put that into perspective. When he stood with his front paws on my shoulders, he could look me straight in the eye. If a car pulled into our driveway, he could look directly in the car window without any effort. I should also tell you that the normal height of a kitchen counter is thirty-six inches. That means that he could see and reach anything on the counter. One Thanksgiving we had a large group of family and friends over for dinner. We were sitting in the living room, which has a good view of the steps leading to the second floor. That is when we saw our Great Dane start up the steps with the turkey carcass in his mouth with grease dropping along the way. I can tell you that we were not happy at the time, but that image is emblazoned in the mind of everyone who was there that day. And, it brings a smile to our faces as we recall that "Kodak moment."

When we scolded him for taking the bones up the stairs, this is what he said, "The hand of the Lord was upon me, and he brought me out by the Spirit of the Lord and set me in the middle of a valley; it was full of bones…I will make breath enter you, and you will come to life…' This is what the Sovereign Lord says: Come from the four winds, O breath, and breathe into these slain, that they may live.' So I prophesied as he commanded me, and breath entered them; they came to life and stood up on their feet—a vast army." (Ezekiel 37:1-10) Then Josh said to me, "that's my story and I'm sticking to it."

See you tomorrow, God willing!

November 23 — Thanksgiving Feast

"Thanksgiving is traditionally the heaviest travel weekend of the year, with the Sunday after Thanksgiving taking honors for the heaviest travel day bar none." We saw it every year as we traveled back and forth to celebrate the holiday with our parents. After a few very bad experiences returning home on the Sunday after Thanksgiving, I learned to take an extra day of vacation and make the drive home on Monday.

Have you ever considered why Thanksgiving travel is ahead of all other holidays? Here is my analysis. First, it is the only holiday that all colleges let out on the same day. Since it is also spaced at a nice gap from the time school starts, nearly all college students travel home for the celebration. Second, it is the last holiday that persons living in cold weather climates can be relatively sure that the weather will be okay for travel. For those people, it is the "last chance" holiday for several months. And, because it is a four-day weekend it gives people a chance to travel at a more relaxed pace. And, last but not least, it is one of the most significant "family" holidays on the calendar.

Thanksgiving meals in our family were out of this world. Since both sets of grandparents (parents) lived in the same town, we got the opportunity to have two feasts in the same day. Typically, my wife's family would schedule the initial meal around 1:30 p.m. If all went well, we would be away from the table by 3 p.m. Then it was time to go to my family's house for meal number two. I would like to tell you that we paced ourselves at the first meal to leave plenty of room for more food at the second feast, but I was never able to discipline myself to do so. So instead of truly enjoying the second meal, I was forced to stuff myself to make sure I didn't hurt anyone's feelings. The food at both locations was so good that it wasn't hard to stuff myself. In later years after my dad passed away, we were able to combine the two families at one Thanksgiving feast.

I am proud to say that daughter and her family do not have to suffer through two separate feasts. Our very first Thanksgiving in North Carolina was celebrated by the families and that custom has held true every year. Some years we eat at my daughter's house, some years at her in-laws house and some years we eat at our house. One thing, however, is the same – there is still more food than you can imagine and it is still out of this world.

On this Thanksgiving Day, let us heed the words of the prophet Isaiah, "Give thanks to the LORD, call on his name; make known among the nations what he has done, and proclaim that his name is exalted." (Isaiah 12:4)

See you tomorrow, God willing!

November 24   A Thanksgiving Prayer

The story that needs to be written on Thanksgiving is the story of God's love for all mankind. It is a story that has no beginning and no end and it is a story that includes each of us in the main plot. "No eye has seen, no ear has heard, no mind has conceived what God has prepared for those who love him." (1 Corinthians 2:9) That Bible verse tells me not to attempt to tell the story, so I will simply use the opportunity to thank God for including me in His story of love.

Dearest Heavenly Father, there are no words that I could ever speak that would fully express the gratitude that I have for all the blessings that you have poured out on me and my family. I am not worthy nor have I done anything to earn your favor. Yet, today I will have a feast with my entire immediate family and I praise you for putting each one of them into my life. First, you blessed me with a wife who has been my suitable helper for over forty years. Then you blessed with me two wonderful children and gave to each of them suitable helpers. Then came more gifts – five beautiful, charming, smart, loveable grandchildren. I thank you for each and every one of my family.

Lord, you have also granted me good health all of my life and that has enabled me to enjoy all you have to offer. I thank you that you have given me a keen mind and a soft heart. When my tears flow, Lord, I know that someone's garden is being watered. Especially this Thanksgiving, I want to praise you for allowing me to serve your children in the Dominican Republic. It is a stern reminder of my responsibility to serve the Least, the Lost, and the Last.

As we enjoy the fruits of the greatest nation in the world, I pray that this "lost nation" will turn back to you. "If my people, who are called by my name, will humble themselves and pray and seek my face and turn from their wicked ways, then will I hear from heaven and will forgive their sin and will heal their land." (2 Chronicles 7:14) That is my prayer, Lord that we will turn back to you.

To everyone who reads this letter, I pray blessings on you and your families. May this Thanksgiving be a new beginning.

See you tomorrow, God willing!

November 25 — Macy's Day Parade

My wife and I always wanted to attend a Macy's Thanksgiving Day Parade. The annual parade is a three-hour event held in New York City starting at 9:00 a.m. EST on Thanksgiving Day. In 1996, we finally decided to make our desire a reality. Along with friends we took a bus into New York City arriving early enough to get a good viewing site for the parade. Since the parade route was through Times Square down Broadway, we walked the short distance from Port Authority Bus Terminal and set up shop around 38th and Broadway. There were only two problems with our plan. First, we had picked one of the coldest Thanksgiving Day's in many years to be standing outdoors for several hours. Although we had arrived early enough to get a first-row view of the parade, we had not counted on the challenge of holding onto those spots for several hours. How could we leave to get a cup of coffee or go to the bathroom? By the time the parade finally reached us, the people were five or six rows deep making it virtually impossible to leave, even if we wanted to.

The parade was great fun. The floats are even more majestic when you see them from twenty-five feet rather than on television. The music also happens to be better perhaps because it is bouncing off the large buildings all along the route. We happened to be situated at a spot on the parade route where the bands would stop and serenade us and that was a real treat. The wind that swept through the streets between the skyscrapers made it very difficult for the handlers to maintain control of the large helium-filled balloon characters. That same wind chilled us to the bone and made the long morning seem even longer. However, we survived and it was an experience we will never forget.

There was a first rate parade that took place during King David's reign. "So David went down and brought up the ark of God from the house of Obed-Edom to the City of David with rejoicing. When those who were carrying the ark of the Lord had taken six steps, he sacrificed a bull and a fattened calf. David, wearing a linen ephod, danced before the Lord with all his might, while he and the entire house of Israel brought up the ark of the Lord with shouts and the sound of trumpets." (2 Samuel 6:12-15) There was only one float in that parade, but it was incredibly beautiful because of what it contained. And, like most parades, it was complete with dancers and music. And, that group of revilers didn't have to worry about cold weather – David only wore a linen ephod.

Next time you see a parade, think about David and the Ark of the Covenant; it should bring a smile to your face

See you tomorrow, God willing!

November 26 — Meaning of Names

When we spent a week with my wife's family in the fall, her nephew came down from Richmond on Thursday evening to spend the last couple of days with us. Since her nephew's wife is expecting in February, all of us were anxious to know if they had selected a name for the baby. My wife's sister-in-law suggested a few names for their consideration, but I could tell that her son was politely listening without committing to anything.

When our daughter was born, we wanted to name her after everybody and we tried. The first name covered my sister and my dad since my sister's name is the feminine version of my dad's name. The second name covered her maternal grandmother and the third name covered her paternal grandmother. While we didn't realize it until later, we also noticed that her initials also captured the name her maternal grandfather often used for his business correspondence. In three names, we had covered all four grandparents and my sister.

When our son came along nearly four years later, we didn't have so many people to cover. His first name just happened to be a name we both liked. His second name is from me and the third name is the Irish variant of for my sister's husband. We used the Irish variant because he was born on St. Patrick's Day.

In Biblical times, a person's name often carried a description of the person's character or something about the person. I took the time to look up the meaning of all both of our children's names. Lorena Elizabeth Gretchen means, "Crowned with Laurel," "Consecrated to God," and "Pearl." What a wonderful description of our lovely daughter! Christopher William Sean means "Christ-Bearer," "Protector," "God is Gracious." He is living into that beautiful name.

In Henry Blackaby's book, "*Experiencing God*", he talks about the importance of getting to know God personally. Blackaby notes that in the Bible, God reveals many sides of himself and He takes on many names. Do you recognize some of them? "My witness" (Job 16:19), "Wonderful Counselor" (Isaiah 9:6), "Almighty God" (Genesis 17:1), "My hiding place" (Psalm 32:7), "The Good Shepherd" (John 10:11), and "Good Teacher" (Mark 10:17). I want to know Him by all these names and more. When Moses asked God to tell the Pharaoh who had sent him, "God said to Moses, 'I AM WHO I AM'. (Exodus 3:14) Perhaps that is the most descriptive name that we can ascribe to Him. He is "I AM!" He is everything to me.

See you tomorrow, God willing!

November 27　　　　　　　　　　　　　　　　　　　　Ballet Dancer

When our daughter was a little girl, she had a pink ballerina dress that she wore around the house and pretended that she was a prima ballerina. I suppose that is common for little girls and I have seen the same kind of behavior as we watch our granddaughter grow up. When our granddaughter and her mom and dad were with us for the Thanksgiving holiday, my wife put on *The Nutcracker* video for our granddaughter to watch. We weren't sure whether or not she would watch it, but over the years, my wife has taken a multitude of little girls to watch holiday performances of the ballet and little girls are always spellbound by the story and the dancing. Our granddaughter was no exception. She not only watched; she danced.

As she danced to the music of "*The Nutcracker,*" she invited her daddy to dance with her and he did. He cabrioled; he devanted; he pirouetted; he piquéd; and he pliéd. I don't think that he knew he was doing all of these things, but it didn't matter because his daughter was thoroughly spellbound by this special moment with her daddy.

We recently went to see the Christian movie, "*Courageous,*" and there was a scene in the movie where a father chose not to embarrass himself by dancing with his young daughter in the parking lot of a bank building. After his young daughter tragically died in a car accident, he went back to that parking lot and danced with her in his memory regretting that missed moment in time. My son, who also saw the movie, said that he would have danced the first time, and I know he was telling the truth. When I saw him doing ballet with his daughter in our family room, I saw the scene replayed in my mind.

We saw a tee shirt the other day that reminded us of the special relationship that exists between fathers and daughters. On the front of the tee shirt it said, "Daddy, so easy to operate a daughter can do it."

There are too many times in our lives when we let our pride get in the way of doing something special. Are we afraid of what people will say about us? Are we afraid to stand up for those people and things that we love? How often do we get a chance to be a witness for God, yet we hold back for exactly the same reasons? The next time you have a chance to be a witness, remember what Paul said, "I am not ashamed of the gospel, because it is the power of God for the salvation of everyone who believes…For in the gospel a righteousness from God is revealed, a righteousness that is by faith from first to last, just as it is written: The righteous will live by faith." (Romans 1:16-17)

See you tomorrow, God willing!

November 28 — Come with Me

Close you eyes and come with me. We are walking down a slight incline on a smooth path that feels like poured concrete. I see a large garage door directly in front of me and there seems to be a small door built into the large door. It's a bit strange because the door on the lower left is too small to let anyone in the garage without stooping over. Nevertheless, the little door is opening and I immediately feel warmer as I enter the enclosed area. There is a small coal-burning pot belly stove directly to the left as you enter the garage area.

What is this place? Over to my right, I can see a bunch of smashed aluminum cans on the concrete floor of the garage, and there are tools everywhere. There is a lawn mower, a trimmer and a wheel barrow. There are what seems to be an infinite number of screw drivers, hammers, files, and pliers. After glancing around a little more, I finally find a string that I can pull to turn on some lights.

Now that the place is lighted I see some really neat stuff. In the far back corner, it looks like a pool hall. There is a regulation pool table complete with its own pool table light hung directly over the table.

Now things are getting even more interesting. There is a contraption not too far from the pool table and there are walnut shells all over the floor. And, there were a couple of large vices that seemed to be holding polished pieces of wood that appeared to be limbs from trees or something of that nature. Each of the polished pieces of wood was about three feet long and each had a small white rubber tip on one end and a curve at the other end. They were handmade canes made by my wife's dad.

You can open your eyes now. Those in my family know where they are and have their own memories of the place. My wife's dad left us memories all over the place. Sometimes we just have to open one of the doors in our minds and take a little peak.

This story about the garage was brought on by an innocent remark that my wife made about a devotional she had read in "Guideposts" about a man who made canes. Do you know that every time a rainbow appears in the sky, it is a reminder of one of God's promises? "Never again will the waters become a flood to destroy all life. Whenever the rainbow appears in the clouds, I will see it and remember the everlasting covenant between God and all living creatures of every kind on the earth." (Genesis 9:15b-16)

I hope the next time you see someone walking with a wooden cane it will remind you of this stroll.

See you tomorrow, God willing!

November 29 — Coal Miner

"Man puts an end to the darkness; he searches the farthest recesses for ore in the blackest darkness." (Job 28:3) Job is believed to have lived some time between 1900 and 1700 BC. That means that mankind had already learned to tunnel into the earth in search of ore. Verses four through six from chapter 28 go on to say, "Far from where people dwell he cuts a shaft, in places forgotten by the foot of man; far from men he dangles and sways. The earth, from which food comes, is transformed below as by fire; sapphires come from its rocks, and its dust contains nuggets of gold."

That is where my dad spent most of his career "far from where people dwell." He worked down in the deep recesses of the earth as a foreman responsible for the work of his crew in bringing coal to the surface. I know the work was hard and dangerous, but it was the one way he could support his family, so he made the sacrifice. Although he didn't talk too much about the working conditions, I do remember a few things. When he got home from work he was covered in coal dust from head to toe. I specifically remember his eyes; it was as if he had black eye liner on the top and bottom of his lids. He also told stories about working in seams of coal that were very small. In those cases, the men could not stand upright, but worked for many hours in semi-crouching positions. Oddly enough, it was this wear and tear on his knees that finally caused him to take disability. As most coal miners of his generation, dad also got Black Lung from breathing coal dust for too many years. Many coal miners died from this disease, but fortunately my dad's Black Lung was only bad enough to cause him to quit smoking.

At several points in his life my dad left the tough working conditions of the mines to try his hand at other occupations. He ran a hotel for a few years; he leased a gas station and ran it for a short time; and he even tried his hand at strip mining for awhile. However, none of those professions proved to be successful so he always returned to what he could do best.

Dad searched his whole life for the right profession for him. In his own way, he was looking for wisdom. "He tunnels through the rock; his eyes see all its treasures. 'But where can wisdom be found? Where does understanding dwell?'... And he said to man, 'The fear of the Lord—that is wisdom, and to shun evil is understanding.'" (Job: 10-12, 28) By the time dad died in 1986, he had found true wisdom. He was at peace with God.

See you tomorrow, God willing!

November 30   Ground Nesting Yellow Jackets

For many young boys, fear is not a word in their vocabulary. I have told many stories about stupid things I have done that would certainly demonstrate that I did not understand the word. On our farm in Illinois, mother had a clothes line that was used to dry the wash. It so happened that our clothes line was made of hollow metal so it was possible for wasps to build their nests inside the clothes line pole. One of my favorite pastimes was to take a baseball bat and whack the clothes line pole to disturb the wasps. The key was to strike the pole once and then run away as fast as possible to avoid being stung.

We destroyed many wasps' nests in that clothes line pole and in other locations around the house. As I think back on that activity, I now know why I have been repaid by wasps over the years for this demonic activity. My first payback occurred at golf when I was about fourteen years old. I was walking through a creek bed when I stepped in a ground nest of eastern yellow jackets. As I began to feel the stings on my legs, I tossed my golf bag aside and began to run, all the while flailing at the wasps on my legs. Those who were playing with me at the time nearly fell down in laughter at the sight of me running and flapping my arms. When they found out that I had been stung by wasps about thirty times there was some sympathy, but not much.

Over the years, I have stepped in many ground nests of yellow jackets while working in the yard. It happened several times in my yard in Pennsylvania and just recently in my yard in Greenville. Much to my surprise, the last time I was stung, I had an allergic reaction to the stings and the fingers on the hand that was stung began to swell and there was pain in the joints. The sting on the face, or perhaps the multiple stings all over my body, caused me to develop a short term difficulty in breathing. I began to understand that the immunity that I seemed to have over the years had gone away.

My past immunity was God given and is similar to the protection the psalmist noted in Psalm 118. "They swarmed around me like bees, but they died out as quickly as burning thorns; in the name of the Lord I cut them off. I was pushed back and about to fall, but the Lord helped me. The Lord is my strength and my song; he has become my salvation. (Psalm 118:12-14) God is my strength and my song, but I don't want to push my luck. I'm going to do my very best to stay out of yellow jackets' nests from now on.

See you tomorrow, God willing!

DECEMBER

December 1 — Nutcrackers Are Coming

It's just about that time of year. For eleven months of the year, our collection of nutcrackers rests comfortably in their individual boxes waiting for their thirty days of glory. I can tell you that the first visitor came in the late 1960's after some friends had taken our daughter to see "The Nutcracker Ballet." For Christmas that year, they gave her what turned out to be the first in our collection of fifty characters.

There is a story behind each of our nutcrackers, but I will spare you the reading of all fifty. If you ever take the time to look at all of the nutcrackers that are available, you might wonder why certain one's get in the collection while others are left in the store. Here is our reason; we like to pick out nutcrackers that reflect the character of family members. For example, in 1993, we found a cute little blonde girl, Claire, who was actually the lead character in the ballet. She reminded us of our daughter and since you don't find a lot of female nutcrackers we bought that one in a hurry. We only have one other female nutcracker that is entitled, Garden Lady; guess who that is? There is also a Sea Shell Hunter for my wife. One year we added a snow skier and that, along with the Fisherman, was our son. When our son-in-law came into our family, we added a Navy man to represent him in our army of toy soldiers. It seems that my personality and interests made it far too hard to represent me with just one nutcracker. Here are a few of my family – there is the Old Hippie, the Cookie Baker, the Golfer, Ophah and one of my favorites, The Phantom of the Opera. Most of the family nutcrackers receive a place of prominence on the fireplace mantle.

There is another set of nutcrackers that also receives special display privileges. Those are our Biblical characters. They include – St. Peter, Noah, Moses, Joseph and his coat of many colors, and the Magi.

It is always fun to get the nutcrackers out of storage each Christmas season, because they bring back wonderful memories of past Christmases. However, they are not the reason for the season. "Of what value is an idol, since a man has carved it? Or an image that teaches lies? For he who makes it trusts in his own creation; he makes idols that cannot speak. Woe to him who says to wood, 'Come to life!' Or to lifeless stone, 'Wake up!' Can it give guidance? It is covered with gold and silver; there is no breath in it. But the Lord is in his holy temple; let all the earth be silent before him." (Habakkuk 2:18-20) The Lord is in His Holy Temple; let all earth be silent before Him. That is very profound.

See you tomorrow, God willing!

December 2   From My Journal

Last January when I began to write my daily letters, I marked a page in my calendar with a note that said "use your favorite verse in the Bible, Romans 12:2 as the topic of your letter on December 2nd. Well, today is December the 2nd and I have been searching for a meaningful story for nearly a year. Last night, I went up to my office to try one last time. First, I tried looking in some old daily devotionals hoping there would be some magic on a previous 12:2. It was to no avail. Just when I was about ready to give up, I pulled an old journal of mine from 2003 and began to read some of my daily entries. On January 19, 2004 I found what I was looking for. It was meant for this day.

January 19, 2004 – Today is the beginning of Covenant's "40 Days of Purpose" and I am keeping a separate journal that captures my thoughts and revelations on this aspect of my walk with Christ. However, after I finished my first day and returned to my regular devotions, I read with new revelation Ephesians 1:17, part of Paul's prayer for the Ephesians. It says, "I keep asking that the God of our Lord Jesus Christ, the glorious Father, may give you the Spirit of wisdom and revelation, so that you may know Him better."

I have read this verse many times, but I missed a significant point. I read it to mean, little "s" spirit. In other words, give me a spirit of wisdom and revelation so I can independently get understanding. It says, "Give me the SPIRIT." Through the Spirit I will be given wisdom and revelation. That knowledge helped me understand why it is so important for us to call on the Holy Spirit for help.

This verse also puts the punctuation mark on another verse that God recently drew me to (Romans 12:2). "Do not conform to the patterns of this world, but be transformed by the renewing of your mind. Then you will be able to test and approve what God's will is – His good, pleasing, and perfect will." Allow the Holy Spirit to guide and direct you and He will show you His will for you – His good, pleasing, and perfect will.

Then came yet another verse, 2 Corinthians 5:5, "Now it is God who has made us for this purpose and has given us the Spirit as a deposit, guaranteeing what is to come."

Here is the summary for today. When we invite Jesus into our life, the Holy Spirit resides in us. That Spirit brings wisdom and revelation. Once we establish that on-going relationship, we are able to see with more clarity the perfect plan God has for our lives. Furthermore, that same Holy Spirit is a deposit guaranteeing our inheritance.

That is the story God wanted me to tell you today.

See you tomorrow, God willing!

December 3 — The Trinity

I love the way God works. Yesterday, I sent out an unconventional letter that included my favorite Bible verse (Romans 12:2). When I started writing the beginning and end of the story, I had no idea that the focus of the story would be on the Holy Spirit. On December 1st and December 2nd, I wrote two other stories that are in my "story inventory" to be sent out some time before the end of the year, or so I thought. Both of the new stories are seemingly unrelated and had no apparent connection to the verses from yesterday's story.

As I drove to work yesterday morning, I wondered about the two new stories because both of them seemed to come out of nowhere. One is about a gala event that my wife and I attended while we were in London and the other story is about some trouble that I got into when I was in high school. In my mind, the three stories were not connected in any way whatsoever and they just happened to be random stories that God was allowing me to tell.

I was wrong and God showed me the connection and encouraged me to send out the next two letters as part of a series. Tomorrow, you will receive a story titled "The Invitation" and it will talk about Jesus' invitation to a new life with Him. The next day you will receive a letter titled "Wrong Place at the Wrong Time" and that letter is about God the Father as Judge.

Without knowing what I was doing, I had written three letters about the Trinity – God the Father (the Judge), God the Son (the one who invites us to the feast) and God the Holy Spirit (the one who guides and direct us). I am not a theologian so I beg your forgiveness for the simplicity of these letters with regard to the Trinity.

I started this letter with the phrase "I love the way God Works." Let me end in a similar manner, "And this is love: that we walk in obedience to his commands. As you have heard from the beginning, his command is that you walk in love." (2 John 1:6) When you love God and allow Him to work in your life, you will see amazing things.

See you tomorrow, God willing!

December 4 — The Invitation

It may seem strange to you that the story I am about to tell is so far off in terms of the calendar. Nevertheless, it is a story I need to tell because the message is timeless. Are you ready?

During the summer of 1985, I was working in Europe and the rest of the family had joined me for the summer. There is almost nothing in London that reminds you of the United States. The architecture is old and incredibly different from what we see here. The houses are generally stacked on top of each other and they have no yards. To make matters worse, it rains all the time. During that summer it rained virtually every day. Not only was it wet, it was downright cold all summer. The temperature only exceeded eighty degrees Fahrenheit one day the entire summer.

It is a great place to visit, but it isn't home. There was one event that took place that summer that made us feel at home. Around the third week in June, we received this beautiful invitation to attend the annual 4th of July Ball sponsored by the U. S. Chamber of Commerce in London. The invitation actually came from the president of our European operations who was also an American.

Since the event was a gala affair, we had to obtain the proper clothes for the evening. For me it was easy; I simply rented a tuxedo. For my wife, it was not that easy. She had to shop for a formal gown, shoes, etc. and find a place to get her hair done. The evening turned out to be a wonderful time and it was good to have our feet symbolically on home soil.

There is a wonderful story in the Bible that parallels our experience in London.

"The kingdom of heaven is like a king who prepared a wedding banquet for his son. He sent his servants to those who had been invited to the banquet to tell them to come, but they refused to come… 'Tell those who have been invited that I have prepared my dinner'… But they paid no attention and went off—one to his field, another to his business… Then he said to his servants, 'The wedding banquet is ready, but those I invited did not deserve to come. Go to the street corners and invite to the banquet anyone you find'… But when the king came in to see the guests, he noticed a man there who was not wearing wedding clothes. 'Friend,' he asked, 'how did you get in here without wedding clothes'…? Then the king told the attendants, 'Tie him hand and foot, and throw him outside, into the darkness, where there will be weeping and gnashing of teeth. For many are invited, but few are chosen.'" (Matthew 22:2-14) When your invitation to the "wedding feast of the Lamb" comes, please accept His invitation and get yourself ready.

See you tomorrow, God willing!

December 5 — Wrong Place, Wrong Time

Growing up in a small town often means there isn't too much to do on the weekends. If you aren't careful, you can end up at the wrong place at the wrong time. That is just what happened to me one evening during my high school years.

One of my good friends happened to have a nice convertible with a white top. On summer evenings, it was great fun to simply ride around with the top down and enjoy the warm weather. Of course, when the sun went down the top went up as the evening cooled. Evenings also brought mischief.

I don't know when the bad feelings developed between my friend and another teenager, but I do know it spelled trouble for me. One fall evening, my friend had left his car parked on the street because we were running around with some other friends. When we returned to his car, there was motor oil all over the white top of his convertible. He suspected who the culprit was so we looked around town to see if we could find him. While we couldn't find him, we did see his car parked at another spot in town. When we looked in the back seat of the car, he saw an open can of motor oil. Rather than call the police to handle the situation, my friend poured the remainder of the oil all over the cloth seats of the car.

I wish that the story ended there, but it didn't. When I returned home from playing golf the next day, I had an arrest warrant waiting for me. I was in the wrong place at the wrong time. To make a long story short, we had to go before a judge at the county seat to have the charges against us heard. When our lawyer filed counter charges against the other boy, the judge did the wise thing and dismissed both sets of charges.

It was the only time in my life that I have ever had to face a judge for any reason. I know one day, I will face another judge and that time, I will not be innocent. Fortunately for me, I know the judge personally, and He has already paid for my wrongdoings ahead of time. He will pay for yours, too, if you let Him. "If we confess our sins, he is faithful and just and will forgive us our sins and purify us from all unrighteousness." (1 John 1:9) "For as high as the heavens are above the earth, so great is his love for those who fear him; as far as the east is from the west, so far has he removed our transgressions from us." (Psalms 103:11-12)

Sometimes you can't do too much about being in the wrong place at the wrong time, but you can be sure that your sins are wiped away before you see The Judge.

See you tomorrow, God willing!

December 6   Fire Down Below

Back in 2002, when we first moved to Greenville, our daughter had an accident at her house that caused major damage to her kitchen and smoke damage to the rest of her house. Fortunately, no one was harmed, but the house was not livable for an extended period of time. Apparently, God knew ahead of time what was going to happen (He always does) because the house we were renting at the time had an upstairs with plenty of room for the whole family to live with us while their house was being refurbished.

While the fire itself was a bad thing, the time they lived with us had some wonderful memories. Here are just a few of them. Her two boys were both going to a private Christian school at the time. Every morning, it was my pleasure to drive them to school. They loved to be chauffeured to school in the Blue Cadillac that we had inherited from my wife's dad. Both of them recall those early morning rides with great affection.

Another memory of their stay involved my son-in-law's guitars. There is no one who takes better care of his musical instruments than he does. He will not leave his instruments in the car for any period of time, not fearing for the safety of the guitar, but not wanting them to be subjected to any temperature extremes. When they came to stay with us, we had generally kept the upstairs of the house at cool temperatures since we rarely went upstairs unless it was to get something that we had stored there. When our daughter and the rest of the family came to stay, we had to dramatically increase the temperature, not for them, but for the guitars.

I don't remember exactly how long they stayed with us. As best I can remember it was about six weeks. This is what I do remember; we had a wonderful time. "When you pass through the waters, I will be with you; and when you pass through the rivers, they will not sweep over you. When you walk through the fire, you will not be burned; the flames will not set you ablaze." (Isaiah 43:2) God protected His children during the fire and gave us a special blessing to go with it.

See you tomorrow, God willing!

December 7 — Who Decorated That Tree?

As we approach the Christmas season, I recalled an incident with my mother-in-law after her Alzheimer's had progressed well along and she had been bedridden for about six months.

We had gone to visit to give her caregiver a few days off and recharge her batteries. During the time the caregiver was away, we got out her artificial Christmas tree and decorated it with all of her favorite ornaments. When the caregiver returned and saw the decorated tree she said, "Granny the tree looks beautiful, when did you have it decorated?" Without blinking an eye or hesitating for even a second, she told her that she had decorated the tree all by herself. When I mentioned this story to my wife, here is what she had to say, "I wish there was a way for others to see the look of joy on her face as she told us she had decorated the tree. Even when the caregiver ask her how she got upstairs to carry all the boxes down! She said 'I just walked up and down the stairs!'" We all enjoyed the moment. It didn't matter in the least who had decorated the tree, for one moment my wife's mother remembered previous Christmas's when she had indeed decorated the tree for our arrival.

One of my favorite pastimes when we went to help care for my wife's mom was to sing with her. There was an old Baptist hymnal at the house and I would go through the hymnal and find hymns that were familiar to me. She loved for me to sing to her and much to my dismay she would often sing along even in the last days when it seemed as if she couldn't remember anything from her past. Later I would learn that it is common for late stage Alzheimer patients to respond in a very positive manner to music. They will remember words to songs from their past even though nothing else from that era of their life can be recalled. Singing to her was one way I could repay the love she had shown me for many, many years.

If you read the Bible often, I would dare say that you do not spend a lot of time reading the book of Leviticus. I will admit that it can be a bit dry, but don't forget that every Word of God is flawless so if He put a particular book in the Bible, there must be a reason. Try this verse on for size, "Rise in the presence of the aged, show respect for the elderly and revere your God. I am the Lord." (Leviticus 19:32) It is very sound advice and I am glad I listened.

See you tomorrow, God willing!

December 8 — Potluck Dinner

I got an email the other day from church that notified me about a meeting that will be held on December the 14th. The invitees are individuals within the church that are active on one of several outreach committees. The email also notified me that there will be a "potluck dinner" as part of the meeting. Wikipedia says "a potluck dinner is a gathering of people where each person or group of people contributes a dish of food prepared by the person or the group of people, to be shared among the group.

Wikipedia went on to say that potluck dinners are most often organized by religious or community groups, since they simplify the meal planning and distribute the costs among the participants. Smaller, more informal get-togethers with distributed food preparation may also be called potlucks. The only traditional rule is that each dish be large enough to be shared among a good portion (but not necessarily all) of the anticipated guests. In some cases each participant agrees ahead of time to bring a single course, and the result is a multi-course meal. Guests may bring any form of food, ranging from the main course to desserts. In the United States, potlucks are associated with Crockpot dishes, casseroles (often called hot dishes in the upper Midwest), dessert bars and Jell-O salads.

Going back to the email announcing our "potluck" dinner, there was a line in the note that said we were to go to www.PerfectPotluck.com to see what we might bring. I love technology, but this is going too far. Whatever happened to letting God do the planning? He has fed me for over fifty years at potluck dinners and I never had a bad one with too much or too little of anything. What would my mother have done if too many people had signed up for desserts before she checked on the list? People would have been deprived of her black skillet cherry cobbler or other people's specialties. Technology is a good thing, but some things need to be left alone and let God take care of them

No matter what happens in the arena of technological development, there is one form of communication that no computer, cell phone, or I Pad will ever replace. If you guessed prayer, you are right on the money. You can get right down on your knees and use the words Jesus taught His disciples nearly two thousand years ago. "This, then, is how you should pray: 'Our Father in heaven, hallowed be your name, your kingdom come, your will be done on earth as it is in heaven. Give us today our daily bread. Forgive us our debts, as we also have forgiven our debtors. And lead us not into temptation, but deliver us from the evil one.'" (Luke 11:2-4) You don't need to go to www.whattopray.com to figure that one out.

See you tomorrow, God willing!

December 9 — Date Night

The concept of a date night was probably invented by an aspiring young husband who was neglecting his bride by spending too much time at work and not enough time with his wife and children. Wikipedia defines date night as an opportunity for a married couple, especially one with children, to go out on a date.

One of my favorite stories from my wife and her brother was about "date night" in their family. Every Saturday night when they were youngsters, the kids would get a very early dinner and be sent off to bed. As my wife recalls their dinner, it was more like peanut butter and jelly sandwiches than it was a real dinner. Once the youngsters were in bed, they could smell the steaks and potatoes being cooked in the kitchen. After a hard week of work, it was time for her to relax and they did – salad, steak, and potato, a meal fit for the king and his bride.

It wasn't until my mother had lived with us for a couple of years that my wife and I decided that a date night would be a good idea. Since someone always needed to be with mother, we would ask her caregiver to spend the night on some Saturday nights to give us the opportunity to go out for dinner and a movie. If we didn't feel like going out, we would still have her come over and we would rent a movie in order to keep the night free.

Personal relationships do not stay alive and healthy if you don't take the time to be with the one you love. Date nights are great, but it is like going to church on Sunday, if that is all you ever did to have a relationship, the relationship would fail. Spend time with your spouse every day to see how she is doing. Did she have a good day? What made her day special? What problems did she have that she would like for you to hear about (NOT SOLVE)? What can you do to make her day a little easier or brighter?

God wants to have the same type of relationship with us. He wants us to talk to Him daily and He wants to talk to us through His written word. Going to church on Sunday is good, but it is not enough. The one hundred nineteenth Psalm uses the word "precept" twenty times. It is a Psalm about dedicating time to understanding God's ways. Here is my favorite verse from that Psalm, "Let me understand the teaching of your precepts; then I will meditate on your wonders." (Psalm 119:27) A daily walk with God will result in a relationship that is built on understanding, obedience, trust, and love. That's what God wants from each of us. It is better than a date night.

See you tomorrow, God willing!

December 10   Arrowheads

My father-in-law loved to hunt and he bagged his share of deer, "wild turkeys" and even squirrels. He also loved to fish and during trout season he would put on his wet gear and head for the nearest trout stream. When he wasn't hunting or fishing, he might just be walking through the woods looking for ginseng root or simply enjoying the outdoors by hiking a well-known trail. All of those activities were enjoyable, but there was one other outdoor activity that that he dearly loved – looking for arrowheads and other Indian relics.

He had a framed picture on the wall in the living room that displayed some of his best finds. There was an assortment of different shapes and sizes and he had done his homework and could tell you quite a bit about them. For example, I wasn't aware that there were different sized arrowheads for different sized game. If the Indians were hunting small game, they used small arrowheads. If they were hunting large game, the arrowhead would be much larger.

His collection contained far more than arrowheads. There were also many different heads from tomahawks. While the smaller tomahawk heads went on those weapons for throwing, the larger heads were used in hand to hand battle. It is interesting to see that each tomahawk head was carefully ground around the upper third of the rock to allow a piece of wood to be inserted around the groove and attached to the stone.

Much to my surprise, his collection also contained a number of pieces of flint that had been made into tools such as drills and hatchets. The American Indian did not lack ingenuity. In fact, raw pieces of flint that came from their quarries were also used for currency or trading between various tribes.

The Bible is full of references to arrows, mostly related to warfare. Obviously, these sharp objects could penetrate through shields and armor to cause serious damage or death. For example, King Ahab of Israel was killed when an arrow "hit the king of Israel between the sections of his armor." (1 Kings 22:34) What I found most striking was not the references to war, but the comparisons of the tongue to the piercing power of an arrow. "Their tongue is a deadly arrow; it speaks with deceit. With his mouth each speaks cordially to his neighbor, but in his heart he sets a trap for him." (Jeremiah 9:8) Likewise, the prophet Isaiah described himself as a weapon of God, "He made my mouth like a sharpened sword, in the shadow of his hand he hid me; he made me into a polished arrow and concealed me in his quiver." (Isaiah 49:2)

Here is the question I leave you to ponder. Is your mouth a sharp arrow of destruction or a powerful weapon in the fight against Satan?

See you tomorrow, God willing!

December 11 — Black Ice

The weather in Pennsylvania had been snowy and very cold for several days. When I came home from work that day, the snow had melted off the roads to the point that they were passable. I got home about six p.m. from work and had dinner with my wife before I headed out for a meeting at church. As I went out the door, my wife told me to be careful, it was turning colder again and the moisture on the road would very likely refreeze creating black ice. Black ice, sometimes called glare ice or clear ice, refers to a thin coating of glazed **ice** on a surface that is virtually invisible.

I thanked her for reminding me of the possibility of slick roads and left for my meeting. When I turned onto the main highway, everything seemed to be okay. However, after driving about a mile I noticed a string of brake lights in front of me. When I tapped on my brakes to stop, nothing happened. I tapped again, but the car continued to move forward and the stopped cars in front of me were now only a few feet away. By now, I realized I was going to be the victim of "black ice." The car was not going to stop so I did the only thing practical at the time, I turned the car onto the shoulder of the road, which was still snow covered, and managed to keep the car under control as I passed six or seven cars on my left. Just about the time that the available shoulder of the road was to run out, a space appeared between two cars on my left and to my amazement the traffic was moving again. I jerked the car back onto the road and proceeded on my way as if nothing had happened.

I can imagine what was on the mind of the cars I passed. They had to be thinking "what a jerk, why can't he wait patiently like the rest of us for the road to clear?" There was one driver on the road that had something different on his mind. I was thinking about how God took the wheel of my car and kept it under control until He could make a space for me.

The road of life is full of potholes, crazy drivers, and unsafe surfaces. While Satan wants us to crash and burn, God wants us to be safe to glorify Him. "We know that anyone born of God does not continue to sin; the one who was born of God keeps him safe, and the evil one cannot harm him." (1 John 5:18) The evil one, "black ice," was no match for the God of the universe. I am still here to sing God's praises because He looked after me.

See you tomorrow, God willing!

December 12 — Basketball Star

When my son and his wife came to visit during Thanksgiving, I made it a point to talk to her about her basketball career at the now defunct St. Paul High school. As old-timers say, back in my days at St. Paul High School, they didn't even have a girl's basketball team. However, one of the few intelligent things that our government has ever done was to force colleges to make equal opportunity for girls to participate in sports. It wasn't too long after that edict that high schools also began to offer more sports opportunities for the ladies

Back to the story. I didn't know too much about her basketball career before I talked to her. I did know that was she was a very good player. When she graduated from high school, she was the leading scorer in the school's history. She held that record for only a few years until her sister came along and broke the record. As we talked about her career, I found out that my basketball career and hers had some common themes. According to her own account, she was a "ball-hog." If you don't happen to be familiar with the term, it means someone who handles the ball a lot and shoots even more. If you happen to be on a lack-luster team and you handle the ball a lot and you are a really good shooter, you will almost always end up being a ball hog. As we talked about basketball, I told her that I had the same reputation. In fact, I was accused of shooting so much that I would even shoot when I didn't have the ball.

There was also one other thing that she and I had in common with respect to basketball. We spent hours in the gym to enhance our skills. I spent even more hours in my backyard where I had a backboard and rim attached to a tree. It wasn't pretty, but practice makes perfect. There is the lesson for the day. Whatever is important in your life, practice to make yourself better. If you want to be more like God wants you to be, practice loving on people. The Christmas season is a great time to reach out to those in need. You will be better for it. "Whatever you have learned or received or heard from me, or seen in me—put it into practice. And the God of peace will be with you." (Philippians 4:9)

See you tomorrow, God willing!

December 13 — Griswold Lights

When my mother lived here in Greenville with us and after she moved to assisted living, she loved for us to drive her around Greenville during the evening before Christmas to see all of the Christmas displays. I suppose we are all guilty to some degree of getting carried away with Christmas decorations that fail to tell the real Christmas story. Here is a little story that emphasizes my point. When our children were small the outdoor lights were not the same size as they are today. The bulbs were huge and multicolored. There were no ice sickle lights or light blankets for the bushes. There were no tiny light sets to hang in the trees or fancy stars or colored balls. There were only strands with these huge bulbs. If you remember the movie "Christmas Vacation" with Chevy Chase, you know exactly the type of lights I am talking about. In fact, the outdoor lights that we owned became known as our "Griswold" lights after the family in the movie. They were antiques to be laughed at, but never displayed or so our daughter told us.

The first year we lived in North Carolina we visited her house one evening when we knew they were out. We decorated the bushes around the front of their house with the Griswold lights. Boy, were they surprised when they came home that night. Being good sports, they saved the lights for the next Christmas and played the same trick on one of their friends. I lost track of the lights after that.

Christmas displays and family traditions are all a part of enjoying the Christmas season. As long as we never forget that without Christ, there is no CHRISTmas. Our lights at Christmas time should burn to remind us that "Light has come into the world, but men loved darkness instead of light because their deeds were evil." (John 3:19) "When Jesus spoke again to the people, he said, 'I am the light of the world. Whoever follows me will never walk in darkness, but will have the light of life.'" (John 8:12) Walk in the light.

See you tomorrow, God willing!

December 14 — Dancing with the Star(s)

One of our favorite television shows is "Dancing with the Stars." We never miss an episode because my wife tapes both the show where the participants perform and the results show which comes on the following night. By taping the shows, we can avoid the myriad of commercials and reduce the viewing time down to a reasonable time. I'm not sure why we have become such fans of the show, but I suppose there are many reasons. Since I am a lousy, two-left foot dancer myself, I suppose I enjoy watching other not so talented dancers trying to learn the difficult art of ballroom dancing. As the season progresses, the less talented participants fall by the wayside and some of the individuals improve significantly.

Over the years, my wife and I have taken dance lessons on numerous occasions. While I don't want to seem too old, our first dance lessons were disco, which was popular around the end of the seventies. I only remember the timeframe because our son's first grade teacher was also in the class. We actually got to the point where we could dance in public without embarrassing ourselves, but we got too little practice so what little skills we did have quickly eroded.

Several years later, we enrolled in another set of dance lessons at a studio in East Greenville, PA. Those lessons were weekly and lasted approximately six months. We learned the Cha-Cha, the Linde Hop, the Foxtrot, the Jitterbug, Salsa, and the traditional Waltz. I do not remember how to do any of those dances today and I would be embarrassed to try. The scope of my dancing is now limited to the Chicken Dance at weddings and the Hokey Pokey with children.

I think that I want to do my next dancing in heaven. In the Book of Revelations, it gives us a glimpse of what it will be like in heaven. "All the angels were standing around the throne and around the elders and the four living creatures. They fell down on their faces before the throne and worshiped God, saying: 'Amen! Praise and glory and wisdom and thanks and honor and power and strength be to our God for ever and ever. Amen!'" (Revelations 7:11-12) It doesn't say specifically that there was dancing going on, but if I were a betting man I can't imagine how anyone could stand still in the presence of the Almighty God. By the way, to insure your future participation, you don't have to practice the dance steps, just the belief steps.

See you tomorrow, God willing!

December 15 — Snowstorms

Snowstorms in North Carolina, like the three inches we had last Christmas, are a bit of a misnomer. They are treated like snowstorms because their impact on traffic flow is more serious than a blizzard in Eastern Pennsylvania or worse yet, western New York State. Snowstorms in Eastern Pennsylvania are a bit more serious. A three to six inch dusting of snow is not enough to slow down traffic. To be treated in a serious manner, the snowfall needs to reach a foot or more. In Eastern Pennsylvania where we lived for twenty-five years the average snowfall for a winter was about thirty-five inches, but in the winter of 1996 we got one snowfall in early January that nearly reached that depth. The snow fell over a period of two days with a total accumulation of twenty-six inches.

Since our house was located on a private road shared with four other families, we had to hire private contractors to plow our gravel road. However, because of the volume of work created by a large storm it was often difficult to get rapid response. Therefore, I often took it upon myself to shovel the three hundred feet of private road between our house and the state road. It was a chore, but if I took my time it was manageable. However, the day I dug out of the big storm I encountered a problem that broke my heart.

On the morning of January 8, 1996, I got up early, had my morning coffee, and then dressed in warmly to attack the job at hand. The snow was very dry which made the shoveling somewhat easier and the sun shining brightly on the new snow made the chore bearable. In a period of about three hours, I completed my task and, since the main roads were already plowed, I went back in the house to get ready to go to work. While I was showering, the state snowplow came by and pushed several feet of snow across the entrance to my private road. The task I had finished early was ruined and I was broken-hearted.

Trying to dig yourself out of a mammoth snowstorm is about like trying to get to heaven by your good works. It is a novel attempt, but it just won't get your there. "Why not? Because they pursued it not by faith but as if it were by works. They stumbled over the stumbling stone. As it is written: 'See, I lay in Zion a stone that causes men to stumble and a rock that makes them fall, and the one who trusts in him will never be put to shame.'" (Romans 9:32) The stumbling block, of course, was Jesus Christ, and we will soon be celebrating His birthday.

See you tomorrow, God willing!

December 16   Star or Supernova

As a chemistry major in college with a mathematics minor, I didn't get to take too many easy courses. Fortunately, at the University of Virginia you were forced to take a sprinkling of liberal arts courses to help make us better rounded students. There are two or three of those courses that I remember all too well. One of those courses was anthropology. I only remember the course because I ended up with my only "D" in my life. I missed one of the three exams during the semester on one of the golf team's southern swings and the professor gave me a zero on the test, even though he had promised to exclude the grade from my final mark.

The second liberal arts course I remember was "Art Appreciation." That course truly lived up to its name. I learned quite a bit about great art and I have spent many hours since those days walking through some of the world's greatest museums "appreciating" the art of the Masters.

The third liberal arts course I took was "Astronomy." Frankly, I took that course because every one knew that upperclassmen could take the course and with very little effort could get an "A" or at worst a "B." The professor graded on a curve so if no one got too smart, we would all be in good shape. We smelled trouble on the first day of class when a nerdy looking, red-headed freshman walked into the class and we discovered that his hobby was astronomy. On the first quiz, he made a hundred and the next best score was around eighty. Much to our dismay and pleasure, the professor threw out his high score and curved the grades from the next highest score on the test. About the only thing I can recall from the course was the life-cycle of stars and information about supernovas.

No one knows whether or not the star of Bethlehem was a real star or a supernova, but it doesn't really matter. If God wanted it to be a star, it was a star. If it indeed was a supernova, it still performed its task of leading the wise men to the place of our Savior's birth. "We saw his star in the east and have come to worship him... Then Herod called the Magi secretly and found out from them the exact time the star had appeared. He sent them to Bethlehem and said, 'Go and make a careful search for the child. As soon as you find him, report to me, so that I too may go and worship him.'" (Matthew 2:2; 7-8) When the Holy Spirit leads you to the Savior, worship Him, don't try to destroy Him as Herod tried to do.

See you tomorrow, God willing!

December 17 — Little Rocking Chair

My wife and I enjoy having dinner parties during the Christmas season and we generally do not know exactly who will attend these parties. We do not plan the parties well in advance of the scheduled date because it would ruin the attendance. Our objective is to plan the dinner party on very short notice and thereby allow God to determine who is available and who isn't. We call the attendees, God's Guest List.

While the food is always very good and enjoyable, it is the fellowship that makes the evening special. Our favorite time during the evening is when we ask each person at the table to share a Christmas story with the group and why the story is so special. The stories which are told are amazing.

One year, my wife shared a story with the group that I had not heard before. When she was about four years old, she received a tiny rocking chair for Christmas along with a small ironing board and play iron. Little did I know, it was the same green wicker rocking chair that sits in our family room. It has been through three generations of little girls and if all goes well it will make it through many more generations.

A few years ago, we did repaint the chair from white to green. We replaced the cushion with a nice new one and we repaired the supports making the rocking chair as good as new. Isn't it funny, that is exactly what God does for us when we receive Him? He makes us as good as new and we are guaranteed of life eternal. While our earthly body will some day wear out, we will simply replace it with a new one that will be far superior. The Bible often refers to our body as our earthly tent. "I think it is right to refresh your memory as long as I live in the tent of this body... (2 Peter 1:13) "Now we know that if the earthly tent we live in is destroyed, we have a building from God, an eternal house in heaven, not built by human hands." (2 Corinthians 5:1) In that new house, we'll get a fresh coat of paint, new cushions and new supports. When you get to be sixty-five, some days it feels like you already need all of those things.

See you tomorrow, God willing!

December 18   When Does Santa Claus Come?

This is not a trick question. When does Santa Claus come to your house? If you have little kids I suppose you will answer that Santa Claus always comes during the night on Christmas Eve. That is a pretty good answer, but for millions of children who go to see their grandparents for the Christmas holiday, the correct answer is "it depends."

When our children were little, Santa Claus actually came three different times. It is amazing how smart he is. Santa always came to our house a few days before Christmas. It varied depending upon where Christmas day fell any given year. Santa appeared a second time on Christmas Eve to my parent's house. He finally showed up a third time at my wife's parent's house on Christmas morning. Our kids learned at a very early age that it didn't matter whether or not they got what they wanted for Christmas during Santa's first visit or even his second visit. They simply had to be patient until Santa was exhausted from all of these separate deliveries for them. If the present they wanted didn't arrive on the third try they were out of luck. Frankly, I doubt that they ever went through all three visits without getting everything they wanted and more.

Looking back at the number of presents that you get for Christmas, I'm not sure we did our kids any favors. When you get too many presents, it diminishes the value of each one. Which one is the favorite? Which one should I play with? How do I act excited each time I unwrap another present? The answers to those questions are not easy, particularly for children.

I will never forget the Christmas that our son was two years old (almost three) and all he wanted for Christmas was a football helmet. When it was the first present he opened, he was content to stop and enjoy his Cincinnati Bengals helmet. When we told him he had more presents to open he was surprised and not really expectant of more presents. After that year, it was open one, throw aside the present and go for another one until the pile was completed. Even then, it was "is that all?" We had created the expectation, now we had to live with it.

To paraphrase Solomon in the book of Ecclesiastes, "Whoever loves presents never has presents enough; whoever loves presents is never satisfied... (Ecclesiastes 5:10) Solomon was actually talking about money, but the same point applies. When we love the number of presents more than the individual gift, we have lost track of value. It also causes us to take our eyes off of the real gift of Christmas, our Lord and Savior Jesus Christ. He only came one time, on Christmas Day. If you invite Him, He will come a second time, right into your heart forever.

See you tomorrow, God willing!

December 19 — Eeny, Meeny, Miny, Moe

Back in the good ole days, kids wandered around their neighborhoods looking for other kids to play games that involved quite a number of players. Games such as "hide and seek," baseball, basketball and "kick the can," all had one thing in common – you had to choose up sides or choose some one to be "it.". Generally speaking, there were always two kids who were willing to be captains of their respective teams. Once these kids were chosen, the next step was to determine which captain got to choose first.

There were several popular methods for making that determination. One way was to go "eeny, meeny, miny, moe; catch a piggy by his toe; if he hollers, let him go; eeny, meeny, miny, mo. By alternating words between each captain, the one who got the last word "mo," was allowed to select first. If it were a baseball game, the captains generally alternated hands on the bat going upwards until there was no more room for a hand. The person with his or her hand on the very top of the bat got to choose first. For a game like hide and seek where there was no team to choose, we might draw straws to determine who was "it" when the time came for everyone to hide.

In the Bible there were also incidents that required a similar type of decision making. Drawing of lots was the most common method of making these types of choices. When the Israelites entered the Promised Land, they divided the new territory among the tribes by the casting of lots. There was even the casting of lots at the foot of the cross. "When they had crucified him, they divided up his clothes by casting lots. (Matthew 27:35)

In the first chapter of the Book of Acts, the disciples met in Jerusalem and one of their responsibilities was to choose a replacement for Judas. "For," said Peter, "it is written in the book of Psalms, ...May another take his place of leadership...They prayed, 'Lord, you know everyone's heart. Show us which of these two you have chosen to take over this apostolic ministry, which Judas left to go where he belongs. Then they cast lots, and the lot fell to Matthias; so he was added to the eleven apostles.'" (Acts 1: 20, 24-26)

Frankly, I don't want my fate in any situation to come down to the drawing of straws or the casting of lots. I think I will stick to the process I now use. I will just continue to pray for God's guidance and wait for Him to answer.

See you tomorrow, God willing!

December 20   Physical and Spiritual Health

Yesterday, I had my annual physical exam. Because of my position when I was working, I was required to get an annual physical exam once I turned fifty years old and I continued to get an annual physical once I retired in 2001. Since I turned sixty-five this year, I was eligible for my first Medicare sponsored physical which included a few more bells and whistles. I am happy to report that all systems are sound, if not a bit worn out. Even the results of my EKG were good. The doctor did tell me one thing; "You need to lose about fifteen pounds."

Since I had my hip replaced in August of 2009, I have been lax in doing any cardiovascular exercises. I do walk on the golf course a couple of times a week, but since I am not allowed to run any more, I have not been able to force myself to get on the elliptical to get the kind of exercise I really need. It is a discipline that I need to start. Perhaps if you say a little prayer for me, it will give me the nudge I need to get started. Routine exercise will definitely help me lose the fifteen pounds and help get me back in shape.

I started my daily spiritual exercises right around the age of fifty. Part of my spiritual exercise is daily time in the Bible. Every morning, no matter where I am, I start the day with God. There is a daily devotional – I love Charles Stanley's "In Touch" Magazine – and there is also time in the Word and time on my knees. Each of these exercises helps me stay in good spiritual shape. Like physical exercise, I could always do more, but the daily discipline helps insure that I never get too far out of shape.

I can assure you that your spiritual health is far more important than your physical health. Good physical health will likely extend the duration and quality of your life on this earth. However, good spiritual health will extend your life for eternity. "Let us draw near to God with a sincere heart in full assurance of faith, having our hearts sprinkled to cleanse us from a guilty conscience and having our bodies washed with pure water. Let us hold unswervingly to the hope we profess, for he who promised is faithful. And let us consider how we may spur one another on toward love and good deeds…So do not throw away your confidence; it will be richly rewarded. You need to persevere so that when you have done the will of God, you will receive what he has promised." (Hebrews 10:22-24, 35-36)

See you tomorrow, God willing!

December 21   Proud and Teary-Eyed

My office in Cincinnati was on the 35th floor of the 45-floor Carew Tower, one of the tallest buildings in the city. The lower floors of the Carew Tower were home to the Netherland Hilton Hotel and Pogue's Department Store. There was a large enclosed arcade that ran down the center of the Carew Tower with entrances to both Pogue's and the Hilton. During the Christmas season, there was much hustle and bustle in the arcade some of which was to entice people into Pogue's to do their Christmas shopping.

One lunchtime when my daughter was about three years old, she and my wife hopped on the bus and came downtown to have lunch with me and do a little shopping. I remember the day like it was yesterday and I even remember what my daughter was wearing. She had on a darling camel-colored wool coat and cap that she had received for Christmas the year before. To get another season out of the tiny coat, my wife had added fur to the end of the sleeves and to the bottom of the coat to extend the length. The coat was beautiful, but my daughter was even more beautiful.

As we walked through the arcade, we heard Christmas music being played. As we walked into the crowd, we saw a bass fiddle player, a violinist, and a guitarist playing and singing. I put my daughter up on my shoulders so she could have a good view of the musicians. As she swayed to the music and bounced on my shoulders, she caught the eye of the musicians and before I knew it they were right beside us with her as the focal point of their serenade. I was proud as a peacock and possibly a little teary-eyed at the turn of events.

Can you imagine how the shepherds must have felt when the angels came to serenade them on the night Christ was born? "And there were shepherds living out in the fields nearby, keeping watch over their flocks at night. An angel of the Lord appeared to them, and the glory of the Lord shone around them, and they were terrified. But the angel said to them, 'Do not be afraid. I bring you good news of great joy that will be for all the people. Today in the town of David a Savior has been born to you; he is Christ the Lord. This will be a sign to you: You will find a baby wrapped in cloths and lying in a manger.' Suddenly a great company of the heavenly host appeared with the angel, praising God and saying, Glory to God in the highest, and on earth peace to men on whom his favor rests." (Luke 2:8-14) By the time the shepherds got to the manger, I bet they were proud to have been invited and more than a little teary-eyed.

See you tomorrow, God willing!

December 22   Bear Fruit

When the temperature of nitrogen in the air is reduced to minus 320 degree Fahrenheit, the nitrogen turns from a gas into a liquid. The liquid can them be stored in specially insulated tanks or transported in tank trucks that have similar insulation. There are many industrial applications for the cryogenic properties of liquid nitrogen; among them is the flash freezing of foods. I had the good fortune to manage a business unit at my company which sold the liquid nitrogen for this application.

The largest user of liquid nitrogen for freezing was McDonalds who required all of their hamburger patty suppliers to use cryogenics to freeze the patties. Traditional slow freezing of a hamburger patty allowed ice crystals to grow too large within the cell structure of ground hamburger which damaged the cells and led to dryer meat – and thus a degradation of quality.

Another very large user of cryogenic freezing was the poultry industry. Again, the culprit for traditional freezing was moisture loss. Once poultry companies, such as Tyson Foods, began to market skinless, boneless breast meat, they had to switch to cryogenic freezing to keep the meat from freezing to the conveyor belt. If the breast stuck to the metal conveyor belt, it was nearly impossible to remove the product without damaging the appearance of the product or causing loss of product.

One of my favorite applications was the freezing of fresh strawberries in baths of liquid nitrogen. California is the largest source of fresh strawberries in the United States. When the strawberries begin to ripen in the spring, most of the berries are sold into the fresh market. To keep the plants bearing fruit, the strawberry must be cut off the stem. Later in the season as the berries begin to transition to the frozen market, the growers must be careful to manage output from the fields to avoid overproduction and a subsequent drop in commodity prices. To keep the strawberry plant from continuing to bear fruit, the strawberries are plucked off the cap. This fools the plant into thinking that the fruit is still there so it stops producing.

If we allow Satan to pluck us from the vine, Jesus tells us that we will no longer bear fruit. "Remain in me, and I will remain in you. No branch can bear fruit by itself; it must remain in the vine. Neither can you bear fruit unless you remain in me. I am the vine; you are the branches. If a man remains in me and I in him, he will bear much fruit; apart from me you can do nothing." (John 15:4-5) I don't know about you, but I'm going to stay attached to the vine

See you tomorrow, God willing!

December 23   Blessings and Obedience

It has been my practice to keep my letters to about five hundred words, so I won't try to include all of the blessings I have received this year while being obedient to God's call. When you are obedient to God's will, you will be the one who receives the most blessings, not those He has called you to serve.

As the year rolled forward, I commented many times about what was happening. On January 29th, I wrote, "Writing to my family on a daily basis has opened my eyes to things I would never have seen or discerned before. It has also opened up lines of communication to levels I never thought possible." (Day 29 – The First Milepost)

Again on March 12th, I wrote, "Today is the 71st day of 2011. Normally, that would have no particular meaning for me. In fact, in previous years, I would never have known that March 12 was the 71st day of the year, except for leap years. Nothing is normal for me this year. Every day I am looking at the world through a new set of lenses; I am remembering things buried deep in the recesses of my mind; and I am feeling emotions once untapped." (Day 71 – What's in a Number)

On the 10th of April, I mentioned blessings yet another time, "My desire was to tell you stories of the past and relate the stories to God's wonderful presence in all that we do. Guess who is getting the most blessings? Yes, it is I. I can't begin to tell you how many times I have received a return email from someone letting me know that the message they received that day had been meant for them. The letters have required me to open my mind to all possibilities in terms of input for the letters. I can tell you with no fear of contradiction that when I begin to write I am unaware of where the story is leading me or rather where the Holy Spirit is leading me. (Day 100–Old One Hundred)

Finally, on the 15th of September, I tied obedience and blessings with the same bow. "Obedience is defined as "compliance with someone's wishes or orders or acknowledgment of their authority." Most of us are not thrilled with the implications that the word implies. Yet, obedience to God's will is our most essential act of worship.

"If you are willing and obedient, you will eat the best from the land; but if you resist and rebel, you will be devoured by the sword." For the mouth of the Lord has spoken." (Isaiah 1:19-20) The prophet Isaiah says it very succinctly. If you are obedient you will eat the best of the land; if you are not, you will be devoured by the sword." (Day 258 – Broken Wrist, Not Broken Spirit)

Each of you has been a blessing to me. Thank you for your kindness and attention.

See you tomorrow, God willing!

December 24 — Christmas Pageant

It is that time of year when children all over the world are preparing for the big day. You probably think I am talking about Santa Claus's annual appearance, but I am not. I am talking about preparations for the annual Christmas pageant that takes place in churches from Greenland to Greenville. The pageant is almost always the retelling of the Christmas story as told in the Gospels of Matthew and Luke. To get the full story used in most Christmas pageants you need to read Matthew 1:18 – 2:12 and Luke 2:1-20. These two versions combined give you all the characters you need to have a first class pageant. There are wise men and shepherds; there are angels; and there are Mary, Joseph, and Jesus. If you throw in a few animals from the stable you got yourself a nice sized cast.

Can you smell a story coming? In our small church in Pennsylvania, the Christmas pageant was held every Christmas eve at four p.m., and it was standing room only. While there was a different lady just about every year who took responsibility for the casting, costumes, and training, the pageant was never an afterthought. Plenty of time and effort went into the pageant to make sure everything went off perfectly.

One year when our daughter was ten years old, she was asked to be Mary. I don't think she was thrilled with the limelight, but she agreed to play the role. If I am not mistaken, our son was a little drummer boy (a part you won't find in the Bible), but nevertheless appropriate in our culture. Oddly enough, it wasn't the enacting of the events of the story that jogs my memory. It was some very specific costumes. One of the matriarchs of our congregation was a sheep farmer. She donated several sheepskins, two white and one black that were laid over the backs of three small children. As those three children processed up the main aisle, there was a murmur that spread through the congregation noting how precious those innocent children were. In a strange way, the essence of Christmas had been captured – the precious nature of a newborn baby in a manger.

Isaiah foretold the event seven hundred years before it took place, and we are still celebrating the birth of Jesus two thousand years later. "The people walking in darkness have seen a great light; on those living in the land of the shadow of death a light has dawned…For unto us a child is born, to us a son is given, and the government will be on his shoulders. And He will be called Wonderful Counselor, Mighty God, Everlasting Father, Prince of Peace. Of the increase of His government and peace there will be no end." (Isaiah 9:2, 6-7a) Because He lives today, we no longer have to walk in the darkness.

See you tomorrow, God willing!

December 25 — Poof-Ball Christmas

For about the last twenty years, we have had a family tradition of getting a family picture taken on Christmas Day or Christmas Eve of everyone who is present. Here is the catch, that means we have to find a way to have the camera "click" the picture with no one standing there holding the camera or pushing the button. When we started the tradition in Pennsylvania, I had a 35-mm camera and tripod so it was easy to set up the picture with every one in the frame. Once the shot was in focus and there was a spot for me in the photo, I simply went to my appointed spot and squeezed the "poof ball" that was attached to the camera and "voila" we had our shot. Because we could not view the quality of the shot on the spot, we normally took several pictures to make sure that we had one with every one smiling.

When digital cameras came along a few years later, the process got easier in some respects and yet a layer of difficulty crept into the process. I could still place the camera on a tripod to set up the picture, but now I couldn't use my "poof ball." Not to worry, all of the digital cameras have a feature that allows you to push the button and wait five or ten seconds for the picture to flash. That gives you plenty of time to focus the shot and run to the spot you have left for yourself in the picture. It sounds pretty easy doesn't it? It would be except for two reasons. One, I have lost the tripod so I am forever looking for a place to set the camera that will not interfere with the photo but will still allow me to get everyone in the picture. Secondly, I forget every year how to set the camera up for the delayed flash. By the time I rediscover how to set the camera, every one has lost interest.

Several times in the last few years, our daughter has brought her camera and taken the group photo. She has a nice 35-mm digital camera, and she knows how to set the camera for delayed flash, and furthermore, she remembers from year to year how to do it.

The Christmas pictures give us a year-to-year record of new family members and lost family records. They are truly a treasure. There is nothing on earth that is more important than family. The Gospel of Luke says, "For where your treasure is, there your heart will be also." (Luke 12:34) Between our biological family and our Christian family, it is true. That is all the treasure we need because God is the Father of our family. I think He already has a picture of us.

See you tomorrow, God willing!

December 26   The Journey

It is going to take me a few days to wrap up "365 Love Letters." The journey has been incredible to say the least. I set out to tell stories about our family and I did so. Beginning from the third year of my life, the time when children begin to develop long-term memory, there are stories about me. There are stories from the farm in Illinois. There are many stories about growing up in Virginia. And there are many stories about our life in Cincinnati, Allentown and Greenville. Would you believe that the stories cover exactly one hundred years? Until I was going through the chronological order of the stories I didn't realize that the oldest story was about my father-in-law at age twelve. Coincidence? I don't think so. On January 19th there was a story entitled "Coincidence or God" that expressed my views on this topic. This is a quote from that story, "I recalled many times in the Bible where God caused things to happen in such a powerful manner to demonstrate that He alone is God, there can be no coincidence, no other explanation for the events." God is alive and well in our lives.

Here is another statistic that may surprise you. I have written stories about 15 different countries during the past year. That is just another reminder of God's blessings in my life. I have had the good fortune to see a lot of the world. Some of it is visually beautiful, like Niagara Falls, Paris, London, and the Caribbean Islands. Some countries and locations are not so pretty visually. The barrios and bateys of the Dominican Republic, the slums of San Pedro Sula, Honduras and the bleak life style in Bulgaria are examples. However, I learned that even in the seemingly bleak places of the world you can see God's beauty, particularly through the eyes of a smiling child.

On February 22nd, I wrote a letter about the children we saw in orphanages in Honduras and Bulgaria. Here is an excerpt from that story. Two verses in the Gospel of Mark give us a picture of how Jesus felt about children. Mark 9:37 says, "Whoever welcomes one of these little children in my name welcomes me; and whoever welcomes me does not welcome me but the one who sent me." A little later in Mark 10:14, Jesus clarifies His attitude even more, "Let the little children come to me, and do not hinder them, for the kingdom of God belongs to such as these."

And, speaking of geography, I have actually sent letters out from all over. My letters were sent from St. Maarten, New York City, Myrtle Beach, Emerald Isle, Columbia, South Carolina, and then the Dominican Republic. No matter where I was I had to find a way of getting Internet access in order to keep the letters flowing.

Stay tuned; there are still things to tell you.

See you tomorrow, God willing!

December 27   The Journey – Continued

"In the beginning, God created the heavens and the earth." That is the very first verse in the Bible, Genesis 1:1a. Actually, it isn't even the complete first verse; it is only the first sentence. When I began writing the letters, I had no particular objective when it came to covering the whole Bible in my letters. However, as I kept up with the verses I used on a daily basis, it became apparent to me that God did have an objective for me. He wanted to touch every book in the Bible. A little over a year ago, I read a book by Larry Crabb titled "66 Love Letters." In his book, he likened the Bible to God's continuous love story to his people. Every book in the Bible delivered the next saga as God unfolded His story to mankind. As you no doubt have figured out by now, I borrowed from his title because my letters also unfolded my own story and my own personal walk of faith.

If you happened to keep track, you would have seen that by August 23rd, I had quoted verses from every book in the Bible. Of the 1188 chapters in the Bible, verses have been included from nearly 400 different chapters. Whether you know it or not, you have been exposed to a major portion of God's Word. Since God's hand has been leading me the whole time, I can only assume that He has had you pay particular attention to the verses that fit your own personal needs. On January 7th in a letter titled "God's Guest List," I quoted this verse from Proverbs 30:5, ""Every word of God is flawless; He is a shield to those who take refuge in him." In another letter on March 9, I quoted another famous verse that talks about the sanctity of God's Word, "All scripture is God-breathed ...." (2 Timothy 3:16) and "no prophecy of scripture came about because of the prophet's own interpretation. For prophecy never had its origin in the will of man, but men spoke from God as they were carried along by the Holy Spirit." (2 Peter 1:21) The verses that I have included in the letters were carried along by the Holy Spirit for your sake and mine.

When I went back through every letter, I found that I had included most of the "favorite" Bible stories that we have all heard since we were children – Noah's ark and the Great Flood; Jonah being swallowed by a whale; Daniel in the lion's den; the Christmas story; Good Friday and Easter; and many more. Like Larry Crabb said, the Bible is just one big love story for mankind.

Here is one last verse for you to ponder. "The grace of the Lord Jesus be with God's people. Amen." In case you don't recognize the source of that verse, it is Revelations 22:21, the last verse in the Bible.

See you tomorrow, God willing!

December 28   The Journey of Life

Over the last few days, I have been looking back over my letters to see if I have missed anything. The last two days, I have written about some of the more obvious topics. In this nearly final letter, I want to cover some other important content. Today, I want to talk about life and death. As each family member's birthday rolled around, I tried to tell a story that would celebrate that special day. However, on September 22, I wrote a story, "A Baby Changes Everything," that talks about a birth that is still in the future. Only God knows what stories will be told about that precious child.

Starting on April 21st and continuing through April 24th I wrote a series of stories about death. The stories chronicled my own journey of understanding about death and the final letter in the series was sent out on Easter Sunday. Here was the final paragraph, "Death has been swallowed up in victory. Where, O death, is your victory? Where, O death, is your sting?" (1 Corinthians 15:54b-55) "...in a flash, in the twinkling of an eye, at the last trumpet. For the trumpet will sound, the dead will be raised imperishable, and we will be changed." (1Corinthians 15:52).

As the rest of the year unfolded, I wrote additional stores about friends who had passed away during the year or friends who were no longer living who had made a mark on my life. Each of them taught me something profound. The one I remember the most was a story I told on February 12, which oddly enough was one of the shortest stories I wrote all year. The story, "Give Thanks in All Circumstances," was the third in a series of letters about verses from Thessalonians 5:16-18, "Be joyful always; pray continuously; and give thanks in all circumstances." It was a story that encouraged us to look for the goodness in every situation. Instead of grieving over the loss of a friend or loved one, we should thank God that He placed that person in our lives.

For the last few days, I have been telling stories about Christmas. How strange! This letter began with stories of birth and ended with the most important birth in the history of the world. In Solomon's wisdom he wrote "a time to weep and a time to laugh…" (Ecclesiastes 3:4) It is the "Circle of Life" and it awaits us all. As one of our friends told people before she died, "Aren't you jealous?"

See you tomorrow, God willing!

December 29 — Faithful, Encourager

Are you going to keep writing letters after December 31st? That is a question that I have been asked many times over the past couple of weeks. My answer has always been "probably not." However, it wasn't my idea to write 365 letters in the first place so I will just have to wait and see.

I have been reminded of many wonderful things about God's character–foremost among them is His faithfulness. When God asks you to do something, you can be sure that He will equip you. Every time that I thought that there were no more stories in me, I prayed fervently for God to open up the recesses of my mind. He did, every time. Here is how I knew it was Him. The stories seemed to come from nowhere and on consecutive days the stores would be totally unrelated with absolutely no apparent connection. He wanted me to know that He was in charge and that He would provide the material I needed.

Here is another element of God's nature that I saw repeatedly during the year. Many times Satan would whisper in my ear that I was wasting my time and that no one cared if I sent them or not. Just when I was at my lowest points, God would encourage me. Out of nowhere, several people would reply to one of my letters telling me that what they had read that day had encouraged them in some way. I can't begin to thank you enough for your kind responses. It was God's way of encouraging me and reminding me that I was being obedient to Him and the letters were part of His plan, not mine.

In March, I commented on the presence of the Holy Spirit in my writing. "Since I began writing "365 Love Letters", I have received many compliments on the quality of my writing and the interesting and thought provoking ideas I have presented. I chuckle to myself every time I receive one of these comments because I know that I don't deserve them. I have coined a new word to describe writers like me – most of whom are graduate students compared to my status as a child in kindergarten. The new word is Spiritwriter and here is the definition. A Spiritwriter is a person who writes messages inspired by the Holy Spirit, but puts his or her own name on it. In fact, the Holy Spirit enables the Spiritwriter to see circumstances and people from a divine perspective. (Day 68 – Ghost Writer or Spiritwriter)

I am not a theologian. I am not a Biblical scholar. I am not even a very astute Biblical student. In fact as early as 15 years ago, I would have been classified as Biblically illiterate. I am just a hillbilly (or hill Bill) from the mountains of Southwest Virginia whom God has chosen to help tell His story of mercy and grace.

See you tomorrow, God willing!

December 30   What Did YOU Say?

Throughout the year, I received responses from many of you that let me know that the stories I had written were helping you recall your own memories of a particular event or an event that happened in your own life that sounded a lot like the one I had written.

Sometimes the responses were very short and to the point–"Love them all, but this is one is extra special. It both touched and encouraged me. Others were much longer.

This response reminded me that my stories are very much like the rest of you. "Wow, you really hit a cord today! My dad died in June 1985. We were in Michigan, Dad and Mom in VA; I didn't have the opportunity to drive home. The times I've thought of things I'd like to have said, and discussed with my dad. As I didn't grow into my faith until after Dad died, I never really had the chance to ask him a bunch of questions about his faith. We attended church when I was younger, but you know how that goes."

Another friend was so moved by a story about "Night Seasons" that he (she) replied. "By the way, in my most recent darkest time, I had a cup. It was aluminum with a plastic casing. I took it everywhere with me back then. Other than 5 days of clothing, it was the only thing I was allowed to take once I was removed from my home. I drank water from that cup everyday, whether at home or at work. One day before I left, my cup had disappeared. I searched everywhere and I was absolutely beside myself. At one point I broke down and began praying... Please let find the cup. Just then, a peace washed over me. The next morning, my cup was sitting in the empty sink. I don't know who took it. I don't know who put it there. I only knew that God had influenced someone to return it to me. If you ask any of my close friends now to describe the cup, they would tell you it serves as a memento of God's love for me and how he watched over me and walked with me during that time."

And finally, a good friend responded early in the process, "Thank you for your time and your passion in writing these, but most of all for your example of a yielded heart."

There were so many touching responses from all of you that it was really hard for me to pick out the most important one. So, I went to the Bible, as I always did to find the answer. I found it in the Gospel of Mark. "'The most important one' answered Jesus, 'is this: Hear, O Israel, the Lord our God, the Lord is one.'" (Mark 12:29) That pretty much sums up my message for the year.

See you tomorrow, God willing!

December 31   New Year's Eve 2011

On this day one year ago, the Holy Spirit spoke to me in my inner being and said to me, "I am pleased with the way you have continued to pray earnestly and faithfully for the well being of your children. God hears your prayers and now He wants you to step out in obedience and tell them how much you love them and how much God loves them. Here is what God wants you to do. He wants you to send them a message every day during the following year to remind them. Tell them stories. Stories about your childhood. Stories about their grandmothers and grandfathers. Stories about their mother and other members of the family. Stories about their own childhood. Finally, tell them stories about God. In fact, show them how God is intertwined in all of this."

I started on January 1st with a letter that committed me to the three hundred and sixty-five letters. By the 3rd day of the month, it dawned on me what I had promised. It was a little scary, but I knew if God called me to send the letters, He would provide the material.

For the last three hundred and sixty-five days I have been faithful to His call and He has kept His end of the bargain. It has been one of the most fulfilling journeys of my life and has taken me back to many memories that were hidden in the recesses of my mind. I have laughed and cried. I have called family members to get more details about stories that I had too little knowledge to tell. I have accessed the Internet regularly to add details about people, places and things that were unfamiliar to me. And, I have searched the Bible daily to find the connection between my stories and God's Word.

I can also tell you that as the days and months dragged on, there were days when I wondered if anyone was even reading my daily missives. When I was at my lowest, God would always have multiple people reply to me with encouragement. Something I had written had caused them to tell me that the message had been special for them personally on that day. I knew it was God's way of telling me to stay the course.

During the process, I have given up many hours of sleep and spent way too many hours composing letters on the computer, but I wouldn't trade those hours for anything in this world. All I want to hear is this "Well done good and faithful servant." (Matthew 25:21).

May the words of my mouth and the meditation of my heart be pleasing in your sight, O LORD, my Rock and my Redeemer. (Psalm 19:14)